MENZIES
The Shaping of
Modern Australia

MENZIES

The Shaping of Modern Australia

J.R. Nethercote

Editor

Connor Court Publishing

in association with the

MENZIES RESEARCH CENTRE

Connor Court Publishing Pty Ltd

Copyright © J. R. Nethercote 2016

PO Box 7257
Redland Bay QLD 4165
sales@connorcourt.com
www.connorcourt.com

ISBN: 978-1-925501-01-8 (pbk.)

Cover design by Vanessa Schimizzi
Cover portrait by Godfrey Argent (National Portrait Gallery, London)
Printed in Australia

CONTENTS

Foreword

Heather Henderson

My father told me once of a conversation he had with Sir Winston Churchill in Churchill's old age. Churchill had spoken about the "clever young men" criticising him and belittling his achievements. It had upset him. Don't worry about it, my father told him, it happens to all of us. In time a balance will be struck.

When I heard that the Menzies Research Centre was putting this book together I thought: "How marvellous for me to know that, fifty years after my father's own retirement and after so many untrue and unkind things have been said and written about him, such a resounding blow is being struck on his behalf."

There are very few people left who were able to meet and talk to my father. This book will provide a great opportunity for us all to learn more about what he thought and believed and did. It shows what a well-endowed and interesting man he was. A wide range of authors has found plenty to write about him, about different aspects of his beliefs, ideas, and achievements.

I am grateful for the enthusiasm and diligence and skill with which John Nethercote and the Menzies Research Centre have compiled this book. It is an important one.

Preface

The Honourable Josh Frydenberg, MP
Member for Kooyong
Minister for Resources, Energy and Northern Australia

Nearly five decades on since Sir Robert Menzies left the Lodge his legacy looms large.

His policies on foreign affairs and defence, education and economic reform left Australia more prosperous and secure. But perhaps the most enduring aspect of Menzies' legacy was his conviction, his civility, his principles. "If you stand on principle you will never go far wrong", he would often say.

Menzies approached the complexity of government with a firm set of values that guided him through peace and war. He promoted the individual, freedom and free enterprise and railed against Labor's class warfare while appealing to the unheralded middle-class.

For Menzies, politics was a battle of ideas not a clash of warring personalities. He never sought to destroy his opponents but simply to defeat them. This approach not only earnt him the respect of his colleagues from across the political divide but also were emphatically endorsed by the Australian people at a record seven consecutive elections.

Menzies' significant achievements meant he was a political giant not only at home but also abroad. Internationally, his reputation preceded him with Richard Nixon once famously remarking, "If I were to rate one post-war leader it wouldn't be Chou Enlai or de Gaulle it would be Sir Robert Menzies".

Despite Menzies' stature and his list of achievements, there is always the danger that with the passage of time memory of his record will fade.

That is why this book is so important. With distinguished contributors bringing their expert eye to the various aspects of Menzies' policies we can ensure that all that he did to strengthen the fabric of our nation will not be forgotten.

I strongly commend the Menzies Research Centre and editor John Nethercote for putting together this significant publication and I hope you enjoy it as much as I have.

Contributors

Peter Edwards, historian and biographer, has degrees from the University of Western Australia and Oxford (DPhil). He has held many posts in universities and has worked in the Historical Section in the Department of Foreign Affairs. His books include *Prime Ministers and Diplomats* (1983), *A Nation at War* (1997), *Arthur Tange: Last of the Mandarins* (2006) and *Australia and the Vietnam War* (2014).

Margaret Fitzherbert, a Liberal member of the Legislative Council of Victoria, previously worked as a ministerial adviser to Judi Moylan and Dr David Kemp. Educated at Monash University, she is the author of *Liberal Women: Federation to 1949* (2004), followed in 2009 by *So Many Firsts: Liberal Women from Enid Lyons to the Turnbull Era*.

Henry Ergas wrote *Wrong Number* in 2008. He has had various posts in universities and had assignments with the OECD, the Australian Competition and Consumer Commission and the Productivity Commission. He is, among other things, a columnist with *The Australian*. His essay on "Tocqueville, Hancock and the Sense of History" will be published shortly in William Coleman (ed.), *Only in Australia* (2016).

Lionel Frost graduated from Monash University where he is now Associate Professor in the Faculty of Business and Economics. Author of many articles on diverse aspects of Australia's economic and social history, he wrote *Immortals: Football People and the Evolution of Australian Rules* (2005).

David Headon is a cultural consultant and historian. Now a Visiting Fellow, ANU Research School of Humanities and the Arts, he has previously been Director of the Centre for Australian Cultural Studies (1994-2004) and Advisor on the Centenary of Canberra in the ACT Chief Minister's Department. His many books include, *The Symbolic Role of the National Capital* (2003), and, as editor, *Best Ever Australian Sports Writing – a 200-Year Collection* (2001) and *Canberra Red* (joint editor, 2013).

Anne Henderson, educated at the University of Melbourne, is Deputy Director, the Sydney Institute, where, among other things, she edits *The Sydney Papers*. Her many books include *Enid Lyons: Leading Lady to a Nation* (2008), *Joseph Lyons: The People's Prime Minister* (2011) and *Menzies at War* (2014).

John Howard, Prime Minister of Australia, 1996-2007, is a graduate in law from the University of Sydney. He represented Bennelong in the House of Representatives from 1974 until 2007. He held several ministerial posts before appointment as Treasurer in 1977. He was Deputy Leader of the Liberal Party from 1982 to 1985; and Leader of the Liberal Party and Leader of the Opposition, 1985-89 and 1995-96. His autobiography, *Lazarus Rising*, was published in 2010, followed in 2014 by *The Menzies Era: The Years that Shaped Modern Australia*.

David Kemp was a member of the House of Representatives for the Melbourne seat of Goldstein from 1990 until 2004. A front-bencher for most of his time in the House, he was Minister for Education, Training and Youth Affairs, 1998-2001, and Minister for the Environment and Heritage, 2001-04. Educated at the University of Melbourne and Yale, from which he holds a doctorate in politics, he was a Senior Lecturer in Political Science at Melbourne before appointment as Professor of Politics at Monash University, 1979-90. He was a Senior Adviser to Prime Minister Malcolm Fraser, 1975-76, and later Director of the Prime Minister's Office, 1981. Subsequently he was president of the Victorian Division of the Liberal Party from 2007 until 2011. His book, *Foundations for Australian Political Analysis*, was published in 1988. With D.M. White, he edited *Malcolm Fraser on Australia* (1986); and he wrote the Introductory Essay to a new edition of *Robert Menzies, The Forgotten People and Other Studies in Democracy* (2011).

Greg Melleuish was educated at the University of Sydney and subsequently took a doctorate at Macquarie University. He now teaches politics and history at the University of Wollongong. Author of *Cultural Liberalism in Australia* (1995), he has also written *A Short History of Australian Liberalism* (2000), *The Power of Ideas* (2009) and *Despotic State or Free Individual* (2014) as well as editing a number of other books.

J.R. Nethercote is Adjunct Professor, Canberra Campus, Australian Catholic University. He studied at the University of Sydney before joining the Australian public service where he worked for 30 years, mainly for the Public Service Board and the Department of the Senate. As well as editing the *Canberra Bulletin of Public Administration* from 1980 to 2000, he was a joint editor of *The Menzies Era* (1995) and editor of *Liberalism and the Australian Federation* (2001).

Mikayla Novak, Senior Research Fellow at the Institute of Public Affairs, has worked for both Commonwealth and State government agencies. Her publications include *School Autonomy* (2006) and *Towards a Healthy Productivity Reform Agenda for Australia* (2007). She writes extensively in newspapers.

Jonathan Pincus is Professor Emeritus of Economics at the University of Adelaide where he previously held the George Gollin Chair in Economics. Educated at the University of Queensland and Stanford, he has held academic posts in, among others, the Research School of Social Sciences, Australian National University, and Flinders University. He has lately been Principal Adviser Research at the Productivity Commission. He wrote *Pressure Groups and Politics in Antebellum Tariffs* (1977) and jointly authored *Government and Capitalism* (1982).

Graeme Starr studied at the University of Sydney, Carleton University (Ottawa) and the University of West Virginia from which he obtained an award-winning doctorate. In addition to teaching at several universities in New South Wales, he has been senior private secretary to the Minister for Communications (and later Minister for Defence). He is also a former State Director of the Liberal Party (NSW Division). He edited *The Liberal Party of Australia – a Documentary History* (1980). His biography of Sir John Carrick, *Carrick – Principles, Politics and Policy*, was published in 2012.

Anne Twomey is Professor of Constitutional Law at the University of Sydney. She has worked for the High Court of Australia, the Commonwealth Parliamentary Research Service, the Cabinet Office of NSW, and has been Secretary to the Senate Committee on Legal and Constitutional Affairs. Her publications include *The Constitution of New South Wales* (2004), *The Chameleon Crown: The Queen and her Australian Governors* (2006) and *The Australia Acts 1986: Australia's Statutes of Independence* (2010).

List of Photos

Second Set, pp. 223-230

Menzies with the Prime Minister of Japan, Nobusuke Kishi, at the signing of the historic Australian Japan Commerce Agreement of 1957
(Courtesy of the Menzies Foundation)

Menzies greeted by villagers in Papua New Guinea
(Courtesy of the Menzies Foundation)

Menzies in talks with Indonesian President, Dr Sukarno, in Jakarta 1959
(Robert Menzies Collection, Baillieu Library, University of Melbourne)

Menzies was the first Australia Prime Minister to visit Indonesia
(Courtesy of the Menzies Foundation)

Meeting with US President, John F. Kennedy, in the White House 1962
(Public Domain)

Menzies meets the Press Gallery in his office, Parliament House, Canberra
(The Federal Parliamentary Press Gallery)

Robert Menzies in talks with US President Lyndon B Johnson at the White House, 1964
(Lyndon B. Johnson Presidential Library, University of Austin, Texas)

Menzies outside the Lodge in Canberra with the family dog, Pie, 1962
(Menzies Family Collection)

Menzies, a keen photographer, in action
(Menzies Family Collection)

Menzies with Athol Townley, Minister for Immigration and later Minister for Defence
(Menzies Family Collection)

Political adversaries Robert Menzies and Arthur Calwell share a light-hearted moment at the opening of the R.G. Menzies Library at the Australian National University. The two men enjoyed an amicable relationship outside the parliamentary chamber. Seated to the other side of Menzies is ANU Chancellor, H.C. "Nugget" Coombs.
(ANU Library Collection)

Portrait of Sir Robert Menzies in his robes as a Knight of the Most Ancient and Most Noble Order of the Thistle, 1963
(Stephens Orr)

Dame Pattie and Sir Robert Menzies, 1968, portrait by Godfrey Argent
(National Portrait Gallery, London)

Sir Robert Menzies: Prime Minister of Australia (1939-41 and 1949-66)

J. R. Nethercote

On Thursday, 20 January 1966, Sir Robert Menzies, Prime Minister of Australia, issued a press release, drafted in his own hand in lead pencil on quarto paper:

> I have given careful thought to my future in the light of what seems best for the Government and the country. . . . I have decided to resign from the Prime Ministership forthwith.

A notable premiership thus came to an end. He had been prime minister in total for over 18 years, more than twice as long as any of his predecessors.

Menzies had been at the centre of Australian national politics for three-and-a half-decades, half the history of the Commonwealth up to that time. His retirement, at a time of his own choosing, was an event of great moment.

The 50th anniversary of Menzies' retirement presents a timely opportunity for a retrospective, bringing together a composite portrait of Menzies' own place in history, and that of his governments.

Immediate commentary concentrated on the longevity of his prime ministership. So accomplished had he been at the helm that there was something of a view that government was now much easier than it had been in the first half-century of the federation. The next decade and longer would show that governing still required considerable and diverse skills of a high order.

Other comment was very predictable. His Anglophilia received much attention; in the immediate aftermath of his retirement no-one felt the need to examine the complexity of his approach to Australia's international relations in these years, except to note that Australia now seemed to look to the United States instead of the United Kingdom as principal guarantor of its security. The growing but readily observable cultivation of relations with Asian nations generally went unnoticed as a feature of Menzies' stewardship.

Domestic policy received less attention from commentators, academic or journalistic, but, again the inclination was to grumble that government had not been more active, more interventionist. This was the era when indicative planning of economies, notably as practised in France, was regarded as the model to follow; this sentiment even grew in succeeding years as Japan emerged as a formidable force in economic terms.

It took many years before the Menzies era began to be seen in a better perspective, more informed and more realistic. The foundations had been laid by the Government itself, in its record and in Menzies' own exposition of his achievement in *Afternoon Light* (1967) and *The Measure of the Years* (1970), supplemented by his lectures on *Central Power in the Australian Commonwealth* (1967). Various other books, including memoirs, shed a more personal light on the character of the Menzies years. Among these were Percy Joske's "informal memoir," Percy Spender's two volumes of memoirs, Cameron Hazlehurst's *tour d'horizon* of his career, *Menzies Observed* (1979), and Judith Brett's suggestive *Robert Menzies' Forgotten People* (1992).

With archival sources increasingly becoming available, it was the 1990s which witnessed major re-evaluations, partly occasioned by the centenary of his birth in Jeparit and partly by the 50th anniversary of the foundation of the Liberal Party. A great milestone was reached with A.W. Martin's two-volume biography, *Robert Menzies: A Life* (1993, 1999); and, of comparable importance, Ian Hancock's *National and Permanent? The Federal Organisation of the Liberal Party of Australia 1944-1965* (2000).

Other important sources have been the memoirs and biographies of other leading figures in the politics of the Menzies years. The memoirs include those of Paul Hasluck, Garfield Barwick, Jim Killen and the diaries of Peter Howson. Among the biographies are those of Harold Holt by Tom Frame, Ian Hancock on John Gorton, David Lowe on Percy Spender, W.J. Hudson on Casey, David Marr on Barwick, and Geoffrey Bolton on Paul Hasluck.

John Howard's *The Menzies Era* is a very significant addition to the library on the Prime Minister and his government. Comprehensive in its coverage, it is a notably skilful narrative which embraces probing accounts of the major policies and achievements of the Menzies Government, marked by an acute understanding of the political dynamics of post-war prosperity. It is, indeed, an exemplary illustration of how much a statesman, with long experience of high office, can bring to an understanding of the life and record of another who has previously scaled the highest peaks in a nation's public life.

In recent years, increasingly deep understanding of Menzies has come from the availability of several documents in his own hand. The Victorian Division of the Liberal Party performed a signal service when it published a new edition of *The Forgotten People* in 2011, with a splendid introductory essay by David Kemp.

At much the same time, Heather Henderson edited letters her father had sent to her when she was abroad (*Letters to my Daughter* (2011)). These letters provide incomparable insight into Menzies as a person as well as into the politics of the time. This collection was admirably supplemented by Henderson's own family memoir, *A Smile for My Parents* (2013). And where Henderson essentially wrote about Menzies at home, Sir John Bunting's *R.G. Menzies* effectively provided a parallel account of Menzies at the office.

The 50th anniversary of Menzies' retirement presented a timely opportunity for a retrospective, bringing together a composite portrait of Menzies' own place in history, and that of his governments, mainly, but not exclusively, on the post-war Liberal-Country Party Coalition in office from 1949 to 1966. The purpose has been not simply to provide a narrative of the period, but to examine and recall the principal features of policy. Holding office for so long a period inevitably meant rocky times occasionally. But the broad characteristics were a preference for opening opportunities for individual enterprise and industry, and limiting government to what was essential for social welfare and development. The nationalisation ambitions of Labor gave way to the mixed economy (and, eventually, privatisation in whose advancement in the 1980s and 1990s both parties played a role). Internationally, Australia made its place in the post-Imperial world, concentrating upon East and South-East Asia, and fostering closer relations through trade and social programs of which the Colombo Plan is the most well-known.

This book embraces an exposition of Menzies' political philosophy, the war-time prime ministership and then his crucial post-war term of office. This historical coverage includes examination of the Liberal Party, the principles underlying its foundation, and in particular the attention given to the representation of women.

A series of essays then review major fields of policy: foreign affairs, security and defence; economic growth and development; social welfare; and the fostering of tertiary education. These are followed by various studies of institutions and government in this period.

The book concludes with a recollection of Menzies' central role in the development of Canberra, the national capital.

These deeply researched essays provide firm foundations for considered appraisal of the period and the scope for further research and investigation including into matters not covered, or only lightly covered, in this book.

J. R. Nethercote
Canberra, March 2016

1

The Political Philosophy
of Robert Menzies

David Kemp

Robert Gordon Menzies was the most influential Australian political leader of the twentieth century. His political philosophy is central to understanding his influence. By force of character, courage, political skill and unmatched eloquence he transformed, through his ideas, the culture of his country's politics and the nation's future. He held office as prime minister in total for more than eighteen years, and was the most widely recognised and respected voice of Australia on the world stage. All the national governments that came after him for four decades built on the foundations he had set in place. Without him, today we would be writing a very different history of Australia.

Menzies' ideas reveal to us a rather different person to that often portrayed in popular writing, where interpretations and stories tend to be survivals from the political chatter of the day, press comment, or follow the self-interested political "lines" of friends and opponents. Biographies of the man tell of events, repeat anecdotes, put together a story, but often with little reference to the ideas that give meaning to Robert Menzies' actions and influence over a political life of some forty years.[1]

Menzies believed – as have political leaders before and after him – that politics is a contest of ideas. He wrote: "The art of politics is to convey ideas to others, if possible, to persuade a majority to agree, to create or encourage a public opinion so soundly based that it endures, and is not blown aside by chance winds; *to persuade people to take long-range views.*"[2] His influence on the nation's politics is largely attributable to his articulation and practice of the ideas that guided his political judgment, and that he sought to embed in the political party – the Liberal Party of Australia – of which he was the principal founder.

Menzies' ideas not only had the force that came from their inherent logic and appeal to the cultural values of the Australian electorate, but also from the persistence of expression over time that reflected the self-belief and mastery of language that was Menzies' gift. No previous Australian prime minister had approached Robert Menzies in the depth, coherence and realism of his political philosophy, though George Reid – the tireless advocate of free trade and the liberal economy of the Federation era – perhaps comes closest. In the crisis of momentary self-doubt that followed Menzies' resignation as prime minister in 1941 he did not flee the field but, instead, summoned all his moral courage and intellectual skills to a task that was to make him the great architect of Australia's post-war politics and policy success.

Along the way, his opponents – and, at times, even some of his friends – criticised him, and identified political misjudgments. Much, but not all, of the criticism was shallow, partisan and unfair, and Menzies himself conceded the validity of some of it in his memoirs. Yet, when we reflect on his life, viewed now across the growing distance of the years, it is the depth and scope of his values, his fundamental soundness of judgment, his character, and unwavering commitment to his fellow citizens and his country, that stand out.

It is easier to speak of Menzies' political philosophy than that of many other leaders because he himself regarded his ideas as comprising a "philosophy" and designated them as such, though he would certainly have disowned the description, "philosopher." He sought to impose a logic and coherence on his thinking about politics and life, which he tested in part against analysis, but more generally against his understanding of history and the experience he acquired in the process of implementing his ideas.

The pre-eminent and most comprehensive statement of Menzies' political ideas is to be found in his book of collected and edited radio talks, delivered in 1942, *The Forgotten People*. The collection was, he wrote in the foreword to the published collection in 1943, a "summarized political philosophy".[3] In his first volume of memoirs, *Afternoon Light*, published in 1967, the year after his retirement from national politics, he regarded the great achievement of his political life as "the revival of Liberalism in Australia" through "the creation of a new party with a modern philosophy".[4] Twenty-three years prior to this he had told the founding conference of the Liberal Party that it was a matter of "desperate importance to our country" to work for "a true revival of liberal thought".[5] The name of his new party said just that. He later wrote:

> We took the name 'Liberal' because we were determined to be a progressive party, willing to make experiments; in no sense reactionary, but believing in the individual, his rights and his enterprise ...[6]

Liberal thought

For Robert Menzies, "liberal thought" centred on the equal rights, the capacities and the entitlement to respect and dignity, of each individual person. He later spoke of "the supreme importance of the individual,"[7] and argued that "[t]he test of civilisation is freedom, freedom of the spirit and of the mind and of the body."[8]

The institutions of liberal democracy and the rule of law existed to protect individual rights. The liberal economy based on private enterprise was the expression of those rights in the daily lives of people, demonstrating the dependence of society on the creativity of the individual whose enterprise delivered both jobs and prosperity. Education was the principal road to the empowerment of, and opportunity for, each person. Government had responsibilities to enable this to happen, and to protect the rights of, and to assist, those whom economic or other misfortune had afflicted, and those vulnerable to the prejudice, hatred or the violence of others.

Classes, races, religions, genders, political causes – the collectivities that dominated the political thought of many, and which were often accompanied by hatred of others – had no priority in his view over the rights, and the well-being, of each person. Menzies understood clearly that if all individuals mattered, and if each individual had distinct needs and talents, policy should promote opportunities for each of them. "We must aim at the fullest development of individual capacity", he had told the Liberal Party's founding conference.[9] Treating social collectivities such as classes, races or religious denominations as if they had voices and rights inevitably led to injustice to individual people.

Robert Menzies passionately defended the parliamentary and legal institutions Australia had inherited from Britain, and modeled by the founders in part on those of the United States, which he saw as designed to protect individual liberty. The independent judiciary was an essential element of these institutions. "The guarantee of civic freedom is the certainty and impartiality of justice," he said.[10] Throughout his career he saw the necessity of defending parliamentary government against those interests that sought to dictate national policy from outside the democratically elected governments – the "faceless men" as he characterised them during the 1960s. These interests had their strongholds principally in the Labor Party, but he had been equally alert to repel any parallels on his own side of politics.

He thought broadly about political life and its relationship to the workings of society as a whole. While his liberalism was a policy philosophy, pointing the way to sound decisions and legislation, its scope embraced also the conduct, nature and architecture of political life, and a developed understanding about the way society worked and about human nature. Policy, he believed, could not be properly made, nor good government realised, if the processes and institutions of politics did not function well, and policy would not be effective unless it was based upon a valid comprehension of social life and humanity. His liberalism also encompassed a profound Australian patriotism, and the strategies to guarantee the security of his country in a troubled world occupied a significant place in his thinking.

Menzies' judgment that the revival of "liberal thought" was a matter of "desperate importance" by the 1940s expressed his dismay at the shallowness and destructive character of the ideas that he saw as then dominating Australian political debate. These ideas had eaten away at the economic and social achievements of colonial Liberalism, had undermined enterprise and encouraged dependence on government, had plunged Australia into one of the worst depressions in the world after 1929, and had weakened the nation as it faced external aggression from Japan. Reason in national policy had too often been replaced by prejudice and selfishness, and individual liberties, and individual motivation, had been threatened by a strengthening authoritarian demand for group solutions to industrial and economic problems. The nation's vitality was being sacrificed to illiberal thought.

Illiberal thought

Menzies' intellectual and political targets were ideas which pervaded many aspects of political and national life. He sought to replace the sectarian, class, racial and nationalist hatreds of Australian political life with respect and rationality, to reason with his foes, and to exemplify civility in the conduct of national affairs. He wanted people to think sensibly and in a reasoned way about problems, and had a special distaste for sanctimony and for the "pseudo-intellectual" whose shallow and incoherent thought often promoted social division, or advocated breaching fundamental principles such as the rule of law in pursuit of their causes and ideological concerns. He patiently worked against the parochial nationalism fostered by the protectionist era of White Australia with his immigration, trade and education policies and through the welcome his government offered to students from Asia coming under the Colombo Plan.

Most of all, however, he set himself to defeat the influence of the utopian ideas about the role of government in society then dominating the Labor Party and union Left, and what he called "the foul doctrine of the class war."[11] Among these were the beliefs that successful economies and business corporations could be administered like bureaucratic government departments, that markets, prices and entrepreneurs were unimportant, that profits were against the public interest, that raising production destroyed jobs, that the interests of employers and employees under "capitalism" were fundamentally opposed, and inevitably produced a kind of civil or class war. Likewise, he contested beliefs that the greater the number of businesses run by government the better, that politicians, officials and selected others could be entrusted with vast arbitrary discretions over individual lives, that multiplying the uniform rules imposed by government on everyone could produce progress, that a unified governmental authority in Canberra could be effectively controlled by the people, and that personal security could be obtained through an all-powerful state.

These were all ideas that in the decades in Australia before 1949 went under the name of "Socialism," though in his view they might just as readily be called "fascism," as he told the House of Representatives in the debate on bank nationalisation in 1947:

> The attitude of the Government is: 'We are the rulers of the land. We know better than the people what is good for them'. That is the fascist mind.[12]

Menzies had summarised his refutation of these ideas for the assembled delegates from the liberal organisations at the conference he had called to establish his new party in 1944:

> I see the individual and his encouragement and recognition as the *prime motive force* for the building of a better world. Socialism means high costs, inefficiency, the constant intrusion of political considerations, the damping down of enterprise, the overlordship of routine. None of these elements can produce progress, and without progress, security will turn out to be a delusion.[13]

Through the Liberal Party of Australia Menzies set out to reset the course of Australian history, to expose the fantasies of the Left utopians, and to build a new political culture on a rescued liberal tradition – one not based on class, sectarian or nationalist hatreds, but on mutual respect and faith in the ability of people, making their own choices in life, to create a good society. Government would be recognised as having the responsibility to protect them and to empower them as they pursued their own missions in life.

Without Robert Menzies there would have been no Gough Whitlam, carrying the battle against Left extremism into the darkest corners of the Labor Party, nor a Malcolm Fraser inspired by Menzies' example, pursuing the equal rights of all people regardless of ethnicity, race or religion, supporting those in need, controlling government spending and seeking to re-establish a concept of limited government. It was Menzies' success in restoring "liberal thought" to Australian government that laid the intellectual and cultural foundations for the efforts to dismantle the bloated state of the post-federation decades under Hawke, Keating, and Howard, and for the tax, education and industrial relations reforms of the Howard era. As Australia became the "miracle economy" of the OECD in 2000, a more open, tolerant and good humoured nation than it had ever been before, it was the spirit of Menzies that had brought it there.

Politics as a public service

There are at least three aspects of Robert Menzies' early life to which we can point as providing foundations on which his adult philosophy of politics was constructed.

Throughout his life Menzies saw his involvement in politics as a public service, and politics as an activity whose purpose was to advance the interests of the community as a whole.[14] Politics should never be seen as a selfish activity to better oneself, or to promote some special interest at the community's expense, but to improve the lives of all.

This had been almost the dominant lesson of his childhood.

His parents, he wrote, "were a remarkable pair of people, with great talents, high moral purpose, and an intense and self-sacrificing desire to see their children make some unselfish but competent contribution to life."[15] His father, he said, "was a great one for getting things done. In this he was completely unselfish, for all his greatest crusades were for others."[16] In *The Forgotten People* he defiantly defended the motivation of public service:

To discourage ambition, to envy success, to hate achieved superiority, to distrust independent thought, to sneer at and impute false motives for public service – these are the maladies of modern democracy, and of Australian democracy in particular. Yet ambition, effort, thinking and readiness to serve are not only the design and objectives of self-government, but are the essential conditions for its success.[17]

Menzies would become famous in his own family for his lack of interest in money or personal fortune. As he told a meeting of the Institute of Public Affairs in 1954, when he was prime minister for the second time:

What I ask you to realize is that people like myself – I'm not the only one – go into this life because they have beliefs, because they have a faith, because they believe that there is something that matters for their own country.[18]

Reason, knowledge and logic

The second aspect of his early life that he said came to matter greatly was his reaction to his father James' own political style – a highly emotional platform style that he did not like, and left him squirming in his seat at meetings addressed by his father. At times, he observed, his father's emotionalism could be wounding to others. "We were not a little frightened of him", Robert recalled.[19] He did not doubt the effectiveness of the emotional style but, in response to it, he developed his own style of highly rational and reasoned argument. In his memoirs, when he had retired from politics, he conceded that both approaches had their merits, and that perhaps his cool rationalism had had its downsides as well:

My father's emotional character derived from a deep-seated faith and belief. He had not been through the disciplined experiences of the Law, and so, paradoxically, was nearer to the surface in the expression of things that were deepest in his heart. I wish today that there were more like him. It is one thing to be the coldly reasoning product of the schools; the objectivity thus produced is needed badly in a world in which there is so much passion and prejudice, 'malice, hatred and all uncharitableness'. But there is a great place in life for beliefs so strongly held that they must find utterance and sway the hearts of men.[20]

Without Menzies' logical and rational analysis of the world, he would never have developed the understanding to which his impact on Australian history can be traced, yet, as he looked back, particularly to his alienation from many of his parliamentary colleagues in the early years of the war, when he had resigned the prime ministership and subsequently the party leadership, he could see that Menzian logic could wound as much as Menzian passion.

After the "humiliation", as he called it, of 1941, he decided to adopt more of what he recalled as his mother's "sweet reasonableness," [21] learning from bitter experience that leaving a trail of walking wounded was neither admirable nor politically sensible. As the years went by he became more self-deprecatory, more generous to foes, more attracted to the humorous. But beneath the logic there remained a submerged passion that drove him on and his commitment to enlightened understanding and public service continued to motivate him.

Idealism

The third aspect of his early years that contributed to his future course was his family's political idealism. Both his parental family and the family of his wife, Pattie Leckie, had strong political beliefs. Robert's father, James, and his father-in-law, John Leckie, had been members of parliament and, more than that, they were *Liberal,* in an era when Liberals in Australia were conscious that their great peaceful and reformist tradition – which had culminated in the establishment of one Australian nation in 1901 – was being overwhelmed first by the horrors of war, 1914-1918, and then submerged into a party led by Billy Hughes, then Stanley Melbourne Bruce, that they struggled to recognise as their own.

Robert's brother, Frank Gladstone, had been named after the leader of the British Liberal Party, W.E. Gladstone, who had died in 1898. No statesman had stood more strongly for moral standards in public affairs. The Menzies family believed deeply in this kind of politics, and Robert was to exemplify it in his career. But it was the agony of Australian Liberalism during and after the Great War that sharpened Menzies' political views, and set him on what may seem in retrospect an inexorable course to "revive liberal thought."

The Liberals after 1917 faced two challenges. The "win-the-war" Nationalist Party – created out of the merger of the Liberal Party that had been formed by Deakin with Hughes' National Labor – came increasingly to be seen by many former Liberals as moving away from what they understood by economic and constitutional liberalism. More shockingly, the Left of Australian politics, after the Russian revolution of 1917 – through both the Labor Party and the newly-formed Communist Party – was embracing a utopian anti-capitalist ideology based around class war, inflation of the power of government, and the submergence of the individual. Labor's leader, Matthew Charlton, in his 1925 election policy speech, had declared that Labor "stands for the unity of the mass against the mass power of Mammon. It subordinates the individual to principle."[22] The issue of the relationship between politics and economic and social life was now squarely on the nation's political agenda, and two divergent policy approaches were being promoted.

What troubled the former Liberals was that these two forces were not divergent enough, for the Nationalists showed some signs of moving to a policy convergence. Hughes, despite earlier indications, was plainly not an advocate of liberal thought and made no secret of his distaste for "capitalism"[23] or of his belief in government ownership. Bruce, the Nationalist leader from 1923, was a young businessman who viewed Australia more as a corporate entity and was a policy pragmatist with little regard for federalism or theoretical liberal principles. For those who believed in liberalism, the question was: should the Nationalists be confronted by a revived Liberal party, or changed from within?

A small revived Liberal party, the Liberal Union, was successful in disposing of Hughes after the 1922 election, through the agency of John Latham working with the new Country Party, and in 1926 John Leckie helped to establish an Australian Liberal Party in Victoria. The risk of a new Liberal Party, however, was that it would split the Nationalists and let Labor into government. Robert Menzies chose a second strategy and set out to reform the Nationalist Party from within through a new "party within a party", the Young Nationalists. From the time he entered the State Parliament of Victoria in 1928 he set out to become a voice for his developing philosophy of liberalism based on responsible individualism rather than state intervention.

The formation of the Young Nationalists in 1929 clearly revealed Menzies, for the first time, as an architect of politics, prepared to transform its structures to further his ideas. Functioning political parties were the key. The Young Nationalists became effectively an organisation promoting Menzies' version of liberalism.

Political architect

By the early 1930s Menzies had become one of the most eloquent voices for political liberalism in Australia against those seeking authoritarian solutions through the communism and quasi-fascism that were claiming attention in the English-speaking world. He attacked the danger of political movements identified by the colour of their shirts, and their "idea of primitive justice and wild justice," and felt a genuine sense of mission as the defender and advocate of traditional democratic and parliamentary values in the face of incipient threats, at home and abroad. [24] He constantly stressed the theme that "a strong Parliament was the only protection against dictatorships and Communism," and parliament could only preserve itself through independence and strength.[25] His frequent addresses to Irving Benson's Pleasant Sunday Afternoons were regularly reported in the press.

In the darkest days of the Great Depression Menzies played a key role in engineering the restoration of public confidence in the party system and in parliamentary government. Confidence in parliamentary government depended on a party system that could formulate sensible policies and make a persuasive case to the people. When that system broke down, people searched for non-parliamentary, and threatening, solutions.

In the Depression after 1929, unemployment at almost 30 percent shook confidence in government, political parties, and (what remained of) the liberal economy. National debt was over 125 percent of GDP, and Australia's capacity to borrow internationally collapsed. Political extremism on the fringes, and not just the fringes, was the result. The Premier of New South Wales, Jack Lang, was threatening the socialisation of NSW industry and the repudiation of international debt obligations. The chairman of the NSW ALP's socialisation committee told the Easter Conference of that party in 1931 that "Capitalism has failed and socialism must have its trial ... Parliaments are stinking in the nostrils of the electors". The conference was told: "A people's government must take control."[26] While the Lang Labor Party debated whether revolutionary action was required, simultaneously a middle class revolt arose against the Nationalist Party through the All For Australia League and other organisations, and Menzies, keeping his head when all about him were losing theirs, moved rapidly to consign the old "win-the-war" Nationalists to the dustbin of history.

As the Labor Government led by James Scullin began to fall apart and Joseph Lyons rebelled against its failure to restore fiscal responsibility and balanced budgets, Menzies once again acted. He formed a group of prominent Melbournians to support Lyons' transition to the leadership of a new party – a party that would take the name of the "United Australia Party" to beat the Depression. Unlike Lyons, who initially proposed a break from "the crippling fetters of the party system,"[27] Menzies knew that a new party was necessary to rebuild confidence in the parliamentary process that had frayed badly, as evidenced by the willingness of the union and Labor Left and groups of returned servicemen to organise para-military groups as a protection against violent action. It was Menzies who helped to persuade John Latham to step aside from the leadership of the Nationalists and agree to serve in the new party, and it was a member of Menzies' group, Ambrose Pratt, who wrote notes for Lyons for his resignation speech from the failing Labor Government.

By his role in these events Menzies was already flagging his belief that parliamentary government could not operate without an effective party system, and he was prepared to seize opportunities to reorganise his own side of politics to work better on behalf of his political values.

When he looked back on this testing period from the war year, 1942, Menzies concluded:

> There can be no doubt that this democracy of ours has been very sick. If and when it can be cured, it has great work to do. But it will never be cured unless we see the past clearly, and recognize frankly that we cannot ignore politics and treat democracy as a mere matter of loaves and fishes and demean the politician, and at the same time sensibly demand that 'government of the people, by the people and for the people shall not perish from the earth.'[28]

These years of upheaval also did much to crystallise the substance of Menzies' policy philosophy, and to lead him to emphasise the importance of a policy framework that embraced the encouragement of enterprise, the equal rights of all under the rule of law, well-directed and controlled public spending, and a comprehensive "safety net" based on national insurance for those suffering distress through no fault of their own. Many of the nation's problems arose, in his view, from capitulation to excessive and dangerous demands by special interests – business, farming and union especially – for state intervention in the market, and from irresponsible spending, borrowing and regulation by governments. These were policy ideas that had led to excessive dependence on government by both industry and unions, and to national bankruptcy. The key to a return to sound policy-making and economic health was the recognition that freedom and reward, and the value of personal responsibility, were the sources of creativity and achievement for individuals and the economy as a whole, and that government had a responsibility to revive and encourage these motive forces of economic progress and social health.

In articles in the Melbourne *Argus* in 1929 Menzies had described the idea that judges could regulate the workplace as "grotesque."[29] He would have noted the Brigden report's conclusion that Australian tariffs, which would become the second highest in the world (after the United States), were unrestrained from infinite expansion, threatening the nation's economic health.[30] The conversion of the Deakinite Liberal, Frederic Eggleston, in his seminal study, *State Socialism in Victoria*, to the view that government enterprises had been run not in the public interest, but by the "Interests"[31] was one that Menzies fully comprehended. He would have noted the conclusion of the historian, Keith Hancock, in *Australia,* that what Australian public policy required was a "realistic individualism"[32] in which the interests of individual Australians defined the public interest, not the selfish "swarm of petty appetites" that sought to extract benefits and privileges for themselves from the state.

Principle v. Special Interest

During these years Menzies formulated more clearly his critique of policy decisions based on interest group pressures rather than sound principles of the public interest. He had been concerned with selfish pressures from the Progressive Country Party in Victoria, and from influential businessmen organised in the National Union, a fundraising committee for the Nationalist Party that attempted to interfere in pre-selections. In September 1931, as President of the Victorian National Federation, he had stated his belief that the solution to such a self-defeating politics lay in principled, rather than pressured, policy:

> I believe that a large majority of the public today is perfectly ready to give its adherence to a party which will display political principle and political courage.
>
> ... We have suffered far too much from people who have no political convictions beyond a more or less genteel adherence to our side of politics. That kind of adherence is worthless. We must have people who believe things, and who are prepared to go out and struggle to make their beliefs universal.[33]

He later brought these ideas together in a series of radio talks, published in 1943 as *The Forgotten People and other Studies in Democracy,* and gave organisational expression to them in his main architectural achievement, the Liberal Party of Australia, in 1944. The Liberal Party was a party with an explicit philosophy of the public interest, committed to the interests of the individual citizen, that would control its own pre-selections and its own fundraising, and where the parliamentary party elected by the people would determine policy. It would not be a business-led or controlled party, but a party whose policies of support for a more liberal economy would benefit business along with all other citizens.

In *The Forgotten People* Menzies noted that the inter-war years had seen remarkably few pieces of legislation designed to encourage individual effort, enterprise or personal independence. For two decades the nation seemed to have been travelling down a path that was leading to stagnation, and the submergence of the individual. Without freedom, individual people could not flourish, and without freedom there would never be real progress. The constant political rhetoric which emphasised welfare and state oversight from the cradle to the grave and class war demeaned each citizen, had threatened Australia's democracy during the Great Depression, and would ultimately destroy its vitality as a nation:

> There may be some people who think that the only freedom that counts is to have a roof to sleep under, clothes to wear, food to eat. These are very necessary. Governments must be pledged to do all in their power to assist people to secure them; but they are not freedoms at all. Each can be obtained in a state of utter slavery. The real freedoms are to worship, to think, to speak, to choose, to be ambitious, to be independent, to be industrious, to acquire skill, to seek reward. These are the real freedoms, for these are the essence of the nature of man.[34]

Free enterprise

Menzies' emphasis on the importance of economic freedom was derived from these general principles. His view was that to deprive citizens of this freedom, through unnecessary industry regulation or nationalisation, was nothing short of fascism. Indeed, in the organised marketing arrangements in many industries, and in the demands of extremists in the union movement for compulsory membership of trade unions, he saw, rearing its ugly head, the same corporatist principle that was advocated by fascist movements in Europe.

> There is some tendency today, as there was in the Italy of the early Mussolini, to organize the community by giving to each trade or industry a separate collectivist control of itself through the employers and employees engaged in it. At first sight this seems reasonable. But second sight will tell us that the most important person is the party of the third

part – the member of the general public. He must never surrender his rights. The community is greater than the trade or the business or the craft.[35]

In his talks in 1942 Menzies advocated none of the flagship policies of the Deakinite agenda: industry protection, compulsory arbitration of industrial disputes, nor White Australia. His silence was eloquent. His pre-occupation, in reality, was to deal with the consequences of the failure of these policies, and to return, in many ways, to a more classical liberalism of the kind that had been advocated by the English economist and political philosopher, John Stuart Mill, based on acceptance of minority differences, equal rights, individual liberty and policies that put the consumer ahead of the producer, while acknowledging a positive role for the state and condemning *laissez-faire*.

At the foundation of the Liberal Party two years later, relying on what he described as an "amazing" study, *Looking Forward*, by the Institute of Public Affairs, that embodied ideas from the English economist, John Maynard Keynes, and the political economist, Friedrich Hayek, Menzies set out to identify "the true economic functions of the State." These were, he said:

> First, to assist in preventing the periodic recurrence of large-scale unemployment;
>
> Second, to secure to all responsible citizens (through social legislation) at least a decent and reasonable minimum of economic security and material well-being;
>
> Third, to impose a framework of law which will give the utmost encouragement to the enterprise, resourcefulness and efficiency of individuals and groups, and which lead to the greatest possible output of the goods and services which the community needs;
>
> Fourth, to conserve in the long range interests of the community, those natural resources fundamental to the life and future prosperity of the nation.[36]

Although Menzies' training was in the law, and his reforming zeal in government was to be more in areas such as education, health and foreign policy, he never departed from his view that economic and financial policy lay at the very heart of liberal thinking. The great political debates of his time were centred on economics, which he recognised as inextricably entwined with all those aspects of life he held dear: the rule of law and the liberty of people to control their own lives. It became a central proposition of his political philosophy that government could, by unwise interventions, damage and even destroy the productive working of the economy, and foster corrupt and authoritarian concentrations of power. Neglect of this area, in his view, had been one of Churchill's flaws, and of this neglect he had written:

> No political leader known to me ever knew less of the complexities of economics and finance. His grasp of domestic peacetime problems was so imperfect that he had great difficulty, in pre-war years, in holding his parliamentary seat.[37]

Robert Menzies would not make this mistake. Chifley's proposal to nationalise the trading banks in 1947 on the basis that "private banks are conducted primarily for profit, and therefore follow policies that in important respects run counter to the public interest,"[38] confirmed Menzies in his view that Australian democracy was in grave danger from Labor's socialist lack of economic understanding and its corporate state policies. Democracy was based on respect for the capacity and rights of individual people, and personal liberty and economic liberty were indistinguishable. Of Chifley's Banking Bill to nationalise the trading banks he said:

> The Bill will be a tremendous step towards the servile State, because it will set aside normal liberty of choice, and that is what competition means, and will forward the idea of the special supremacy of government. That is the antithesis of democracy. Democracy rests upon the view that the people are the rulers, as well as the ruled; that the government has no authority and no privilege beyond that granted by the people themselves; that while sovereignty attaches to the acts of the parliament, that sovereignty is derived from the people and has no other source. Fascism and Nazism, against which the free peoples of the world have just waged a bloody war in which millions suffered bitterly, both rejected the democratic idea as I have defined it …"[39]

In his memoir, *The Measure of the Years* (1970), he wrote:

> [T]he basic philosophy of Australian Liberalism is that the prime duty of government is to encourage enterprise, to provide a climate favourable to its growth, to remember that it is the individual whose energies produce progress, and that all social benefits derive from his efforts.[40]

Between 1949 and 1966 Australia remained protectionist, and direct export and import controls were used on occasion, though phased out. The industrial relations system was reformed to separate judicial and arbitral powers, compulsory arbitration remained, but strikes were few. The White Australia immigration policy persisted, at least formally. Organised marketing of primary products, and in some primary industries, production licensing, continued. The government retained ownership of the Post Office and telecommunications, a trading and savings bank, an airline, a shipping line, and a radio and later television network. Menzies had judged that the major policies of the Deakinite post-federation settlement were too entrenched to be confronted directly, and that the politics of overt reversal was impossible. All were strongly supported by the Labor Party Opposition, which sought to block change, supported from the mid-1950s by the Democratic Labor Party. The Country Party, essential to coalition government, was protectionist and defended extensive regulation of many primary industries. His liberalism would undermine these policies, nonetheless.

Menzies' assessment of what was possible pointed him to a lengthy reform agenda as the policy framework for economic and social liberalisation was put in place. Wartime rationing and price controls were abandoned and Labor's nationalisation agenda was terminated. The banking system was put on a sounder and less politically vulnerable basis: the uncalled liability of the trading banks was cancelled in 1953, the Reserve Bank established in 1960, and the Commonwealth Trading, Savings and Development Banks separated. The public debt declined from 136 percent of GDP in 1949 to 52 percent in 1966, and international credit was rebuilt. The regulatory activities of the Commonwealth of private economic activity stabilised, and in some respects (direct controls) were withdrawn. Secret ballots were introduced for union elections in 1951; the Commonwealth Industrial Court was established after 1956 and empowered to order compliance with awards and punish for contempt. The Tariff Board began its slow journey to the economic analysis of protection, foreshadowing its ultimate abandonment. Foreign capital was actively sought, national development took off, jobs were plentiful, and unemployment low. After a short surge in the early 1950s, inflation remained under control at low levels.

Menzies' philosophy protected Australia from the fashionable economic panacea of indicative economic planning, then popular in Europe, especially France, rejecting this recommendation of the Government's own Committee of Economic Enquiry (the Vernon Committee) in 1965. He refused to hand over policy-making, he said, to the so-called "experts": "In no case is a political policy the product of purely expert opinion on technical matters", he argued. "We are a private enterprise economy. In such an economy, the demands set up by the people who are the buyers are the normal stimulant for increased industrial investment and activity. What the Committee appears to have in mind is that those demands, where necessary should be redirected." The Committee, he said, had "predicated a degree of planning and direction of the economy which in our opinion would not be either appropriate or acceptable in Australia ... "[41] What Australia, under Menzies' leadership, saw clearly, European countries would also later conclude, and that continent would then abandon its *dirigiste* polices as liberal thought revived throughout the West.

Menzies' liberalism was based on a deep faith in the capacities of each human being, in the desirability of "a fierce independence of spirit" and "a brave acceptance of unclouded individual responsibility."[42] These values would build a better society. Government had an important role, but it was limited in what it could achieve because its services and laws inevitably imposed conformity where progress required diversity. Where socialism meant uniform provision for all, and was justified in some limited cases, Menzies insisted upon the right of each person to exercise judgment and choice in all those aspects of life where people's preferences differ, and where a variety of goods and services can be provided. He wrote: "any activity in which choice and personal confidence are essential is not an activity for which the socialist solution is appropriate." [43]

Such areas included banking, medicine and health care, housing, aged care, media and education services, as well as the normal commercial activities of a liberal economy. As prime minister, Menzies pursued policies in each of these areas designed to foster through private provision the variety citizens were seeking. In strengthening and cementing in human services the mixed character of provision – private and public – he put in place a characteristic pattern of service provision for which Australia still stands out internationally.

The liberalisation of social policy proceeded apace, as significant steps were taken towards strengthening private provision in Australia's mixed public/ private systems in health and schooling and empowering patients and parents with choice. An effective voluntary system of health insurance was established through the historic *National Health Act* 1953. Support for White Australia was eroded by massive immigration, and thousands of students from Asia, and would be effectively ended by Harold Holt in 1966 in the face of opposition from the Labor Party. The Commonwealth took over the major role in the funding and expansion of higher education. Menzies set out to encourage private home ownership and his success was proudly recorded in his memoirs. He wrote that "of all the dwellings in Australia, over forty percent were built" during his term of office after 1949.[44] The foundations for one of the world's (proportionately) largest middle classes were set in place.

The exercise of choice and the freeing of individual creativity would have a profound effect on the structure and leadership of society, Menzies argued. His policy ideas, as he saw it, led to opportunity for individuals in a way that the uniformity of government provision and regulation never could. Opportunity in turn would naturally lead to the strengthening of the middle class, and in Australia the values of the middle class were those that would lead to a progressive, enlightened, humane and prosperous society.

Education, opportunity and the middle class

The key to opportunity and to strengthening the middle class was education, for education was empowerment. Out of his Scottish heritage Menzies saw the realisation of liberal principles and education as linked, because education was the essential basis of a politics based on knowledge and reason, and reason had a central place in liberal thought, coming out of the Scottish enlightenment. The Scottish farmer, he said, sees the future of his child secured not by money but by "the acquisition of the knowledge which will give him power."[45]

> Apart from the winning of the war, the greatest because the most fundamental task in front of us is to educate a new generation, not for mere money-making or to comply with the law, but for an enlightened citizenship based upon honest thinking and human understanding.[46]
>
> ... in the new world we must seek to develop all the intelligence and strength and character in every child. Each one of them must have his chance ... When the war is won, for every hundred boys and girls who now pass into higher schools and universities there must be a thousand. Lack of money must be no impediment to bright minds ... To develop every human being to his fullest capacity for thought, for action, for sacrifice and endurance is our major task; and no prejudice, stupidity, selfishness or vested interest must stand in the way.[47]

Menzies' Liberal Party after 1949 placed education – both school and university – at the centre of its program. His Government overturned the nineteenth century sectarian policy that refused to recognise the public benefit of government support for all schools (and, indeed, hospitals), provided scholarships for university entry and, following the 1957 report of the Committee on Australian Universities (Murray Committee) that he established, introduced revolutionary change into university funding, vastly expanding entry to high education through new universities. Menzies pursued this policy with a passion. As he introduced into the House of Representatives the measures that would lead to the unprecedented development of the university sector, "my emotions", he said, "were deep, and for me, unforgettable."[48]

Menzies' view was that better education would lift the whole society, and the quality of every institution in it. It would improve leadership, it would improve public debate, and it would produce greater equality. The position of women was foremost in his mind. "Higher education for women must come to be regarded as normal," he said, and not as a matter of eccentricity.[49] Working with Elizabeth Couchman, in a striking contrast to Labor, Menzies ensured that the new Liberal Party gave women and men equal positions of leadership in its councils, including in pre-selection conventions.

Though his belief in empowering people through education and the encouragement of a sense of responsibility permeated his thinking, Menzies also supported income redistribution through the government to those whom the vicissitudes of life had injured, and in government established legal frameworks for the provision of services that were necessary on humanitarian grounds that would not be privately provided. This, too, was part of empowerment. He objected vehemently to "false humanitarianism which does not strengthen but corrupts," that asserts that one person should be another's keeper. His programs would be aimed to encourage individual responsibility.

Under his Government social security spending continued to rise. He was proud of the Commonwealth entry into improving care for the aged through the *Aged Persons Homes Act* 1954; the provision of free life-saving drugs, and free medical and pharmaceutical services for old age and invalid pensioners. His Government expanded child endowment to first child and full-time students, and during his prime ministership the Commonwealth entered into capital provision for mental health patients.

Freedom of expression

The freedom to which Menzies gave priority, and without which – he believed – all other freedoms collapsed, was freedom of expression. Freedom of association and freedom of religion were essential elements of his liberalism, but it was freedom of expression to which he gave the greatest importance, because without it all other freedoms were threatened. During the 1930s he had been one of the most liberal voices against censorship on grounds of morality. He wrote in 1942: "The worst crime of fascism and its twin brother, German national socialism, is their suppression of free thought and free speech." [50] Without free speech, error might never be discovered and truth would be suppressed:

> Hence, if truth is to emerge and in the long run be triumphant, the process
> of free debate – the untrammelled clash of opinion – must go on.[51]

He associated himself with the principle stated by John Stuart Mill that the only restraint on the exercise of freedom must be to prevent harm to others. The threats to liberty become greater as society becomes more complex and, as this occurs, "we must be increasingly vigilant for the freedom of our minds and spirits."[52] Menzies was a lifelong advocate of freedom of the press, and he carefully weighed the principles behind wartime censorship in the *Forgotten People* talks. The policy expression of this commitment was perhaps clearest in media policy for radio and television. Chifley's premature attempt to establish a government monopoly in television was overturned by Menzies as consumers were provided with the choice of commercial networks alongside the ABC.

Menzies' attempt to ban the Communist Party in 1950-51 did not conflict with his profound belief in freedom of speech, and did not involve any attempt to ban the expression of communist beliefs by individuals. Subversive associations had been banned on grounds of national security in both world wars though, it was arguable, with limited effect. After 1945 he had resisted, on grounds of freedom of speech, Country Party proposals to ban the party again (as at the time of the Nazi-Soviet pact). His changed view after 1949, as the Cold War was heating up and wider war threatened, was based on his assessment that, in light of new intelligence information, the Communist Party had become an active agent on behalf of the Soviet Union in a subversive attack on Australia. Its members had penetrated the highest levels of politics and government and had passed secrets to the Soviets. Chifley had acted against this penetration and set up the Australian Security Intelligence Organization (ASIO), and the Petrov Royal Commission in 1954 established its extent in detail, including into H.V. Evatt's office. Banning the party would enable the Government to force Communist Party members out of the public service and out of leadership positions in unions in industries vital to the security of the country. The prospect of a fifth column operating inside Australian government and in vital industries in time of war was not to be contemplated. It could prevent the Government acting effectively and, if this happened, Australia might not survive.

The Labor Party, fearful of a threatened double dissolution of the House of Representatives and the Senate, supported Menzies' initial bill. During the Petrov affair the Cabinet acted deliberately and effectively to ensure that witch-hunts of the kind that had occurred in the United States under Senator Joseph McCarthy were not replicated in Australia. But the pressure of Menzies' proposal on a Labor Party, divided as it was between anti-communists and the secular, utopian and sectarian Left, would lead in 1954 to an irrevocable split in that party, and to the long-term realignment of Australian politics.

In the event, armed conflict between the major powers did not eventuate and the potential fifth column Menzies had identified never had its opportunity. Communist Party members at senior levels in the public service fled, recanted or ceased their activities, and the party's ideological rigidity and popular uprisings against communist governments in eastern Europe (Hungary 1956, Czechoslovakia 1968) drained support from communism in Australia.

By his steadfastness on principle, Menzies had not only reconstructed his own side of politics, but had helped to force a realignment of his foes, securing to his party an unprecedented twenty-three years in office.

National security

Menzies' political realism led him to give a very high priority to the security of Australia. Adam Smith, the Scottish moral philosopher and founder of economics, had in 1776 described the first duty of government as "protecting the society from violence and invasion of other independent societies." As Prime Minister, 1939-1941, Menzies clearly recognised that Australia's security might come to depend on America. He valued the Empire at a policy level because it gave Australia military support, vital intelligence links, and a seat at the Cabinet table during wartime of one of the greatest powers in the world. It was a seat Menzies used forthrightly to speak truth to power.

It was nevertheless evident from his first period as prime minister that his respect for Britain and love of British traditions did not stand in the way of his determination to defend Australian interests against Churchill's strategy, nor to underestimate the potential importance of the United States to Australia's survival if the onslaught should come. He established in the United States Australia's first diplomatic appointment to a foreign country (R.G. Casey), bought the Australian Residence in Washington as a permanent seat for the mission, visited America to gain assurances that it would support Australia's security and followed up with diplomatic appointments to Japan (J.G. Latham) and China (F.W. Eggleston).

In government after 1949 Robert Menzies used his diplomatic skills, and those of his colleagues such as Percy Spender and Paul Hasluck, to build a network of alliances that would stabilise the Pacific and East Asian region, and pursued trade and aid policies to promote economic progress and political leadership throughout the same area. Alliances would secure Australia where the United Nations could not. The Colombo Plan was negotiated in 1950; the ANZUS Treaty in 1951; the South East Asia Collective Defence Treaty in 1954; the comprehensive trade treaty with Japan in 1957; and the free trade agreement with New Zealand in 1965.

Menzies believed that Australia could make a significant contribution to regional security through its alliances. He overturned the suspect moral principle that Australian conscripted forces could only serve in a limited geographical zone – a principle that had humiliated Australia in the Second World War as American conscripts died to defend Australia in areas where Australia would not require its own citizens to fight. His Government established the principle that Australian forces could be garrisoned outside Australia, and major re-equipment of the Royal Australian Air Force undertaken with Hercules and Mirage aircraft.

Menzies' diplomatic skills were recognised throughout his prime ministerial years. Lee Kwan Yew attributed the successful launch of the State of Singapore in 1965 to Menzies' good relations with Malaysia. "The outcome, without Bob Menzies, might have been disastrous for us," he said.[53] In 1982 former American President Richard Nixon, whose own reputation rested heavily on his skill in foreign affairs, wrote: "If I were to rate one postwar leader ... it would not be one of the legendary European or American figures. It would be Robert Menzies."[54] He wrote of Menzies' "extraordinary intelligence and profound understanding of issues, not only in the Pacific but throughout the world."[55]

Equal dignity for all

Menzies believed that he knew from his own family culture and experience that the morality that supported ethical and respectful relations between citizens was principally a product of the home, not the state, and that insofar as the state could contribute to a moral social order, it was by providing the rule of law and a model of leadership characterised by honesty, integrity, good humour and mutual respect.

The great moral problems that Menzies had set himself to address were those that arose from prejudice and ideology – sectarianism, racialism, and national and class hatred – the answer to each of which was respect for all. His education and health policies, and the openness of his Liberal Party to people of all faiths, dissipated decades of religious hostility in Australia between Catholics and Protestants. His Liberal Party would seek to hammer the nails into the coffin of Protestant/Catholic sectarian political hatreds.

The abhorrence of racialism that had underpinned his immigration and education policies found expression in his attitudes to the conduct of foreign relations on a number of occasions. When, during the infamous Kristallnacht, 9-10 November 1938, Jewish properties were attacked and burnt throughout Germany at the instigation of the Nazis, the Lyons Government decided that Australia must respond to the demand to admit refugees, and in the year leading up to the war some 5 000 Jewish refugees were admitted, along with other victims of persecution.[56] Menzies was repelled by anti-Semitism and racialsm in all its guises and remained a firm friend of Jewish communities.

In the *Forgotten People* talks Menzies had attacked the deliberate fostering of race hatred against the Japanese in wartime propaganda as "fantastically foolish and dangerous":

> If this war with all its tragedy breeds into us a deep-seated and enduring spirit of hatred, then the peace when it comes will merely be the prelude to disaster, and not the end of it.[57]

Menzies' appointment of Paul Hasluck as Minister for Territories in 1951 committed Australia to the long journey of achieving equal rights and opportunities for Aboriginal people. Social services were extended to aborigines; in 1962 voting rights were established; and in 1965 Menzies met with aboriginal leaders and introduced legislation for a referendum to abolish section 127 of the Constitution, so that aborigines could be included in the census. It was a provision, Menzies said, "completely out of harmony with our national attitudes".

In relation to apartheid he would warn the South African Prime Minister, Verwoerd, that its failure was inevitable:

As I said once to Verwoerd, 'The more the policy succeeds in the short run, the more certain it is that it will fail in the long run.' For the more successful the education and health services provided for the Bantu (and they are better than those provided in other African nations), the more surely the day will come when the Bantu will no longer be content to be treated as second class citizens. There may well be a horrible explosion, and with the backing or encouragement of some intransigent northern African nations, much blood may be shed.[58]

Conclusion

As Robert Menzies had intended, the freedoms and incentives of the liberal economy, civil liberties, limited government and widening education led to the vast expansion of the middle class, and, with his policies, the educational level of the population rose dramatically. His policies strengthened the foundations for individual independence and individual freedom. His immigration programs produced a marked and relatively harmonious shift in the character of the country's population. Australia turned towards the Asia-Pacific in both security and commercial terms. The banking question was settled for several generations. He laid educational foundations for an economy that could embrace the shift from manual labour to service, science and new technologies, and he steered Australia away from public ownership, strengthening its private enterprise character. As a consequence of such changes, public debate on policy was transformed.

His egalitarian and respectful attitudes restored the political culture. Religious, class and racial hatreds died away and the growing legions of Robert Menzies' forgotten people began to influence the Labor Party itself as it sought their support. In the new knowledge-based society Menzies had foreseen and worked to bring about, the very issues of politics evolved. The policies of the old Liberalism were replaced by the policies developed out of the new Liberalism that Menzies had espoused.

Robert Gordon Menzies was not just *at* the turning point in the ideas governing public policy in Australia in the twentieth century. He *was* the turning point, the most remarkable Australian political leader of his generation, indeed of the century.[59]

Endnotes

[1] This is beginning to be recognized. See Elena Pasquini Douglas, "Robert Menzies' Stolen Legacy", *Australian Financial Review*, 24 January 2014.

[2] R.G. Menzies, *The Measure of the Years*, Melbourne, Cassell, 1970, 8.

[3] Robert Menzies, *The Forgotten People and Other Studies in Democracy*, Melbourne, (1943), 2011, Liberal Party of Australia (Victorian Division), 29.

[4] Sir Robert Menzies, *Afternoon Light: Some Memories of Men and Events*, Melbourne, Cassell, 1967, Ch. 12.

[5] *Forming the Liberal Party of Australia, Record of the Conference of Representatives of Non-Labour Organisations, convened by the Leader of the Federal Oppositiion, Rt. Hon. R.G. Menzies, K.C., M.P., and held in Canberra, A.C.T., on 13th,14th and 16th October 1944*, Melbourne, 1944, 2.

[6] Menzies (1967), 286.

[7] R.G. Menzies, *Speech is of Time*, London, Cassell,1958, 219.

[8] Ibid., 211.

[9] *Forming the Liberal Party of Australia*, 10.

[10] Ibid., 222.

[11] R.G. Menzies, Policy Speech, 1946.

[12] Rod Kemp, Marion Stanton (Eds.), *Speaking for Australia: Parliamentary Speeches that shaped our nation*, Allen & Unwin, Sydney, 2004, 143.

[13] *Forming the Liberal Party of Australia*, 11.

[14] A.W. Martin, "Menzies the Man", in Scott Prasser, J.R. Nethercote, John Warhurst (eds), *The Menzies Era: A Reappraisal of Government, Politics and Policy*, Sydney, Hale & Iremonger, 1995, 22.

[15] Menzies (1967), 5.

[16] Ibid., 11.

[17] Menzies (2011), 36.

[18] Institute of Public Affairs, *The I.P.A. Review*, Vol. 8, No. 2, 1954, 50.

[19] Menzies (1967), 9.

[20] Ibid., 12.

[21] Ibid.

[22] *Argus*, 10 October 1925.

[23] L.F. Fitzhardinge, *William Morris Hughes: A Political Biography*, Vol. II, Sydney, Angus and Robertson, 507.

[24] A.W. Martin, *Robert Menzies: A Life*, Melbourne University Press, 1993, Vol. I, 109.

[25] Martin, op. cit., 108.

[26] *Sydney Morning Herald*, 6 April 1931, 7.

[27] David Bird, "The Annus Mirabilis of a Subdued Radical", *Quadrant*, Vol. 53, No.11, November, 2009, 49-50.

[28] Menzies (2011), 178-9.

[29] *Argus*, July 1929.

[30] Alf Rattigan, *Industry Assistance: The Inside Story*, Melbourne University Press, 1986, 11.

[31] F.W. Eggleston, *State Socialism in Victoria*, P.S. King & Son, London, 1932.

[32] W.K. Hancock, *Australia,* Jacaranda Press (1930), 1961, 120-1.

[33] Martin (1993), 99.

[34] Menzies, Policy Speech, 1949.

[35] Menzies (2011), 188.

[36] *Forming the Liberal Party of Australia*, 12.

[37] Ibid., 6.

[38] Kemp & Stanton, 135-6.

[39] Kemp, Stanton, 141.

[40] R.G. Menzies, *The Measure of the Years*, Cassell, 1970, 55.

[41] Kemp & Stanton, 180.

[42] Menzies (2011), 35.

[43] Menzies (1970), 121-2.

[44] Ibid., 129.

[45] Menzies (2011), 35.

[46] Ibid., 157.

[47] Ibid., 186-7.

[48] Menzies (1970), 86.

[49] Menzies (2011), 159.

[50] Ibid., 41.

[51] Ibid, 42. See also Menzies (1958), 218.

[52] Ibid., 43.

[53] *Sydney Morning Herald*, 14 September 1998, 9.

[54] Douglas, *AFR*, 24 January 2014.

[55] Richard Nixon, *The Memoirs of Richard Nixon*, Macmillan, 1978, 120-1.

[56] Michael Blakeney, *Australia and the Jewish Refugees, 1933-1948*, Croom Helm, 1985, 141-7.

[57] Menzies (2011), 79-80.

[58] Menzies (1970), 282.

[59] I have repeated at several points in this essay some of the phrasing (with slight modifications) used in my introduction to *The Forgotten People* (2011). These concluding words are from that essay.

2

Robert Menzies

War and Peace

Anne Henderson

Anzac Day 1939 was, indeed, a full news day. The ministry of the new United Australia Party government of Robert Menzies was announced alongside reports of tens of thousands of returned servicemen marching in capital city streets, watched by many more. The following day, the *Argus,* in Melbourne, reported that 100 000 had watched the march to the Shrine of Remembrance, that city's monument to the fallen of the Great War, opened before a crowd of 300 000 in November 1934.

This mixture of war and politics on Anzac Day 1939 would define the government of Australia's new prime minister, Robert Menzies – April 1939 to August 1941. Described in the *Argus* as a person with a career of "sheer brilliance" and "an Australian Birkenhead,"[1] at age 44 Robert Menzies remains one of the youngest members of the Australian Parliament ever to take the prime ministership – only Chris Watson (1904) and Stanley Melbourne Bruce (1923), among his predecessors, were younger. Menzies came to the position on the sudden death of his predecessor, Joseph Lyons, the inaugural UAP prime minister after winning government in an historic landslide in December 1931. The years of Lyons' leadership of Australia were marked by depression and a battle to draw the economy back to prosperity. Menzies entered the Lyons Government after the 1934 election and soon became Attorney-General and Minister for Industry. By the time of Lyons' death, disunity in the UAP was barely under control, papered over by the still popular Lyons. With his death, rivalries became exposed.

The press reports surrounding announcement of Menzies' first cabinet emphasised the youth of many of its members. It was to be a fresh start after the appearance of disunity and tiredness in the last months of the Lyons administration. The *Argus* noted that no fewer than six of the men chosen were new to "Cabinet work" and that "most of the Cabinet are relatively young men." Menzies added that he attached "importance to the factor of youth" and that "the future of Australia rests largely on the shoulders of youth – so youth should be given its fair chance of influencing the policies amid the results of which it will have to live."[2] Menzies had also increased the size of Cabinet to sixteen by creating a new portfolio of Supply and Development under Richard (Dick) Casey. The prime minister explained that he felt the enormous task of organising the war effort was too much for one minister. Casey was soon given an assistant minister.

In time, well into the future, Robert Menzies would become Australia's most successful prime minister, outlasting opponents over a term of office spanning sixteen years and retiring at a date of his own choosing. But, in April 1939, this was a distant chapter in the Menzies' life story. The much younger Robert Menzies who announced his ministry on that Anzac Day did so against a backdrop of uncertainty. A row with the leader of the Country Party, Sir Earle Page, had split the Country Party and ended the agreement for coalition with the UAP. Menzies was left to lead a minority government, albeit one that could be assured of parliamentary support from its former partner on crucial issues. It would be almost a year before the UAP would again resume coalition with the Country Party. Menzies told the Governor-General, Lord Gowrie, wryly, when asked how long the new government could last, that he might only manage "six weeks."[3]

Robert Menzies was one of Australia's most astute politicians, moving, in 1928, with the help of strong political connections in the Nationalist Party of the day, from his remarkable and early success at the bar as a constitutional lawyer to Victorian State politics. Although self-made as a scholarship lad, Menzies had also grown up among a divergent clan that included his Sampson grandfather who had helped to pioneer Victoria's trade union movement, and Uncle Syd Sampson who ran regional newspapers where, as a boy, Menzies had helped after school. Syd Sampson also became the federal MP for Wimmera. In addition, Menzies' own father, James, had entered Victorian State politics as member of the Legislative Assembly for Lowan from 1911 to 1920. As he moved to university, Menzies made further contacts when editor of the *Melbourne University Magazine* and, with an impeccable Presbyterian background, as a Young Nationalist.

It was also a step up when Menzies married Pattie Leckie, the daughter of well-known businessman, and later senator, Jack Leckie. Further support came with his notable work at the bar – especially in matters before the High Court.

All this gave the political Robert Menzies a dream run. But he was also developing a persona in danger of attracting the average Australian's negative reaction to a "tall poppy." Added to this was Menzies' young man's and barrister's lack of tolerance for those not so well-endowed intellectually, especially at a time when most politicians on both sides of the House were without a university education.

Unlike his predecessor, the likeable and diplomatic Joseph Lyons, who had been schooled in the rag and tag of early Labor politics and carried the scars of his defection from Labor in 1931, Menzies came to the prime ministership in April 1939 a touch thin-skinned. His personal records, in letters and diaries from the time, indicate that as he faced enormous stress both internationally and domestically through 1939-41, the weight of office left him in doubt about his choice of career.

But Menzies' resignation, a few months over two years from announcing his first Cabinet, was as much about giving in as about his belief that playing politics was not appropriate in a time of war. The effect of these short years of political blooding, and those in opposition to follow, would mould the successful and more mature prime minister that Menzies became during his second chance in the Lodge. These were also years of resilience, lessons learned, dice rolled and opportunity knocking. Menzies made the best of all of them.

Undoubtedly, the Menzies years, from December 1949 to January 1966, were so successful they have come to overshadow, even extinguish, the performance of Menzies' first prime ministership in the historical record. Historians with Liberal Party sympathies have largely ignored the first Menzies prime ministership as not being part of the Liberal legacy. Pro-Labor writers have done likewise for different reasons. Paul Hasluck's war history volume is the best record, along with the first volume of Allan Martin's biography of Menzies. Hasluck's detailed study of the first Menzies Government led him to judge its legacy as "considerable" and "a major factor in Australian survival under Japanese threat."[4] Hasluck was also an admirer of John Curtin. But, in the popular histories – most often written by Labor-leaning academics – it is as if the Menzies Government of the early war years had no impact. Like the successful years of Prime Minister Joseph Lyons, it appears not to have existed.

It is a surprise, then, to read – in the papers of Frederick Shedden who served as permanent head of the Defence Department to both Robert Menzies and John Curtin – that the success of the Curtin administrations, covering the later war (1941-45), owed much to the legacy of the Menzies Government, 1939-41. Frederick Shedden described it plainly in the draft of a book he would never publish, writing:

> Some critics have charged the United Australia Party with lack of vigour in defence preparations since 1933, when the Nazi threat began to emerge, but many overlook the economic situation at the time ... The effects of the world depression on the Australian economy, and the demands for the restoration of cuts made to the budget had a restrictive influence on what could be devoted to defence. Admittedly, Australia entered on vast expenditure on the entry of Japan into the war but ... he would be a bold person who would assert that more might have been done. The military results of Curtin's miraculous conversion through responsibility when he came to power, and the measures he took at great personal political risk to have the Defence platform of the Labor Party amended, could not have been immediately effective, but for the foundations laid by the Defence Programme of the preceding United Australia Party Governments. Curtin generously acknowledged the inheritance he had received.[5]

Australians, like most in Western nations just two decades after the end of the Great War, carried contradictory feelings about fighting Adolf Hitler. The years of the 1930s had witnessed calls for negotiated peace as never before – even when the work of the League of Nations proved increasingly futile as the dictators of Europe moved to annex further territory. The reminders of the Great War carnage filled graveyards across Europe and were echoed in the scars and losses carried by hundreds of thousands in families and communities throughout Australia. The Munich Agreement of 30 September 1938, giving Hitler the Sudetenland in return for "peace", had been celebrated as a defining moment. The Prime Minister of the United Kingdom, Neville Chamberlain, was invited by the King to stand with the Royal couple on the balcony at Buckingham Palace as thousands celebrated below. In Australia, the Lyons Government had strongly supported Chamberlain. Then Hitler launched *kristallnacht* against the Jews within weeks and invaded the rest of Czechoslovakia a few months later. Negotiating with the Fuhrer, or following policies of appeasement, would eventually become a term of derision. Yet, in government circles – in Whitehall and beyond – hope still held that there would be a line drawn at some point that Hitler would not cross.[6]

Among what would become the "Allies", no one wanted war. President Franklin D. Roosevelt told a crowd in the 1940 presidential election campaign, as Britain faced potential defeat by Germany, "I've said this before, and I'll say it again and again and again, your boys are not going into any foreign wars."[7] Declaring that Australia was at war, on 3 September 1939, Robert Menzies spoke of it as his "melancholy duty." But, in Australia, those most opposed to armed conflict abroad were to be found in the Australian Labor Party. Where so-called appeasers had attempted to negotiate a line on the map of Europe – and later South-East Asia – that the aggressors would not cross, Labor was not interested in any sort of brinkmanship. Labor had spent the 1930s intensely pacifist and, even as war was declared, was prepared to argue that Australian troops should never be sent to fight Nazi Germany.

Labor's cry of home defence alone was to argue that Australia should stay out of any international involvement. Curtin, a long-time believer in the defensive strength of air power, opposed Australian trainee airmen being involved in the Empire Air Training Scheme. Against this somewhat parochial position, Robert Menzies' outlook – as that of Lyons before him – was internationalist, acknowledging Australia's alliance responsibilities as a member of the British Empire alongside a practical understanding that any defeat of Britain meant a dangerous future for Australia with its Imperial links to a mother country defeated by the Nazis.

Read today, John Curtin's arguments late in 1939 and even in 1940 smack of isolationist fervour. In May 1939, in a debate on the international situation in the House of Representatives, Curtin opined: "The efforts of the British Government in its negotiations for peace were to some extent made difficult by the partisan activities of those who are more concerned, as it were, with fighting Hitler than with establishing peace."[8] Curtin was opposed to war – and, in this, he had considerable backing in Australian public opinion. Curtin argued that the fascist countries had been partly pushed that way by the actions of democratic nations. And no war was justified to overturn repression in another country – "No war," said Curtin, "even in Europe, should be a war fought either to defend or to create political systems against other political systems."[9] The years of financial downturn had left a long shadow; the aggression of a European dictator towards countries many Australians had barely heard of – what John Curtin referred to as "remote parts of the world"[10] – did not especially resonate. As appeasers went, Labor was ahead of the pack.

In spite of Labor's opposition to sending Australian troops to fight Germany, on 4 January 1940, thousands of enlisted Australians marched through Sydney's streets to make up the 6 000 Diggers embarking for the war in Europe, the Middle East and North Africa.

The Menzies Government had also introduced compulsory military training for able bodied, unmarried men aged twenty-one. In mid-June 1939, after a robust debate in Parliament, the Menzies Government had established a National Register Board to oversee the allocation of manpower. Labor had opposed the bill on grounds of industrial conscription and a faction in the UAP led by Menzies' disgruntled colleague, Bill McCall, had tried to move amendments. Using the guillotine, the Government eventually shut down debate and the legislation passed easily with the Country Party falling into line. But division in the non-Labor ranks was clearly on display.

By September, Earle Page, who had stood down as Country Party leader, was replaced, unexpectedly, by the mercurial Archie Cameron from South Australia. Artie Fadden and other breakaway Country Party members rejoined the party fold, which strengthened their party's criticism of a government in which Country Party members secretly desired portfolios. Cameron's hostile correspondence with Menzies from October 1939 to early 1940 vented scuttlebutt and hyperbole, from exaggerated accounts of the Prime Minister's unpopularity throughout the nation and local grudges of wheat farmers in Western Australia to demands for action against "aliens" and dramatic increases in the enlistment of men.[11] Cameron even went so far as to suggest Menzies was holding shares in manufacturing industries in his wife's name. Menzies, in reply, described Cameron's intemperate communications as "a farrago of injurious gossip" and cautioned him that such outbursts did not make a good case for trusting the Cameron-led Country Party to observe cabinet solidarity.[12] As 1939 ended, Menzies expressed some of his misgivings to his son, Ken, writing, "The only piece of fatherly advice I can think of at the moment is that it is much better to be a good lawyer or even a good agricultural expert than an indifferent prime minister."[13]

On 2 March 1940, at the by-election in the seat of Corio to replace Dick Casey, who had left the House of Representatives to become Australia's first minister [ambassador] to the USA, the Government lost yet another seat. Sensing it was no time to bear grudges, within a week Menzies had brought the Country Party into a coalition where the Prime Minister agreed to consult Cameron on his choice of portfolios for Country Party members but would retain the right to choose them. At the same time, large increases in the numbers of troops for the Second AIF, with a squadron of the RAAF to be attached to it, were announced. In May, the Government appointed Essington Lewis, the Managing Director of BHP, as a wartime industrial overlord, making him Director of Munitions, with the same access to the War Cabinet as military chiefs of staff. Lewis's success in decision-making and industrial progress was such that John Curtin as prime minister increased his powers, making him also director-general of the Department of Aircraft Production.

Early in 1940, however, the national mood reflected a divided nation. War had affected many but not all. Political division, between and inside the parties, made politics uncertain. For Menzies, press advocacy that his Government had not made more strenuous efforts to support the war clashed with Labor's message that home defence was the real option. Labor, meanwhile, was caught in a divide that had split it throughout the 1930s, with divisions in NSW continuing around populist anti-communist Jack Lang and his opponents on the left, a divide made worse by the pact between Germany and the Soviet Union in August 1939 (commonly known as the Nazi-Soviet pact). It was an alliance that, by May 1940, had helped the Germans to advance through Norway and, elsewhere, into Belgium, the Netherlands and France.

Germany's advance pushed Curtin to unequivocal support for Australia's involvement in the war. But, in Labor ranks, Communist Party influence argued the Moscow line that the Soviet Union was not at war with the Allies, and that Australian troops were simply being used by "Imperialists" to further capitalist interests. Curtin condemned the Australian Council of Trade Unions (ACTU) in caucus as the unions tried to force Labor to support their campaign to defy the National Register laws. Industrial dispute dogged the nation.[14] Labor's Eddie Ward later estimated that some 855 disputes – on average eight a week – occurred between September 1939 and Menzies' resignation in August 1941.[15] By mid-April 1940, the Government had been forced to censor communist press comments on the war; after the fall of France, the Government declared the Communist Party of Australia, along with other groups, illegal.

As Paul Hasluck has chronicled and documented in *The Government and the People 1939-1941*, the first Menzies Government oversaw radical reform of the public service and federal administration, much of it forced on Australia by the demands of a war economy. The 1930s, with financial depression alongside technological changes in travel (aircraft) and communications (radio), had seen the Lyons Government take the first steps for a properly educated public service. At the outset of the war, however, the Federal Government was still saddled with a lowly-educated public service. During the war public service numbers would double with the most rapid growth during the Menzies years. As Hasluck has written, "in the course of two years, administrative functions that had been originally in the Defence Department had been greatly expanded and spread over [nine] departments – Defence, Navy, Army, Air, Munitions, Supply, Aircraft Production, Home Security, Labour and National Service".[16] In July 1941, after returning from the UK and the USA, Menzies and Defence supremo Shedden oversaw a complete reorganisation of the federal administration. Five new departments were created. Meanwhile, as a young federation, government was conducted between three cities, one of which (Canberra) saw many employees housed in makeshift huts.

Limitations aside, progress was made, much of which advanced Australia's federation notably. A wartime situation forced a more rapid response from government – often to situations that were constantly changing. The Menzies Government was also forced to connect parliament more directly with the war effort. And, notwithstanding party differences, a reasonable amount of co-operation developed between Government and Opposition in many wartime decisions. Under Menzies, that co-operation came with creation of a War Cabinet, an Advisory War Council (which included members of the Opposition) and an Economic Cabinet. Much of the reform of the public service at this time, and the subsequent and more developed administrative procedure that was undertaken, was overseen by Shedden who had learnt much at the Imperial Defence College (London) and from the retired secretary of the UK Cabinet, Sir Maurice Hankey (by now Lord Hankey). On their return from four months in the UK, in the first half of 1941, Menzies and Shedden set about reorganising departments and expanding the areas of ministerial responsibility. This added to the administrative structure a network of boards and committees which attracted specialised outside expertise and advice to what was, largely, a very inexperienced public service. The significance of the expansion of government in the war years can be seen in the figures: public expenditure grew sevenfold between 1938-39 and 1943-44.

1940 was an election year. The election would be held in very different political times from the previous one in 1937, when hope prevailed that war might be averted. As the press debated the timing of the election, the Menzies Government watched the resignation of Neville Chamberlain in the aftermath of defeat in Norway, the succession of Winston Churchill, and the fall of France. Behind the scenes, in Whitehall, capitulation to Hitler by Britain was narrowly overcome when Churchill outplayed his defeatist Cabinet colleague, Lord Halifax, the Foreign Secretary, who saw surrender and coming to terms with Germany as a way forward. As Britain became preoccupied with its own survival, Menzies sensed insouciance in London about distant Empire concerns over the threat of Japanese expansion.

In a lengthy cable, on 8 May 1940, to the Secretary of State for Dominion Affairs, Anthony Eden, Menzies gave blunt warning that Australia would not tolerate any lack of information on the progress of battles and the war generally.[17] There were worries also that the United States would transfer its Pacific fleet to the Atlantic. At the same time, there was still a belief in London that Japan could be mollified over any desire for territory further south. Menzies was successful in finally gaining British approval for Australia to open a diplomatic mission in Tokyo, to which Sir John Latham, Chief Justice of the High Court and a former Minister for External Affairs, was appointed as minister [ambassador]. Soon after, Australia received a request from Britain to send one division and two squadrons of aircraft to support Malaya in the event of an encroaching Japan, as well as a request from Australia's Brigadier General Thomas Blamey that reinforcements be sent to the Middle East. In the background, the Treasurer, Percy Spender, sought to find increased income with the pressures of growing expenditure. A mini-budget on 2 May 1940 increased taxes substantially.

The 1940 election, when it was finally called, was held against a backdrop of national mourning and tragedy. On 13 August, flying into Canberra, a Lockheed Hudson carrying three senior ministers – Geoffrey Street (Army, Repatriation), Henry Gullett (Vice-President of the Executive Council) and Jim Fairbairn (Air and Civil Aviation) – the Chief of the General Staff, Sir Brudenell White, a staff liaison officer, the Air minister's private secretary and four RAAF personnel crashed and burned killing all on board beyond recognition. Menzies recorded in later life that the tragedy had harmed his first term prime ministership more than anything else.

A week after the crash, Menzies announced that the country would go to the polls on 21 September 1940. A record number of candidates contested the election – a testimony to the divisions within Labor and unsettled allegiances for the major parties. In Kooyong, Menzies faced four independents as well as a Labor opponent.

In the House of Representatives the result of the election was very close. Neither side secured a majority. Labor had won seven seats in NSW. In other States, the Menzies Government held up; in Fremantle, John Curtin had narrowly retained his seat while Menzies in Kooyong attained a record majority. Still, almost a decade after its landslide win in 1931, the UAP was facing loss of government. The Country Party soon deposed its leader, Cameron. Artie Fadden emerged as acting leader and soon after became leader.

The option of a national government was put to Labor at a meeting of all parties on 16 October; Labor rejected the offer a week later. Menzies eventually formed a minority government, supported by two Independents from Victoria – Alexander Wilson in Wimmera and Arthur Coles in Henty. The weeks that followed were full of brinkmanship as the budget was passed. Many felt that the newly-elected Labor parliamentarian, Dr H.V. (Bert) Evatt, a former High Court judge, would stop at nothing to be part of a government. But John Curtin was not so keen to take charge while his own side of politics was rent with divisions. Menzies now had a precarious but, nonetheless, second fresh start.

By late 1940, Menzies had become more than concerned at a lack of communication from the British high command over the progress of the war. When Menzies realised that he had been left to discover from newspapers the defeat in West Africa of the Free French by the Vichy French, in late September he exchanged pointed cables with Winston Churchill.[18] Meanwhile, in Canberra, with Bert Evatt sharpening the tenor of Labor opposition and showing frustration at his lack of immediate advancement, Menzies wrote to Casey on 8 December 1940 that he had "no doubt a first class split [is] developing in the Labor Party."[19] Menzies also registered that Evatt was enjoying warm relations with "the weaker brethren on our own side." At the same time, the situation around expected Japanese advancement south made the lack of British support for reinforcement of its base at Singapore all the more worrying. Menzies' critics, the historian Stuart Macintyre, for instance, have scorned Menzies' dependence on the British alliance at the time, ignoring the fact that there was little alternative.

It was in this mindset that Menzies planned a most ambitious journey across the globe – believing he had a case sufficient to persuade Churchill and the War Cabinet in London of Australia's pressing needs. He also wanted to visit Australian troops abroad to improve their morale and to better inform himself of their situation. Menzies' hunch that the already splintered Labor Opposition had new internal difficulties left him confident he could afford time away from

Australia. There was also something of the hubris of a young and successful barrister turned political leader in Menzies' confidence he could persuade Churchill. Australia's High Commissioner in London, Stanley Melbourne Bruce, the former prime minister, warned Menzies his trip would achieve no change in Churchill's overall view of the war.[20] To Churchill, Australia and the dominions were protected by distance – he had no concept of the world of the Pacific.

Undaunted, and convinced he could change Churchill's mindset to make him see the needs of the Pacific dominions, Menzies left Sydney on 24 January 1941 on a Qantas Empire Flying Boat. Heading out across the Timor Sea from Darwin at dawn on 27 January, Menzies wrote in his diary, "Australia is behind and the great adventure has begun."[21] Back in Australia, Pattie Menzies had told her husband, as he would record in *Afternoon Light*, that he would last six weeks as leader on his return. But Menzies was undeterred, such was his belief in his advocacy.

After an extraordinary journey, hopping his way across Australia's top end to Indonesia, Singapore, Rangoon, Calcutta, Karachi, Bahrain and Basra to Palestine and thence to Egypt and Libya after which a long flight across the Sahara and southern Africa then north to Lisbon, Menzies and his small team arrived in England on 20 February. By the time he began his meetings in London, Menzies had as good a picture of the Empire and its war as any other, and possibly a better one than many. His visit to Singapore had made him even more concerned about Australia's vulnerability: his diary records, "the interesting material at Singapore was human – and disturbing."[22]

If Churchill had no imagination for the Empire beyond India, and its potential peril at the hands of advancing Japanese, then Robert Menzies would be hard pressed to convince him otherwise. The fate of Singapore was simply not on Churchill's horizon – he was looking the other way, to America. His quest by then was to woo the United States, with copious amounts of attention, in the hope it would come to Britain's aid.

Menzies extended his weeks in London in vain hope. He attended the War Cabinet and became known for his temerity in being a lone voice occasionally questioning Churchill's dogmatism. He dined at the prime minister's country residence, Chequers, on several weekends; he met senior Whitehall figures, media barons and business leaders. He travelled to major cities in the quest for trade deals for Australia's manufacturing industries now more isolated and with stiff competition from the United States. He became the darling of some of Churchill's Conservative critics for his readiness to speak up in the War Cabinet. He even visited Dublin and Eamon De Valera in the hope of influencing Eire's refusal to support Britain in the war.

Nothing worked. And, as he stayed in Britain, Menzies recorded how his emotions and regard for Churchill swayed from admiration to annoyance. For all his efforts, Churchill did not understand the situation at Singapore or the vulnerability of Britain's dominions in the Pacific. By 30 April, Menzies was protesting in the War Cabinet that Churchill was not consulting him ("though I was in London!")[23] regarding advice he should give the President of the United States in relation to moving significant sections of the US Pacific fleet to the Atlantic. As he travelled to Canada, after leaving Britain on his way home, Menzies tried to enlist the support of Canada's prime minister, Mackenzie King, for an Imperial War Conference in London. He was not successful.

Menzies returned to Australia on 24 May 1941, only to face the despairing news of the failed Allied campaign in Greece where Australian forces suffered major casualties, followed by their further defeat on Crete. In the days following his arrival home, Menzies was met with large crowds cheering his return. But the mood turned sour as the Government worked to overhaul significantly the administrative framework for a country at war – out of which came an administrative structure that would strengthen the future Curtin Government, but also one in which UAP malcontents like William Hutchinson, Bill McCall and Charles Marr were not given promotion. These three colleagues seriously undermined their own side of politics during the next few months.

The Japanese continued to move south, occupying Indo-China. As ministers and the press urged Menzies to return to London for another attempt at persuading Churchill to reinforce Singapore, the Labor Opposition through the Advisory War Council would not agree to his proposed visit. Losing the support of many Cabinet colleagues who were fearful their minority government might break down, thereby forcing an election, Menzies chose to resign the prime ministership late in August 1941. As Percy Spender has recorded, Menzies could have held on – he had not lost the numbers.[24] In the end, it was his decision that to continue to try to govern against such odds was not in the best interests of Australia in a time of war. Within six weeks, the Coalition Government, now led by the Country Party's Artie Fadden, had lost its majority in the House of Representatives (on the Budget) and John Curtin assumed the prime ministership leading another minority government. At the 1943 election, Labor won one of the greatest election victories in Australian history. It returned to office holding 49 seats, a majority of 23.

The night of his resignation, as he left Parliament House, Menzies was a broken man, leaning on his private secretary, Cecil Looker, and in tears. To his secretary he spoke of having "to bleed awhile."[25] Menzies retained the leadership of the UAP (and the Defence ministry) until the fall of the Fadden Government early in October after which he resigned, on 8 October. His successor as leader of the UAP was the ageing Billy Hughes. The chances of any political role for Menzies now looked bleak – especially as successive representations on his behalf for positions in the British war administration failed. But he did not resign from Parliament and returned to the Bar for extra income to support his family. Then, in January 1942, Menzies began a weekly series of radio broadcasts on commercial radio. These continued through 1943.

Much has been written on Menzies' *Forgotten People* radio talks. For the most part in these talks, Menzies editorialised on issues of government of the day. But, within months, he had expanded his scope to articulate what became a philosophical base for the future Liberal Party of Australia. From May 1943 – over some weeks – Menzies developed a thesis that it was the middle classes, the small entrepreneurs and white collar workers who had no effective political representation within the political party structures. To these people he would speak.

To some extent, Menzies was reliving the headiness of Joe Lyons' win in December 1931 when such citizens had swept Lyons to power at a time of great financial uncertainty. But the UAP had never defined its political platform formally. In his talks, Menzies was putting into words something of an inversion of Franklin D. Roosevelt's fireside chats over the radio that had spoken to the "forgotten man" during the depression years of the 1930s. But where FDR spoke to the poorest Americans, Menzies addressed hard-working middle Australians, voters who paid their way and had no representation from trade unions. While his talks struck a chord, it would be some years before the message would manifest itself in a new political party, much less win over a majority of voters.

For too long, in the historical accounts, Robert Menzies has been depicted as some sort of silver spoon Tory, given government on a plate. In fact, Menzies was always a skilful political operator ready to work from a small base within his political group to build anew. This had been the case when he was a figure in the

Young Nationalists in the 1920s and later one of the driving forces bringing the UAP into existence. In 1930, Menzies had worked with Labor's Acting Treasurer, Joseph Lyons, on a campaign to raise £30 million for a massive loan conversion. Later he was instrumental, through the Melbourne businessman, Staniforth Ricketson, in wooing Lyons away from Labor and installing him as UAP leader. Menzies was a consummate political operative. Whatever ambitions he may have entertained in the law, circumstances and the play of politics would eventually override such feelings. Politics was something Robert Menzies just could not give away. Following his failure to gain the position of Chief Justice of Victoria in January 1944, at a time of great despondency about politics,[26] Menzies set out on a path to lead a movement to create a new non-Labor party. After all, he had done this before – in 1931.

It is true as Ian Hancock has written that "many men and women were involved in the drawn out process" that eventually saw the formation of the Liberal Party of Australia in 1944.[27] But there is little doubt such an achievement would never have resulted without Robert Menzies. Unity among those disparate groups and individuals did not come easily, even after the actual party was proclaimed. In fact, disunity in New South Wales probably cost the Liberals the 1946 election. Menzies was the spearhead – and organiser – that made ultimate success possible.

Menzies began his campaign to form a new party shortly after the 1943 Federal election that saw such a loss for the UAP and Country Party. Out-playing Billy Hughes at the party meeting on 3 October 1943, Menzies emerged again as UAP leader, albeit saddled with Hughes as his deputy. Menzies had made his opposition to Hughes' leadership clear through 1943 when he headed up the National Service Group within the UAP – staying within the party but resolving not to attend party meetings, of which, indeed, there was only one. But there was still a long way to go – and the lacklustre state of non-Labor politics in January 1944 was no doubt the reason Menzies allowed his name to go forward for the position of Chief Justice of Victoria. Then, in 1944, the Curtin Government attempted to extend the wartime powers of the Commonwealth in what became known as the Powers Referendum. This gave Menzies an opportunity to campaign for the "No" case around the country, which he did forcefully through July. The referendum was easily lost, and brought Menzies' name back to the forefront of daily news.

Within weeks of the result, Menzies had written to the leaders of all non-Labor parties and groups loosely aligned with the UAP to invite them to a conference in

Canberra on 13-16 October 1944. This conference and another, two months later in Albury, would see the birth of the Liberal Party of Australia – an achievement of huge proportions given the divisive nature of the groups that came together. In no small way, the inclusion of Elizabeth (May) Couchman's Australian Women's National League gave significant organisational strength to the new party. The AWNL would underpin Liberal Party branch structure throughout Victoria, in particular. And the losses of the 1943 election had swept much of the old UAP away while, in time, as men returned from the war, fresh talent came forward to strengthen the new party's administration and pre-selections.

Robert Menzies returned to the Lodge in December 1949. The battle to wrest government from Labor had not been without its trials. In 1946, Menzies thought he was on the way to victory at the Federal election only to lose badly and win just five seats from Labor. He had been misled by the warmth of his supporters at election rallies – a warmth he had not experienced before. But these were his supporters. A majority of electors, however, had voted Labor. So a longer march had ensued, and Menzies could, in time, thank his rival, Ben Chifley, who had succeeded Curtin as prime minister in 1945. One Saturday, in August 1947, Chifley announced a hasty decision to nationalise Australia's banks. Menzies could also thank Labor's Attorney-General, Bert Evatt, for his unwise judgment in going on to appeal and appear before both the High Court of Australia and the Judicial Committee of the Privy Council in London in support of the bank nationalisation cause. By the time the banking legislation had been rejected as unconstitutional in both courts, it was just months before the 1949 election. Over the two years, Menzies had led protest rallies of his "forgotten people" – bank and insurance workers, small investors and entrepreneurs, other white collar employees – across the nation. Little wonder, at the 1949 election, the Liberal Party prevailed.

It is a testament to his experience of loss, and travails as Leader of the Opposition through the later 1940s, that the Robert Menzies who absorbed his party's success on Sunday 11 December 1949 was a subdued and almost stunned man. "I'm only mildly excited yet," he told reporters. "I should be home in bed. After a night's sleep I'll probably begin to take in what's happened."[28] The heading, "So happy; so tired," accompanied the article.

The "bleeding" which Robert Menzies had spoken of, in August 1941, had lasted less than a decade – and was not to return.

Endnotes

[1] *Argus,* 25 April 1939, 2.

[2] Ibid., 1.

[3] Sir Robert Menzies, *Afternoon Light: Some Memories of Men and Events,* Melbourne, Cassell, 1967, 13-14.

[4] Paul Hasluck, *The Government and The People, 1939-1941,* Australian War Memorial, 1952, 558-65.

[5] Frederick Shedden, Preface, "Book 3: The Notable war record of the Menzies government, 1939-1941", Shedden Collection, NAA, A5954/765/3.

[6] David Dilks (ed), *The Diaries of Sir Alexander Cadogan, OM, 1938-1945.* 212-3.

[7] *The Road to Alamein: Churchill's Desert Campaign* (television documentary) BBC TWO, aired 5 November 2012, see www.bbc.co.uk/programmes/b01nts8p

[8] *CPD,* H of R, Vol. 159, 201-2.

[9] *CPD,* H of R, Vol. 159, 203.

[10] *CPD,* H of R, Vol. 160, 1381.

[11] Cameron to Menzies, 19 October 1939, NLA, MS 4936, Box 582, Folder 31.

[12] Menzies to Archie Cameron, 20 October 1939, NLA, MS 4936, Box 582.

[13] Letter, Robert Menzies to Ken Menzies, 6 December 1939, Menzies family collection.

[14] Hal G.P. Colebatch, "Treachery: the Communist Party and the Labor Party", *National Observer,* no. 59, summer 2004, www.nationalobserver.net/2004_summer_112.htm

[15] Elwyn Spratt, *Eddie Ward: Firebrand of East Sydney,* Rigby, 1965, 67.

[16] Paul Hasluck, op. cit., 436.

[17] R.G. Neale (ed), *Documents on Australian Foreign Policy 1937-49,* Vol. 3, 1940, Document 215, 272.

[18] Anne Henderson, *Menzies at War,* 105.

[19] Menzies to Casey, 8 December 1940, NLA, MS 4936, Box 581, Folder 23.

[20] Neale (ed), *Documents on Australian Foreign Policy 1937-49,* Vol. 4, July 1940-June 1941, Cablegram 14, 325.

[21] Menzies' diary, 27 January 1941, R.G. Menzies (A.W. Martin and Patsy Hardy), *Dark and Hurrying Days,* National Library of Australia, 1993, 20.

[22] Menzies' diary, 29 January 1941, Ibid., 23.

[23] Menzies' diary, 30 April 1941, Ibid., 121.

[24] Percy Spender, *Politics and a Man,* Angus & Robertson, 1972, 164.

[25] Gavin Souter, *Acts of Parliament,* Melbourne University Press, 1988, 340.

[26] Anne Henderson, *Menzies at War,* 183 – information supplied by historian John Paul.

[27] Ian Hancock, "Liberal Party of Australia", in Graeme Davison, John Hirst & Stuart Macintyre (eds), *The Oxford Companion to Australian History,* revised edn, Oxford University Press, Melbourne, 2001, 390.

[28] *Argus,* 12 December 1949, 1.

3

Robert Menzies

The Second Prime Ministership

John Howard

The most remarkable thing about the second prime ministership of Robert Gordon Menzies was that it happened. It is difficult to imagine a more abject political failure than that of Bob Menzies when he left the prime ministership on the 29 August 1941. Australia was at war, and he had been found wanting by his colleagues. It was the first time a prime minister of Australia had lost office in this manner. Betrayed by many previously seen as loyal confidantes, few people saw him with a political future. The saga of his political revival from those dark days to become Australia's longest serving prime minister was a testament to his resilience, intellect and the clarity of philosophical beliefs.

In Federal Parliament for not even five years before assuming the top job, Bob Menzies had always been a highly talented man in a hurry to gain control of the nation's affairs. In the process he did not stoop to conquer. He wrongly assumed that in politics every argument is won by superior logic and force of advocacy, never by accommodating a variety of views and an understanding of the sensitivities of others seeking a place in the political sun. He himself wrote: "I do not doubt that my knowledge of people, and how to get along with them and persuade them, lagged behind. I was still in that state of mind in which to be logical is to be right, and to be right is its own justification."[1]

In planning his return to a leadership role on the non-Labor side of politics, Menzies realised that his brusque personal treatment of many of his colleagues had contributed to his early and painful downfall as prime minister. As he recorded,

I had yet to acquire the common touch, to learn that human beings are delightfully illogical but mostly honest, and to realize that all-black and all-white are not the only hues in the spectrum.[2]

He resolved to remedy this.

Menzies also understood the pressing imperative to unify the non-Labor political forces in Australia. The dismal result for the old United Australia Party (UAP) at the debacle which was the 1943 election, when it lost nearly half its seats in the House of Representatives and all its Senate seats, helped to convince many erstwhile doubters that only a person of the intellect and debating skills of Robert Gordon Menzies could revive the then Opposition forces, by bringing to them coherence and a consistent belief system.

When he returned in 1943 as leader of the UAP, Menzies demanded that, as the UAP was the larger of the Opposition parties, its leader should again become the Leader of the Opposition. He also won a free hand in undertaking the challenging task of unifying the non-Labor groups. In less than two years he had brought about the formation of the Liberal Party of Australia, by any measure the most successful political party in Australia's history. Many played a role in this political transformation, but the force of Menzies' personality and ambition effectively to confront the Australian Labor Party lay at its heart.

A crucial element in Menzies' personal recovery and the birth of the Liberal Party was his *Forgotten People* broadcasts of 1942. These were a series of radio talks covering a range of economic, social and political issues. Their message had near universal application, particularly to the vast bulk of middle class Australians represented neither by organised labour nor large employer groups. In these broadcasts Menzies appealed to the innate value attached to home life by millions of Australians and the simple aspiration they had for a secure and happy future for their children and their nation.

In a notable passage he conveyed the essence of his message:

I do not believe that the real life of this nation is to be found either in great luxury hotels and the petty gossip of so-called fashionable suburbs, or in the officialdom of organized masses. It is to be found in the homes of people who are nameless and unadvertised, and who, whatever their individual religious conviction or dogma, see in their children their greatest contribution to the immortality of their race. The home is the foundation of sanity and sobriety; it is the indispensable condition of continuity; its health determines the health of society as a whole.[3]

The genius of these broadcasts lay in the fact that they provided enough detail to explain Menzies' core values but not so much as to make him hostage to future cynics and nit-pickers. They were an object lesson in direct, simple political communication and persuasion.

Even after the successful formation of the Liberal Party, Menzies' return to the Lodge was by no means assured. While the vote for the Coalition parties increased by 10 percent at the 1946 election, he barely troubled the scorers in terms of seats. The mutterings – especially in Sydney – that "you can't win with Menzies" came back. But Ben Chifley's fatal blunder, launched in August 1947, in attempting to nationalise the private trading banks, gave Menzies a crucial issue. Grabbing the banks was rightly seen as blatant socialisation. An indignant Australian public responded enthusiastically to Menzies when he crystallised the issue as one between state control and individual freedom.

The debate over bank nationalisation saw Menzies at his fighting best. He had a philosophical base – freedom of choice – readily combined with a powerful economic argument that state ownership of the banking system would retard economic growth. The Chifley legislation would fall foul of the Constitution, with both the High Court of Australia and the Judicial Committee of the Privy Council (then available as a final court of appeal) ruling the Labor lunge at our banking system to be unconstitutional. Because this issue had only been settled just before the 1949 election, it remained vivid in the minds of many voters as they went to the ballot boxes in that historic poll.

Menzies' first Government after his 1949 election victory demonstrated just how much he had learnt from past failure. Its cornerstone, and that of all subsequent Menzies ministries, was a rock solid coalition between the Liberal and Country parties. His first Coalition Treasurer was Arthur Fadden, Leader of the Country Party. Without question the second most significant figure of the Menzies years between 1949 and 1966 was the formidable John McEwen, deputy leader of the Country Party who succeeded Fadden as Leader in 1958. Enmity between the two parties had caused constant difficulties in earlier years. Menzies saw to it that this did not happen again.

Difficult questions such as handling the Korean War wool boom, projected entry of the United Kingdom into the Common Market early in the 1960s or emerging dispute about the tariff were all deftly handled. Menzies' mature mastery of politics certainly included the art of coalition.

The personnel of that first post-1949 Government showed Menzies at his pragmatic (and forgiving) best. Old and bitter rivals such as Sir Earle Page were included (as Minister for Health). Secure in the knowledge that his 1949 victory had given him great authority, Menzies was untroubled about giving Cabinet positions to past critics such as Richard Casey (Minister for National Development) and Thomas White (Minister for Air and for Civil Aviation). That some of them had previously been touted as leadership rivals left Menzies unmoved. Having delivered an emphatic win he knew that, if he governed well, his position as prime minister was untouchable.

And, indeed, the ministry he led placed him in a strong position to govern with strength and determination – among them, Fadden as Treasurer; Percy Spender as Minister for External (now Foreign) Affairs; McEwen at the helm at Commerce and Agriculture (later Trade); Harold Holt at Labour and National Service, and Immigration; Casey heading National Development and, later, External Affairs; Eric Harrison, then Philip McBride, in Defence; William Spooner at Social Services, then National Development; Neil O'Sullivan at Trade and Customs; and John Spicer as Attorney-General.

People joining the ministry in the ensuing decade included Paul Hasluck (Territories); William McMahon (Social Services and later Primary Industry); Shane Paltridge (Civil Aviation); Athol Townley (Immigration, then Defence); John Gorton (Navy, then Works and Minister Assisting the Prime Minister on Education matters); Alexander Downer Snr (Immigration); and Hubert Opperman (Shipping and Transport).

The Australia Menzies was elected to lead was vastly different from that over which he had presided ten years earlier. It had come close to suffering enemy invasion; Australia's Asian neighbourhood had been transformed by the emergence of India, Pakistan and Indonesia as independent nations, with European colonialism under pressure to contract even further. Leadership of the democratic world had passed from Britain to the United States. The Cold War between the Soviet-led Eastern Bloc and the American-led West was gathering momentum. The communist takeover in China early in 1949 increasingly focused the minds of all Australians. World communism had become a growing threat. Menzies intuitively understood this and adjusted his political thinking and rhetoric accordingly. The Labor leaders, Chifley and then Evatt, fatally misread this historic development. This failure would haunt their party for years into the future and provide much of the explanation for the historic ALP split in 1955.

Given how long Menzies remained in office it is common to think that after

46

winning in 1949 he was under no electoral pressure at all. This is wrong. His first five years of office were characterised by the loss of a referendum to ban the Communist Party in 1951 and a very close shave at the 1954 election. Only after the Labor Party split in 1955, and an emphatic election win in November of that year, did the belief take root that Menzies would remain prime minister for as long as he chose to stay in politics.

He understood the world-wide threat of communism. He also knew that the influence of communist leaders on unions very dominant in the ALP predisposed many people in the Labor Party to a less strident attitude towards both the domestic and world-wide menace of communism. Industrial disruption on the wharves, in the coal mines and in the electricity industry was a frequent reminder of the communist presence.

Decades after those times it is difficult to comprehend just how threatened many felt both about the communist menace, but also the possibility of World War III breaking out between the United States and the Soviet Union. When Menzies returned from an overseas visit in 1951 and declared that Australia should prepare for war within three years, most people took him seriously.

At Menzies' instigation Federal Parliament passed a law declaring the Communist Party of Australia a subversive organisation. The High Court declared this as beyond the defence power of the Commonwealth and therefore unconstitutional. At a referendum in September 1951 he sought the necessary alteration to our Constitution to ensure that outlawing the Communist Party would be permissible. He over-reached with the referendum question, and fell victim to the historic reluctance of the Australian people to change the Commonwealth's founding document. This was a big setback for Menzies, and a huge win for his new Labor opponent, the former High Court judge, Dr Herbert Vere Evatt – the Labor leader and former Prime Minister, Ben Chifley, having died just after the 1951 double dissolution election.

Fortunately for Menzies, but disastrously for the ALP, Evatt's truly bizarre behaviour, several years later, before the Royal Commission into the so-called Petrov Affair negated any political momentum Evatt might have gained from the 1951 referendum victory and the narrow win Menzies secured at the 1954 election.

Petrov was a Soviet spy, posing as the Third Secretary at the Soviet Embassy in Canberra. He defected and successfully obtained political asylum in Australia along, ultimately, with his wife. This occurred on the eve of the 1954 election and Evatt became convinced that the whole affair had involved a conspiracy to damage him politically. A Royal Commission was set up to examine Soviet spying in Australia. Evatt appeared at the Commission on behalf of some of his staff, and made reckless allegations against the security services as well as Menzies and his colleagues. He was so unbalanced by the issue that he would later write to the Soviet Foreign Minister, Vyacheslav Molotov, asking whether or not Petrov had been a spy. Unsurprisingly Molotov replied that he had not been a spy!

Evatt compounded the agony for his party when, in October 1954, he attacked certain Labor MPs from Victoria whom he claimed were under the control of the so-called Movement, a lay organisation associated with the Catholic Church and very active in fighting communists in unions. It was led by a Mr B.A. Santamaria. He became the most influential figure in post-World War II Australian politics never to enter the Australian Parliament. In reality the MPs attacked by Evatt were staunchly anti-communist; had wanted the Communist Party of Australia banned; and believed that Evatt's handling of the Petrov Affair had done great damage to the Labor Party.

Embarking on a campaign to eject the Victorian MPs and their supporters from positions of influence in the Labor Party, Evatt procured the removal of the then Victorian Executive of the ALP (which supported the MPs, by then dubbed "the groupers") and its replacement by a new, more left-wing body. This made a split in the Labor Party inevitable. It all came to a head at the Federal Conference of the Labor Party in March 1955 in Hobart.

The split was formalised with the formation, first in the Victorian Parliament and, later, in the Federal Parliament, of breakaway Labor parties. These two breakaway parties later became known as the Democratic Labor Party (DLP). The split was catastrophic for Labor in both the Victorian and Federal elections of 1955. The Labor Party was resoundingly defeated in both. In each case the breakaway Labor parties directed their second preference votes to Coalition candidates with painful consequences, respectively for the Cain Labor Government in Victoria, defeated in the Legislative Assembly in April 1955 and vanquished at a general election in May 1955, and the Evatt-led Labor Opposition in Canberra, which lost a bundle of seats to Menzies in November 1955.

DLP preferences in favour of the Coalition would play a crucial role in several elections to come. They proved absolutely vital in preserving the Menzies Government at the close run poll in December 1961. It is incontestable that the

Labor split, with the subsequent emergence of the DLP, kept Labor from power for many more years than would otherwise have been the case.

Thus far I have dealt with the pure politics of Menzies' first decade back in power. But these years saw the Australia he led rapidly changing for the better in so many ways. The 1950s saw the great middle classing of our country. Home ownership began to grow. In 1949 it was a little under 50 percent. By 1970 it had reached 70 percent. Private ownership of motor vehicles multiplied in the early years of the 1950s. Australians began to enjoy better health services and more educational opportunities. They were reassured by extremely low levels of unemployment. The Chifley Government had launched a program of high immigration in the late 1940s. Menzies further expanded this. The fertility trough of the Great Depression meant that large numbers of migrants were needed to fill many of the jobs becoming available in the 1950s.

It is fair to say that the 1950s was the first decade of the twentieth century in which large numbers of average Australians came to enjoy the good life. Despite concern about the threat of communism and the possibility of war involving nuclear weapons, domestically it was a period of growth and considerable prosperity. There were periodic economic challenges, such as the high inflation flowing from the Korean War wool boom, but these were usually dealt with quickly and without continuing disruption to the Australian economy.

On the foreign policy front the Menzies Government aligned Australia with what were then seen as her traditional allies, Britain and the United States. In most cases this did not cause any difficulty as our two "great and powerful friends" usually sang from the same hymn sheet. A painful exception was the Suez crisis of 1956. Egypt nationalised the Suez Canal in July 1956; Israel attacked Egypt in October of that year, with Britain and France intervening purportedly to separate the combatants and thus protect the Canal, which was vital to their trading interests. There was collusion between Britain, France and Israel regarding the Israeli attack on Egypt. The United States opposed the Anglo-French action, and effectively used economic blackmail to force a British withdrawal from Egypt. Relations between London and Washington became poisonous which was stressful for Menzies as, hitherto, he had never imagined that he would need to choose between his heart and his head. The then Prime Minister, although acutely aware that American power now dominated the free world, remained nonetheless intensely pro-British in his values and attitudes.

The most important long-term foreign policy event of Menzies' early years in

Government was the signing of the ANZUS Treaty in 1951. This bound Australia and New Zealand with the United States and has remained the centrepiece of our security ever since. It was very much the work of Percy Spender. Although only External Affairs Minister for less than a year and a half, he achieved a lot. In addition to ANZUS he launched the Colombo Plan whereby thousands of Asian students would study at Australian Universities thus providing an enduring link between our country and future generations of Asian political leaders and business operatives. There was also the South-East Asia Treaty Organization (SEATO) to which Australia was a signatory along with the United States, Britain, France, Thailand, New Zealand, Pakistan and the Philippines. This was a defensive pact against potential communist aggression in South-East Asia.

The late 1950s saw Menzies completely dominate domestic politics. He used this authority to usher in a new era for higher education in Australia. Acting on the recommendations of the Murray Committee, he lifted Commonwealth assistance to universities to a new plane. This produced a massive expansion in the university sector, to be soon followed by greater investment in other parts of tertiary education. He greatly valued university education and, by his actions, made it accessible to tens of thousands of Australians who would otherwise have been denied it. When speaking in the House about the Government's initiative, he said:

> I hope that we will not, under current pressures or emotions, be tempted to ignore the basic fact that civilization in the true sense requires a close and growing attention, not only to science and all its branches, but also to those studies of the mind and spirit of man, of history and literature and language and mental and moral philosophy, of human relations in society and industry, of international understanding, the relative neglect of which has left a gruesome mark on this century.[4]

He added that it was "a rather special night in my political life," recalling his own undergraduate days, and those of Dr Evatt, "when a university student was either a scholarship holder (and they were hard to come by), or the child of poor parents who made huge sacrifices for their children, or one of the small number who were children of the well-off."[5]

It was in this period (1957) that the historic commerce agreement between Australia and Japan was signed. It is difficult to exaggerate the significance of this agreement. Just twelve years after the end of World War II, and in the face of vehement opposition from the Labor Party, and a marked reluctance on the part of the general public, still conscious of the brutal treatment by the Japanese of Australian prisoners of war, Menzies and his Minister for Trade, John McEwen, pushed for this pact which greatly expanded trade horizons between Australia and Japan. It was the true beginning of the trade relationship between Australia and Asia which is so crucial to Australia's current economic prosperity.

In an historic coincidence 1957 was the year which saw the signing of the Treaty of Rome. This document was the foundation of what has now become the European Union. At first Britain did not join what was generally called the European Common Market. In time that would change and, when Britain did join, Australia lost many trading preferences in the United Kingdom, previously guaranteed under the imperial preference system established through the Ottawa Agreement of 1932. Having laid the foundation of a more favourable trading relationship with Japan, Australia was readily able to accommodate the growing Japanese demand for our mineral resources, particularly of iron ore after its discovery in the 1960s. As one door closed another, via the Commerce Agreement of 1957, opened. McEwen and Menzies had been far-sighted.

Although the Commerce Agreement with Japan had lasting consequences for Australia's economic relations with Asia, it was the Colombo Plan inaugurated by Percy Spender, Menzies' first Minister for External (now Foreign) Affairs that established enduring personal links with Australia, through the opportunities it afforded for young men and women from a variety of Asian countries to study in Australia.

These experiences for so many young Asians would prove vital years later in preserving the substance of Australia's bilateral relations with our neighbours, even when at a head of government level the friendship might temporarily sour. A good example was Malaysia during the later years of the prime ministership of Dr Mahathir. Despite his coldness towards Australia (and, indeed, a number of other Western countries) the network of links through commerce, the armed services and elsewhere meant that normal transmission was resumed once Malaysia had a prime minister who was less indifferent to Australia. One of the explanations for this was simply that so many Malaysians in key positions had been educated at Australian universities.

1961 saw Menzies suffer a near-death political experience. He and his Treasurer, Harold Holt, mishandled the Government's response to a booming economy in 1960. A so-called short, sharp shock was applied too severely, and there was a painful reaction to the credit squeeze imposed by the Government.

Unemployment went to 4.1 percent, a level undreamt of for more than a decade. The Government's greatest problem was that it had behaved in a contradictory manner. The 1960 budget spoke of an economy which was running smoothly, yet within a few months the Government had to announce that the economic brakes were being slammed to the floor. Confidence in both the Prime Minister and the Treasurer was eroded.

Menzies' narrow victory at the 1961 election was due to the faithful flow of DLP preferences in Victoria. Although Coalition seats fell like ninepins elsewhere, not one Liberal or Country Party seat was forfeited south of the Murray. This was due entirely to something like 90 percent of DLP preferences going to Coalition MPs. Truly Menzies had been saved by Santamaria.

Although there was much soul-searching in the wake of this near defeat, Bob Menzies' position as leader was not seriously questioned. Within the next two years he would stage a stunning political recovery, go to an early election in November 1963, and be returned with a greatly increased majority.

This was largely due to Menzies' clever exploitation of the outside control of Labor MPs exercised by a Special Federal Conference of the ALP over an issue which left Arthur Calwell and his fellow Labor MPs appearing equivocal in their support for a US communications centre at North-West Cape in Western Australia. This centre was an integral part of the worldwide functioning of the American nuclear deterrent. Using the mantra of "the 36 faceless men", Menzies effectively painted the Federal Conference of the ALP, which had 36 members, but did not include the Leader or Deputy Leader of the Federal Parliamentary Labor Party, as unaccountable outsiders, more in sympathy with left-wing ideology than the national security interests of Australia.

The other winning issue for Menzies in 1963 was that for the first time the Federal Government promised significant financial assistance for independent (mainly Catholic) schools, via grants for science blocks, which were to be made available on a *pro rata* basis to all schools. This historic decision began the process of dismantling what many saw as one hundred years of discrimination against the independent school sector. A remarkable feature of this policy shift was that, despite the majority of Australian Catholics still being Labor supporters, their party of choice had stubbornly refused to remedy the injustice they felt existed in the education system. There was little doubt that this education promise by Menzies at the 1963 election won for the Liberal Party, for the first time, the votes of many middle-class Catholics, especially in New South Wales.

Reflecting Menzies' continuing commitment to home ownership a cash grant of £250 ($500) was promised to young home-buyers who had saved a designated amount towards a deposit on their first home.

1963 was the last general election Menzies would fight. He led the party to a successful outcome in the 1964 half-Senate election and, as widely expected, resigned the prime ministership in January 1966. He thus stood down after seven consecutive election victories, combined with another two for the Senate alone, at a time of his own choosing.

His final two years in government were anything but a lap of honour. It was during this time that his government took two of the most controversial national security decisions of his entire sixteen years in power after 1949. The first of these was the introduction of conscription late in 1964. The other was the decision in April 1965 to commit an Australian combat battalion, to serve alongside the Americans, in defence of South Vietnam.

One of the ironies of these decisions was that possible further aggression from Indonesia, at the time of that country's confrontation of Malaysia, was the principal driver for the introduction of conscription. Yet it was to Vietnam that the conscripts would be sent in the second half of 1965.

Menzies was a staunch believer in the Domino Theory. It held that if one country in South-East Asia fell to communism then it would only be a matter of time before others were overcome. This theory may seem simplistic, indeed erroneous, from the distance of fifty or sixty years, but in the 1950s and 1960s it was a belief strongly held throughout the Western world. There was plenty of field evidence to validate it, particularly in the wake of the French defeat in Indo-China in 1954 which came only a few years after Mao's takeover of mainland China in 1949. Dwight Eisenhower, the President of the United States, 1953-61, held firmly to the Domino Theory, as did Australia's long-serving foreign minister, Richard Casey.

At first Australia's commitment in South Vietnam had strong public support. As time passed, however, this began to wane, particularly after it became apparent that the Americans had concluded that a military victory could not be achieved and peace talks with the North Vietnamese were pursued. It is clear that one of the reasons Menzies committed Australia to a deep involvement in Vietnam was that he saw it as a way of ensuring that the United States would remain committed to the defence of our immediate region and thus, if required, the defence of Australia. Like so many others at the time of the decision to send the infantry battalion, Menzies would have seen it as inconceivable for the United States not to have achieved her military objectives in Vietnam.

Years later, Lee Kwan Yew, the revered founder and leader of Singapore, would argue that American (and Australian) involvement in South Vietnam had bought time for Malaysia and Singapore to emerge as stable, pro-Western nations. He also averred that the allied presence in South Vietnam had given heart to the anti-communist cause in Indonesia.

There is little doubt that the Menzies Government between 1949 and 1966 put down the foundations of modern Australia. It was this period which saw not only a huge increase in Australia's population but also the emergence of a truly middle-class Australian society. It was also a period of amazing economic stability. Low inflation, very low unemployment, and the ready availability of credit for small businesses, accompanied consistent levels of economic growth. Strong immigration flows played a major role. It has been estimated that some 70 percent of the new jobs that became available in the 1950s were filled by migrants. The assimilation policies of that era worked effectively. Great national development projects – such as the Snowy Mountains Scheme (inaugurated by the Chifley Government) – symbolised the easy coming together of newly-arrived migrants in their adopted homeland. Although there had been some tempering of the White Australia policy in the late 1950s, through abolition of the dictation test, it was Menzies' successor, Harold Holt, who, as prime minister, would effectively end this discriminatory policy.

Menzies was the beneficiary of benign post-World War II economic circumstances. It was a period of recovery after the devastation of war. It was also a period when the prevailing economic orthodoxy in Australia was that interventionist policies such as high tariffs, centralised wage determinations and fixed exchange rates were the right policies. Despite rhetoric to the contrary, these policies had bipartisan support. This was because they appeared to work. It was very difficult to challenge an economic framework which seemed to have delivered such economic growth and stability.

It was only the occurrence of such dramatic events as the quadrupling of world oil prices and the collapse of the Bretton Woods era of fixed exchange rates that the established orthodoxy was challenged. It quickly became apparent that a new approach was needed. The old methods would no longer work.

Bob Menzies left politics at a time of his own choosing in January 1966. Although Menzies himself departed politics then, it is fair to argue that the

Menzies era did not truly conclude until the defeat of the Coalition Government by the Australian Labor Party, led by Gough Whitlam, in December 1972. Harold Holt, Menzies' loyal deputy for nearly a decade, was unanimously elected to succeed the Liberal Party's founder. Holt led the Coalition to a massive victory in November 1966, when support for Australia's participation in the Vietnam War was at its peak. His successor, John Gorton, whom I described in *The Menzies Era* as a tory larrikin, succeeded Holt after the former's tragic drowning at the end of 1967. Gorton had immense charm and appeal and was possessed of high intelligence. Yet his lack of discipline and a seeming indifference to some of the ethos of the Liberal Party, especially relating to federalism, led to him being removed as leader by his own party, despite having seen off Whitlam at the 1969 election – albeit with a sharply reduced majority.

Perhaps, as the last man left standing, William McMahon, who for so long had coveted the top job, replaced Gorton. He was perceived as being no match for the flair and flourish of Whitlam. Yet, if there can be anything such as an honourable defeat, he probably delivered one in the 1972 Federal Election. Whitlam's majority was only nine.

Holt, Gorton and McMahon were part of the Menzies era not only because they had all served as ministers in Menzies' ministries. They also presided over essentially the same economic orthodoxy which had operated during the Menzies' years, although it is right to acknowledge that McMahon, as Treasurer, had begun to question the high tariff policies of the Menzies period and especially championed by John McEwen. As a mark of the continuing bipartisan embrace of the old economic approach, the lavish spending plans outlined by Whitlam for the 1972 election presupposed a continuation of the high levels of economic growth enjoyed during the Menzies years.

His critics claim that he succeeded merely because he had the good fortune to be in government during times of uninterrupted prosperity. Not only is this false, but it ignores his capacity to respond effectively to those economic challenges which arose despite the general prosperity of the period. A prime example of this was his Government's response to the Korean wool boom of 1951 which saw Australia's inflation rate reach 23 percent that year. Within 12 months it had returned to more normal levels. History is full of examples of governments falling into error even during times of great economic prosperity.

Menzies triumphed as a political leader for a number of reasons. First of all, he was a conviction politician. There was never any doubt where Menzies stood on issues. He was certainly the best political orator I have ever heard. He knew, intuitively, that politics was a battle of ideas, not a public relations contest. He had an extraordinary intellect. If he had remained in the law, it is very likely that he would have reached the bench of the High Court. Above all, the former Prime Minister had a skilful understanding of the aspirations of middle Australia.

Endnotes

[1] Sir Robert Menzies, *Afternoon Light,* Cassell Australia, 1967, 57.

[2] Ibid.

[3] Robert Menzies, *Forgotten People and Other Studies in Democracy*, Liberal Party of Australia (Victorian Division), 2011 [1943].

[4] Cited in John Howard, *The Menzies Era*, HarperCollins, 2014, 247.

[5] Ibid.

4

On the Political Side

Graeme Starr

At a press conference following announcement of his retirement on 20 January 1966, Sir Robert Menzies was asked: "What do you see as your most lasting achievement" as prime minister? He nominated two broad areas of policy, one external ("Australia's relations with the United States") and one internal ("what has been done about education").[1] It was a fair assessment. Even critics bent on perpetuating the myth of the Menzies era as a time of torpidity usually concede, albeit reluctantly, that foreign affairs and education were the fields of greatest activity.

Before he mentioned policy, however, Menzies stressed what he called "the political side." He said he looked back with most satisfaction and pride on two political achievements without which his successes in particular fields of policy would hardly have been possible. The first was what he regarded as the "highly individual task" of creating a new party of principle from a mass of political fragments, and sustaining that party through more than twenty years, most of which were spent in government. The second was construction and maintenance of the fruitful and enduring coalition with the Country Party, which thereby provided the numbers needed to top-off the majority in the House of Representatives.

Menzies' policy successes certainly deserve appropriate recognition. But they would not have been possible if he had not first applied what he had learned about promoting a genuine and credible image of unity through party-building and coalition-maintenance. Similarly, these achievements "on the political side" were possible largely because of Menzies' exceptional intuitive and developed campaigning skills in Opposition and in Government, which contributed significantly to his record as Australia's most successful national political campaigner and longest-serving prime minister.

Party building

The extraordinarily difficult task of building the Liberal Party was nearing completion when the Menzies Government was elected in 1949. Menzies' first term as prime minister had lasted less than two-and-a-half years. When he regained the leadership of a sadly depleted and dispirited Opposition after the 1943 Federal election, he faced the task of remaking his side of politics. He acknowledged that the party he led, the old United Australia Party, was a spent force with no mass membership, no process for strategic consultation between the parliamentary party and the organisation, and no principles or codes for "rank-and-file finance" which Menzies insisted "ought to be the monetary basis of any true democratic organisation."[2]

Menzies therefore proposed a series of conferences which resulted eventually in the transformation of Australian politics through the founding of the modern Liberal Party. There had been earlier unsuccessful moves to unify the non-Labor side of politics,[3] but the new party was unmistakeably "Menzies' Child."[4] Against the odds, the party came about through his influence,[5] with the party platform and constitution indelibly marked by his words and speeches and standing essentially unchanged until after 1966.

Politics is people

Menzies' leadership in 1949 reflected the valuable lessons of his experience as Prime Minister and his extraordinary record as Leader of the Opposition. A successful government needed the backing of a strong party in which a mass membership had a meaningful role in strategy and policy. A successful party needed a credible funding code to enhance its independence from outside interests. These questions demanded continuing attention if the Liberals were to project the sense of purpose, propriety and permanence necessary for stability and survival.

Menzies saw 100 000 as a reasonable and appropriate target membership for a party in government.[6] He stressed the message that this could be achieved if every joining member should feel that he or she has an effective chance of influencing both policy and organisation.[7] By 1950, with the party newly elected to Federal government, membership rose to 197 984 people in 1 651 branches.[8]

The membership gradually settled around 100 000, where it remained until after Menzies' retirement in 1966. After Menzies, the only significant rise in party membership occurred in 1975 when the unpopularity of the Whitlam Government made it especially easy for the Liberals to attract new members.[9]

Throughout his second prime ministership, Menzies remained actively engaged in party affairs. He worked closely on strategy with the general secretaries in the State organisations through the Staff Planning Committee (the SPC consisted of the senior federal staff and the State general secretaries),[10] and either he or the deputy leader chaired the organisation's Joint Standing Committee on Federal Policy, which brought together relevant ministers and the organisational leaders from all States. As prime minister, Menzies participation in major party activities was not done simply for public relations reasons. Indeed, public relations was only a peripheral aspect of functions like the meetings of the Federal Council, which were held without bells and whistles and with policy debates conducted in closed working sessions to avoid media grandstanding. The time Menzies gave to party affairs was instrumental in development of a substantial strategic and policy role for the organisation and thus in sustaining party numbers and enthusiasm.

Principled party funding

In view of the history and experience of the United Australia Party, the integrity of party funding presented the Liberal Party with more immediate problems. There was no disagreement with Menzies' insistence on "rank and file" finance or with his warning that the fundamental weakness of the older parties had been their dependence on corporate finance through relationships with the external business club (the Consultative Council) which had controlled party funding. Accordingly, Menzies insisted that, as a founding principle, the Liberal Party "would raise and control its own funds ... [and] would be free of any possibility of control from outside itself."[11]

With the party only months old, however, a public controversy erupted. It arose from what was seen as an attempt by another Sydney-based business club[12] to take control of the party's funding efforts.[13] The disintegration of the new party seemed imminent, but this was avoided largely by the success of the State president (and Federal Treasurer of the party), William Spooner, in developing a strict code of finance principles based on those advocated by Menzies. These included: donations would be accepted only from individuals and companies and not from clubs and trade associations, and only when given unconditionally; there would be only one finance-raising body; only authorised persons would handle party money, and proper records would be kept; and parliamentary members and candidates would not engage in the raising and disbursement of funds, thus insulating government policy-makers (especially ministers) from the direct influence of donors.

The finance principles as developed by Spooner and Menzies were subsequently adopted by the party federally.[14] They were applied rigidly and continue to be so by responsible party leaders. There may have been occasional lapses of commitment by individuals and some State parliamentary groups, but throughout the Menzies era and beyond the strength of commitment to the code by the wiser leaders and party officials has served generally to maintain the integrity of the policy process free from undue influence.

Less than two decades after Menzies' retirement, however, the relevance of the finance code was undermined by introduction (first by the Wran Labor Government in NSW in 1981 followed by the Hawke Federal Government in 1983) of laws requiring the disclosure of donations to parties and candidates. Among the consequences, possibly unintended, of these laws were the opening of opportunities for new increments of corruption and extortion in the political system and removal of the mechanism for insulating the policy process from the campaign funding process. Moreover, the new laws provided increasingly generous public funding[15] to political parties (or, through them, to the real beneficiaries in the advertising, media, research and communications industries). Initially, the Liberals, seeing disclosure as a threat to privacy and voluntarism and to the principles of freedom of association, opposed public funding of politics as a mistaken spending priority and refused to be subsidised, but eventually they were forced to join the other parties at the public trough.

By earlier standards, parties and campaigns came to be awash with money, which began to play an increasingly important role in the political process. With the willingness and the wherewithal to pay for professional services, the parties found that they no longer had to depend on the role and enthusiastic activity of members and volunteers. The political environment was transformed and many party functions considered important in the Menzies years declined in relevance.

Coalition building

The architecture of the Liberal Party was crucial to the party's survival in government in the Menzies era, just as it had been to its success in opposition. The organisational question that absorbed the greatest effort was the agreement on relations with the Country Party (now the National Party). In government after 1949, the maintenance of a high level of unity in this relationship was the key to successful political strategy in general and electoral strategy in particular, but it was recognised quite early that formal unity was out of the question and that a close electoral and parliamentary alliance was the only option realistically achievable.

The two parties understood the need to avoid any appearance of disunity, but they approached their relationship from different directions. The Country Party had declined Menzies' invitation to participate in unity conferences. They made it clear their party was resolved to maintain its separate identity.[16] The Liberals retained their ultimate goal of full non-Labor organic unity as advocated by Menzies,[17] with some even calling for elimination of (or amalgamation with) the Country Party. For Menzies, collaboration with the Country Party was a prime task for the Liberals. He emphasised this was vital for the future political stability of Australia.[18] This became the focus of the rolling series of meetings that settled coalition strategies for the capture of government, and the outcomes of these meetings set the stage for subsequent relationships between the coalition parties in office.

Even in government, however, there were significant differences between the coalition parties at all levels, making it extremely difficult to maintain a credible image of unity. There were strong and almost tribal animosities between the parties at the local level, differences over ideology and organisation at the State level, policy and strategy conflicts at the parliamentary levels in the States, and old personal differences exacerbated by policy differences in the Federal parliamentary parties. Further, there was no common pattern in the relationships between the parties from one State to another: a "war of attrition" persisted in Queensland;[19] calls for amalgamation along the lines of absorption in Victoria;[20] and continuing resentment among Liberals in New South Wales who believed the Country Party was systematically trying to exclude them from rural areas.[21]

Government required astute management of these tensions. What the Federal President of the Liberal Party, Richard Casey, called "the virus of antipathy"[22] generated fears in many sections of the party that the ill-feeling might become so acute that the Country Party would withdraw from the coalition.[23] The strategic differences between the two parties seemed irreconcilable. Menzies always sought compromise. As a consequence the parties moved into government with a coalition agreement on joint Senate tickets and faithful exchange of preferences in a minimum number of three-cornered House contests. Moreover, parochial differences were assuaged when Menzies, Casey and the New South Wales and Victorian State presidents (William Spooner and Magnus Cormack both heading for parliamentary honours) reported that working arrangements had been arrived at in each State where coalition relations were relevant.[24]

The coalition agreement included a commitment to a comprehensive common federal policy. In the early years, agreement on policy was specific: the stabilisation of primary industries through guaranteed prices; full encouragement to all secondary industries; encouragement for increased production; public works; reestablishment of servicemen and women; housing; immigration; defence; contributory social services and abolition of the means test; arbitration; and the decentralisation of public administration.[25] Going into government, however, party leaders like Casey and Eric Harrison, Deputy Leader of the Parliamentary Liberal Party, were prepared to announce without qualification that the coalition parties were united in the shared goal of defeating "the Socialists" and that there was no "cleavage or disagreement" between the parties "whose policy in all major matters is identical".[26]

In his Joint Policy Speech for the 1949 election, Menzies announced that "just as we have acted jointly in opposition … we shall set up a combined government if you elect us". The Country Party leader, "Artie" Fadden, declared that his party stood "four square behind the policy stated by Mr Menzies" and would form a strong composite government with the Liberal Party.[27] There was some criticism that the agreement gave the Country Party leaders exactly what they always wanted and reflected their shrewd understanding of the nature and power of smaller parties in political coalitions.

Coalition maintenance

Both parties came to government satisfied with the coalition settlement and with the process that had brought it about. The agreement was a contributing factor in the winning of government and the principles of the agreement were followed in each subsequent electoral contest during the Menzies era, adding meaning and legitimacy to the election victories.

The relationship between Menzies and Fadden had not been an easy one during much of the decade before they became colleagues in government, but as prime minister and deputy prime minister the partnership was marked by a professional mutual respect, reflecting Fadden's public description of Menzies as "the leader of a composite party with a composite platform and a composite policy".[28] Differences between the coalition partners arose from time to time[29] but potential tensions or incidents that might suggest serious coalition disunity were well managed. Those that did become public tended to reflect long-standing disputes over party political interests (such as the impact of electoral laws) or economic policy preferences (such as questions involving exchange rates or, later, tariff policy). Incidents in both categories emerged in the first years of the new government and persisted well beyond Menzies' retirement. Their potential damage was contained by calm, careful attention to coalition maintenance.

There was considerable scope for conflict over political interests. The question of party representation in the Cabinet and the ministry, along with allocation of portfolio responsibilities, was an ever-present sensitivity. Menzies was generous in his inclusion of Country Party ministers – five of the 19 members of Cabinet in 1950 (or two of 12 when the ministry was divided in 1956), compared with 19 of the 74 coalition members of the House of Representatives. Further, Menzies acceded to Country Party demands for influential policy portfolios. Fadden became Treasurer and his deputy, John McEwen, Minister for Commerce and Agriculture (later Trade). Menzies was deft in his management of such issues, helped at the outset by his relationship with Fadden and, except for some agitation for increased representation when McEwen succeeded Fadden early in 1958, this potentially troublesome question never became a critical issue within the Coalition.

The political question that plagued coalition relations in Menzies' time involved competition between the parties in triangular contests. Electoral arrangements, along with policy agreements, had to be settled between the parties before every election. The stakes were high. The Liberals persisted, for example, with their ambition for amalgamation, even offering the Country Party generous terms[30] such as presidency of a combined party and equal numbers for the smaller party on a joint executive, but the Country Party remained wary of Liberal intentions. Similarly, there was suspicion among Liberals that many of their coalition partners shared the view of the leader of the Country Party in New South Wales, Max Bruxner, who told a meeting with the Liberal Party in 1952: "There will be no joint policy if there is a single triangular contest. I prefer to go my own way and win or lose these seats."[31] In this view, a Country Party seat lost to Labor could always be won back at a subsequent election, but a seat lost to a Liberal might become subject to coalition arrangements and possibly be lost forever. Triangular contests, especially in by-elections such as those in Gwydir in 1953 and in Calare in 1960 maximised the non-Labor vote but resulted in a great deal of bitterness between the parties,[32] seriously complicating the process of coalition maintenance.

John Howard's account of the decision of the executive of the New South Wales Division of the Liberal Party to overturn an earlier decision to run a candidate in the traditional Country Party seat of Cowper in 1963 illustrates the political complexities of triangular contests. It also shows the sensitive nature of the relationship between the organisational and parliamentary wings of the Liberal Party on such questions and Menzies' subtle skill in navigating this relationship.[33]

These complications, and the Country Party's sensitivity on electoral matters, were displayed most clearly in 1962 when conditions called for redistribution of federal electoral boundaries. Based on the 1961 census, the House of Representatives would have been reduced from 122 to 120 with an increased proportion of urban to rural seats. Both the Country Party and the Labor Party opposed the redistribution proposals. McEwen condemned them as "intolerable" in the strongest terms and called for amendment of electoral laws "to ensure a sufficient voice for the out-back, for the north and for the great export industries".[34] When it became clear that an embarrassing revolt was imminent and that the Country Party was prepared to vote with Labor to defeat the proposals approved by the Liberals, Menzies had the bills removed to the bottom of the House of Representatives notice paper where they subsequently lapsed.[35] They were replaced in the following year with amendments to the electoral legislation acceptable to the Country Party. Commentary saw this as a defeat on what many Liberals regarded as a matter of important principle.

Economic policy differences between the coalition parties also emerged in the very early days of the Government. Only months before the 1949 election, the Chancellor of the Exchequer in the UK, Sir Stafford Cripps, announced a 30 percent devaluation of the pound sterling. Nine other countries, including

Australia, followed. The new Menzies Government faced an immediate political issue, with commercial interests representing importers calling for an appreciation of the value of the Australian pound. The Chamber of Manufactures defended the existing exchange rate, with primary industry interests joining them in opposition to any revaluation.[36]

Menzies and many Liberals in the ministry were reported to favour revaluation, but a few Liberals together with Fadden and the Country Party were opposed.[37] When some Country Party ministers made it clear that they would rather leave the Government than agree to a revaluation, the proposal was dropped by Menzies and the looming cloud of inflation[38] was dealt with by alternative measures and Treasurer Fadden's "horror budget" in the following year.

There were lessons for the Liberals in these incidents in the Government's first year, especially when subsequent currency valuation decisions became necessary in the face of opposition from Country Party leaders, McEwen in 1967 and Doug Anthony in 1971, following Menzies' retirement. It became clear that the Country Party, voting as a united bloc, had a strategic advantage as potential "balance of power" in the ministry or the joint party room where Liberal opinion was more likely to be divided. Further, it was demonstrated that the concurrence of the Country Party with the majority Liberals in the coalition could not be taken for granted and that principles such as ministerial responsibility and cabinet solidarity had to be weighed carefully in coalition agreements.

These principles came into sharper focus in coalition relations in the later years of the Menzies era after McEwen replaced Fadden as leader of the Country Party. An incident that became known as "the Bury affair"[39] illustrates this. In an address to the Australian Institute of Management in July 1962, Minister for Air and Minister Assisting the Treasurer, Leslie Bury, Liberal member for Wentworth (NSW), said that the effects on Australia's economy of Britain's proposed entry into the European Common Market had been greatly exaggerated and that, but for certain rural industries feeling that they may need to adjust any plans for future expansion, entry could ultimately bring benefits to Australia. As Trade Minister negotiating on the subject and preparing for discussions at a forthcoming Prime Ministers' Conference, McEwen was shocked. He publicly rebuked Bury, claiming that by lightly brushing off the threat to Australian industry he was undercutting the negotiating position agreed by the Cabinet. The fray inevitably involved Menzies as prime minister, who found that with unfeigned regret he had to ask Bury to resign.

Press comment and the political folklore it generated tended to present Bury's resignation as another example of the Country Party leader in a "tail wagging the dog" situation, perhaps because McEwen at the time was thought to be positioning himself to succeed Menzies eventually as prime minister in a coalition government. Menzies appears to have had great respect for Bury, as did his party, which tried to persuade the Prime Minister to retain him.[40] As he said in his letter asking for Bury's resignation, however, Menzies was bound by the principles of ministerial responsibility and cabinet solidarity[41] and he could not allow a situation where his and McEwen's negotiations could be met by the argument that their own government contained and retained a minister whose views were not those of the Cabinet. Further, Menzies wrote that he had tried his best to devise some middle course, even consulting McEwen in search of a way to avoid dismissing his minister. McEwen later wrote that he had advised Menzies not to drop Bury from the ministry,[42] but the Prime Minister found himself in the unfamiliar position where he felt he had no real choice.

As with any government, there were numerous instances of internal disagreement over specific policy interests. Most of these differences were settled in ways agreeable to the Country Party, and only occasionally (such as with rejection of key recommendations of the Vernon Committee of Enquiry into the Australian Economy in 1965) were Menzies' decisions seen to be contrary to the interests of McEwen or the Country Party. Some Liberals became critical of Menzies' approach to the management of the coalition. Sir Garfield Barwick, for example, saw a "fundamental weakness" in coalition government and argued that Menzies "avoided any confrontation" with McEwen, although he conceded that this was part of Menzies' "general practice" of chairmanship by consensus.[43]

Political disagreements in coalitions tend to be settled by compromise or by patience and delay, with the majority preference usually prevailing but with appropriate concessions being made wherever possible to minority opinions, especially in policy areas of vital interest to the minority's constituency. This describes Menzies' approach to coalition maintenance. He had experienced disunity, defeat and Opposition in the 1940s. Near-defeats in 1954 and 1961 hinted at the spectre of minority government, and convincing wins like those in 1955 and 1958 demonstrated how easily disunity can be exploited. It would have been extremely difficult to convince Menzies that a favourable compromise with the Country Party was too high a price to pay for government.

Coalition is a peculiarly difficult form of government and successful coalitions are rare. Few coalitions anywhere have been more successful than the one constructed by Menzies almost seventy years ago between the Liberal and Country parties in Australia. In retirement, the leaders of both parties looked back on the coalition with satisfaction. Fadden wrote approvingly of the Opposition in the 1940s and of the two parties with a common purpose "working well together with a minimum of friction".[44] Menzies described the Country Party as our close and almost indistinguishable ally.[45] To Menzies, the coalition was much more than simply an electoral convenience. It was, as he called it, the basis of a joint government heavily dependent for its success upon the mutual loyalty that he developed with Fadden and, later, with McEwen, of whom he said: "I have had the most tremendous loyalty not only from Country Party ministers, in particular Mr. McEwen, who is a most distinguished man, but also his private members."[46]

At his press conference on retirement, Menzies was asked a supplementary question about his achievements: "Sir Robert ... Do you foresee the day when the Liberal Party may govern in Australia without the assistance of the Country Party?" Menzies replied with a message for his successors:

> I don't. If you are asking me, at any time over these years if I had come back with an absolute majority for the Liberal Party on the floor of the House, I still would have said to the Country Party, "I want you to be in" because I believe it is in this alliance, this conjunction of affairs that a great deal of strength has existed.[47]

Menzies as campaigner

The first really successful Menzies election did not come until 1949, or more than ten years after he first became prime minister. Significantly, he went into that campaign as what would today be called a "two-time loser". The inconclusive result in the 1940 election was hardly a memorable victory. He had gone to the polls as prime minister, and emerged from the campaign without a clear majority in the House of Representatives and subsequently lost the prime ministership. The result was worse in 1943, when Menzies was not leader but campaigned as a sort of Leader of the Opposition-in-waiting. By 1946, Menzies had begun to unify his support throughout the country, but again he lost to Labor. If he was the great campaigner, it was not yet evident.

Apart from occasional warnings that the Liberals could "never win with Menzies," the prognosis for 1949 was much more positive. Numbers, momentum and enthusiasm were stirred by Menzies' campaign against Labor's bank nationalisation measures and the massive "No" vote in every State in the 1948 Rents and Prices referendum. Menzies and the coalition were united and ready for a year of intensive campaigning and displayed enhanced appreciation of the importance of organisation and political strategy. At the electorate level, for example, the Liberals had built a team of some seventy professional field officers to organise the grass-roots campaigns.[48] At the national level, the confidential political appreciations regularly prepared by the party's Staff Planning Committee[49] were the primary source of intelligence for strategic decisions.

Menzies learned to depend on key professionals on the SPC for strategic advice. As he told the general secretary of the New South Wales Division: "It's my job to be distracted. Your job is to focus on the long term."[50] Sir John Bunting provides the best description of the place and value of strategy in a Menzies campaign:

> Government had to be worked for, earned, and earned well. He scheduled meetings with his party advisers well in advance of any possible election, and in collaboration with them settled on an election campaign plan. This was independent of the election date. That was something to be fixed later on, the first thing was strategy. This was no mere programming matter, such as itineraries and visits to marginal seats. It was, in political terms, the intellectual structure of the campaign: issues, problems, policies and so on. And, from the testimony of the advisers, the strategy, once settled, was unchanged.[51]

A Menzies era campaign typically consisted of two parts (the 365 days campaign, and the 31 days campaign). The purpose of the long campaign was to inform and persuade the electorate on policy and performance. This required much more time than was available in the few weeks before polling day. Thus, the year before the election became a period of continuous campaigning with every available medium being used to ensure that the Menzies message was delivered as widely and as fully as possible. Because of limited media in 1949 it was difficult to run a continuous campaign in opposition, but Menzies was able to sustain an effective effort and attract public attention through a tightly organised series of national speaking tours. These won widespread press notice, both because of the popular welcomes Menzies received in unexpected places and because of the incidence of violence from groups determined to disrupt his public meetings. In government after 1949 and in control of the campaign agenda, Menzies further developed the continuous campaigning technique, using Question Time and other opportunities in Parliament to advance his policies throughout the year. This remained a feature of the Menzies style of long-term campaign.

For Menzies, the intensive campaign period (the four weeks immediately before polling day) also had policy information as its main focus. It began with a public meeting usually in a suburban town hall, most often in or near the Leader's electorate or at some similarly friendly venue, and held on a week-day evening with the aim of gaining the best coverage in the morning newspapers. The feature of the launch meeting was the policy speech, usually lasting about an hour, broadcast throughout the nation, and typically setting out the campaign theme, criticism of the Opposition, the positive highlights of the party's record, and four or five "big-ticket" promises in the major policy areas. It was not thought necessary to have anything like a glossy manifesto with details of policy in every area of government as all this had been spelled out in the preceding months. Instead, the policy speech was printed and distributed as a small booklet to serve as the "prayer-book" for candidates and speakers throughout the campaign. The policies announced in the speech could be elaborated upon by Menzies or a minister during the campaign, but any new policy announced after the policy speech was considered a desperation move or a distraction.

Following the launch meeting, Menzies would tour the States, usually with a rally in each capital city and with public meetings in as many marginal electorates as were judged to be necessary, and a major rally with a speech in the character of an address to the nation to end the campaign. With only a few exceptions, politics was to be enjoyed. As his daughter, Heather Henderson, has noted, her father's "political meetings were, like Wirth's Circus, the Greatest Show on Earth".[52] They were the great attractions of the Menzies campaigns and continued to be so into his final elections for the House of Representatives in 1963 and the Senate in 1964.

The town-hall style of campaign clearly suited Menzies' sense of theatre, but the meetings were much more than simply theatrical performances. The public meeting was seen as the best available means of getting the message to the people. It was consistent with Menzies' conviction that "the art of politics is to convey ideas to others" and to persuade a majority to agree.[53] Paul Hasluck explained that, while Menzies liked to do his "bit of showing off" in his lighter speeches, he used his words to convince or persuade others rather than to have the fun of feeling clever.[54] In Hasluck's view, Menzies was successful on the political stump because he had fashioned for himself good tools of trade and handled them like a master craftsman with great skills with a crowd enabling him to overcome rowdy opposition.[55]

As a professional politician, Menzies clearly understood the role of publicity in the modern political contest, but he was wary of stunts and he recognised that too much emphasis on publicity could easily turn the political campaign into a mere marketing campaign. While he preferred to address the people directly at public meetings, Menzies was willing to adapt when new media technologies and tactics were found to be useful in communicating his message. His use of radio in the 1940s, for example, was particularly innovative and successful and his broadcast addresses, notably *The Forgotten People* series, proved to be of lasting significance.[56]

Television was introduced to Australia in 1956 and Menzies first used it to campaign with a fifteen minute talk on all Sydney and Melbourne channels on 3 November 1958. He was initially cautious about television, conscious that it had potential to restrict as well as promote the flow of public information. To him, politics was about words, while television was about images.[57] He was prepared to use television, but he was not prepared to let television use him. Thus, when a Great Debate was organised in 1958, reported to be the first such election event televised anywhere between the leaders of opposing parties,[58] Labor was represented by its leader and deputy leader, Dr H.V. Evatt and Arthur Calwell, while Menzies was happy to leave it to his deputy leader, Harold Holt, and William McMahon. The Prime Minister was always the focus of a Menzies campaign, but he saw no value in providing a platform and an audience for his opponents.

By 1963 and Menzies' final House of Representatives election, the leaders of both major parties, Menzies and Labor's Arthur Calwell, agreed for the first time to launch their campaigns on radio and television. Menzies was reluctant, but he wrote to a friend that television as a "medium is one I detest. I would always prefer to have a live audience (but) I realise this is the way to reach the most people, and allow them to form opinions ..."[59] The forty-minute policy speech was taped before an invited audience of 250 Liberal supporters, kept secret and broadcast four days later. Election campaigning was changed for ever. The public meetings remained an important part of the Menzies campaigns in 1963, just as they had been in 1949 and later, but television had clearly become entrenched in the Australian pattern of electioneering.[60] Menzies accepted this, but insisted on his own style, as described by Sir John Carrick:

> Menzies insisted on looking the television viewer full in the face and simply talking to him. PR people always said we should put some cows or sheep or some other relevant visual in the background but Menzies wouldn't hear of it. He was right, of course. Fortunately, he was good at it.[61]

It was generally agreed that Menzies "mastered television with consummate ease and success,"[62] but he remained concerned that it could easily be used for deceptive advertising campaigns. There would have been no point in asking him to pose in an Akubra and bowyangs, patting a bull on the head and calling it a primary industry policy, but he was more than willing to sit and discuss the details of a complicated policy announcement. The public relations firm and the advertising agency had technical jobs to do, but they had no real role in determining political strategy. The Liberal advertisements in the Menzies era were possibly the worst in any campaign, but flaws in communications and strategy were rare and somehow Menzies and his party kept on winning elections.

According to one adviser, Menzies was similarly "allergic to public relations gimmickry, he never had a public relations officer on his staff, and he spoke with contempt of that particular craft in contemporary Australian politics."[63] In the early days of his party, the Federal President, Richard Casey, sought to persuade him to take "a more professional approach" to public relations in his campaigns,[64] but Menzies was happy to leave that sort of thing to someone else. He was willing to have a press secretary, but, as one of his journalistic biographers noted, what the prime minister really wanted was someone who could keep the press at bay.[65] The style of modern political campaigning that relies extensively on polling, public relations stunts, "spin doctors", and media management techniques owes very little to Menzies.

Conclusions

Robert Menzies did not withdraw from politics when he lost the prime ministership in 1941 and resigned the party leadership shortly afterwards. His leadership was judged a failure, but he still had much to offer in public policy and he was far from ready to retire. He took defeat as a signal to apply himself to politics with greater vigour and he made sure that the value of his experience was not lost. He reinvented himself and his side of politics, redefined the role of Opposition, and returned in 1949 to lead the most successful government in Australian history.

When he retired from Parliament in 1966, Sir Robert Menzies' talents as a political campaigner were widely recognised. His reputation was assured by seven consecutive election wins and holding a record for years spent as prime minister. More importantly, he was also a skilful political architect. As he said on retirement, the achievements which gave him most satisfaction and pride were the design and building of the modern Liberal Party and the maintenance of the Liberal-Country Party coalition, two of the most enduring Australian political edifices. His pride was well placed, for without these achievements it is unlikely that his campaigning skills alone would have been sufficient to win the 1949 election and every House of Representatives election from 1949 to 1963. Menzies' policy achievements in international relations, education and elsewhere certainly deserve appropriate recognition, but they would not be much of a story if Menzies had not first applied the lessons he had learned about promoting a genuine and credible image of unity through party-building and coalition-maintenance.

Endnotes

[1] Department of Prime Minister and Cabinet, *PM Transcripts, Press, Radio and Television Conference Given By Sir Robert Menzies At Parliament House, Canberra On 20th January 1966*, Interview, 20 January 1966.

[2] Menzies itemised and emphasised the defects in the UAP in his opening address to the conference of supporters in Canberra on 13 October 1944. The speech is reproduced in Graeme Starr, *The Liberal Party of Australia: A Documentary History*, Drummond/Heinemann, 1980, 73-7.

[3] There had been earlier moves to unify the non-Labor side of politics, but these had been unsuccessful and were absorbed by the Menzies initiative. See W.H. Anderson, *The Liberal Party of Australia: Its Origin, Organisation and Purpose*, The Liberal Party of Australia (Victorian Division), undated; 3, and John Cramer, *Pioneers, Parties and People: A Political Memoir*, Allen & Unwin, 1989, 59-68.

[4] Gerard Henderson, *Menzies' Child: The Liberal Party of Australia, 1944-1994*, Allen & Unwin, 1994.

[5] As John Howard has noted, the formation of the Liberal Party was anything but a foregone conclusion and "without the galvanising influence of Menzies's intellect, eloquence and political experience it would not have come about". John Howard, *The Menzies Era*, HarperCollins, 2014, 60.

[6] R.G. Menzies, Closing Speech to the Albury Conference, 16 December, 1944. The national membership of the UAP had fallen to unviable levels, probably fewer than 40,000 people.

[7] Ibid. This was more modest than the Inaugural Federal Council's target of "a million members each contributing one pound per annum". Report of the Provisional Executive to the Inaugural Federal Council of the Liberal Party of Australia, 29-31 August, 1945.

[8] Liberal Party of Australia, Report of the Federal Executive to Federal Council, 4 September 1950, 11.

[9] In the Whitlam years between 1972 to 1976 Liberal membership in New South Wales alone rose from a low of just over 15,000 to 39,068.

[10] See Graeme Starr, *Carrick: Principles, Politics and Policy,* Connor Court, 2012, 148-50.

[11] W.H. Anderson, *The Liberal Party of Australia: Its Origin, Organisation and Purpose,* The Liberal Party of Australia (Victorian Division), undated, 3.

[12] The Institute of Public Affairs (NSW) was regarded as heir to the Consultative Council. It had been represented at the Canberra and Albury conferences but unlike the other participating organisations it did not surrender its identity when the Liberal Party was formed.

[13] *Sydney Morning Herald,* 17 April 1945, and 18 April 1945.

[14] Joint Statement by T.M. Ritchie and William Spooner, 18 December 1945, cited in G. Starr, *The Liberal Party of Australia: A Documentary History,* Drummond/Heinemann, 1980, 113.

[15] In 1984 Commonwealth public funding provided 60 cents per House of Representative vote and 30 cents per Senate vote. By 2015 the entitlement had increased to 259.405 cents per eligible vote.

[16] Don Aitkin, *The Country Party in New South Wales,* ANU Press, 1972, 42-3; Paul Davey, *The Nationals; The Progressive, Country and National Party in New South Wales, 1919 to 2006,* Federation Press, 2006.

[17] Liberal Party of Australia, *Forming the Liberal Party of Australia,* Record of the Conference of Non-Labour (sic) Organisations, undated, 2.

[18] R.G. Menzies, Closing Speech to Albury Conference, 16 December 1944.

[19] Letter, J.B. Chandler to Liberal Federal Secretariat, 6 December 1945.

[20] Letter, W.H. Anderson to the Director of the Liberal Federal Secretariat, 4 December 1945.

[21] Report of the NSW State Executive of the Liberal Party, 27 August 1948.

[22] Letter, R.G. Casey to the Director of the Liberal Federal Secretariat, 17 August 1948.

[23] Letter, R.G. Casey to the Director of the Liberal Federal Secretariat, 20 August 1948.

[24] Report of the Federal Executive to the Federal Council, 15-16 August 1949.

[25] Joint Statement by T.M. Ritchie and Sir Earle Page, 8 April 1946.

[26] Hon. E.J. Harrison and Mr. R.G. Casey, Press Statement, 9 November 1948.

[27] A.W. Fadden, Policy Speech, 17 November 1949.

[28] *Sydney Morning Herald,* 11 November 1949.

[29] A useful analysis of many of the major issues on which the coalition parties differed in the Menzies years is presented in B. Costar, "The Politics of Coalition", in S. Prasser et

al (eds), *The Menzies Era: A Reappraisal of Government, Politics and Policy*, Hale & Iremonger, 1995, 98-107.

[30] "Proposal For Amalgamation: Lib – C.P". Meeting of the Executive Committees of the Liberal and Country Parties on Thursday, 25 January 1951.

[31] Minutes of the Meeting of the Negotiating Committee of the Liberal and Country Parties, 29 April 1952.

[32] See K. West, *Power in the Liberal Party*, Cheshire, 1965, 250-2.

[33] John Howard, *The Menzies Era: The Years that Shaped Modern Australia*, HarperCollins, 2014, 318-9.

[34] *Commonwealth Parliamentary Debates*, Vol. H of R 37 new series, 2877-9.

[35] K. Richmond, "The National Country Party", in G. Starr et al, *Political Parties in Australia*, Heinemann Educational Australia, 1978, 115.

[36] *Sydney Morning Herald*, 15 June 1950.

[37] *Sydney Morning Herald*, 3 September 1950.

[38] U. Ellis, *A History of the Australian Country Party*, Melbourne University Press, 1963, 286.

[39] R.G. Menzies, letter to L.H.E. Bury, 27 July 1962, in G. Starr, *The Liberal Party of Australia: A Documentary History*, Drummond-Heinemann, 1980, 179-180.

[40] See G. Starr, *Carrick: Principles, Politics and Policy*, Connor Court, 2012, 142-3.

[41] R.G. Menzies, letter to L.H.E. Bury, 27 July 1962, (in G. Starr, op. cit.), 180.

[42] *Sydney Morning Herald*, 1 February 1963.

[43] Sir Garfield Barwick, *A Radical Tory*, The Federation Press, 1995, 117.

[44] Sir Arthur Fadden, *They Called Me Artie*, Jacaranda Press, 1969, 94-5.

[45] Sir Robert Menzies, *Afternoon Light: Some Memories of Men and Events*, Cassell, 1967, 295.

[46] Department of the Prime Minister and Cabinet, PM Transcripts, Press, Radio and Television Conference Given By Sir Robert Menzies At Parliament House, Canberra On 20th January 1966, Interview, 20 January 1966.

[47] Ibid.

[48] G. Starr, *Carrick: Principles, Politics and Policy*, Connor Court, 2012, 135-6.

[49] Ibid., 149-50.

[50] Ibid., 150.

[51] Sir John Bunting, *R.G. Menzies: A Portrait*, Allen & Unwin, 1988, 49.

[52] Heather Henderson, *A Smile for My Parents*, Allen & Unwin, 2013, 22.

[53] R.G. Menzies, *The Measure of the Years*, Cassell, 1970. Menzies' theme was also taken up by John Howard and cited in *The Menzies Era: The Years That Shaped Modern Australia*, HarperCollins, 2014, 242.

[54] Hasluck, *Sir Robert Menzies*, MUP, 1980, 15.

[55] Ibid.

[56] See R.G. Menzies, *The Forgotten People: And Other Studies in Democracy*, Liberal Party of Australia, Victorian Division, 2011.

[57] This view was confirmed in the US presidential election debates in 1960 when those who listened on radio saw Richard Nixon as the winner while those who viewed it on television gave the honours to John F. Kennedy.

[58] *Sydney Morning Herald,* 15 November 1958.

[59] Cited in A.W. Martin, *Robert Menzies: A Life*, Vol. 2, MUP, 1999, 473.

[60] *Age,* 5 November 1963.

[61] Sir John Carrick, cited in G. Starr, *Carrick: Principles, Politics and Policy,* Connor Court, 2012, 184.

[62] S. Cockburn cited by Heather Henderson in *A Smile for My Parents,* Allen & Unwin, 2013, 78.

[63] E. Holt cited in P.Hasluck, *Sir Robert Menzies*, MUP, 1980, 28.

[64] Martin, op. cit., 73-5.

[65] K. Perkins, *Menzies: Last of the Queen's Men,* Rigby, 1968, 175.

Select Bibliography

Aitkin, Don, *The Country Party in New South Wales*, ANU Press, Canberra, 1972.

Anderson, W.H., *The Liberal Party of Australia: Its Origin, Organisation and Purpose,* The Liberal Party of Australia (Victorian Division), undated.

Barwick, Sir Garfield, *A Radical Tory*, Federation Press, Sydney, 1995.

Bunting, Sir John, *R.G. Menzies: A Portrait,* Allen & Unwin, 1988.

Cramer, Sir John, *Pioneers, Parties and People: A Political Memoir,* Allen & Unwin, Sydney, 1989.

Davey, Paul, *The Nationals; The Progressive, Country and National Party in New South Wales, 1919 to 2006*, Federation Press, Sydney, 2006.

Ellis, Ulrich, *A History of the Australian Country Party,* Melbourne University Press, 1963.

Fadden, Sir Arthur, *They Called Me Artie*, Jacaranda Press, 1969.

Hancock, Ian, *National and Permanent: The Federal Organisation of the Liberal Party of Australia 1944-1965,* Melbourne University Press, 2000.

Hasluck, Sir Paul, *Sir Robert Menzies,* Melbourne University Press, 1980.

Henderson, Anne, *Joseph Lyons: The People's Prime Minister,* New South Publishing, Sydney, 2011.

Henderson, Gerard, "Why Menzies Still Matters", *Quadrant,* No. 452, December 2008.

Henderson, Gerard, *Menzies' Child: The Liberal Party of Australia, 1944-1994,*

Allen & Unwin, Sydney, 1994.

Henderson, Heather, *A Smile for My Parents,* Allen & Unwin, 2013.

Howard, John, *The Menzies Era: The Years That Shaped Modern Australia,* HarperCollins, 2014.

Martin, A.W., *Robert Menzies: A Life,* Vol. 1, Melbourne University Press, 1993.

Martin, A.W., *Robert Menzies: A Life,* Vol. 2, Melbourne University Press, 1999.

Menzies, Sir Robert, *Afternoon Light: Some Memories of Men and Events*, Cassell, Melbourne, 1967.

Menzies, Sir Robert, *The Measure of the Years,* Cassell, Melbourne, 1970.

Menzies, Robert, *The Forgotten People: And Other Studies in Democracy*, Liberal Party of Australia, Victorian Division, 2011.

Perkins, Kevin, *Menzies: Last of the Queen's Men,* Rigby, 1968.

Prasser, S., Nethercote, J.R. and Warhurst, J., (eds), *The Menzies Era: a Reappraisal of Government, Politics and Policy*, Hale & Iremonger, 1995.

Richmond, Keith, 'The National Country Party,' in G. Starr et al, *Political Parties in Australia,* Heinemann Educational Australia, 1978.

Starr, Graeme, *Carrick: Principles, Politics and Policy,* Connor Court, Ballan Vic., 2012.

Starr, Graeme, *The Liberal Party of Australia: A Documentary History,* Drummond/ Heinemann, Richmond Vic., 1980.

Tiver, Peter, *The Liberal Party: Principles and Performance,* Jacaranda Press, 1973.

West, Katharine, *Power in the Liberal Party,* Cheshire, 1965.

5

Menzies and the Representation
of Women

Margaret Fitzherbert

Robert Menzies is not perceived as a champion of women, yet he was instrumental in Liberal women taking an unprecedented role in a major political party – both within the organisation, and later as members of parliament. This helped the Liberal Party build an election-winning lead with women voters that it cultivated for years, providing an electoral advantage that lasted until the defeat of the Fraser Government in 1983. The large number of female members of the Liberal Party, and the quota that gave them assured roles throughout its organisational wing, in turn drove the party's continuing focus on women as voters, as party members, and subsequently as members of parliament. Menzies championed this approach for several, intertwined reasons. Some were political, others were more personal. Menzies' liberal philosophy and commitment to equality were undoubtedly the most important.

A philosophy that supports the innate rights and responsibilities of the individual logically applies to both men and women. Menzies spoke directly of this on several recorded occasions, and it was his own experience of the political organisations that he worked within, as a volunteer and as an MP, and through the Nationalists and the United Australia Party (UAP).

By the time he became prime minister for the first time, Menzies had worked side by side with the women of the Australian Women's National League (AWNL) for decades. His own organisation, the Young Nationalists, was closely aligned with the AWNL and Menzies developed a close friendship with its last president, May (later Dame Elizabeth) Couchman that endured for decades. This, too, was to be critical to the formation of the Liberal Party, and the role of women within it.

Today Menzies is most usually associated with what some unkindly characterise as the malaise of the 1950s, the decade eponymous with his own name. Menzies' own views on women and politics were strongly influenced by his thoughtful response to the social impact of the Second World War. Menzies realised early that unlike the years immediately after the Great War, when women returned to the home after the war effort was over, the Second World War would bring permanent change to the role of women. He correctly judged that their involvement in paid work, and heightened involvement in politics, would not completely cease when the war ended. He also knew this had implications for political parties. It was a world view that looked past the decade or so after the war ended and well into the future.

It is not a coincidence that the Liberal Party was formed in the dislocation and upheaval of the Second World War, as Australia began to grapple with the consequent social change – especially for women. This atmosphere permeated the formation of the party. It particularly affected how women fitted into the new party and, in turn, their activities as members of the new Liberal Party, especially in the 1940s and 1950s.

In other words, from the outset it was clear that women would have an unprecedented role in the Liberal Party. Menzies and Dame Elizabeth were two of its architects. The AWNL joined because it wanted to be at the heart of policy formation. It did so on the condition that it had equal representation throughout the organisation, and maintained the right to participate in preselections that it had jealously guarded since the Deakin era. Members of the AWNL, including Dame Elizabeth, had sought preselection in the years before the formation of the Liberal Party. As members of the new Liberal Party, former members of the AWNL and women who were newly recruited to the party influenced policies and campaign techniques. Both were designed to have clear appeal to women voters. In the 1940s and for long after, this was radical stuff – and it worked.

The AWNL was a product of Federation. The debates that preceded Federation triggered a surge in political activity and discussion, and women were an important part of the national conversation. By the time the constitutional conventions were held in the 1890s, women already had the right to vote in two colonies: South

Australia and Western Australia. As a consequence, women's suffrage had to be on the agenda for discussion: should the women who already held the State franchise be given the Federal franchise, and, if so, on what basis?

The question was formally considered at the Constitutional Convention held in Adelaide in 1897. Edmund Barton, who subsequently became first Prime Minister of Australia, was among those who believed that women who were entitled to vote in two colonies (and later States) should logically be entitled to vote in Federal elections. At the same time, their inclusion would create a disproportionate number of voters in the two States if women were not allowed to vote elsewhere. The South Australians threatened to abandon Federation rather than sacrifice the women's franchise.

The question was settled in Adelaide on 15 April 1897, with the vote in favour carried by a margin of only three. It was agreed that women who had the right to vote in State elections would not be excluded from voting in the first Federal election. Later that year in Sydney, and in Melbourne in 1898, it was agreed that all white women would get the right to vote in Federal elections as one of the first acts of the Commonwealth Parliament. Unusually, women also had the right to stand for election to the Australian Parliament from its first election, which was held on 29-30 March 1901.

Women had been part of the campaigns for suffrage before Federation, and afterwards they continued in the States that had not yet enfranchised women – such as Victoria, where white women were not allowed to vote until 1908. Women had, ironically, also campaigned against the vote for women. Once the question was settled at a federal level, women took their campaign skills into other organisations.

In New South Wales, women in favour of suffrage formed the Women's Liberal League. In Victoria, many women who had been part of the campaign against women's suffrage began to form the AWNL in 1903. Carrie Reid and Freda Derham were daughters of members of Victoria's Legislative Council and members of the Anti-Suffrage League. Over eight weeks, the two women wrote to the *Argus*, ran a public meeting in Melbourne and collected a petition of nearly 23 000 signatures, from throughout Victoria, of those opposing women's suffrage.[1] Carrie Reid and Freda Derham were both foundation members of the AWNL, which was modelled on the British Conservative Party's Primrose League. The Victorian Employers' Association helped its formation.[2]

The AWNL was set up to be a political organisation for women, educating them on political issues and enabling them to be involved in debating policy and campaigning. A pamphlet from around 1904 outlined its philosophy:

> Freedom for both employer and employee is essential to the progress and welfare of a nation. Their mutual interests should not be interfered with by restrictive legislation. We are against all government proposals of that nature. We are opposed to state socialism, or, in other words, to government trading, on the ground that it deadens the private enterprise of the community, and in the end must destroy the energy and self-reliance of the people ... the League will watch state as well as Commonwealth politics, with the desire of protecting the country from rash legislation and profligate expenditure, which would be a burden on posterity ... We recognise no class, believing in the independence of the individual ...[3]

The AWNL emerged at the same time as a number of other political organisations or, as they were known, leagues. Many engaged in political activities of the sort we see today in political parties, but were usually based on a single issue, or narrow set of issues. The AWNL was unusual because it was a league for women. It was not the only league for women; there were others in New South Wales (the Women's Liberal League) and Queensland (the Queensland Women's Electoral League), as well as another branch of the AWNL in Tasmania. The WLL disbanded in the 1920s but QWEL and the AWNLs in Tasmania and Victoria all became part of Menzies' Liberal Party.

The other way that the AWNL was unusual is that it was large and strong and, as a result, it lasted for decades. At its peak during the Great War, its membership was around 50 000.[4] By the time the AWNL wound up and directed its members to join the new Liberal Party, its membership was about a quarter of this. Even so, it was bigger and lasted longer than almost all the other leagues with which it worked and, at times, battled.

The other source of its power was that the AWNL built a reputation as a slick election campaign machine. With its numbers, the AWNL could provide an army of women to do the time-consuming and labour intensive work of any successful election campaign. In the first decades of the twentieth century this meant direct contact with as many voters as possible: door-knocking, canvassing, taking voters to polling places, organising and speaking at public meetings, and distributing printed material. The women did all of these tasks through a branch structure that was later taken over by the new Liberal Party – and, in Victoria, largely survives to this day.

Robert Menzies worked side by side with the women of the AWNL from the start of his involvement in party politics. The federal seat of Kooyong, which Menzies held from 1934 to 1966, was one of its strongholds, and most of its members transferred to the new party on its formation. In 1930, two years after he was first elected to parliament as a member of the Victorian Legislative Council, Menzies helped to form the Young Nationalists, the youth wing of the Nationalist Party. The Young Nationalists argued that the Nationalists were too beholden to the National Union and its business interests. They also demanded that it have a better standard of candidates for election. By 1931, by which time Menzies had moved to the Legislative Assembly as the member for Nunawading, he led the Young Nationalists, which was allied with the AWNL within the Nationalist organisation. Elizabeth Couchman led the AWNL from 1927 until it merged into the Liberal Party.

Menzies and Dame Elizabeth first met years before this, and well before Menzies was first elected to parliament, but their respective leadership roles meant they spent increasing amounts of time together. They had much in common and in many ways had lived parallel lives in politics. Both despaired over the organisational failings of their party, at that time a relatively loose coalition of groups and individuals. They also led groups with reputations as skilled campaigners. The Young Nationalists and the AWNL could deliver a seat in parliament to a hopeful candidate. At a time when Nationalists often ran several candidates for one seat, this kind of support could be critical to a candidate's success.

In many ways, Couchman's own life showed how women's education, opportunity for paid work and political aspirations changed during the first decades of the twentieth century. She was born in Geelong in 1876 as Elizabeth Tannock. Her family was not affluent. Her widowed mother ran the family's confectionary business in Malop Street. She was educated at Geelong Girls' High School and became a school teacher before later matriculating at the University of Melbourne in 1895, at the relatively late age of 21.[5] During her teaching career she taught at Melbourne's Methodist Ladies College and Tintern.

In 1913, May Tannock travelled to Perth, where her sister lived. She started an Arts degree at the University of Western Australia, the only university at that time that did not charge fees. She was 37, but claimed to be 30. In 1914, she was elected Vice-President of the UWA Guild; in 1991, the Guild named the May Tannock Room in her honour. She became engaged to Claude Couchman when she was still living in Perth, and married him in Melbourne in January 1917.

Couchman was a member of the AWNL before the Great War and resumed her involvement when she returned to Melbourne from Perth. She was at the forefront of the battle within the AWNL to change its position on whether women should run for election to parliament. In 1924, women obtained the right to stand for election to the State Parliament and the AWNL began actively to support women as candidates. Couchman became president of the AWNL in 1927. She sought to become a Senate candidate three times between 1930 and 1940 and was candidate for the safe Labor seat of Melbourne in 1943. By this time she was prominent in many community organisations and a member of the Australian Broadcasting Commission. In 1934, she had been part of the Australian delegation to the League of Nations, having been nominated by the National Council of Women.

Immediately before travelling to Geneva, some of the UAP's most senior members (including the Prime Minister, Joe Lyons, and the Attorney- General and Minister for External Affairs, John Latham, as well as various State premiers) had left a Premiers Conference to attend her farewell party. It was on this triumphant occasion that Menzies described her as "one of the greatest fighters we have on our side of politics."[6] Decades later, he told Dame Margaret Guilfoyle that Couchman "would have been the best Cabinet minister I could have wished for."[7] For her part, Couchman regretted that she never had the opportunity to be a member of parliament. Well into her 80s, she worked to help in the election of other women – including Guilfoyle when she first sought preselection for the Senate. She was, to use Menzies' apt phrase, "a great loyalist."[8]

Menzies and Couchman were confidantes for decades. In 1960, at a dinner in her honour, Menzies described Couchman as "the presiding genius ... of the Australian Women's National League", a great organiser, clear-headed, brave "and with an imagination for the future". He explained that she had become involved in politics at a time when it "was not a fashionable occupation ... There were relatively few people of high qualifications who concerned themselves with politics". Menzies also admired her intellect:

> If you go back to the beginning of her association with these things you will find she – as I will always believe – created a fashion, a jolly good fashion, among intelligent people, educated people, people who were concerned with public affairs. So she got a number of women who were

not just doing it as a sort of mildly background sentimental activity, but were doing it because, intellectually, they felt convinced that this was a good thing to do. And it is the intellectual leadership that May Couchman has given which is another claim to our respect.[9]

Menzies credited Couchman with bringing the AWNL into the Liberal Party. He was conscious of the AWNL's long history and the pride it had taken in its independence. It had resisted merger talks with Alfred Deakin and his Liberal Party, and during the years of the Nationalists and the United Australia Party. By the time Menzies suggested a new Liberal Party in 1944, part of the AWNL's culture and folklore was its refusal to relinquish its own identity. Dame Elizabeth's leadership was critical in changing this. As Menzies said in 1960, "Of all the things that had to be done at that time, the one that required the greatest degree of courage was for her to bring her own organisation to the Party, literally to the Party."[10]

One of the main reasons the AWNL merged into the Liberal Party was so that it could be at the heart of policy development. As Dame Elizabeth said to members of the AWNL during its heated discussion about merging, she usually saw policy announcements shortly before they were made public, when it was too late for any changes. "On our side of politics there has not been a party council where women in sufficient numbers could give their ideas on the spot."[11] In truth, their membership was well down on its peak of 50 000 during the Great War; it had fallen victim to non-political competitors like the Red Cross. The merger was also timely because of the effect of the war on the role and expectations of women. Menzies recognised this as a permanent change well before the war had ended.

In January 1940, as First Lord of the Admiralty, Winston Churchill called for a million women "… to enter the war and industry" in a speech at the Free Trade Hall in Manchester: "This is not the time for ease and comfort. It is the time of war. The cost of living must be kept down. Work must be found for all men and women …"[12] More than three years later, Churchill reflected on his words during a speech to 6 000 women at the Royal Albert Hall in London. On this occasion, he argued that it was not peaceful times that caused greater equality between men and women: "War is the teacher, a hard, stern, efficient teacher. War has taught us to make these great strides forward towards a more complete equalisation of the parts to be played by men and women."[13] Churchill succeeded in drawing some two million women out of their homes and into civilian work in support of the war effort and paid employment, and a further half a million joined the armed forces.[14]

From his vantage point as a war-time prime minister, Menzies saw that the contribution made by women in Britain, as "fighting daughters of their country", was creating a fundamental change there and in Australia, but believed that this was far from any cause for regret.[15] He made this argument after losing the prime ministership in 1941, during what became known as the *Forgotten People* radio broadcasts. In 1942, Menzies described the kinds of work that women were taking on, and doing well, in Britain as part of the war effort. His comments were part of a war-time conversation about the role that women should be play in the workplace:

> We have grown up with what might be called all sorts of taboos and superstitions and conventions on this matter. We say, perhaps a little artificially, that women should not do this or that kind of work, and that if the circumstances do require that they should work, the task should have a quality of gentility. Now what is the truth of the kind of work that women can do? And particularly the kind of work that women can do in war?[16]

Menzies admired the women who had joined the armed forces, including those doing work well beyond administration and nursing: "As I saw them they were cheerful, with good nerves, with the right enthusiastic spirit." Women were working in all kinds of jobs, in the city and on farms:

> At the Fire Stations of London, scattered right through the blitz area, there were hundreds of women – young and not so young – dressed in the blue overalls of the auxiliary fire service; not merely standing around and looking picturesque, but working hard and fast, reporting fires, telephoning, doing a mass of work which before the war was done by men. And it did not end there. When bombs came down and the fires started, there were young women in the auxiliary fire service driving cars, driving other vehicles, operating courageously in the fire-lit target areas, coping with incendiary bombs … grimy, but playing a part worthy of any man.[17]

Menzies continued in a similar vein. He spoke of the women working in munitions factories and in the land army. He paid particular tribute to:

> … millions of women who, while they form part of no army and work in no factory, are doing a superb job in an entirely unadvertised and often unnoticed way. Today's housewife in Great Britain has had the whole order of her life disturbed. She has become a great improviser, a person

of almost infinite resourcefulness. If the bombs fall and the electric light system is interrupted or the gas mains set on fire or the water pipes burst, she must be able to at almost a moment's notice to turn her hand to getting, by what means a man can never understand, a hot meal for her family, because the day's work must go on and the day's workers must be fed. After dinner at night, sitting with her family in her suburban street, she may find herself called upon to go out with sand bag and stirrup pump to help extinguish incendiary bombs in her area. What a life! What amazing courage that this can take daily danger almost as common place.[18]

Menzies described "this great movement of women into the defence of the realm" as a "formidable breaking down of old barriers and old ideas," including some elements of life that people may have wanted to keep. He warned that it would be "completely unrealistic" to see that when the war was over there would be no return to the status quo for women. It was a "… formidable breaking down of old barriers and old ideas." This, he argued, was nothing to be feared – Australia would be better off with the benefit of the full contribution of its women.

In the long run, won't the country be a stronger, better balanced and more intelligent community when the last artificial disabilities imposed upon women by centuries of custom have been removed? There is no equality so ennobling as an equality in sacrifice. There is perhaps nothing that we need more as a corrective to the patent ills of democracy than a full brotherhood and sisterhood in action and sacrifice.[19]

This was an early example of Menzies' excellent and inclusive use of language – and here, content – to include women in his audience. Exiled for a time from party leadership, Menzies used his radio broadcasts to make and maintain an intimate connection with those listening. His fireside chats were then a distinctly different way of communicating with voters. At a time when most political speeches were made at formal meetings in town halls, Menzies' words were relatively informal and friendly, and reached voters in their own homes. His subjects were national issues, but made to be personal. As with his famous *Forgotten People* speech, which was also part of this series of radio talks, Menzies was consciously speaking to women as well as to men.

In 1943, Menzies used his radio talk to give his views on Women for Canberra, a local version of Britain's Women for Westminster, a wartime drive to see more women elected to parliament. Menzies gave a view that largely stands the test of time: he saw no reason to elect women simply because of their gender, but equally, and unlike many of his contemporaries, he did not believe women should not be supported as candidates because of their gender. He openly claimed women as equals ("No educated man today denies a place or a career to a woman because she is a woman"), and did not subscribe to the idea of "a female perspective" in politics:

> I know that it may be said in answer that there is, particularly on social problems, a special woman's point of view. But again, quite frankly, I am sceptical. When I am asked, for example, what men think about such and such, my only reply is that I have no idea, since almost all men have different experiences and different points of view. Is this not equally true of women?[20]

In expressing such views, Menzies showed an awareness of women as citizens and voters that was radically different from the then prevalent approach which the Labor Party continued to follow. The difference would not have been lost on the women of the AWNL, who extracted a good deal when they agreed to merge into the new Liberal Party. Elizabeth Couchman negotiated with Menzies along with Edith Haynes and Ivy Wedgwood, who later became the first woman elected as a Senator from Victoria.

The three women persuaded members of the AWNL to wind up the organisation. Its branch structure, with a minimum of twenty members, would be used for the new party. Crucially, women would have half the delegateships for branches, the State executive, the new State council (with its emphasis on policy) and in the bodies that preselected candidates for elections. It appears that a majority of the AWNL's membership joined the new party, although not without some very public rancour. Former members of the AWNL took over a majority of senior roles for women in the new party and remained firmly in control until well into the 1960s.

The new party made an unprecedented pitch to women voters, starting in elections in the 1940s. This had a similar tone and approach to that of Menzies in his radio talks, and was also the result of having women in the Liberals' campaign teams. Women were addressed directly and explicitly in advertising and in speeches.

In the 1940s, the Liberals' Public Relations and Political Education Committee ensured that election pamphlets were created for women voters in both State and Federal elections. Campaign advertising included pictures of men and women, and this extended well beyond policy matters that until then had been considered of interest to women. For instance, in the 1946 Federal campaign, a series of printed advertisements about the Liberals' policy to reduce tax were directed to men and women. In one advertisement, a woman takes the lead and explains to her husband that only the Liberals are offering tax cuts. Some advertisements for the Liberals' industrial relations policy were addressed only to women, explaining that industrial action had led to food shortages. Even advertisements for policies about post-war rehabilitation were addressed to servicemen and service women. No women were depicted in ALP advertising, which showed only men, and cartoons of Robert Menzies.

Menzies always held that the political issues of interest to men and women were generally the same:

> We have never accepted the view that men and women have an entirely distinct interest in politics, or that only some of its problems are for the consideration of women. The truth is that all the great questions of policy and administration affect men and women in equal degree.[21]

Nevertheless, from the first election it contested, the Liberal Party developed many policies based on the platforms of the women's leagues that were specifically directed at women. These included "elimination of anomalies in employment opportunities for women," including an assessment of unequal wages; the appointment of women to government committees and commissions; and, controversially, divorce law reform. For the first time in Australian politics, the Liberal Party produced a policy statement for women in each election.

These initiatives were unusual for Australian politics but they were consistent with the approach taken through the women's leagues. Now they had the imprimatur of a major party, as well as the party leader.

Menzies was not personally supportive of every policy but was obliged to support them once they were adopted by the party. He did not support extension of child endowment to first-born children (the Liberals' centrepiece policy for women in the 1946 and 1949 elections) but lost a vote in the party room on the policy to Dame Enid Lyons, its champion. Like many of his colleagues, he was very wary of reforming divorce laws, which varied from State to State and usually were more onerous for women. The women's leagues had long argued for reform, and in the Federal Parliament this was advanced by the member for Balaclava, Percy Joske, QC, a contemporary of Menzies at university and the bar.

Joske's private member's bill to reform divorce law was eventually replaced by a government bill, which passed in 1959 as the *Matrimonial Causes Act*.

Similarly, along with many of his ministers, Menzies resisted changing the requirement that women retire from the public service on marriage (the so-called marriage bar), but it was actively supported by Liberal women MPs, and legislative change followed shortly after Menzies' retirement in 1966.

While Menzies proved to be a traditionalist in relation to these policies, his support of women as candidates and MPs meant that he had encouraged into the parliament a cohort of women who generally supported the policies of the women's leagues, despite Menzies' reluctance in some instances. Elizabeth Couchman was a candidate in the 1943 election (the Women for Canberra election, conducted before the war ended), but failed in her last bid for election. Instead, Dame Enid Lyons became the first woman elected to the House of Representatives; Dorothy Tangney (Labor, Western Australia) was the first woman to be elected to the Senate. Both were elected at the 1943 Federal election.

Dame Enid famously supported the Liberals' child endowment policy in the Liberals' party room against Menzies and then in the party's advertising. Annabelle Rankin, elected to the Senate in 1946, was responsible for developing the women's policy for the party at the 1949 election. The package ultimately included the child endowment policy, housing initiatives and abolition or reduction of sales taxes on domestic appliances and food.

The first women in most parliaments in Australia were either Liberals or members of its predecessor parties. After the election of Lyons and Tangney, the next six women elected to the Senate were Liberals. By contrast, it was only with the election to the Senate of Ruth Coleman in 1974 that another woman was elected on a Labor ticket. This was not an accident. As well as creating a party that provided a springboard for women into parliament, by giving them real experience in campaigning and in the party organisation, the women's sections in most State divisions actively campaigned to have a female Liberal senator in each State – a forerunner, perhaps, of the ALP's quota. The push worked.

Dame Annabelle Rankin entered the Senate in July 1947 and served until 1971. Agnes Robertson, in Western Australia, was elected in 1949 and served from 1950 to 1956. When she lost Liberal Party preselection, she joined the Country Party, was re-elected to the Senate and finally retired in 1961. Ivy Wedgwood, a veteran of the AWNL and one of the team of three who negotiated its merger with the Liberal Party, was also elected in 1949. She retired in 1971 and was succeeded by Margaret Guilfoyle. In 1975 Senator Guilfoyle became the first woman in Australia to be a Federal Cabinet minister with portfolio (Social

Security; later Finance).[22] For several years, Senator Rankin served alongside Senator Marie Breen, another former AWNL member from Victoria. Nancy Buttfield was elected to the Senate for South Australia in 1955.

Under Menzies' leadership, Liberals achieved a range of electoral firsts for women. Agnes Robertson became the first woman to lead a Senate ticket for a major party, in Western Australia in 1949. That same year, Dame Enid Lyons became the first woman to be a member of the Federal Cabinet, as Vice-President of the Executive Council.[23] In 1951, Senator Annabelle Rankin became the first woman to be a party whip in the Federal Parliament. Much later, as part of the first Holt Government after Menzies' retirement in 1966, Dame Annabelle became the first woman to administer a federal department when she was appointed Minister for Housing.

In 1955, Nancy Buttfield was elected to the Senate and became the first woman from South Australia to be a member of the Federal Parliament (and then the first woman to drink in the Members' Bar, on advice from Menzies that she should definitely do so). That same year, Senator Ivy Wedgwood became the first woman to become a member of the Joint Committee of Public Accounts, a position she held until her retirement from the Senate in 1971. Senator Agnes Robertson became the first woman to be a member of the Joint Parliamentary Committee on Foreign Affairs.

The Menzies years also saw enactment of a number of policies that were directed at women and were undoubtedly popular and well received, however dated some may appear today. These include extension of child endowment to first-born children and introduction of free milk for school children in 1950. More critically, the *Matrimonial Causes Act* 1959 was a brave and controversial move that gave greater equality to women seeking separation and divorce. In 1962, the Women's Bureau was created in the Department of Labour and National Service to research policy in relation to women in the paid workforce.

More generally, however, the Menzies Government took an equal opportunity approach to policy development. To paraphrase what Menzies said on more than one occasion, generally women had similar policy interests to those of men. Given the very visible role of the AWNL, it is perhaps easy to overlook Menzies' important role in creating an unprecedented degree of opportunity and equality for women within a modern political party. The weight of evidence over many years shows that Menzies saw women as political equals in organisational politics. He worked closely with women in the volatile world of Liberal politics, as a

Nationalist and then as a member of the UAP. He did so in the two electorates he represented in the Parliament of Victoria and then in the House of Representatives seat of Kooyong, and he did so in his activities in the broader organisation. Along the way he developed a trusting working relationship with Elizabeth Couchman, as well as a warm friendship. The respect and friendship between Couchman and Menzies was crucial to the women of the AWNL choosing to wind up the organisation that they treasured, and move into the new Liberal Party.

Menzies acceded to the AWNL women's demands that, in exchange for joining the new party, they would have 50 percent of all delegateships, from branch level to the party's State executive. There was no good reason for him to not do so. He trusted Couchman and respected the women, and their campaigning skills. Moreover, he realised that the role of women was changing, and they were destined to exert a greater influence on politics and government. This idea became part of Menzies' stump speech in campaign meetings in town halls around the Australia.

> Tonight I speak to the women of Australia with profound respect and gratitude. They have established an unanswerable claim to economic, legal, industrial and political equality. I hope the time will come when we can say truthfully that there is no sex discrimination in public or private office, in politics or industrial opportunity. We are all, men and women, citizens with a common interest and a common task.[24]

His words, he would say, were addressed not only to men but to women and, indeed, even more to women, because the war had changed their role in Australian society forever. It was, in fact, Menzies who led the way in changing the approach of major parties to women in Australia, as voters and as members of parliament. Menzies said that at the time of the Liberal Party's formation, his great friend and colleague, Dame Elizabeth Couchman, had been "... clear-minded and brave and with an imagination for the future." The words apply equally to Menzies himself.

Endnotes

[1] Frances Fraser and Nettie Palmer, *Centenary Gift Book*, Robertson & Mullen, Melbourne 1934, 106.

[2] John Rickard, *Class and Politics: New South Wales, Victoria and the Early Commonwealth 1890-1910*, Australian National University Press, 1976, 180.

[3] Australian Women's National League (Melbourne) publication, c. 1904. Battye Library, PR 2275/2-3

[4] *The Woman*, 1 March 1929, 4.

[5] Student records of May Ramsay Tannock, 9573, University of Western Australia.

[6] *Argus*, 23 February 1934.

[7] Interview by author with Dame Margaret Guilfoyle, 23 March 2002.

[8] Speech by the Prime Minister, the Rt Hon R.G. Menzies, at Dinner in Honour of Mrs May Couchman on Friday 18 March 1960. Sir Robert Menzies Papers, National Library of Australia, MS 4936.

[9] Ibid.

[10] Ibid.

[11] AWNL Council meeting, Tuesday 20 February 1945, Couchman Papers, La Trobe Library, MS 8713.

[12] *Daily Examiner*, "There can be no turning back", 29 January 1940.

[13] http://www.ibiblio.org/pha/policy/1943/1943-09-28a.html

[14] Sonia Purnell, *First Lady*, Aurum, 2015, 223.

[15] Broadcast by the Right Honourable R.G. Menzies, KC, MP, Friday 20 February 1942 at 9.15pm, "Women in War", Papers of Sir Robert Menzies, NLA 4936.

[16] "Women in War"; Robert Menzies, *The Forgotten People*, Liberal Party of Australia (Victorian Division), 2011 [1943], 105-7.

[17] "Women in War".

[18] "Women in War". The story of a woman looking after her family despite the effects of the war, and personally dealing with bombs, is a good description of the author's grandmother and namesake, in London during World War Two.

[19] "Women in War".

[20] Broadcast by the Rt Hon R.G. Menzies, KC, MP, 29 January 1943, "Women for Canberra", Sir Robert Menzies Papers, NLA, MS 4936.

[21] *Sydney Morning Herald*, 12 November 1949.

[22] When Ivy Wedgwood joined the Senate, she was the first of a continuous chain of female, Liberal Senators that lasted without a break until Helen Kroger's defeat in 2013; Senator Wedgwood was followed by Senator Guilfoyle, then by Senator Kay Patterson and, finally, Senator Kroger.

[23] The first woman minister in Australia was Florence Cardell-Oliver, a Nationalist and later Liberal, who became a minister in the Western Australian in 1947.

[24] Robert Menzies, Liberal Party Policy Speech, 20 August 1946, Liberal Party of Australia (Victorian Division), University of Melbourne Archives 74/63.

6

Foreign Policy, Defence and National Security

Peter Edwards

A principal responsibility of any national government is to ensure its security in the wider world. The Australian public has generally expected its political leaders to contribute effectively to maintenance of an international order that protects and promotes Australia's political, economic and other interests. How they do so has often been left largely to the leaders. Strategic, defence and foreign policies have seldom been salient in Australian political debate, but such debate as there has been has, since the 1850s if not earlier, generally revolved around two poles. Some argue that, as a small population with limited resources occupying a large island continent in a volatile part of the world, nothing is more important than keeping close relations with powerful allies, with whom Australians share interests, values and even a sense of cultural identity. Australians should be able and willing to send expeditionary forces to conflicts, whether close or distant, if these commitments help to maintain our alliances and thereby a stable global order. On the other hand, critics have always contended that this approach is expensive and demeaning, leading to costly commitments to distant conflicts that are not in Australia's interests, reducing Australian forces to the status of janissaries of a powerful imperium. Instead, these critics argue, Australia should adopt a more independent stance, concentrate on making as many friends and as few enemies as possible in our own region, and deploy armed forces only within or close to its shores and only in its direct and immediate national interests.

Governments have traditionally argued that, while they may place more emphasis on one or other approach at a particular time, they acknowledge the importance of both Australia's historical alliances and its geographical position. They usually claim to manage their external policies in such a way that Australia's global alliances and its regional relationships support each other. The real test of a government's strategy is whether it strikes the right balances between the global and the regional, between alliance and independence, between resources and commitments.

During Robert Menzies' long, peacetime term as prime minister, from 1949 to 1966, the international order was dominated by two great historical processes – the decolonisation of the European empires, especially in Asia and Africa, and the Cold War between the communist East and the anti-communist West, led respectively by the Soviet Union and the United States. These interacted in complex, but often threatening, ways, not least in Southeast Asia, a region the strategic importance of which had been brought home to most Australians by the Second World War, especially after Japan's entry in 1941.

The response of the Menzies Government was to develop a strategy generally known as "forward defence." Menzies and his colleagues placed heavy emphasis on the importance of alliances: anything smacking of independence or "self-reliance" (to use the term widely adopted in the 1970s) was considered to be beyond Australia's resources, simply impossible in a world dominated by great powers. Menzies also ruled out the idea of collective security managed through the United Nations, the great aspiration of Dr H.V. Evatt, the Minister for External Affairs in the Labor governments of the 1940s. The only collective security that Menzies supported was from organisations that included the United States, Britain, or preferably both. Menzies also had little time for those who thought that Australia could easily make friends with the new regimes in post-colonial Asia, if their leaders were closely aligned with the Soviet Union, China and other communist powers.

Both at the time and long afterwards, critics cited Menzies' emphasis on the importance of "great and powerful friends", together with the attention he devoted to meeting leaders in London and Washington, his comparative reluctance to visit Asian capitals, and his manifest affection for the monarchy and other traditional British institutions, as evidence that he was unduly deferential to the policies of the government of the day in London or Washington. According to the critics, "forward defence" exemplified the flaws of Menzies' foreign and defence policies, as he committed Australia to "other people's wars," with inadequate assurance that these great and powerful allies would give Australia support when called upon. The enemy, according to the critics, was a largely imaginary threat from Asian, especially Chinese, communism.

I have argued elsewhere that, contrary to this critique, "forward defence" was a respectable strategic policy to adopt in the geopolitical circumstances of the time, with the crucial proviso that it had to be accompanied by skilful statecraft.[1] By statecraft I mean the co-ordination of military, diplomatic and other resources; the exercise of independent diplomacy in regional capitals; and the ability and willingness to gain information about and, when appropriate, to challenge, the military and diplomatic approaches of the relevant allies. "Forward defence" was based on the premise that Australia would act militarily only in Southeast Asia, not in the Middle East or any other distant theatres. Australian forces would only intervene in a country with the explicit permission of the relevant government: they would not take part in invasions designed to effect regime change. Australia would act only in close collaboration with powerful allies, but not in obsequious subservience. As far as Menzies and his colleagues were concerned, "forward defence", and Australia's external policies in general, were not about fighting "other people's wars": his aim was to ensure that great and powerful friends would fight Australia's wars. The ability of the Menzies Government to strike the right balance between global alliances and regional relationships, and between resources and commitments, depended largely on striking the right balance between strategy and statecraft.

This essay begins by noting a frequent critique of Menzies' strategic policies and commenting on the influence of the passage of time; it notes the importance of Menzies' relationships with key ministers and departmental officials; it then examines, in turn, Menzies' relationships with Britain and the (British) Commonwealth, with the United States, and with post-colonial Asia; and it brings together many of these themes in a further assessment of "forward defence," before a concluding analysis.

Time and the critics

In the half-century after his retirement, when "the self-reliant defence of Australia" was the dominant mantra of strategic policy-makers, a standard critique of Menzies' foreign and defence policies was often expressed. The critics alleged that Menzies' romantic commitment to an outdated concept of Britain and the British Empire-Commonwealth was translated into ill-advised support for British policies and ambitions. The most notable examples were Menzies' granting the use of Australian territory, at Maralinga and elsewhere, for British nuclear tests and his rash support for Britain's deceptive and disastrous policy over the Suez crisis in 1956.

Menzies' support for Australia's other great and powerful friend, the United States, was often portrayed as a simple transference of Australian loyalty and dependence from London to Washington. According to the detractors, his uncritical devotion to the American alliance culminated in Menzies' commitment, in the last year of his long peacetime tenure as prime minister, of Australian troops to the Vietnam War, thus associating Australia with Washington's greatest strategic error of the twentieth century. This was frequently cited as the classic example of Australia's misguided willingness to fight "other people's wars," in the interests of seeking strategic insurance from those powerful, but distant, allies.

According to his critics, the obverse of Menzies' deference to "great and powerful friends" was his neglect of Asia. For Menzies, said the critics, Asia was merely what he flew over on his way to meetings at Buckingham Palace or 10 Downing Street or to watch a Test match at Lord's. Menzies supposedly failed utterly to understand the strength or validity of the decolonisation movement, which was turning a small number of European empires into a large number of independent countries in Asia and Africa. Menzies, it was said, saw Asia only as a source of a largely imaginary threat of Asian communism, conflating the traditional Yellow Peril with the newer Red Peril. Menzies therefore based Australian strategic policy on "forward defence," which was simply a way of saying that Australia would prepare itself to fight a supposed Asian enemy "up there" before we had to fight them "down here."[2]

This critique of Menzies' policies, like a cartoonist's caricature of a politician's facial features, has enough contact with reality to be recognisable, at times even plausible, but is based on exaggeration of some elements and the suppression of others. In the light of much that has been written in the past half-century, the critique can be seen as excessive and unbalanced.

Menzies clearly placed a great priority on good relationships with powerful allies, with whom Australia shared common interests and values, even a sense of identity. Attention to powerful allies in the 1950s and 1960s was hardly surprising given the experience of the world in the 1930s and 1940s. The global order before, during and after the Second World War was determined primarily by relations between the great powers. When the elephants of the jungle argued, lesser animals were mercilessly trampled. Menzies was right to see the great powers of the world as the principal forces in shaping the post-1945 world order. He was right to regard blind faith in the United Nations, or simple trust in friendship with the new, post-colonial nations of Asia, as inadequate safeguards for Australian security. But he was slower than he might have been to grasp many of the characteristics of the post-1945 world: the decline in Britain's status as a world power, the unique importance of the United States as the guarantor of security for Western nations in the Cold War, and the inexorable power of decolonisation, creating a more complex international environment in the region as well as around the world. It was understandable, but regrettable, that Menzies, like many of his generation, should instinctively seek to return after 1945 to the pre-1939 world, where Australian security lay in European control of the Southeast Asian territories. He clearly regretted the departure of first the Dutch, then the French, and then potentially the British from their Southeast Asian territories.

Nevertheless, his reactions were, for the most part, those of a conservative rather than a reactionary. Once he had accepted the nature and importance of these and other changes, he sought to manage them in the best interests of Australian security. Moreover, Menzies knew that much of his success lay in reassuring a generally conservative electorate that, amid turbulent change and new challenges at home and abroad, he would ensure that Australia preserved as much as was possible of its traditional links and relationships. A good deal of his backward-looking rhetoric was about reassurance rather than reaction. At the same time, Menzies often displayed more than a hint of nostalgia for the pre-war era in which he had developed his political views and, for the first time, reached the Prime Minister's Lodge.[3]

Menzies' critics often implied that his policies and attitudes were entirely consistent and unchanging during his record-breaking term as prime minister. They were not. The Menzies of 1950, newly returned to The Lodge and still aged in his mid-fifties, was markedly different from the septuagenarian Menzies of 1965, the victor of seven successive elections, possessing unchallengeable authority in the ministry, the Liberal Party, and the Parliament, honoured and respected abroad. The former, seeking to establish himself after the humiliation of losing office at the hands of his own party in 1941, displayed a genuine search for fresh approaches, for solutions to the new challenges. After a decade and a half in office, many of his colleagues saw "the old man" becoming more rigid and resistant to changes in the social and political climate, both at home and abroad. The hinge-point came in the mid-1950s, when the Labor split and creation of the Democratic Labor Party gave the Liberal-Country Party coalition a huge electoral advantage, provided it maintained its strong opposition to communism at home and abroad. From that time onwards, the innovations of the early 1950s too often became consolidated into formulaic responses to international challenges, with insufficient attention to the strength or importance of changes in the international environment.

Menzies and his Ministers for External Affairs

Closely related to this change with the passage of time was Menzies' relationship with key ministers, especially the Ministers for External Affairs (as Foreign Affairs was known until 1970). Much of the innovation and modernisation of foreign policy between 1949 and 1966 came from the successive Ministers for External Affairs – P.C. (later Sir Percy) Spender, R. G. Casey (later Lord Casey), Sir Garfield Barwick and Paul (later Sir Paul) Hasluck. All four were among the most important Liberal politicians of their day; each was at some time considered a potential prime minister. None achieved that goal, but two subsequently became Governors-General, one the Chief Justice of the High Court, and the other ambassador to Washington and President of the International Court of Justice. In short, Menzies did not appoint tailenders of the ministry to External Affairs, as some of his successors were inclined to do.

These appointments were important because the success of the Menzies Government's international policies depended to a substantial extent on the balance established between the Prime Minister and the Minister for External Affairs. As a broad generalisation, Menzies kept his focus on the crucial relationships with Britain and the United States, while the Minister for External Affairs devoted more attention to the rest of the world, especially Southeast Asia and adjacent regions. The foreign policies of the Menzies Government usually worked best, striking an effective balance between global alliances and regional relationships, when he listened to his ministers, giving them scope to explore new initiatives or engaging in constructive argument with them; and the policies were least successful when he overruled his colleagues or disregarded their advice and recommendations.

The clearest examples of the former came in the short but highly productive term of Menzies' first Minister for External Affairs. Percy Spender brought to the portfolio clear goals – to gain a security treaty with the United States and to combat communism in Southeast Asia and adjacent regions by means of social and economic assistance to the emerging independent nations.[4] In only fifteen months as minister, Spender was the key Australian figure in the negotiation of both the Colombo Plan and the ANZUS Treaty. As early as March 1950 Spender, in a major speech to the House of Representatives, laid down the bases for Australian foreign policy for the next generation. Menzies was skeptical about the prospects for a security treaty with the United States, famously describing it as "a superstructure on a foundation of jelly," and he was fortuitously out of contact with Canberra when Spender took a crucial step towards this goal (discussed further below). Nevertheless, Menzies went along with the decisions once made and, after his retirement, claimed ANZUS as one of his greatest achievements. Similarly, he was never closely identified with the Colombo Plan (which at one time was known as "the Spender plan"), but he tolerated the enthusiasm of both Spender and Casey for this project, albeit with less tangible support than either would have wished.

Menzies displayed similar tactics during negotiation of the Australia-Japan Commerce Agreement of 1957, which contributed greatly to Australia's post-war economic development. The agreement was very much the achievement of John McEwen, the Minister for Trade, who soon afterwards became leader of the Country Party and the first person to be designated Deputy Prime Minister. To establish close relations with Japan, albeit economic rather than political, so soon after the horrors of the Pacific War, was courageous, and Menzies ensured that McEwen took the lead, at a crucial time seeming to distance himself from the endeavour. Had the venture failed, McEwen rather than Menzies would have paid the political price. But McEwen, aided by a team of officials led by J.G (later Sir John) Crawford, succeeded, The agreement paid off handsomely, both economically and politically, for Menzies and his government.[5]

Richard Casey, Australia's longest serving foreign minister until his record was overtaken by Alexander Downer early in the twenty-first century, was a less effective Cabinet minister than Spender or McEwen, but he was instrumental in bringing Australians to a better understanding of their regional environment. With considerable assistance from a cohort of young and talented officials in External Affairs, Casey wrote a book describing the countries in Australia's near north as *Friends and Neighbours*, and he oversaw not only a considerable expansion of Australia's diplomatic representation in the region but also some of Australia's earliest initiatives in cultural diplomacy and the exercise of what we today know as "soft power."[6] Menzies often adopted an attitude of amused tolerance of Casey's contributions to Cabinet discussions, which tended to be inconclusive *tours d'horizon* or comments on "chaps with whom we can do business." Nevertheless, Casey took a genuine interest in the countries to Australia's north, seeing them as much more than simply pawns in the global Cold War, and encouraged Australians to share that interest.

One of the clearest examples of the dangers incurred when Menzies overruled his Minister for External Affairs was when he disregarded Casey's firm warnings against Australian identification with Britain's disastrous policies in the Suez crisis of 1956. Casey could see, better than Menzies, what damage this would do to Australia's standing in the Commonwealth, in many African and Asian countries, and not least in the United States. It was significant that Australia's entanglement with British policies began when Menzies, who happened to be abroad at the time, attended a meeting of foreign ministers. When Menzies undertook a mission to Cairo to negotiate with President Nasser, he took with him, among others, the head of Casey's department, Arthur Tange, but excluded him from any role in shaping or implementing policy.[7]

A prominent feature of recent writing on Australia's foreign ministers has been the esteem given to Sir Garfield Barwick, Minister for External Affairs from 1961 to 1964.[8] Barwick's reputation suffered from some of the decisions taken in his subsequent term as Chief Justice of the High Court, including his advice to, and support for, the Governor-General, Sir John Kerr, over the dismissal of the Whitlam Government in 1975. Garry Woodard, a diplomat-turned-historian, has described Australian policy towards the Indonesian "Confrontation" of Malaysia, the dominant international issue of the time, as "best practice" in diplomacy.[9] Australia's sophisticated, nuanced and ultimately successful policy towards Confrontation was largely shaped by Barwick and External Affairs officials, but not without considerable debate with Menzies and senior officers of the Prime Minister's Department. Woodard may have overstated Barwick's superiority to his successor, Paul Hasluck, and underestimated the effects of Barwick's clumsy handling of relations with the United States. But there is certainly a strong contrast with the Government's immediately subsequent handling of a military commitment in support of American policy in Vietnam.

In that case, Menzies effectively sidelined most of his Cabinet and disregarded prudent advice from experienced officials such as Sir John Bunting and Sir

James Plimsoll, relying almost exclusively on a particularly bellicose Chairman of the Chiefs of Staff Committee, Air Chief Marshal Sir Frederick Scherger.[10] Many of the problems suffered by Menzies' successors over the Vietnam commitment can be attributed, not so much to the essential strategic principles that Menzies applied, but to the way in which he handled the crucial decisions between December 1964 and April 1965. In this case, he seems to have decided that the crucial goal was to ensure that the United States did not withdraw from Vietnam, and consequently shaped Australian policy single-mindedly towards that goal. Some form of Australian commitment to Vietnam was probably both justified and inevitable early in 1965, but more prudent handling of the issue may have reduced the costs to Australia by making possible an earlier exit from the commitment. Menzies' later reputation suffered from the opprobrium attached to Suez and Vietnam, and in both cases Menzies gave too little attention to the information and advice available from ministerial colleagues and departmental officials.

The crucial importance of this relationship was underlined by the often forgotten period from January 1960 to December 1961 when Menzies took the External Affairs portfolio himself. As many Liberals feared at the time, this was neither wise nor successful. An attempt by Menzies at the United Nations General Assembly in October 1960 to promote a summit conference of "the Big Four," the leaders of the United States, the Soviet Union, Britain and France, as a tactical move intended to assist President Eisenhower, exposed Menzies to vitriolic criticism from Asian leaders, including India's Prime Minister, Jawaharlal Nehru, who portrayed Menzies as a tool of the great powers.

Menzies also alienated many Asian and African countries by an unsuccessful attempt to prevent the expulsion of South Africa from the Commonwealth after the apartheid regime's police killed 67 demonstrators at Sharpeville. While the world's attention was given to events such as the disastrous attempt by anti-communist Cuban exiles to overthrow the revolutionary government in Havana, the building of the Berlin Wall, and the "Sharpeville massacre," a series of crises was developing in Laos, in effect early rounds of the Vietnam War. Although little was discussed publicly, the Cabinet under Menzies' leadership on three occasions between 1959 and 1961 decided that Australia would, if necessary, support an American intervention in Indochina to support a pro-Western regime that was in danger of being overthrown by communists, even if this meant that Australia would, for the first time in its history, not fight alongside

Britain. This would have important implications for the Government's approach to intervention in South Vietnam in 1964-65. We can only speculate whether the Cabinet would have adopted a different attitude if, for example, Barwick had been appointed Minister for External Affairs in January 1960 rather than December 1961.

Menzies and departmental reform

Menzies developed policies not only through his ministers, especially his most senior colleagues, but also through senior departmental officials, especially the departmental secretaries, then known as "permanent heads."[11]

His general reaction to foreign policy crises during the 1950s, for example, was to convene a meeting with the External Affairs and Defence ministers, and the heads of the External Affairs, Defence and Prime Minister's departments. As the Defence Department was located in Melbourne, until it gradually moved to Canberra from the late 1950s, and as Casey spent much of his time as Minister for External Affairs travelling, this often meant that major decisions were taken by Menzies, the Minister for Defence, and the Secretaries of the Prime Minister's and External Affairs departments. With the passage of time, better policy-making structures were introduced. A Chiefs of Staff Committee was formed with a four-star officer as Chairman; the principal official advice came from the Defence Committee which brought together all the service chiefs with the civilian heads of the Prime Minister's, Defence, External Affairs and Treasury departments; and, in 1963, amid growing crises in Southeast Asia, a Foreign Affairs and Defence Committee was formed of about six senior Cabinet ministers, a precursor to today's National Security Committee of Cabinet.

Although the growth in size and influence of the External Affairs Department in the 1940s was associated with Dr H.V. Evatt, the minister in both the Curtin and Chifley governments, Menzies oversaw continuing growth in numbers and professionalism of Australia's young foreign office and diplomatic service. With the expansion of diplomatic missions, especially in Asia, and departmental positions, a cohort of young diplomats advanced rapidly to senior positions. After being appointed head of department in 1954 at the age of 39, Arthur Tange did much to turn a disparate group of mostly talented individuals into a coherent department, better able to give professional advice and to implement nuanced policies. Although the increasingly competent and confident department developed a policy approach that differed from his rhetoric, urging greater emphasis on relations with Asia and less on the importance of great and powerful friends, Menzies at least acquiesced in the growing status of External Affairs in the departmental pecking order, manifest in decisions such as the inclusion of the departmental head as a full member of the Defence Committee. Menzies tired of Tange as he clung to office for a decade, but he did not turn against the department as a whole, even granting it the ultimate accolade for public servants, sanctioning the award of knighthoods, roughly one each year, to senior diplomats. Throughout his term the special status of relations with the United Kingdom was marked by the linking of the Australian High Commission in London and the British High Commission in Canberra with the Prime Minister's Department, while all other diplomatic missions, including those to or from other Commonwealth countries, dealt with the Department of External Affairs. But with the passage of time, this mattered less and less, until relations with Britain came under the minister and department of External Affairs, renamed Foreign Affairs, in 1970.

While External Affairs was growing in size, status and effectiveness, Defence remained constrained by structures, appointments, doctrines and attitudes that had been shaped by the 1939-45 war but were clearly obsolescent. Structurally, Defence was a group of six departments – one for each of the services, one each for Supply and Defence Production, and a small central Defence department. Each had its own minister and departmental secretary; moreover, each of the services had its own uniformed chief and board of senior officers, who often had more knowledge of, and influence on, policies than their respective ministers and departmental heads. Rivalries between the services, between departments and between civilian public servants and military officers were thus institutionalised, greatly reducing the capacity of officials, whether in suits or uniforms, to give coherent advice on strategic and broad defence policies.

Menzies did not appoint ministers or departmental heads in Defence who gave an effective lead in either policy or administration. The long-serving Minister for Defence in the 1950s, Sir Philip McBride, was a South Australian pastoralist who generally supported Menzies' policies, except during the Suez crisis, but without imposing himself on the complex administration of Defence. His successor, Athol Townley, was also a Menzies loyalist. Townley died a few weeks after leaving office, as did his successor but one, Senator Shane Paltridge. Sir Frederick Shedden, who had been appointed secretary of the Defence Department in 1937, remained in that post until 1956, continuing to dominate the policy-making machinery but increasingly inclined to reminisce about his wartime association with Prime Minister John Curtin and General MacArthur rather than to develop ideas for the post-1945 world.[12] His successor, Sir Edwin Hicks, who was promoted from the Department of Air, also showed no great inclination towards administrative reform or policy innovation.

After public criticism of the state of defence administration, Menzies appointed a high-level committee, chaired by a respected citizen-soldier, Sir Leslie Morshead, but the Government, facing legal and political obstacles, did not adopt its major recommendations, including the merger of the three service departments into a single Department of Defence. Menzies seemed unwilling to confront the supporters of the single services, including the ex-service organisations and some of his own parliamentary colleagues. Not until the 1970s would a government grasp the nettle of introducing major reforms to the structure of Defence and confronting the inevitable controversy.

This mixed record left Menzies with the ability to dominate policy-making on foreign affairs and defence. When satisfied with the outcomes, he was willing to have policy shaped by the appropriate military, official and ministerial committees. But he was also capable of by-passing these committees and shaping policy unilaterally with the aid of chosen individuals, whether ministers, officials or military chiefs.

Menzies, Britain and the British Commonwealth

The reality of Australia's relationships with Britain and the United States differed markedly from the glib critique that Australia simply deferred to one, and then the other, powerful but distant ally. In the first place, Menzies and his colleagues were only too well aware of the differences between London and Washington, often on matters directly affecting Australian interests. In his efforts to remain close to both, Menzies was often like a circus performer trying to ride two horses, which displayed a disconcerting tendency to head in diverging directions. At times Menzies tried to use his personal influence to bring the two together; at other times he sought to use one to persuade the other to adopt the policy that suited Australian interests. The real distinction between Menzies and his critics was the degree to which he was prepared to make these initiatives public. Menzies usually took the view that differences of opinion within the Commonwealth, or within the ANZUS alliance, should be kept behind closed doors: to advertise them would only benefit the West's enemies (and probably his political opponents at home, as he constantly stressed the value of Australia's "great and powerful friends"). He therefore disregarded the advice of officials in the Department of External Affairs that Australia, while supporting its great power allies on fundamental issues, should differ publicly on lesser matters, so that "our other friends" could see that Australia had its own mind, especially on Asian affairs.[13]

Menzies' relations with Britain, in particular, were far more complex than the caricature of the deferential imperialist would suggest. He was genuine in his assertions that the Empire-Commonwealth was most effective when it spoke with one voice, but he wanted that voice to mingle the accents of Australia, Canada, New Zealand, South Africa and others with those of the mother country. At first, Menzies wanted the benefits of membership of the British imperial system, while seeking to maximise Australia's national benefits from that system. In June 1950 he called for a "common Empire foreign policy" to be shaped by a committee in London with a secretariat in each Dominion capital. He was following a tradition that linked many of his predecessors from Alfred Deakin to John Curtin, but this was the last hurrah for the ideal of the diplomatic unity of the empire.

The idea of a closely co-ordinated, if not totally shared, defence policy within the Commonwealth was similarly short-lived. In the public mind, the Labor Prime Ministers John Curtin and Ben Chifley, and their External Affairs Minister, Dr H.V. Evatt, are usually associated with Curtin's statement that "Australia turns to America" and Evatt's strained relations with British and American leaders, in contrast to Menzies' supposedly uncritical loyalty to Britain. The irony is that the defence policies of Labor governments of the 1940s were centred on the Commonwealth, but under Menzies defence relations between Canberra and London grew apart. In the early 1950s Australian and British defence leaders engaged in extensive discussions about the relative priorities of the Middle East and Southeast Asia. Menzies was sympathetic to the British desire that, in the event of a third world war against the Soviet Union, Australian forces should once again make its contribution in the Middle East, defending the Suez Canal and Arabian oilfields. But Australians were also concerned about what Menzies in 1939 had called the "near North." From these early discussions emerged ANZAM, a British-Australian-New Zealand agreement for defence coordination in the Malayan region. After 1953, when Stalin died and the Korean War ended, Australia directed its defence policies almost exclusively to Southeast Asia, not least to encouraging Britain to remain committed to the region.

Menzies' British race patriotism, manifest in his public displays of admiration for institutions such as the monarchy, the Westminster parliamentary system, and Test cricket, and his proud assertions that he was "British to the bootstraps," did not translate into uncritical deference to the policies of the United Kingdom Government. On the contrary, the more he extolled British ideals, the more critical he could be of those who held office in Whitehall or Westminster for failing to live up to those ideals. As prime minister in 1939-41, Menzies had strongly criticised British leaders and their policies, albeit usually in private.[14] In his peacetime tenure, this attitude was even more pronounced. An early example was his reaction in 1950 to the British request for support in combatting the communist-led insurgency in what became known as the Malayan Emergency. Menzies and his colleagues challenged British political assessments and military strategies. He despatched a high-level military mission to Malaya to make its own assessments and even to advise the British on how to conduct jungle warfare. Menzies sent RAAF aircraft, but resisted pressure to send Australian troops until 1955, by which time the back of the insurgency had been broken.

One of the most criticised manifestations of Australian-British relations in the 1950s was the use of Australian soil, most notably at Maralinga, for British nuclear tests. The conduct of the tests and the subsequent clean-up was deeply flawed, showing little respect for the personnel involved or for Australia's Indigenous peoples. It was not, however, a simple matter of Menzies' sacrificing Australian interests in misguided deference to the mother country. In a world dominated by great powers, and not least by those with nuclear capacity, the Menzies Government saw Australia's interests being best served by restoration of Britain to its pre-war status at the top table of world powers. It seemed better to have two "great and powerful friends" with "the bomb," not merely one. Australia, like Britain and other Western countries, did not wish to be entirely dependent on the United States for its security. Moreover, Australia had the potential to benefit directly. In a united or, at least, a well co-ordinated, Empire-Commonwealth, a "British bomb" would be available for the defence of all its member nations, not least a Dominion placed uncomfortably close to the cauldron of Southeast Asia. The British tests were seen, for a time, as a step towards Australia's own, independent nuclear capacity.[15]

Disillusion with British policies arose on several grounds. One was the communist threat to all of Southeast Asia, including Indochina. In the late 1940s and early 1950s British officials had strongly supported the "domino theory," seeing a communist advance in Indochina as a threat to Britain's own interests in Malaya and Borneo. By 1954 the British had changed their minds. The government led by Winston Churchill, with Anthony Eden as Foreign Secretary, now favoured a diplomatic solution to Indochina, including the partition of Vietnam into a communist north and an anti-communist south. Australia faced an agonising choice between American and British policies in the "united action" crisis. Menzies and his colleagues played for time, with Casey playing an active role, but finally came down on the British side, while giving minimal offence to the United States.[16]

Britain's decolonisation of the empire on which the sun had never set proceeded rather too rapidly for the comfort of Menzies and his colleagues, who were conscious of the implications for Australia's own mini-empire on the island of New Guinea. All too often Australia was left isolated in votes at the United Nations on colonial issues, siding with a handful of countries like Portugal against the growing tide of anti-colonial sentiment in Africa, Asia, Latin America and, indeed, much of Europe. As David Lowe has shown, the distance between Canberra and London on colonial issues tended to break down the centrality of the British connection in many other aspects of Australia's foreign policy. Especially when Percy Spender was ambassador in Washington, frequently leading Australian delegations to the United Nations in New York and acting as if he were still the Minister for External Affairs, the Washington embassy had a greater role than the high commission in London on a wide range of foreign policy decisions.[17]

Menzies' attitude to the new, multi-racial Commonwealth evolved during his long tenure. In the mid-1950s he showed some skill in using his authority, and his well-known fondness for the game, to persuade the governing body of Australian cricket, the Australian Board of Control, to accept, in the interests of "British-Commonwealth relations", a tour of the West Indies in 1955, after similar requests had been rejected in 1947 and 1950. As that tour took place, Menzies successfully supported a similar request, conveyed by the Indian High Commissioner, from the Board's counterpart in India. The terms in which Menzies wrote to the Australian Board exemplify his approach:

> You will at once see the international political advantages for Australia in building up goodwill in India; but you will also, of course, be familiar with other problems with which I am only dimly acquainted ... Do make it clear [to the Board] that I am not seeking to make an impertinent intrusion on matters which are their affair, and which they are much better qualified to deal with than I am. But the reasons I have indicated earlier, plus my own enthusiasm about the game, will, I hope, constitute a respectable excuse.

As the historians of Australian Test cricket observe, "it says something that the most conservative of Australian prime ministers was still more expansionary and international in perspective than the Australian Board of Control."[18] Much the same could be said of other conservative elements of the Australian electorate. As late as 1968, for example, the State president of the Returned Services League in New South Wales publicly described the Commonwealth as "a polyglot lot of wogs, bogs, logs and dogs."[19]

As the years passed, Menzies' views on the Commonwealth seemed to harden, while Britain's attitudes and policies evolved in a different direction. When the British Prime Minister, Harold Macmillan, spoke of "the winds of change" blowing through Africa, leading among other things to the expulsion of South Africa from the Commonwealth, he received no support from Menzies. One unpleasant gust of the winds of change came in 1962 when Macmillan had to leave a meeting of the Commonwealth Prime Ministers for another commitment. He asked India's Jawaharlal Nehru, and not Menzies, to take the chair, to the Australian's deep chagrin. Macmillan, it seemed, was more attuned to the new Commonwealth, symbolised by Nehru, than to the old white dominions, epitomised by Menzies.

The most disruptive force on the Anglo-Australian relationship was Britain's first attempt in 1961 to join what was then called the European Economic Community.[20] Before the venture was vetoed by President De Gaulle's famous "Non" in 1963, Australia had to adapt to the reality that Britain was, in political and security matters as well as economic, turning away from the Commonwealth and its global role, especially "east of Suez," towards closer engagement with Europe. To many in Australia, it seemed that it was Britain, not Australia, that was deserting the principles and values that had underpinned Australia's identity and sense of its place in the world. Menzies sought to delay, even to deny, this trend as long as possible, by his "British to the bootstraps" rhetoric. The Macmillan Government privately hoped that they could use Menzies' Anglophilia to bring Australia round to accepting the new direction of British policy, but they encountered John McEwen's profound opposition to Britain's attempts to enter Europe, with its implications for Australian exports. As David Goldsworthy has recorded, when forced to choose between Macmillan and McEwen, Menzies chose McEwen.[21]

McEwen did not often interfere in foreign policy but, when he did so, he was forceful and effective. McEwen's opposition to Britain's move towards Europe was unbending. When a junior minister, Leslie Bury, tentatively suggested that Australian concerns were overstated, McEwen insisted that he be sacked. Ministerial sackings were rare under Menzies. As already indicated, he allowed a degree of freedom that would be unimaginable today, when ministers and even backbenchers are expected to be "on message" to the last syllable every minute of the day. Bury's dismissal was a mark of the strength of McEwen's influence on the policies of the coalition government.

Menzies and the United States

From the outset, the Menzies Government faced difficulties in reconciling its relationships with the two great and powerful friends. The British Government, especially after Winston Churchill returned to 10 Downing St in 1951, was strongly opposed to the concept that Australia and New Zealand could enter a security treaty with the United States to which the United Kingdom was not a party. It brought considerable pressure on Menzies and his ministers, but the Australians insisted that they wanted direct access to Washington, and prevailed. A major step in the Australian campaign for the treaty, the commitment of troops to the Korean War, was motivated by a change in British policy. In London the Attlee Government told Menzies that it was not about to commit troops, and Menzies agreed to follow suit. Then, while Menzies was crossing the Atlantic and virtually incommunicado, the Australians heard that London was about to reverse its stance. The agile Spender arranged that Australia would announce a troop commitment before Britain to make it clear that Australia was acting independently and not as a mere British acolyte. We will never know how Menzies would have reacted if he had received the news of Britain's policy shift before Spender, but the brilliant barrister adapted swiftly and adroitly to the changed circumstances. Menzies, however, played the Korean commitment card skilfully in the United States, gaining a World Bank loan, which underpinned Australia's economic development during the post-war boom.[22] This was the first, but by no means the last, occasion on which the government would use a relatively small military commitment – far smaller than those of the two world wars – to achieve policy goals that supported domestic prosperity.

Achievement of a security treaty with the world's greatest superpower did not mean that Australia was immediately and uncritically deferential to its new ally. From the start there were reservations about the value of the ANZUS alliance. Officials were well aware that the commitment in ANZUS was a commitment to consult in certain defined circumstances, whereas the signatories to the North

Atlantic Treaty Organisation (NATO) alliance agreed to act on the basis that an attack on one was an attack on them all. No less important, from Canberra's perspective, was the fact that ANZUS did not give Australians access to the confidential thoughts of Washington's military, political and diplomatic planners, especially those of the Joint Chiefs of Staff in the Pentagon. Throughout Menzies' term in office, access to what one Cabinet minute called "the inner political thinking and defence planning"[23] of American leaders remained an unfulfilled ambition. Menzies' public rhetoric, lauding the Americans for their staunch defence of Western interests around the world, was designed both to assure the Australian electorate that the Liberal-Country Party coalition was better able to ensure that the United States remained committed to Australia's part of the world; and to convince the Americans that Australia was a reliable and useful ally which had limited defence resources of its own but was worthy of the protection of the global superpower.

Seldom mentioned or even hinted at in public was what might be called "the MacArthur factor" – the fear that, while the military strength of the United States was enormous, Washington's allies could not always rely on wisdom and prudence in the application of that strength. Australians had their own reservations about General Douglas MacArthur dating from his service as Commander-in-Chief of the South-West Pacific Area in the Second World War. The Korean War demonstrated to the world both the strengths and the weaknesses of his strategic decision-making. MacArthur spoke loosely of the possibility of using atomic weapons in Korea, raising the prospect of a third world war in which both sides would have "the bomb." His ill-advised "push to the Yalu" led to the intervention of Chinese forces, with almost catastrophic effects on the tide of the war. The UK Prime Minister, Clement Attlee, dashed across the Atlantic (at a time when intercontinental air travel was still a novelty, not without risk) to speak personally with President Harry Truman. Menzies, typically, was more discreet: but, through diplomatic channels, he made it clear that his sympathies lay with Attlee.[24] In subsequent years an undercurrent of concern that the Americans might risk nuclear war ran through Australians' private assessments of American policy.

Somewhat similarly, in what was known as "the off-shore islands crisis," Menzies also took the British side when it appeared that a conflict over some tiny islands in the Taiwan Straits might lead to all-out war between the United States and China. Menzies acted as a virtual envoy of three Commonwealth nations,

Britain, Australia and New Zealand, in a mission to convince Washington that these tiny scraps of territory were not worth a third world war.[25]

One major question dividing London and Washington was recognition of the People's Republic of China, installed after the communist victory in October 1949. The United Kingdom quickly recognised the new government and maintained trading links: the United States, under the influence of a powerful "China lobby," opposed both recognition and trade relations. The Menzies Government acceded, albeit reluctantly, to American pressure not to recognise "Red China," but the strength of the Country Party in the coalition was reflected in the decision to continue trade. Sales of wheat to China made an important contribution to Australia's balance of trade, allowing Menzies and his colleagues to shrug off accusations of hypocrisy in trading profitably with a regime that it denounced politically.

For a time, especially during the early 1950s, Menzies shared the widespread view among conservative Australians that while the Americans had the military and economic strength to be the world's dominant power, the British, with their long imperial experience, had the greater wisdom in knowing how, where and when to apply their power. This idea lost ground as disillusion set in over British policies towards Europe and Southeast Asia, as noted above, although for some time Australian diplomacy had the goal of "quadripartite talks," allowing the United States, Britain, Australia and New Zealand to co-ordinate their strategic policies. The Americans, however, deprecated giving the impression that "a white man's club" was trying to guide the fate of Asian nations; and when such talks were held, Americans made pointed comments about the weak state of Australia's armed forces.

Menzies and his colleagues therefore formed the view that Australian military commitments, which would be focused on Southeast Asia, should, if possible, be conducted within a multi-national coalition, preferably under the authority of a multi-racial international organisation such as the United Nations or the Commonwealth. The United States would supply the essential military strength and therefore leadership, but the collaboration of other nations, preferably including Britain as well as Asian nations, would bring strategic wisdom and local knowledge, while demonstrating that Australia was contributing to a genuinely international campaign, not supporting American or Anglo-Saxon imperialism.

With these ideas and attitudes, it is understandable that the South-East Asia Treaty Organisation (SEATO) appealed greatly to Menzies and his colleagues.

Intended, as the name suggested, to be a regional counterpart to NATO, SEATO was founded after the partition of Vietnam in 1954 to establish a defensive arrangement for the non-communist countries of the region, particularly South Vietnam, Laos and Cambodia. Its members were the United States, Britain, France, Thailand, the Philippines, Pakistan, Australia and New Zealand; its headquarters, including a military planning office, were in Bangkok. On the face of it, SEATO combined the power of North Atlantic allies with the local knowledge of Southeast Asian nations; it offered the comfort of traditional Commonwealth allies as well as American power; it implied access to the military plans of the United States; and it suggested that any ill-advised use of American military might would be constrained by the wisdom of several other nations, including Britain. Australian military planning was centred on the development of several SEATO Plans. The last position held by John Wilton before his long-planned appointment as the head of the Australian Army was to lead the SEATO Military Planning Office in Bangkok. Menzies and his colleagues spoke more about SEATO than about ANZUS in the late 1950s, and Menzies' commitment remained even as the alliance's flaws became increasingly evident in the early 1960s. It became clear that Britain and France had no intention of fighting in Indochina, while Pakistan was only interested in its rivalry with India. SEATO was little more than an American-Thai alliance by 1965, but Menzies continued to assert that the commitment to Vietnam was "consistent with" Australia's SEATO obligations.

The strength of the ANZUS guarantee and the judgment of American military commanders were not Menzies' only concerns over the American alliance. In the late 1950s, with SEATO offering the prospect of security in Indochina and with the Malayan Emergency heading for a successful conclusion, Australia's principal concern in the region was Indonesia's campaign to incorporate West New Guinea, the only part of the former Dutch East Indies that had not been included when Indonesia gained its independence in 1949. Australia, which administered the eastern half of the island under a United Nations mandate, opposed the Indonesian claim, seeing President Sukarno as a major potential threat to regional security. Indonesia was receiving arms from the Soviet Union and the Indonesian Communist Party, the third largest in the world, was pushing Jakarta ever closer to Beijing. Australia hoped that the Australian and Dutch halves of the island would move together towards independence, keeping all of New Guinea out of Indonesian hands. The problem for Canberra was that the United States, under both the Eisenhower and Kennedy administrations, regarded

West New Guinea as an acceptable price for keeping Indonesia from moving even closer to the communist bloc. In 1961 the Kennedy administration, after discussion with the Macmillan Government in Britain, moved decisively to allow Indonesia to incorporate West New Guinea (today the Indonesian provinces of Papua and West Papua). Menzies spoke publicly of his disappointment at having to acquiesce in a joint decision of both great and powerful friends.

This concern about the direction of American policy towards Indonesia, as much as the general concept of paying a premium for strategic insurance, underlined the necessity, as Menzies and his colleagues saw it, to curry favour with the United States. The Menzies Government let it be known that it would be happy to make available tracts of Australian territory for American communications and intelligence facilities, so that Washington would have a strong national interest in the security of Australia. This initiative led to creation of the "joint facilities" at North-West Cape, Pine Gap and Nurrungar. These were not "American bases," as critics generally called them, but the extent of Australian influence or control was minimal. The Menzies Government made a calculated decision that the assurance the facilities gave of American protection outweighed the risk that Australian territory might become a Soviet target in any nuclear exchange.

While eager to offer the use of Australian territory to the Americans, the Menzies Government was reluctant to accede to Washington's pressure to increase its military capacity. In 1959 the Defence Committee recommended that the Government seek a degree of independent military capacity so that it could act at least for a short time without having to rely on allied support. The officials cited concern over Indonesian policy, and the divergence between American and Australian attitudes towards Indonesia, as a principal reason behind this recommendation. The Menzies Cabinet firmly rejected the advice. Fully independent or (to use the term adopted in the 1970s) "self-reliant" foreign and defence policies were seen as beyond Australia's resources. Menzies and his colleagues laid down that Australia would only undertake military commitments in Southeast Asia, and only if Australian forces were fighting alongside those of the United States, Britain or, preferably, both. Menzies evidently felt that a move towards independent military capacity would not only be prohibitively expensive but also undermine public confidence in SEATO and ANZUS – and the electorally valuable idea that only the conservative coalition could manage these alliances in Australia's interests.

More pragmatically, alliances provided defence on the cheap. After the expensive and inflationary commitment to the Korean War, Menzies placed a ceiling of £200 million on defence expenditure, representing a declining proportion of gross domestic product as the economy grew. Menzies told our great and powerful friends that Australia's best contribution to global security was to encourage "national development," such as modern manufacturing and economic infrastructure. London and Washington were not always impressed. Well before President Richard Nixon enunciated what became known as the Guam Doctrine or the Nixon Doctrine, in 1969, senior American officials frequently urged Australia and other allies to undertake a greater share of the defence burden.

The Menzies era is often cited by Australian critics as the classic period of fighting "other people's wars"; but it was equally a time when those "other people," the political and military leaders in Washington and London, said that Australians were guilty of "talking a good war," of free-riding on their allies, or of seeking to fight to the last British national serviceman or American draftee. It was years of pressure along these lines, combined with the growing number of actual or potential commitments in Southeast Asia, that led the Menzies Government in 1963-64 to undertake significant increases in defence expenditure, and to introduce a controversial system of selective national service that would lead conscripts to fight in Vietnam. These developments came only in the last years of Menzies' long term as prime minister: it was his successors who would have to bear the fiscal and political costs.

Menzies and Asia

Menzies' relations with Asian countries, like those with his great allies, were far more complex and nuanced than various caricatures suggest. For a start, it is simply not true that he never visited Asia, as was implied in a recent biography of Gough Whitlam.[26] He paid official visits to several Asian countries, including India, Pakistan, Indonesia, Japan and Malaya. But he was clearly uncomfortable there, in sharp contrast with the ease that he evidently felt in Britain and the old white Dominions. His discomfort was as much cultural as political. As Alan Watt, who served Menzies as both Secretary of the External Affairs Department, commissioner in South-East Asia and ambassador to Japan, put it:

> ... the philosophy and religion of Asia were almost closed books to a
> man of his temperament, just as tropical climates oppressed his massive

physical frame. His imagination at fullest stretch could not comprehend what induced an Indian fakir to lie down on a bed of nails, or a Japanese samurai to commit suicide out of loyalty to his lord. Actions such as these were to him simply irrational, evidencing a lack of any sense of proportion, or humour. His own faith was in the pragmatic life of action and of reasonable compromise, seeking equity in this present life, not immortality in the next or oblivion in Nirvana.[27]

The personal animosity between Menzies and the Prime Minister of India, Jawaharlal Nehru, was vehement and undisguised on both sides, but establishment of close relations between India and Australia has eluded the leaders of both countries before and since, including prime ministers who have reached a personal rapport with their Indian counterparts. As Meg Gurry has pointed out, Menzies and Nehru had fundamentally opposed attitudes towards crucial issues such as the colonial experience, the Commonwealth, the Cold War and other fundamental issues of the day.[28]

Even admirers and confidants, such as Sir Walter Crocker, saw Menzies as simply "anti-Asian." Menzies' private comments on Nehru and the president of Egypt, Gamal Abdel Nasser, have been cited as evidence of an underlying racism.[29] He certainly spoke of Nasser and Nehru in terms that would not be politically acceptable today, but these need to be balanced against some other evidence. Menzies clearly did get on well with Tunku Abdul Rahman, the first Prime Minister of both Malaya and of Malaysia. The Tunku, sometimes described as "a brown Englishman,"came from royal stock in a Malayan sultanate and had studied law at Cambridge. His demeanour and attitude towards the British colonial heritage were markedly different from Nehru's. Menzies was also admired by another Cambridge-educated lawyer with a different ethnic background and political style, the founding father of Singapore, Lee Kuan Yew. After the bitterness of Singapore's expulsion from Malaysia in August 1965, Lee expressed some public disappointment that Menzies had not done more to mediate between the aristocratic Malay statesman and the dynamic young Chinese leader in order to preserve the inclusion of Singapore in Malaysia; but that feeling evidently dissipated, as the two nations worked better apart than together. In his memoirs, Lee recorded the view that Menzies was the Australian prime minister he most admired, ahead of those like Whitlam who proclaimed their greater affinity with Asian values and aspirations.[30]

The difference between Menzies' relationships with Nehru and Lee owed much to fundamentally different geopolitical attitudes. Lee was a prominent supporter of the American and Australian stance in Vietnam, while Nehru, as a leader of the non-aligned bloc, a critic of the war and a quasi-ally of the Soviet Union, was highly critical. Discussions of Australian attitudes to "Asia" too often overlook the breadth and diversity of that vast continent. Menzies clearly had little sympathy for the version of post-1945 Asia exemplified by Jawaharlal Nehru, but a great deal more for that expressed by Lee Kuan Yew.

For Menzies and many Australians of his day, "Asia" principally meant Southeast Asia, extending westwards into South Asia and northwards towards Japan, China and Korea. Even within Southeast Asia, Australian knowledge and interest was only partial. Like most Australians of his era, Menzies was both more concerned about, and more knowledgeable about, maritime Southeast Asia, the band of islands and peninsulas that stretched from the western tip of Sumatra to the eastern end of New Guinea, than about the Southeast Asian mainland, especially the former French Indochina. Not only the Australian prisoners-of-war in Changi but also travellers, officials and businessmen had some acquaintance with the local dynamics of the British and Dutch colonial possessions that would become Malaysia and Indonesia. The French territories of Indochina and their neighbour, Thailand, appeared in Australian thinking principally as territories through which the Japanese had rapidly advanced in 1941 and 1942, threatening Australia's northern neighbours and perhaps Australia itself. This contrast would play an important part in Australian policy in the last years of Menzies' term in office.

"Forward defence"

Nothing figures more prominently in the collective memory of a prime minister's term in office than the military engagements to which he or she has committed forces. Many of the themes discussed above were evident in the four military commitments of the Menzies era – the Korean War and the Malayan Emergency early in his term, the Indonesian Confrontation and the Vietnam War in its last years – and the way they were linked by the strategic concept of "forward defence". "Forward defence" was rather more than a simple assertion that "we must fight them up there before we have to fight them down here", with the presumed enemy being a conflation of the Red Peril and the Yellow Peril, although his supporters should concede that some of Menzies' rhetoric and Liberal Party electoral advertisements laid the policy open to this critique.

"Forward defence" evolved organically in reaction to events: its successes and its failures owed much to the statecraft with which it was applied. Many of its underlying principles arose from Australia's experience in the Korean War of 1950-53. Here Australian forces were operating in an Asian region with a direct relationship to national security as well as alliance maintenance; they fought in a 16-nation coalition, in which the United States provided the major part of the military strength and leadership; Australian leaders had, for the most part, confidence in the political and military strategies employed; the coalition also included Britain and other members of the Commonwealth, with whose forces Australians were closely integrated at the operational level, allowing Australians to fight according to tactics and doctrines with which they were familiar and giving command experience to senior Australians; the coalition included countries from several continents; it operated under the aegis of the United Nations; it fought in defence of a government which had invited external forces, rather than being an invasion force seeking regime change; and the Australian government accompanied its military involvement with independent political and military assessments and diplomatic action.

Throughout the 1950s actual or potential military commitments were assessed against this template, almost as if there were a checklist of criteria of which the government sought to satisfy as many as possible. At its best, when "forward defence" was accompanied by good statecraft, military commitments were carefully co-ordinated with independent diplomacy and other forms of "soft power"; policy was formed in a "whole of government" process, involving a wide range of ministers and their military and civilian advisers; the Government was able and willing to form its own assessments of the region in which it was operating; the Government's leaders were well informed about, and had confidence in, the military and political strategies of its allies, and understood how Australia could contribute effectively, without exposure to excessive risk, to the strategic aim. Most, albeit not all, of these criteria were met by the Menzies Government's commitment to the Malayan Emergency. The success of this commitment, which was declared over in 1960, gave the Australian military confidence that it knew how to operate in Southeast Asia, and it gave Menzies and his Cabinet colleagues confidence that Australia could intervene successfully, in support of a great and powerful friend and ally, in a post-colonial conflict to ensure that the new independent government was sympathetic to the West in the Cold War.

The greatest challenge for the "forward defence" strategy came in the early

1960s as Australia was torn between its two great allies over two separate, but not completely unrelated, conflicts in Southeast Asia. Britain pressed its Commonwealth allies for support in opposing Indonesia's Confrontation of Malaysia, while the focus of the United States was on the increasingly precarious state of the anti-communist Republic of Vietnam (South Vietnam), facing a challenge from an insurgency that was inspired, directed and increasingly implemented by the communist regime in North Vietnam. The British Government, while clearly determined to avoid any entanglement in Vietnam, portrayed Indonesia's President Sukarno as a Southeast Asian Hitler with expansionist ambitions throughout the region. Washington, meanwhile, was urging the Commonwealth countries to handle Indonesia with extreme restraint, while pressing for "more flags" to join in their support for South Vietnam. As the twin crises developed in 1963-64, most Australians were more concerned with Confrontation than Vietnam, but it was proving increasingly difficult to manage the distinction. When Australian leaders pressed senior American officials to state at what point they could expect support under ANZUS over Confrontation, the response was disappointing. The Americans indicated not only that any support would be extremely limited, but also that it would be affected by Australian support for the United States in the theatre of conflict that Washington considered vital – Vietnam.

Ostensibly, Australian policy in both crises was based on the strategy of "forward defence", but their different outcomes reflected the differences between the statecraft with which they were handled. In the case of Confrontation, policy was developed in vigorous, sometimes acerbic, debate between ministers and departmental officials in the relevant departments, based on extensive knowledge of the local politics; the commitment of military assets, especially of ground forces, was made with considerable caution, and only when the Government was confident that their deployment would only occur in accordance with tactics and doctrines approved by Canberra; and the military engagement was accompanied by vigorous independent diplomacy in the key regional capitals (Jakarta and Kuala Lumpur), and by equally vigorous argument with our major ally, Britain, over political and military strategy.

The contrast with policy-making over Vietnam is striking. Here Menzies, in the last year before his retirement, dominated the policy-making process, excluding or disregarding ministers and officials who urged caution in his words and deeds; there was no independent diplomacy and much less knowledge of the real intentions of leaders in Hanoi and Beijing, where Australia had no diplomatic representation; Australia made no attempt to challenge Washington's strategy – or lack of strategy; far from exercising caution in making the commitment of ground troops, the Government pressed an infantry battalion on to the Americans when they had only expressed a vague desire for more advisers; and there was no "exit strategy," no limit on the size or duration of the commitment. Menzies seemed to think that all that mattered was to ensure that the United States remained committed to the region: an American defeat or failure was unthinkable. It was an understandable attitude for a man who, as a young man of military age, had seen the United States wait until 1917 to enter the Great War, and who, as prime minister in 1939-41, had once again seen the perils faced when British countries stood alone against a totalitarian aggressor without the support of the United States; but it did not reflect a deep understanding of the dynamics of Southeast Asia in the mid-1960s. Some Australian commitment in 1965 was both explicable and necessary, but a more carefully handled decision would have reduced the military, financial, political and social costs to the nation.

Conclusion

"History," as C.V. Wedgwood famously observed, "is lived forward but is written in retrospect. We know the end before we consider the beginning and can never wholly recapture what it was to know the beginning only." The observation is particularly apt in considering the foreign and defence policies of the Menzies governments of 1949-66. The history of those policies is often written through the prism of the commitment to the Vietnam War and what W. J. Hudson called his "blind loyalty" to Britain during the Suez crisis of 1956.[31] To do so is to exaggerate the flaws and rigidities in Menzies' policies, while overlooking their more creative and successful aspects. He was right to insist that the Cold War was a crucially important feature of global politics, and that alliances with great powers were vital assets. When he listened to, and gave continuing support to, his ministers and departmental advisers, Menzies often established a fruitful balance between alliances and regional relationships; but when he became overconfident in his own judgment and abilities, complacently applying approaches that had previously proved successful without adjusting to changing geopolitical circumstances, he could go seriously astray, damaging his own reputation as well as the nation's standing. Menzies was slow, emotionally as much as intellectually, to adapt to major changes in the world, such as the decolonisation of the European empires, the dominance of American power, and the changing nature of the Commonwealth. But when changes in Australian policy were initiated, often at the recommendation of influential ministers such as Percy Spender and John McEwen, Menzies generally adopted them as his own. His nostalgia for the days when Britannia ruled the waves and when meetings of the Empire-Commonwealth meant club-like gatherings of the old white Dominions was often a brake on Australian adjustment to a new international order, but his attraction to anachronistic honours and posts, such as being appointed a Knight of the Order of the Thistle or the Lord Warden of the Cinque Ports, were often about symbolism and nostalgia as much as *realpolitik*, helping a conservative electorate to accept the more radical changes. Menzies' latter-day supporters would be wise not to make excessive claims for his policies, but the old critique, of obsequious subservience to Britain and the United States and antipathy to Asia, cannot be allowed to stand without challenge. An examination of the realities, rather than the symbolism and the rhetoric, suggests that, more often than not, Menzies, with the aid of his principal ministers and departmental officials, struck an effective balance between the global and the regional, between alliance and independence, and between resources and commitments.

Endnotes

[1] See Peter Edwards, *Learning from History: Lessons from the Forward Defence Era*, Australian Strategic Policy Institute, Canberra, 2015. Fuller discussion of the "forward defence" strategy, and related aspects of the foreign and defence policies of the Menzies Government, may be found in Peter Edwards, *Australia and the Vietnam War*, NewSouth Press, Sydney 2014; Peter Edwards with Gregory Pemberton, *Crises and Commitments: The Politics and Diplomacy of Australia's Involvement in Southeast Asian Conflicts 1948-1965*, Allen & Unwin in association with the Australian War Memorial, Sydney, 1992; Peter Edwards, *A Nation at War; Australian Politics, Society and Diplomacy during the Vietnam War, 1965-1975*, Allen & Unwin in association with the Australian War Memorial, Sydney, 1997.

[2] See, for example, John Murphy, *Harvest of Fear: a history of Australia's Vietnam War*, Allen & Unwin, Sydney, 1993.

[3] Frank Bongiorno, "The Price of Nostalgia: Menzies, the 'Liberal' Tradition and Australian Foreign Policy", *Australian Journal of Politics & History*, Vol. 51, No. 3, September 2005, 400-17.

[4] David Lowe, *Australian Between Empires: The Life of Percy Spender*, Pickering & Chatto, London, 2010; Percy Spender, *Exercises in Diplomacy: The ANZUS Treaty and the Colombo Plan*, Sydney University Press, 1969. See also David Lowe, *Menzies and the "Great World Struggle": Australia's Cold War 1948-1964*, UNSW Press, Sydney, 1999.

[5] Roderic Pitty, "The Postwar Expansion of Trade with East Asia", Ch. 6 in David Goldsworthy, (ed.), *Facing North: A Century of Australian Engagement with Asia*, Vol. 1, 1901 to the 1970s, Melbourne University Press, 2001, esp. 235-44.

[6] R.G. Casey, *Friends and Neighbours; Australia and the World*, Cheshire, Melbourne, 1954. See also Jeremy Hearder, *Jim Plim Ambassador Extraordinary: A Biography of Sir James Plimsoll*, Connor Court, Ballarat, 2015; W.J. Hudson, *Casey*, Oxford University Press, Melbourne, 1986.

[7] W.J. Hudson, *Blind Loyalty: Australia and the Suez Crisis, 1956*, Melbourne University Press, 1989; Peter Edwards, *Arthur Tange: The Last Mandarin*, Allen & Unwin, Sydney, 2006, 116-23.

[8] See especially Garry Woodard, " 'A Radical Tory': Sir Garfield Barwick, 1961-64", Ch. 6 in Joan Beaumont, Christopher Waters, David Lowe, with Garry Woodard, *Ministers, Mandarins and Diplomats: Australian Foreign Policy Making 1941-1969*, Melbourne University Press, 2003. See also Garry Woodard, "Ministers and Mandarins: The Relationships between Ministers and Secretaries of External Affairs 1935-70", *Australian Journal of International Affairs*, Vol. 54, No. 1, July 1997, 157-69.

[9] Garry Woodard, "Best Practice in Australia's Foreign Policy: 'Konfrontasi' (1963-66)", *Australian Journal of Political Science*, Vol. 33, No. 1, 1989, 85-99.

[10] See Edwards (1992), 358-60.

[11] This based on *Arthur Tange*, Jeremy Hearder, *Jim Plim Ambassador Extraordinary: A Biography of Sir James Plimsoll*, Connor Court, Ballarat, 2015. Woodard, *AJIA*.

[12] David Horner, *Defence Supremo: Sir Frederick Shedden and the Making of Australian Defence Policy*, Allen & Unwin, Sydney, 2000; Edwards (2006), 72.

[13] See Edwards (2006), ch. 5, especially 73.

[14] Peter Edwards, "Menzies and the Imperial Connection 1939-1941" in Cameron Hazlehurst (ed.), *Australian Conservatism*, Australian National University Press, Canberra, 1979, 193-212.

[15] Wayne Reynolds, *Australia's Bid for the Atomic Bomb*, Melbourne University Press, 2000.

[16] See Edwards (1992), Ch. 8.

[17] David Lowe, "Australia at the United Nations in the 1950s: The Paradox of Empire", *Australian Journal of International Affairs*, Vol. 51, No. 2, July 1997, 171-81. See also the essays in David Lowe (ed.), *Australia and the End of Empires: the Impact of Decolonisation in Australia's Near North, 1945-1965*, Deakin University Press, Melbourne, 1996.

[18] Gideon Haigh and David Firth, *Inside Story*, News Custom Publishing, 2007, 113.

[19] Edwards (1997), 166.

[20] See Stuart Ward, *Australia and the British Embrace: The Demise of the Imperial Ideal*, Melbourne University Press, 2001; David Goldsworthy, *Losing the Blanket: Australia and the End of Britain's Empire*, Melbourne University Press, 2002.

[21] David Goldsworthy, "Menzies, Macmillan and Europe", *Australian Journal of International Affairs*, Vol. 51, No. 2, July 1997, 157-69.

[22] Robert O'Neill, *Australia in the Korean War 1950-53*, Vol. 1, *Strategy and Diplomacy*, esp. Chs. 4 and 5.

[23] Cabinet decision 204, 1 May 1962, quoted in Edwards, *Crises and Commitments*, 237.

[24] O'Neill, *Australia in the Korean War,* Vol. 1, *Strategy and Diplomacy, passim.*

[25] Edwards (1992), 168.

[26] Jenny Hocking, *Gough Whitlam: A Moment in History*, Miegunyah Press, Melbourne, 2008, 299.

[27] Alan Watt, *The Evolution of Australian Foreign Policy 1938-1965*, Cambridge University Press, London, 1967, 110.

[28] Meg Gurry, *Australia and India: Mapping the Journey 1944-2014*, Melbourne University Press, 2015, Ch. 2.

[29] See F. Bongiorno, "The Price of Nostalgia", 409.

[30] Lee Kuan Yew, *The Singapore Story: Memoirs of Lee Kuan Yew*, Times editions, Singapore, c.1998.

[31] W.J. Hudson, *Blind Loyalty: Australia and the Suez Crisis, 1956*, Melbourne University Press, 1989.

The Menzies family with Robert (third boy to the right)

Menzies aged five

Menzies commences secondary school in Ballarat, 1907

Menzies in 1927 announcing his intention to nominate for the seat of East Yarra Province in the 1928 Victorian State Election

Menzies, newly-elected member of the Victorian Parliament, 1928

The Menzies family in 1936, from L-R, Ken, Robert, Heather, Pattie and Ian

Menzies speaking at Kurri Kurri sports oval to striking miners, 1940

The
Forgotten People

By

THE RT HON. R. G. MENZIES

From the standpoint of a true patriot and in the spirit of man to man, Mr Menzies examines, in *The Forgotten People*, many of the problems arising from our present state of war such as:

The Forgotten People

Freedom of Speech and Expression

Freedom of Worship

Freedom from Want

Freedom from Fear

What the British are Doing in This War

Scrap Iron for Japan

The Censorship

Our American Allies

Lend-Lease

Women In War

Paying for the War

Rationalization of Industry

Taxing the Shareholder

Has Capitalism Failed?

The Drink Problem

Is Inflation a Bogey?

Compulsory Unionism

The Nature of Democracy

The Sickness of Democracy

The Achievements of Democracy

The Task of Democracy

The Importance of Cheerfulness

Cover of 1942 edition of Menzies' collection of Forgotten People speeches

Formation of the Liberal Party of Australia, 1944

Portrait of Elizabeth (May) Couchman (1876-1982), the President of the Australian Women's League and Liberal pioneer who helped Robert Menzies establish the new Party in 1944. Menzies considered that Couchman "would have been the best Cabinet minister I could have wished for".

Menzies casting his vote in the all-important Federal Election of 1949

Menzies tosses the coin at the inaugural Prime Minister's XI v West Indies match, October 1951. With him are the two captains, Jack Fingleton and John Goddard.

7

The Wealth of the Nation

Henry Ergas and J.J. Pincus

The post-war Menzies governments presided over creation of a modern Australian economy, one firmly based on private enterprise, not the nationalisation of finance and industry; one with millions of "little capitalist" home-owners, not renters dependent on the continuous largesse of the state for shelter; one with a greater emphasis on science and university education than on railway workshops; one no longer held to ransom by communist-controlled unions in coal mining, electricity generation and the wharves; one with its external trade focus shifting from the North Atlantic towards Asia; and one with many of the basic elements of the welfare state.

Yet the successive governments Menzies led (referred to collectively as "the Menzies Government") secured those achievements largely within the framework of institutions they had inherited and that they entrenched. Respectful rather than subversive of Australian traditions, they relied heavily on the arbitration system to define and implement a wages policy; on tariff protection to promote secondary industry and to assist the more labour-intensive parts of agriculture; and on the Commonwealth's fiscal strength to underwrite a system of federalism that, over time, weakened the independence and fiscal responsibility of the State governments.

Each of those aspects of policy was an important element in formation and persistence of the political and social coalition that underpinned the Menzies era – a coalition whose bedrock lay in the rapidly expanding urban middle class but which stretched from rural interests through to the conservative trade unionists who formed the Democratic Labor Party. And along with the newly-developed instruments of Keynesian macroeconomic policy, those institutions were also crucial in the way the Menzies Government managed the recurring tension between its central goal of accelerating national development and the constraints the balance of payments imposed on an economy which had a fixed exchange rate but was largely dependent on primary exports and on sustained capital inflows, making it especially vulnerable to external shocks.

In turn, the question of how that tension should be managed was at the heart of the economic policy debates of the time, which largely accepted the desirability (and feasibility) of "fine tuning" – that is, of using monetary and fiscal instruments so as to control short-term fluctuations in the macro-economy – and the intellectual premises on which Australia's distinctive approach to longer term economic policy relied. Central to those premises was the belief that primary commodities could not in future generate the export income required to fund the level of imports that, without protection, a rapidly expanding economy would demand; the commitment to a wages policy as a way of allocating national income and so helping to absorb shocks to productivity and world prices; and acceptance of the inherent desirability of increasing Australia's population, which inevitably privileged extensive over intensive growth (that is, an increase in GDP, rather than an increase in *per capita* income). Although the period was rich in intellectual disputes, they generally involved implementation of policy: the *weltanschauung* within which the Menzies Government's economic policy proceeded was very broadly accepted, embodying an almost universally shared consensus.

In some respects, that consensus reflected the spirit of the age, not only in Australia but overseas: in particular, the beginnings of the Keynesian approach to securing and preserving full employment, the use of interventionist measures to guide aggregate supply, and the commitment to providing returned soldiers, the old and the ill with some degree of social security. However, the distinctive feature of the Menzies era – that differentiated it from the stance then adopted by the Australian Labor Party and from the approach pursued in much of Europe and even more so in the developing economies – was that its core beliefs were consciously implemented through policies which relied primarily on stimulating private initiative rather than replacing it, and that were shaped by institutions largely independent of executive government (such as the Arbitration and Conciliation Commission, the Industrial Court (after 1956), the Commonwealth Grants Commission and the Tariff Board).[1] The Menzies Government resisted the siren calls of nationalisation on the one hand and of indicative planning on the other: the role of executive government was mainly to facilitate private economic development, rather than plan it, with the most important exception being the active immigration program. And the goals of social welfare policy were largely pursued by an emphasis on job creation rather than through transfers.

In all of those ways, Menzies adopted and adapted the Deakinite legacy to the circumstances of the post-war world in a manner comparable to Canada rather than the United Kingdom or other West European countries.[2] But protectionism remained a defining element, vigorously intensified to include import licensing when it proved necessary (but not, as in New Zealand, to be retained virtually indefinitely) and with assistance extended to primary industry, including through "orderly marketing" schemes for agricultural produce: "protection all round" received strong support from the Coalition partner, the Country Party, especially under John McEwen. Protection had multiple economic roles: to create jobs with good wages, thus helping to absorb the inflow of often unskilled migrants; to diversify the economic base; to preserve foreign exchange; and to garner public revenue.

There were, however, two elements of the Deakinite package that were modified almost to the point of abandonment: Imperial Preference and the White Australia policy. Through trade treaties with Britain (1956) and Japan (1957), the Menzies Government adapted international commercial policy to the UK's relative decline and its turn towards Europe, as well as to the incipient rise of the first of the Asian miracle economies (then specialising in textiles and crockery, not ships and steel). Meanwhile, the Government changed the national composition of immigrants towards Southern Europe, established the Colombo Plan to bring Asian students to Australia (1950), and progressively relaxed the restrictions on non-European settlement, including abolition of the dictation test in 1958. (Through the *Migration Act* of 1966, the Holt Government established legal equality between British, other European and non-European migrants.)

Before the end of Menzies' parliamentary career, there were mounting claims that protectionism had caused Australia to slip down the rankings of countries by *per capita* income; and even the Tariff Board confessed itself unable to offer any convincing economic rationale for the pattern of rates of protection, except differential success in lobbying, or what later was called "rent seeking".[3] In addition, financial repression – that is, tight controls over the price, quantity and allocation of bank credit – seemed increasingly unsustainable in face of the rise of non-bank financial intermediaries that acted as "fringe" suppliers of loans. And the Bretton Woods system of fixed exchange rates was coming under ever-greater pressure, as the United States financed the escalating war in Vietnam on credit and as international capital movements undermined governments' ability to manage monetary policy without exchange rate flexibility.

Taken as a whole, the period was one of sustained prosperity – prosperity all the more striking for being largely unexpected. The economic policies of the Menzies Government – including accelerated migration, openness to international capital inflows, the promotion of wage moderation, and a prudent fiscal policy that strictly limited the public sector's call on national resources, freeing up the savings needed to finance very high levels of private investment – all helped stimulate that growth and permitted it to persist. And the low tax burden, the steady fall in public debt and the refusal to allow social transfers and entitlements to rise as rapidly as they were rising internationally, all made it easier for Australia to bear the costs imposed by the more profligate governments that followed and, more generally, to manage its way through the years of slower and more volatile growth.

Yet it is also true that the economic policies of the Menzies Government contributed to Australia's later difficulties, both by promoting the growth of an ultimately uncompetitive manufacturing sector and by strengthening institutions, such as the arbitration system, which could (and, in later years, did) impede the economy's ability to respond to shocks.

To say that is neither to minimise the achievements nor to denigrate those who called them into being. As we show below, the policies that are now viewed as counterproductive were then almost unanimously endorsed by the country's leading economists; and, far from repudiating those policies, Labor believed they did not go far enough. Labor's program promised far-reaching nationalisation, controls over capital inflows and even greater protection. Had Labor prevailed, the adjustment problems Australia faced in the 1970s and 1980s would have been more intractable and even more costly to resolve.

In considering the economic record of the Menzies Government, we begin by examining economic performance during the period; we then review the intellectual premises that underpinned policy; and proceed to discuss how policy was implemented. On that basis, we consider the trade-off that was made between extensive growth – which expanded the economy by increasing its use of factor inputs – and intensive growth, which required making better use of resources (rather than simply using more of them). A concluding section draws together the threads of our argument.

Overview of economic outcomes

In the 1950s and well into the 1960s, Australia, together with much of the Western world, experienced a long economic boom – of steadily advancing living standards, remarkably low unemployment and fulfilled expectations of low inflation – which erased many of the ill-effects the traumas of the 1930s Depression and the Second World War had inflicted on the cohorts that experienced them.[4] Thanks to that boom, the Australia of 1966 was vastly more prosperous than that of 1950; it was also more equal in terms of the distribution of income and wealth.[5]

Table 1 Population and Economy, 1950 and 1965: selected data

		1950	1965	Annual growth rate
1	Population (m.)	8.3	11.5	2.1%
2	Real Gross Domestic Product ($b, 2010-11 prices)	156	295	4.1%
3	Real Gross Domestic Product per head ($'000)	18.8	25.6	2.0%
4	Overseas Born (% Population)	9.8 (1947 census)	18.4 (1966 census)	
5	Openness ({Exports + Imports}/GDP, as %)	36.3	22.9	
6	Private Non-dwelling Investment/GDP (%)	7.4	11.9	
7	Taxation/GDP (%)	23.0	23.4	
8	Public Debt Outstanding/ GDP (%)	120	52	

Sources: Rows 1-6: M. Butlin, R. Dixon and P. J. Lloyd, "Statistical Appendix: selected data series, 1800-2010", in S. Ville and G. Withers, eds, *The Cambridge Economic History of Australia*, Cambridge University Press, Port Melbourne, 2015. Rows 7, 8: W. Vamplew (ed), *Australians. Historical Statistics*, Fairfax, Syme & Weldon Associates, Broadway, NSW, 1987, GF6, 256.

And it was far larger also, in economic and social terms. During the Menzies era, the Australian population grew by almost 40 percent, faster than in the world as a whole (34 percent) or the United States (30 percent). This was the height of the post-war "baby boom": the fertility rate peaked in 1961 at 3.55 – Menzies had introduced child endowment for multiparous families in 1941, in an effort to postpone an increase in the Basic Wage; it was extended to all children in 1950. But even with the "baby boom", net immigration contributed almost four-tenths of the population increase over the whole period, and over half in the late 1940s and early 1950s – a far higher proportion than in Canada or the United States – as the Menzies Government adapted and extended Labor's immigration program. Reflecting the impact of migration, there was a doubling in the proportion of Australians born abroad (to more than 18 percent) between the census of 1947 and that of 1966. As the migration program proceeded, the sources of the foreign born population changed too, with "New Australians" increasingly coming from Southern Europe.

At the same time, national production, measured as GDP adjusted for inflation, almost doubled in size: this implies a growth rate twice as fast as that of population, and that had not been experienced for an extended period since the boom that followed the gold rushes.

Table 2: Rates of output increase in Australia (percentage rates of increase per annum in real G.D.P.)

1861-70	4.3%
1871-80	5.1%
1881-90	4.0%
1901-10	4.0%
1920/21-1927/28	3.5%
1948/49-1953/54	3.7%
1953/54-1962/63	4.1%
1962/63-1968/69	5.1%

Source: W.A. Sinclair (1976). *The Process of Economic Development in Australia.* Melbourne: Cheshire, 212.

Given the rapid growth of population and production, it is remarkable that GDP per head, an admittedly imperfect index of living standards, grew at two percent a year: as fast as during the period from 1991 to 2010, which is widely considered to have been a period of great prosperity. (A full discussion of the rise in living standards can be found in chapter 8.)

With the economy growing strongly, unemployment was extraordinarily low in absolute terms – in one month in 1951 (admittedly at the height of the wool boom), the number of registered unemployed in South Australia was down to only three people[8] – as well as compared to other high income countries. Despite a slight fall in the participation rate, the supply of labour was increasing rapidly, but demand for labour was also growing fast, boosted by the private and public infrastructure demand of immigrants[9] and especially by private non-dwelling capital formation, which rose from 7.4 percent of GDP in 1950 to almost 12 percent of GDP in 1965.

Figure 1: Unemployment Rate

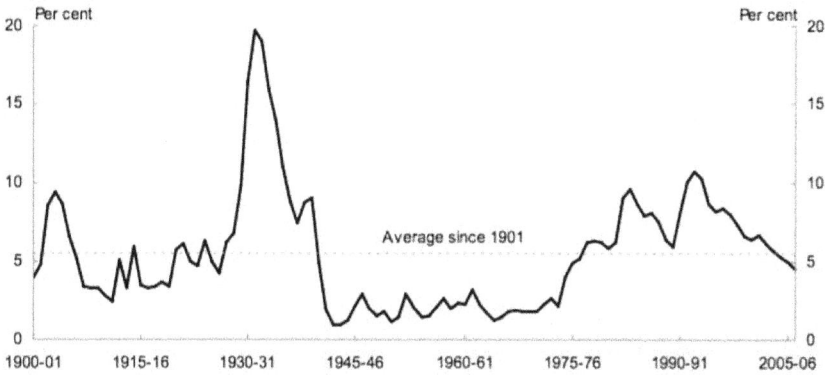

Source: Henry (2007) from ABS Catalogue Number 6204.0.55.001, 6202.0 and Reserve Bank of Australia

Figure 2: Prices and wages (year average)

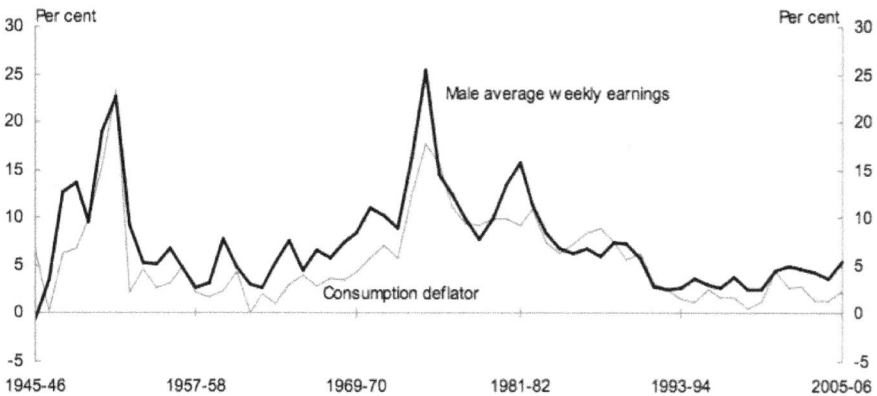

Source: Henry (2007) from ABS Catalogue Number 5204.0, 6302.0 and Reserve Bank of Australia.

Yet, once Arthur Fadden's "horror budget" of September 1951 had brought the inflation unleashed by the 1949-50 surge in wool prices under control, low unemployment was accompanied by low inflation, especially in the 1960s (when Australia's inflation rate was well below that of the other advanced economies).[10] In 1953, the Arbitration Commission abandoned automatic quarterly indexation of the basic wage, as being inconsistent with application of the "capacity to pay" principle to an open economy, such as Australia's.[11] In the event, although the metal trades industries became the wage setting leader, and despite the rise in claims for "margins for skill" (and later in the period, in over-award payments, which provided some flexibility in wage setting), there was no serious "wages breakout" until the Whitlam Government came to office. On the contrary, as Blanche d'Alpuget reported, "when the Minister for Labour, Billy MacMahon, travelled abroad, he was lionized by foreign counterparts who wanted to know how Australia managed things so well".[12]

Far-reaching changes in the structure of the economy accompanied rapid growth. Over the period to 1965, agriculture declined markedly, shrinking from 24 to nine percent of GDP (Figure 3);[13] but rural industries still dominated Australian commodity exports, with wool alone accounting for almost 30 percent of exports by value at the end of the period. The terms of international trade were moving against primary exporters like Australia; moreover, within Australia, the prices of the inputs farmers purchased increased more rapidly than the prices at which they sold their outputs. However, with mechanisation, innovation in varieties and techniques, and application of science, especially of pest control – myxomatosis (although invented much earlier) was introduced in 1950 – productivity in the farm sector was still growing faster than in the non-farm market sector at the end of the era.[14]

Rapid productivity growth affected relative incomes. Despite a decline in the "product" terms of trade (that is, the ratio of prices farmers received to prices farmers paid), rapid productivity growth in agriculture meant that the "factor" terms of trade – the factors of production Australian farmers had to devote to paying for the factors of production embodied in the goods and services they purchased – did not deteriorate by anywhere near as much, and especially when the growth in agricultural productivity was at its peak, may actually have been improving.[15] That encouraged agricultural output to expand, which it continued to do even as prices fell. So notable was the resulting growth that a Treasury retrospective, published in 1966, confidently concluded that:

… Despite the fears voiced from time to time about the future of Australia's exports of primary products, results so far seem to show that increases in production can more than offset the effect on export proceeds of falling prices. Whereas the future of export prices is problematical, experience in Australia and elsewhere suggests that the upward trend in productivity in the main primary industries can continue.[16]

Figure 3: Industry Shares

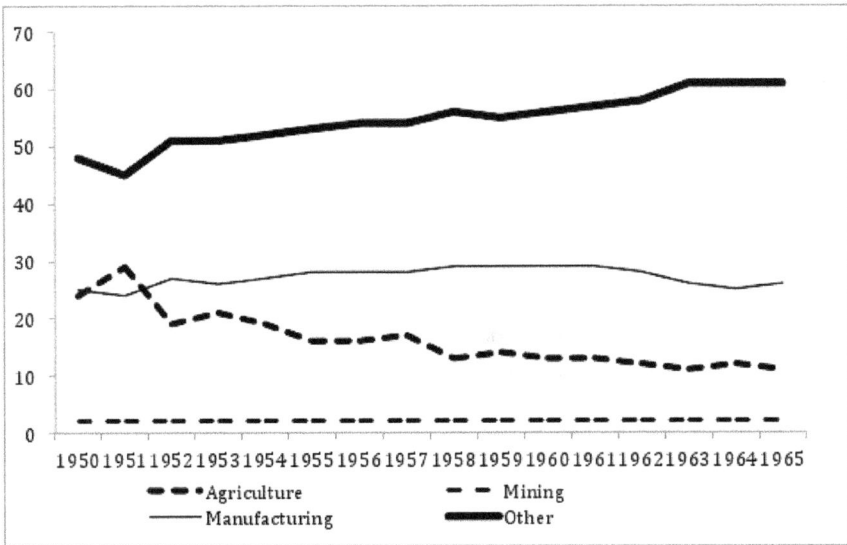

Source: Ville and Withers (2015), Table A1, 559

Figure 4: Terms of Trade and Inflation Rate

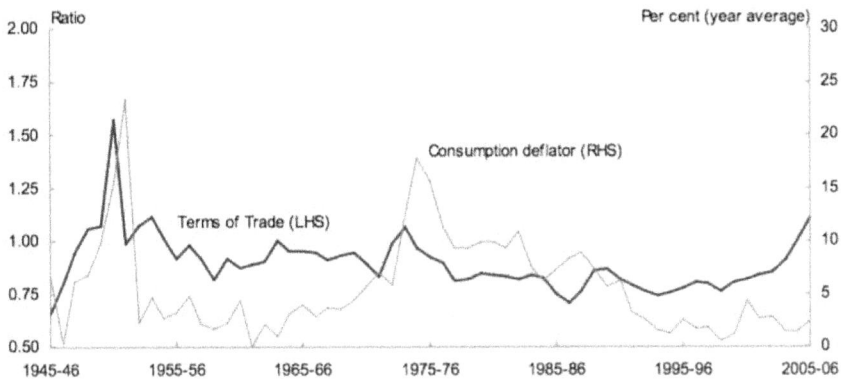

Source: Henry (2007) from ABS Catalogue Number 5204.0 and Reserve Bank of Australia.

Even so, the most rapidly growing productive sector was "Other" – services and construction, which rose from 48 to 63 percent of GDP. It was also notable that manufacturing reached its century peak share of 29 percent of GDP in 1958; and that, despite the stirring of a minerals boom at the end of the period, mining barely grew from two percent of GDP.[17]

Overall, this was a rare period – only repeated in the 1990s – when strong growth in Australia did not coincide with a sustained increase in world demand for its natural resources, and hence when growth was not led by the resource industries.

Rather, the growth process was largely inward-looking. Although the economy was made more open to the inflow of capital and labour from abroad, high levels of import protection meant that international trade fell in importance. This can be seen from the sharp decline in the degree of (trade) openness, measured by the ratio of exports plus imports to GDP that is shown as line 5 of Table 1 and in Figure 5.

Figure 5: Trade intensity (nominal exports plus imports as a share of GDP)

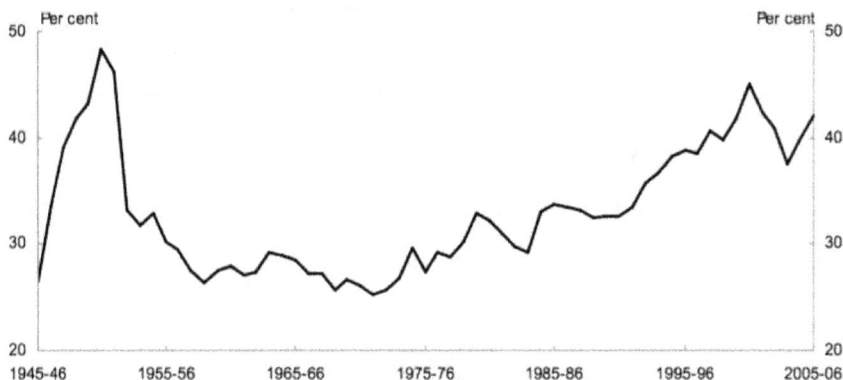

Source: Henry (2007) from ABS Catalogue Number 5204.0 and Reserve Bank of Australia.

Elsewhere, in the USA, the UK and most advanced economies, openness rose or held steady.[18] World trade grew faster than world production, in part due to the efforts of the United States to encourage countries to reduce their import barriers, especially in the various "rounds" of negotiations under the General Agreement on Tariffs and Trade. Australia held back, pleading that it was an intermediate economy: rich but still developing, and reliant on primary rather than manufacturing exports. The refusal of most advanced economies to bind (that is, commit to not increase) the tariff and non-tariff barriers they imposed on agricultural trade, much less reduce them, entrenched Australia's reluctance to scale back its own protectionist measures. Moreover, Australia preferred bi-lateral to multi-lateral trade agreements, or took unilateral action.[19]

But it would be dangerous to view openness too narrowly. Although the economy's trade intensity fell, inflows of factors of production – capital, labour and technology – increased materially, greatly influencing the course of economic development (discussed further below). Additionally, despite the decline in openness to international trade, the economy remained highly vulnerable to external constraints; these manifested themselves in balance of payments crises in 1951-52, 1954-55 and 1955-56, and then 1960-61. Each of those crises, in which the country's holdings of foreign exchange dropped suddenly, was associated with internal booms that caused a surge in imports. Given the constraint of a fixed exchange rate, governments responded by using monetary and fiscal policy to dampen economic activity; the 1951-52 crisis also led the Government to impose quantitative import restrictions in March 1952 (which remained in place until 1960) as a way of stemming the loss of foreign exchange. Tightening fiscal and monetary policy inflicted a cost in terms of economic growth: GDP shrank by about one percent in response to the 1951 "horror budget" and by two percent in 1960-61, while growth came to a standstill in the downturn that followed the balance of payments crisis of the mid-1950s.[20]

The result was to highlight the tension between the Government's central goals of rapid growth and full employment, on the one hand, and the maintenance of external balance – fundamentally, the ability to defend the exchange rate – on the other. How that tension could be resolved was at the heart of economic policy, to which we now turn.

The premises of economic policy

Economic policy during the Menzies era reflected a view of the world that was widely shared by policy-makers and by policy-influencers alike. This was the height of the power of the "Seven Dwarfs": the mandarins who rose to prominence during the war, but retained their dominating influence on public policy for the following two decades.[21] Especially important were Sir Roland Wilson, who was Treasury Secretary from 1951 to 1966, and H.C. "Nugget" Coombs, Governor of the Commonwealth Bank and then of the Reserve Bank from 1949 to 1968; and they were merely the two most prominent public officials with formal training in economics – including, at senior levels, Sir Richard Randall (Treasury), Sir John Crawford (Commerce and Agriculture; Trade) and Sir Leslie Melville (Commonwealth Bank; Tariff Board), along with a growing inflow of economics graduates – who provided government with an analytical capacity that did not exist in the 1930s. This capacity was periodically supplemented by secondments of academic economists, including Trevor Swan (Department of Post-War Reconstruction and, in 1949-50, Chief Economist in Prime Minister's) and Wilfred Salter (Prime Minister's, from 1960 to 1962). However, the circle shaping the broad direction of economic policy was broader than that, as the "official family" was attentive to "outside" expert economic opinion, all the more so given the perception, born of the Keynesian revolution and reinforced through the planning of post-war reconstruction, that the tools were being forged for guiding economies to prosperity.

That is not to exaggerate the impact external views had on policy – this was, after all, the period when the public service's "monopoly" over policy advice was at its peak, and its most senior members, notably Wilson, were notoriously self-sufficient.[22] Additionally, with financial markets relatively underdeveloped (and in any case, heavily regulated), ongoing review by "market economists" of economic policy developments was very limited, the AMP's Dr Harold Bell being virtually the only prominent commentator.[23] Yet it would be equally wrong to dismiss or ignore the climate of opinion. Even in the early 1950s, and yet more so as the Menzies era progressed, Canberra was anything but a "hermit kingdom", impermeable to the weight of ideas, which were also reflected in the evolving debates in institutions such as the Tariff Board and in the economic evidence presented in national wage cases. Moreover, the mere fact that, by and large, expert opinion was generally supportive of the thrust of policy made the broad direction the Government steered easier to justify and maintain.

That was all the more the case as Australian policy discussions in the period were very well served by the economics profession. Especially from the mid-1950s, the profession's leading lights were active in the policy debates, publishing timely, thoughtful and well-researched surveys of the economy and of economic policy, both at the macroeconomic level and on specific policy-relevant topics.[24] Those surveys, which were in many cases commissioned by the Economic Society of Australia and New Zealand for the *Economic Record* – and eventually reprinted, along with complementary pieces, in 1963 as *The*

Australian Economy: A volume of readings, edited by H.W. Arndt and W.M. Corden – provide a strikingly clear guide to the thinking of the time.

Naturally enough, there were disagreements; and there were some dissenting voices within the profession, most notably that of Colin Clark, who emphasised the high costs of protection. Even so, what is remarkable is the extent to which the period's most prominent economists agreed in general terms on what was happening, how to interpret it, and what policy recommendations to make. Moreover, albeit with varying emphases and occasional sharp differences, they shared a common understanding of the longer-term challenges Australia faced and of the broad approach governments should adopt – one that largely accorded with the way in which senior officials saw the world, and with the thrust of government policy.

Four elements were at the core of that view of the world. The first, and by far, most important, was the underlying commitment to the objective of national development, which meant not merely the pursuit of sustained economic growth and of full employment, but of growth at a significantly higher rate than could have occurred simply on the basis of domestic factor accumulation. Associated with that commitment was acceptance of a high level of immigration as desirable both as a means to economic ends and as integral to ensuring full realisation of Australia's national potential.

Development was not seen solely as an economic imperative. Rather, it was also viewed as an indispensable element in the "great world struggle" between freedom and communism. As Percy Spender, the Minister for External Affairs, put it in his famous statement to Parliament on 9 March 1950, to prevail in that struggle, the world's democracies had to ensure they were "politically stable and economically prosperous".[25] It was therefore not a coincidence that the Department of National Development was created in the same month as Spender's statement, with R.G. Casey, its first minister, describing national development as the means "to increase our national security to a maximum".[26] Nor did this broader emphasis wane in later years; instead, as Harold Holt argued, "growth is our watchword as a government on behalf of the people of Australia. It is also the password for the sentry at the gate to our security and our prosperity".[27]

A second element was the emphasis on the external constraints that could nonetheless limit the sustainable rate of growth and hence slow national development.

In part, those constraints were the natural corollary of the commitment to a fixed exchange rate, as that gave rise to a recurring tension between supporting domestic demand at high levels, on the one hand, and the need to finance any resulting shortfall in the balance of trade, thus protecting the exchange rate, on the other.

In turn, fixity of the exchange rate was largely taken as a given. It was, after all, required by the then articles of agreement of the International Monetary Fund, which Australia had joined (after contentious debate within the ALP) in 1947.[28] Indeed, even those academic economists who were critical of fixed exchange rates were cautious in recommending any alternative: for example, James Meade, a future economics Nobel laureate who visited Australia and wrote perceptively about its balance of payments problems, argued in 1956 that it would be better if Australia, the United Kingdom and other countries used a "generalised system of exchange rate variation or wage-rate adjustment rather than the limitations of imports to deal with their difficulties".[29] Especially in view of Meade's long discussion of the conditions necessary to make exchange rate flexibility possible and for a depreciation to improve the balance of trade or payments, his was hardly a clarion call to free up the exchange rate unilaterally, or even for more frequent adjustments of the exchange rate "peg" (which, as is noted below, is what Coombs advocated).[30]

Yet while exchange rate fixity was widely accepted, it was also apparent that it removed a policy instrument which would otherwise have helped reconcile internal balance – essentially, the maintenance of full employment – with external balance, that is, a sustainable balance of payments position. The resulting trade-offs were first illuminated by Trevor Swan in two papers that were only published long after they were written and circulated, but that were enormously influential both in the academic debate and in Canberra.[31] As well as making a number of important analytical contributions, those papers highlighted the role that a national wages policy could play in simultaneously achieving internal and external balance, with adjustments to what was then known as the "cost ratio" – a measure of competitiveness defined by the ratio of an index of the prices of imports and exports to an index of Australian wages – emerging as the instrument that could be used in place of variations in the exchange rate.

Because of its focus on the "cost ratio", the conceptual framework Swan set out (and which rapidly became the distinctively Australian approach to analysing the balance of payments) cemented the view of wages policy, and so of the arbitration system, as a potent weapon in the armoury of stabilisation policy. The machinery of wage-setting therefore came to be seen as serving a crucial macroeconomic purpose, rather than as an institution whose primary purpose – in the Australian tradition of "accommodative" adjudication[32] – was to manage industrial conflict. Swan's model thereby fanned a debate about the rules to be applied in setting wages, with that debate's key outcome being that wages policy should cushion the impact on employment levels of external shocks – a goal which could be achieved by linking wages (and, more broadly, earnings) to overall productivity, measured correcting for changes in the terms of trade.[33]

As well as the concern with short-term stability, however, there was also a longer-term element in the emphasis on external constraints. In particular, economic policy was marked by a pervasive "balance of payments pessimism" – the conviction that, were the economy left to its own devices, Australia's exports would not expand sufficiently rapidly, over the longer term, to finance the demand for imports that would result from sustained economic growth.[34]

At least initially, that pessimism was shaped by the "characteristic Australian assumption that rural production cannot be increased significantly": and, in any event, that farmers would not expand output materially even if doing so became more profitable.[35] As the terms of trade continued to deteriorate, however, greater emphasis was placed on the worsening relativity between the price Australia paid for its largely manufactured imports – which increased by ten percent over the period from 1953 to 1961 – and the price it received for its (mainly primary) exports, which, over the same period, declined by more than 25 percent. In the late 1950s, a prestigious panel of experts established by the GATT had found that "it would be unwise to count upon any improvement in the terms of trade" for agricultural exporters;[36] surveying the prospects for Australian primary exports a few years later, F.H. Gruen echoed that panel's findings, concluding that:

> ... Disregarding the possibility of a world conflict which would make export prices one of our less important worries, there are very few factors in sight which seem likely to counteract those making for a continuation of the long-term downward trend in export prices for farm products.[37]

That relatively bleak view of Australia's potential export income persisted throughout the Menzies era. It culminated in the Vernon report (discussed further below) which, despite Sir James Vernon's crucial role in the Mount Newman project and more generally in the development of iron ore in the Pilbara,[38] largely ignored the mining boom that by then was getting underway. The report presented pessimistic projections of Australia's balance of payments, based on assumed poor prospects for rural exports and on rising dividend payments for foreign capital.[39] Like the earlier analyses, those projections proved unduly grim; but the fact that they were endorsed by so eminent a committee underscores the degree to which a gloomy outlook for primary exports formed part of the mental map that shaped policy.

That gloomy outlook helped to frame the third element in the policy consensus – the need to:

> ... intensify the efforts that have already been made to increase Australian exports and to economise on imports, both by developing new import-replacing industries and by increasing the efficiency of existing home producers. Although primary industry should be encouraged to increase its output and exports (especially those sections of primary industry which are not dependent on heavy subsidy), it would be wise to place greater emphasis in future on the development of manufacturing exports.[40]

In that sense, despite the significant misgivings some expressed about the design and implementation of tariff policy,[41] the desirability of diversifying the structure of the economy was broadly accepted throughout the Menzies period. Indeed, the transition away from reliance on primary industry was viewed as an indicator that Australia had "graduated to the point where it bore a stronger resemblance to the industrial nations of the world than to the regions of recent settlement of the nineteenth century".[42]

Finally, there was a widely shared belief in the ability of governments both to pursue sensible long-term economic objectives and to manage the internal and external shocks any economy undergoing rapid growth was sure to experience. The risks of rent seeking were more frequently recognised than emphasized; they were certainly not regarded as fatal to an activist policy stance.[43]

That is not to suggest there was an indifference to the dangers of government intervention: on the contrary, the Institute of Public Affairs, in its highly influential 1944 pamphlet on post-war reconstruction, *Looking Forward*, had stressed the importance of not attempting to displace private enterprise and the profit motive, which were both the guarantors of individual freedom and "the most powerful of all stimulants to industrial and commercial effort and economic progress". But the Institute also recognised the need for government to "dig the broad channels in which individual organisations can be allowed to flourish", and in that way to "plan private enterprise".[44] This essentially pragmatic approach was later echoed by Menzies, when he said that his government had:

... no doctrinaire political philosophy. Where government action or control has seemed to us to be the best answer to a practical problem, we have adopted that answer ... But our first impulse is always to seek the private enterprise answer, to help the individual to help himself, to create a climate, economic, social, industrial, favourable to his activity and growth.[45]

As for shorter-term economic management, this was what John Hicks later called, albeit with some exaggeration, the "Age of Keynes":[46] the feasibility of "fine tuning" was rarely questioned, and the future was seen as one in which governments would "learn to control aggregate levels of expenditure in the economy much more finely and promptly than has been the case in the past".[47]

Interestingly, despite the stress on government's role, there was very little discussion of social welfare policy, much less of using taxing and spending to redistribute income on a substantial scale. From time to time, proposals were made for taxation and expenditure reform, heavily influenced by social democratic thinking in the UK;[48] but in an era that saw economic growth and full employment as the primary means of meeting social aspirations, these were never rated as priorities.

In short, the conceptual lens through which economic policy was viewed emphasised economic growth by means of rapid factor accumulation; managing that growth so as to avoid balance of payments crises; using tariff and non-tariff measures to diversify the economy, thus reducing reliance on rural exports; and relying on the capacity of government not merely to set the broad direction in which the economy should head but also to steer it actively through any turbulence. There was correspondingly less emphasis than would be the case today on making efficient use of resources; and even less on the danger that instead of serving the public interest, interventionist governments would end up redistributing income from one group in the community to another, squandering some of that income at each step along the way.

The implementation of policy

How successful did that view of the world prove? It could be said that the outcomes spoke for themselves; if full employment with price stability was ever achieved in Australia, it was in the Menzies years, to an extent not seen again until the Howard Government. And the Vernon Enquiry's contention, that sustained growth "endows the community with a sense of vigour and social purpose", was certainly borne out by the lived experience of the time.

There is, however, a risk in attributing to policy what it might not have caused; moreover, the signs of success may simply have hidden problems that were being bequeathed to the future. A more prudent evaluation would be that there were both hits and misses: put simply, Australia became a larger and far richer country, but efficiency was sacrificed for growth.

The area where the goals of policy were achieved to the greatest extent was in attracting factor inflows – of labour, capital and technology – that could lift the economy's potential growth rate well above levels that would otherwise have been feasible, and in ensuring those additional resources were indeed used.

The most socially and politically salient inflows were of labour. Between 1945 and 1965, Australia received more than two million migrants, a majority with their fares to Australia paid or heavily subsidised by the Commonwealth, in return for having to remain in Australia for at least two years and to work in whatever jobs the Government gave them. Immigrants accounted for about 70 percent of the increase in workforce in the 1950s, falling to around 40 percent in the next decade: the fall in birth rates in the 1930s boosted the contribution of immigration in the 1950s, whereas in the 1960s, the baby boomers – including children of migrants – started to join the workforce in large numbers.

There was strong support for a large immigration program and, until the early 1960s, for the White Australia policy. As W.D. Borrie wrote in his masterly study of "The peopling of Australia":

> By 1945 there were few opponents of the theory that a much larger population was urgently required in the interests of security … there was a new confidence in the future which contrasted sharply with the pessimism of the 'thirties … it seemed clear that rapid population growth could only come from immigration. And finally, if pre-war theories were correct, many of the new immigrants would have to come from sources other than the United Kingdom.[49]

The post-war immigration program commenced under Labor: between 1947 and 1953 the Australian Government assisted more than 170 000 Displaced Persons to migrate from Europe (with most of that migration occurring in 1949 and 1950). Once the post-war shortage of shipping had eased sufficiently, Chifley and Calwell's longer-term scheme, to recruit many more immigrants not only from Northern but also from Southern Europe, could come into effect. Their

Figure 6: Natural Increase and Net Immigration (number per thousand of end-year population)

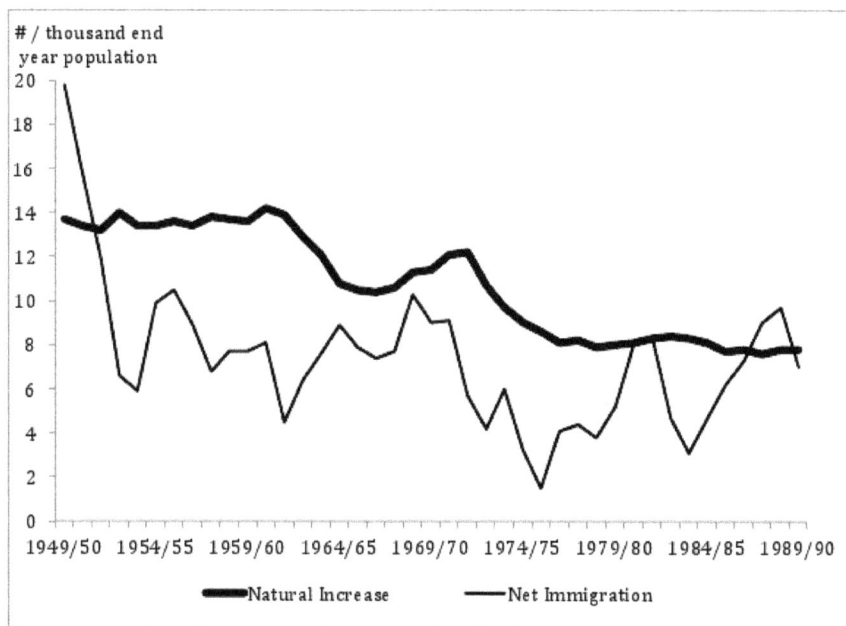

Source: Foster & Stewart 1991, Table 4.1

motivation was to facilitate transition to a peacetime economy, by reducing bottlenecks in essential industries and so avoiding price and wage inflation, especially after the defeat in 1948 of the referendum to vest the Commonwealth with power to control rents and prices.[50] Immigration Minister Calwell set an immigration target of one percent of population, of "persons most needed for national developmental and other essential undertakings of Commonwealth and State Governments and of local government authorities".[51]

Yet once Labor went into opposition, it continually criticised the Government for not halting large-scale immigration whenever there was unemployment or a housing shortage.[52] In contrast, Menzies, who had strongly advocated an expanded immigration program as part of post-war reconstruction, maintained that commitment once in office, although the scale of the program varied from time to time. Periodically, immigration targets were set, which were generally undershot in the early post-war years, and over-filled later.[53] The important point was that the migrants turned out to be, as Borrie put it, "ideal settlers" who, under the terms of their contract, "could be directed to points where labour was most needed, such as developmental projects, extractive industries, iron and steel and so on". Public spending on resettlement within Australia was minimal: Borrie estimates it at less than £40 per head, with most migrants being housed in accommodation that had been built as part of the war effort. Moreover, as they brought few funds with them – Borrie estimated about £90 per head – and (non-British subjects) were excluded from unemployment benefits, they had very strong incentives to find and retain work, all the more so as a record of steady employment was crucial in securing access to a mortgage. Although there has been surprisingly little analysis of the matter, it seems reasonable to suggest that they ensured a high level of mobility and flexibility in the labour market.[54]

The inflows of labour were paralleled by inflows of foreign capital. In 1949, the world was still experiencing an excess of demand over supply, manifest as "the dollar shortage". Many countries, and not only the former belligerents, were looking beyond reconstruction, towards development: the aim was not merely to restore living standards but to improve them materially. This required large-scale investment in productive capacity, in infrastructure, in housing and in motor vehicles.

Within this world economy, Australia sought to achieve one of the fastest rates of economic growth. This involved adding more to world demand than to supply, with the gap reflected in imports that exceeded exports, to be financed through net foreign borrowing and investment, or by sales of Australian assets to foreigners. But the lesson drawn from past experience was that, although public borrowing had financed an impressive railway system, servicing the debt imposed large costs in the depressions of the 1890s and the 1930s. A common interpretation was that, even putting aside the business cycle, public borrowing internationally had not generated a structural improvement in the balance of trade – more additional exports than imports – sufficient to provide the foreign exchange needed to service the debt.

Private borrowers and investors, on the other hand, were more driven by profits than by politics, and so were more likely only to incur liabilities when matched by assets with net revenue-generating prospects. Additionally, in bad times, private borrowers either defaulted on or re-negotiated their debts; and, for direct investment in Australian enterprises, foreign owners suffered the loss of equity when downturns occurred. As a result, private inflows were less likely to lead to situations in which governments had to impose fiscal contractions, thus slashing the economy's rate of growth, so as to service commitments to foreign providers of funds. And as well as involving less risk, foreign investment could serve as a means of transferring technology and know-how, including modern managerial methods.[55]

Nonetheless, in 1948, the then Prime Minister Chifley stated that his government was opposed to overseas borrowing, and that Australia should live within its sterling and dollar incomes.[56] And although Labor welcomed General Motors' investment in General Motors Holden, it remained cautious about foreign private capital, unless directed or stringently regulated by government. Even in 1961, the Leader of the Opposition, Arthur Calwell, said that "It's time for a change" in a long list of matters, including "the open-door policy for foreign capital with no Government plan for the protection against take-over bids of Australian-owned enterprises, and of our great national assets".[57]

In contrast, as with immigration, the Menzies Government welcomed capital inflow, the vast majority of which was on private account: 92 percent, from 1948-9 to 1962-3; three-quarters was in manufacturing, especially chemicals and oil refining (21 percent); founding, engineering and metal working (14 percent); and then in vehicles, electrical goods, food and related, and, finally, "other", each accounting for around 10 percent of the total share valuation.[58] Foreign ownership rose in line with the injection of foreign capital: in 1952, foreign firms accounted for 12 percent of the assets of the top 100 non-financial companies; by 1964, that share had risen to 41 percent.[59]

Significant as these inflows were, it is important to keep their scale in perspective: between 1948-49 and 1964-65, the balance of overseas capital account averaged less than two percent of GDP – that is, foreign capital inflows added one-fiftieth to the pool of Australian-produced goods and services, available for exports or absorption as consumption and capital formation.[60]

As a result, more than 90 percent of capital formation was financed through domestic savings. That was all the more remarkable given the high investment rate, with gross domestic fixed capital investment rising to account for nearly a quarter of GDP in the decade from 1953-54 to 1963-64, compared to 17 percent for the United States and just 15 percent in the UK. Private non-dwelling investment, which had rarely exceeded five percent of GDP in the years subsequent to federation, climbed from 6.8 percent of GDP in 1949 to 12.5 percent of GDP in 1966.

The tightly regulated financial system played a marginal role in mobilising the savings that financing such sustained investment rates required: financial intermediation, measured by the ratio of financial assets to GDP, seems to have fallen over the period and, in any case, was at low levels by international standards.[61] Rather, business investment was financed primarily by retained earnings, which were high in an economy with buoyant demand and in which wage moderation, cartels and trade protection ensured many producers earned substantial rates of return. As for households, consumer credit began to emerge, largely from non-bank institutions such as finance companies, but real interest rates were relatively high.

That is not to suggest financial markets remained unchanged. On the contrary, markets for government and non-government securities became larger and deeper; foreign merchant banks expanded their presence; and rising competition from non-bank financial institutions prompted a competitive response from the established banks, including in terms of lobbying, reasonably successfully, for regulations to be relaxed. Moreover, and importantly, the Government, despite sustained opposition from Labor, separated the Reserve Bank from the Commonwealth Bank, establishing the Reserve Bank of Australia on 14 January 1960. As its historian has noted, that "proved to be a fundamental turning point in the history of central banking in Australia", providing the basis for an increasingly sophisticated approach to the implementation of monetary policy.[62]

Those developments were significant but they were less important to the pace and direction of economic growth than was the ability of firms and households themselves to save the funds they needed to finance the investments they wanted to undertake. That ability was assisted by the broad stance of fiscal policy, at least in the sense that the aggregate call Australian governments made on national savings was relatively tightly managed.

Growth placed significant pressure on infrastructure, not solely because of greater population but also through rapid increases in the number of cars on the roads, in electricity demand and in the stock of homes, many of them in new, outer-lying suburban areas. And adding to those pressures, the jump in the birth rate in the late 1940s soon necessitated a progressive extension of buildings to accommodate the increased intake at succeeding levels of education. (On Menzies and education, see the chapters in this volume by Melleuish and by Pincus.)

But despite those pressures, public borrowing, as managed through the Loan Council, fell from 8.2 percent of GNP in 1951-52 to 4.5 percent of GNP in 1965-

66.[63] With public borrowing at relatively low levels, and inflation gradually eroding the quantum of public debt in real terms, public debt, which had peaked at 120 percent of GDP in 1946, declined steadily to 52 percent in 1965 (Table 1), setting the basis for its further fall to barely 8 percent of GDP in 1974.[64] As a result, government made space for households and the private sector to use domestic savings to finance their investments, rather than using those savings for its own purposes.

To that extent, the "structural" fiscal position assisted economic growth; but whether the attempts to sustain rapid expansion by "fine tuning" the economy over the course of the business cycle succeeded is more contentious. As Figures 1 (unemployment) and 2 (inflation) indicate, the macro-economic record is remarkably good when considered in a longer historical perspective. This was not, however, the ruling contemporary opinion; and much of the academic commentary has been relatively critical: for instance, Artis and Wallace,[65] in an informative and extended budget-by-budget account, concluded that policy action was never quite right in terms of its timing and extent.[66]

A full assessment of the controversy – including the struggle for supremacy in setting and implementing macroeconomic policy between the central bank, headed by Coombs, and the Treasury, headed by Wilson – would require a more detailed treatment than can be given here. Nonetheless, there were two crucial episodes in which macroeconomic policy was used for the purposes of short-term stabilisation – the Korean War boom and bust, and the 1951 "horror" budget; and the boom, credit squeeze and bust of 1959-61 – with each highlighting the broader point.

The circumstances of the first episode are well known, especially given the debates surrounding the sharp improvement in Australia's terms of trade that began in 2003-04. In September 1949, the Chifley Government had devalued the £A by 30 percent against the US dollar (copying Sterling and so maintaining the parity between the Australian and British currencies). Following the outbreak of the Korean War in 1950, however, export income rose almost two-thirds, as the US aggressively entered the market for wool and other resources, driving up Australia's external terms of trade by 50 percent in one year (Figure 4). Inflation rose sharply, and under the system of quarterly indexation which was then in place, the increased prices were soon followed by higher wages. Monetary tightening, which was the initial response to the acceleration in inflation, proved insufficiently effective; and since the Treasurer, Arthur Fadden, accepted the advice of his department (which both suited his party, the Country Party, and was consistent with the approach recommended in the 1945 White Paper on full employment[67]) not to appreciate the currency, the Government imposed what the Opposition called "the Horror Budget" in October 1951, which budgeted for a substantial surplus to be achieved mainly by means of tax increases. Additionally, so as to restrain domestic demand, woolgrowers were required to deposit 20 percent of their earnings into restricted accounts.

Fadden also accepted departmental advice against a rise in interest rates – as advocated by Coombs – chiefly on the grounds that the consequent fall in the market price of government securities would violate promises made to the lenders, including many small savers who had patriotically bought those securities during the war years at the cost of considerable sacrifices. Moreover, it was not clear how great a rise was needed, given the extent of "credit rationing" (which meant that the demand for loans greatly exceeded supply at current rates, reducing the efficacy of a rate increase) and the thin market in government securities.[68]

As a result, the emphasis was placed on fiscal adjustment. Seen in terms of its immediate goals, that approach was relatively successful. Inflation was quickly squeezed out of the system, at some, but highly transient, cost to output.[69] And, as well as quelling inflation, it can also be argued that the sharp fiscal tightening eliminated the risk that a temporary improvement in the terms of trade would be translated into a permanent increase in public expenditure.[70] Whitwell, having noted the dismay and anger that this budget elicited, nonetheless praised it as a positive, decisive step: the first explicit use of Keynesian fiscal policy for anti-cyclical purposes, this was an event of major significance in Australia's budget history.[71]

That said, it is also clear that the timing was poor, in that the tightening coincided with a broader slowing that came as the terms of trade began to fall. Moreover, there are also persistent claims that the Government should have responded through a revaluation,[72] although (for the reasons already noted) these claims bear little relation to the debate at the time or to the broader international circumstances.

Similar issues of timing and extent arise with respect to the tightening in 1960-61, variously referred to as the "Holt jolt" (Harold Holt having succeeded Arthur Fadden as Treasurer in December 1958) or, more broadly, as the "credit squeeze". Designed as a response to a pickup in inflation in 1959, which in turn had been associated with a real estate boom whose origins lay in domestic credit expansion, the package ultimately comprised removal of import licensing, a series of deflationary fiscal measures and a substantial and sustained monetary tightening, including – unusually – an increase in interest rates. At the time, the effects were seen as exceptionally severe, both because GDP fell by some two percent and because the unemployment rate rose to what was then considered an unacceptably high 3.2 percent.[73] Moreover, the impacts were made all the more visible by some spectacular corporate failures, especially of real estate developers and non-bank credit providers, which were blamed on the sudden removal of tax deductibility for certain fixed interest payments.[74]

Subsequent analysis has qualified the harsh judgments contemporaries passed on the "credit squeeze", which was widely held responsible for the Government's near defeat in the 1961 election.[75] As with the "horror budget", the proximate goal of reducing inflation was achieved, while both output and employment recovered relatively promptly. Nonetheless, it is also clear that the impact on economic activity was greater and more adverse than expected, leading to a corrective mini-budget in February 1962.

Overall, both episodes highlight the limitations on stabilisation policy. At the time of the 1951 Budget, ironing out the economic cycle was a goal not only recently enunciated, but yet barely attempted anywhere in the world. Keynes in the 1930s had been concerned with the scope for using fiscal policy to combat a huge slump, not for smoothing out relatively minor periods of excess or deficient demand.[76] The outgoing Labor Government – despite the caution expressed in the 1945 White Paper – fondly believed that it could, whenever the economic environment required, quickly switch public infrastructure projects on and off; experience, including in recent decades, suggests that it over-generalised from the efficacy of economic controls during wartime. Even Keynes's jest of stimulating the economy by having the unemployed digging for bottles that were purposefully buried with pound notes inside, would take time to organise and turn on and (especially) to turn off.

Moreover, government then lacked what would now be regarded as basic up-to-date economic data (such as quarterly national accounts, which only became available in 1960) and the tools with which to analyse them. Nor was the state of the art much more advanced at the time of the "credit squeeze", where predicting the likely effects was rendered all the more difficult by its reliance on a far broader suite of monetary and fiscal instruments than had been used in 1951. Policy was therefore being set under highly imperfect information; as

Treasury itself noted in connection with the 1962 mini-budget, some degree of "stop/go" was inevitable, since the Government had to "adapt its measures to changing circumstances," given that "the effect of economic measures cannot be calculated in advance with close precision".[77]

Expecting "fine tuning" to prove successful may therefore have been asking too much; that it was so extensively used attests more to the era's confidence in government than to a recognition of the constraints within which governments must operate.

In short, the greatest success of economic policy was in making the resources available for sustained growth, ensuring that government's call on those resources did not crowd out private uses, and, more generally, in establishing and maintaining public confidence in the Government's commitment to keeping growth at high levels, which in turn encouraged firms and households to make long-term investment commitments of their own. Yet policy did far better at mobilising capital, labour and technology than at promoting their efficient use. In other words, a price was paid, in terms of the efficiency with which resources were allocated and employed, for the commitment to super-rapid expansion.[78]

The costs to efficiency

Although the economy expanded rapidly, much of the growth was extensive— that is, achieved by increasing the volume of factors consumed – rather than intensive, that is, derived from making better use of given resources. According to one study, undertaken at the end of the 1970s, some 70 percent of the output increases secured during the years of rapid growth were attributable to the growth of labour and capital inputs, with a "residual" of only 30 percent coming from growth in the productivity with which inputs were used.[79] Those proportions are roughly similar to the experience in Canada; in contrast, estimates for the United States attribute around 50 percent of economic growth during this period to greater productivity, while the share due to productivity was even higher – at around 65 percent – in Western Europe, leaving only 35 percent or less of growth coming from increased factor usage.[80]

In part, the small size of the productivity component reflected the fact that while aggregate growth rates were high, they had been obtained at the cost of especially high levels of investment. Taking account of changes in working hours, N.G. Butlin estimated that labour input had risen – over the entire period from 1939 to 1961 – at an annual rate of 1.8 percent; in contrast, the annual rate of increase in capital inputs was 2.8 percent, implying that while labour input by the end of the period was 48 percent greater than it was at the beginning, capital inputs had grown by 84 percent.[81]

The inference is that capital formation yielded relatively little "bang for the buck", with one study estimating that if, over the period from 1953-54 to 1964-65, Australia had had the same level of capital productivity as the major advanced economies, the annual growth rate of GDP would have been 2.3 percentage points higher.[82] Even accepting the many caveats so high an estimate invites, it is reasonably well-established that capital was not as efficiently used as it might have been; W.A. Sinclair noted that while much of the "return to a more rapid rate of economic growth in Australia [in the post-war years] can be attributed to a marked increase in aggregate investment measured as a proportion of gross national product ... the contribution made by capital formation ... derived much more from its high aggregate level than from the fruitfulness of its components".[83]

Although not readily proven, there is every reason to believe that the predominance of extensive, rather than intensive, growth reflected the institutional arrangements the Menzies Government had inherited and retained – and, most especially, protection. The greatest effects were in manufacturing, whose share of GDP at constant prices rose from 19 percent immediately before the Second World War to around 30 percent in 1960-61. Productivity levels in manufacturing grew rapidly during this period, with output per employee-hour three-quarters higher in 1963-64 than in 1949-50. The increases, however, occurred from a very low base, both in international terms and compared to the rural sector: in 1948, output per unit of labour input in agriculture was 2.5 times greater in Australia than in the UK, while Australian labour productivity levels in manufacturing were only 70 percent of the UK's.[84] Substantial as they were, the productivity increases that occurred in the Menzies era were not sufficient to close the international gap, given that productivity growth rates in the other advanced economies were also especially high.

At the heart of the problems was that so much of the investment in manufacturing went into import replacement, rather than into export-oriented activity. As the German economist, Gottfried Bombach, put it, in surveying Europe's own post-war episode of ultra-rapid growth, "export demand is uncomfortable demand as compared with home demand", requiring "competitive product prices, high productivity levels and a continuous adjustment of the product mix"; it is, as a result, "an important learning process" that triggers efficiency improvements in the economy as a whole.[85] But, instead of being oriented to world markets, made-to-measure protection, which set tariffs so as to offset the cost penalty associated with domestic production, encouraged a focus on "leaping over the tariff wall".[86]

In theory, protection was only to be granted to "economic and efficient" production; but, in practice, the impossibility of determining, through an administrative process, what was "economic and efficient" and what was not, together with the political pressures producers could and did bring to bear, ensured protection was extended far more broadly. Moreover, with reasonably ready access to finance, entry into protected activities was likely to occur up to the point where any rents had been dissipated in excess costs, compounding the inefficiency. And collusion, reported to be widespread,[87] would then have allowed otherwise marginal producers to remain viable, as they could shelter under the umbrella of prices set to provide supra-normal returns to the more efficient firms.

The result was to encourage a proliferation of small plants. Relatively high domestic transport costs (arising from State government controls over road haulage and Commonwealth government controls over shipping) and State government policies modelled on those adopted by Sir Thomas Playford, Premier of South Australia from 1938 to 1965, accentuated the problem,[88] as even quite small production runs were dispersed between the States. With domestic producers "covering the waterfront" in terms of the range of products they supplied, production runs already too short were further fragmented into myriad product varieties.

For example, by the mid-1960s, five international companies producing a dozen models competed for a motor vehicle market of about 350 000 units a year, which was arguably insufficient to support two firms operating at anywhere close to minimum efficient scale. Similarly, in oil refining, where economies of scale were also important, a study found that "the Australian market for petroleum products must be treated as five or more separate areas. Within each of these marketing areas the demand for petroleum products at present is insufficient to support one refinery which would be taking full advantage of the economies of large-scale production".[89] And a detailed analysis of the steel industry in the early 1960s concluded that "for years, the industry has suffered from the inability to apply large-scale technology which, moreover, is not stagnant and on balance is probably favouring increasing scale".[90]

Manufacturing, although its output nearly trebled in volume terms during the period, therefore continued to have extremely low productivity levels compared with the United States and Canada, despite the benefits of technology transfer via direct foreign investment, and even though the industrial composition of manufacturing broadly mirrored that of the United States.[91] Many economists believed the main benefit from immigration would be increasing returns to scale:[92] as far as manufacturing was concerned, protection seems to have negated that benefit.

Manufacturing was not the only sector where protection undermined efficiency. Primary exporters bore a large share of the costs of manufacturing protection, which imposed a tax equivalent to some 20 percent of gross export returns;[93] and although some of the more efficient primary producers – such as the national Woolgrowers' Council – opposed protection, many others had instead long sought it for themselves. As W.K. Hancock famously observed decades earlier:

> It might have been expected that the primary industries which produce
> for export would have revolted against this system. Instead, the weaker
> of them have adopted the policy of the French nobleman, who declared,
> while the old monarchy went riotously bankrupt: "When others hold out
> their hands I hold out my hat."[94]

Pressures for assistance intensified as agriculture likewise experienced an upsurge in investment. Gross annual agricultural investment, measured at current prices, was about ten times higher in the first half of the 1950s than it had been in the pre-war years.[95] In some unprotected sectors, notably wool, substantial increases in output were achieved by the larger Australian producers at costs that, by world standards, were relatively low; but that was not the case for the smaller and more marginal wheat-sheep farmers, who were squeezed between rising domestic costs and world prices that fell as competition from synthetics intensified. Those smaller farmers, who operated with less than half the number of sheep per person employed by the larger producers, earned incomes that already by the early 1960s could not have covered investment costs;[96] they provided the most vocal and effective support for the repeated attempts – promoted by the Country Party and especially by John McEwen – to introduce a reserve price scheme, with that scheme coming into effect, eventually with disastrous consequences, in November 1970.

The panoply of schemes that benefited the more labour-, land- and water-intensive parts of agriculture, going from dairying and poultry farming to sugar and dried vine fruits, were no less harmful. For example, the ubiquitous home-price schemes, which sought to stabilise producers' incomes by setting a price to domestic consumers that at least partially offset fluctuations in export prices, not only discouraged the use of other forms of risk management but also induced sharp shifts into the supply of the products covered by home price schemes when export prices were low (and supported home prices high), reducing national income.[97] At the same time, subsidies to agricultural inputs, ranging from preferential loans to provision of irrigated water and transport at charges that were far below cost, both distorted the input mix and shifted output towards those forms of primary production that made the most intensive use of the subsidised inputs.[98]

In short, although productivity growth, evaluated at domestic prices, was high, a substantial share of the greatly increased supply of labour and capital was being diverted into protected, relatively inefficient, uses.

Whether the arbitration system, the other major plank of the Menzies Government's institutional legacy, compounded the inefficiencies is much harder to say. Union membership, which stood at 54 percent of the workforce in 1945, had climbed to 58 percent by 1950 and then rose further to peak at 63 percent of the workforce in 1953.[99] Coming to office after a major strike wave, the Menzies Government legislated a number of changes to the industrial laws, including facilitating the imposition by the then Commonwealth Court of Conciliation and Arbitration of penalties on striking unions, as well as making a series of significant appointments to the Court itself.[100]

It would be incorrect to assume those appointments were determinative in the Court's controversial decisions of the period, including the decision in 1953 to abandon indexation of the basic wage. Those decisions were largely shaped by the Chief Judge, Sir Raymond Kelly, who had been appointed under Labor.[101] Indeed, Harold Holt, the then Minister for Labour, was impatient with Kelly's "inflexibility" and regarded the Court's tendency to clash with the unions as a menace to industrial peace. So as to reduce the risk that posed, the Menzies Government actively sought to improve its relations with the ACTU, and used the High Court's 1956 decision in the *Boilermakers'* case[102] both to reduce Kelly's role and to appoint Richard Kirby, widely viewed as sympathetic to the unions, to head the newly-established Conciliation and Arbitration Commission.

In short, the Menzies Government, although it was deeply concerned about illegal strikes, did not seek to challenge or otherwise undermine the industrial relations system, all the more so as it did not want to be cast as a government dominated by "big business". Moreover, especially given the strengthening of the penal powers, the system was seen as useful in promoting moderate unions while imposing some constraints on those unions that remained under communist control. There was, as a result, certainly the potential for the system to influence the course of economic growth significantly.

In practice, however, a number of factors mitigated its impact, reducing, if they did not entirely avert, the distortions it later caused. These included the sustained number of new entrants into the labour market, and the mobility and willingness to adapt of the migrant workforce; the reduction in commuting costs associated with the rapid increase in car-ownership; and the growing concentration of employment in the major urban centres, all of which made it easier for workers to switch jobs. At the same time, the split in the ALP, and the even more bitter struggle between communists and anti-communists in the union movement, may have made a number of union leaders, as well as the ACTU, less inclined to challenge a government whose commitment to resisting communism they admired.

Exactly how much effect each of these factors had is difficult to say. Nonetheless, what is clear is that the basic wage – which in 1966 was replaced by a "minimum wage" – barely increased in real terms from November 1952 to November 1967,[103] while, during the same period, the real product wage – that is, average earnings deflated by the GDP deflator – rose at an annual rate of two percent,[104] which was only 60 percent of the increase in GDP per labour hour.[105] This was, in other words, a period of sustained wage moderation, which, along with the factors already noted, made for labour market flexibility and underpinned the exceptionally low rates of unemployment.

It was also clear that serious headwinds were building up. By the mid-1960s, wage cases were becoming increasingly contentious; the number of industrial disputes edged up, initially in manufacturing before leaping to a higher plateau for all industries in 1968; and wages drift became more pronounced, as wage increases were secured outside the arbitration system. These trends may partly have reflected generational change – as the entry into the labour force of younger cohorts, who had not experienced depression and war, brought a revolution of rising expectations – as well as structural change within the union movement, with the larger unions gaining members at the expense of smaller ones and the divisions associated with the Labor split fading into the background. Be that as it may, they set the groundwork for the Whitlam Government's ill-judged wages policy, with the "wage explosion" of 1974, when average weekly earnings increased by 26 percent, signalling the end of full employment. Just as the industrial relations system may well have prolonged wage moderation in the Menzies era, so it now became a way of securing and protecting wage increases that in a more decentralised labour market would probably more promptly have been unwound.[106]

It was therefore hardly irrational for the Menzies Government, notwithstanding an at times fraught relationship with individual members of the Court and later of the Commission, to view the Deakinite industrial relations system as highly successful, especially compared to the widely publicised problems being experienced in the UK. In preserving and entrenching it, the Menzies Government created risks that, as with industry protection, played themselves out, at high cost, in the years to come.

The balance

Overall, economic growth, sustained though it was, was distorted by the Deakinite framework, contributing to the severity of the crises that began in the 1980s. To that extent at least, it remained the case that, as Hancock had suggested in 1930, "the Australians had not grown rich because of their policies, but ... being already rich, ... have been able to afford them".[107]

Nonetheless, the harshness of that judgment needs to be balanced in several important respects. To begin with, the heavily assisted segments within manufacturing and agriculture probably never accounted for more than a fifth of output and employment. Moreover, by preserving an economy based on free enterprise rather than pervasive nationalisation, the Menzies Government created room for the diversity and entrepreneurship that would help to ease the transition away from those segments, and also ensured at least some of the capital losses that transition involved fell on private investors instead of taxpayers.

At the same time, the politically courageous trade treaty with Japan in 1957 began the re-orientation of Australian trade towards Asia that would, in time, prove crucial to the move to a more outward looking economy;[108] and that re-orientation was also encouraged and greatly assisted by the lifting of the export embargo on iron ore and by the welcoming attitude to Japanese investment in Australia's natural resources. Additionally, the deepening and gradual liberalisation of financial markets allowed those markets to begin playing a more significant role in allocating savings to their most productive uses and enhanced the effectiveness of monetary policy, as did creation of the Reserve Bank.

In all of those ways, the Menzies Government, although it perpetuated a legacy of protection, contributed to putting in place the foundations that made it possible for the Deakinite legacy to be at least partly overcome. Its cautious fiscal policies also helped. In the immediate term, they freed up savings for use in the private sector, underpinning high levels of private investment. And, seen over the longer term, their result was that when growth began to slow and became more volatile, the Commonwealth had little debt; much like the Howard Government, that meant the fiscal errors made by the governments that succeeded Menzies did not lead to levels of indebtedness that could not ultimately be brought under control.

Moreover, far fewer costly commitments had been made in areas such as pension and health care than in Europe: expressed as a share of GDP, Australian spending on social transfers, above the OECD average at the start of the period, was nearly a third below it in 1970, and actually fell slightly in the course of the 1960s.[109] With a much narrower base of entitlements to start from, not even the more profligate governments that followed could readily mandate transfers and taxes on a scale comparable with the European welfare states.

Last but not least, the Menzies Government retained, at times notwithstanding strong pressures to the contrary, the Australian tradition of delegating to entities independent of executive government a crucial role in the public policy process.[110] Although that could entrench vested interests – as in the industrial relations system – it could also provide policy entrepreneurs with an institutional platform from which to promote far-reaching reform, with the Tariff Board and the Reserve Bank being spectacular examples.

Those mitigating factors are substantial; but they do not end the list of considerations that must be weighed in the balance. It is, in particular, important to stress that the alternative government was committed to aggravating, rather than correcting, the inward-looking orientation of policy – and, in addition, to nationalising large parts of the economy, including banking, the steel industry and aviation. Nor was it supportive of the developing economic relationship with Asia, and it voiced strong opposition to the 1957 trade treaty with Japan, as well as to Japanese investment in Australia's natural resources. Given those policy commitments, no matter how great the adjustment costs future generations bore for the Menzies Government's policies, they must pale into insignificance compared to those a Labor government would have imposed, had the promises Labor made at successive elections been adopted.

Conclusion

The 1950s and 1960s were a golden age of Australian economic growth: output rose at a rate not experienced since the aftermath of the gold rushes; unemployment and inflation were extremely low, both in absolute terms and compared to overseas; as incomes increased, a sense of confidence and of economic security, so seriously damaged in the inter-war years, became the norm, encouraging business and households to make long-term investment decisions.

The international economy more broadly was experiencing a period of exceptional prosperity. But with the Australian economy's trade intensity declining, domestic prosperity was by no means simply the consequence of global buoyancy. The dynamic of growth was largely internal and economic policy played an important role in making rapid expansion possible. High levels of immigration brought millions of "New Australians" who were strongly motivated to work and save. Sustained inflows of foreign capital brought technology and management skills, especially from the United States, that allowed local industry to meet rapidly expanding demand for consumer and capital goods. And a cautious fiscal policy, which kept public spending under tight control and avoided the unfunded promises that characterised the European welfare state, ensured the growing pool of savings could be used by the private sector to finance a sharp rise in the share of investment in GDP.

As well as setting those foundations for growth, the Menzies Government, drawing on the Deakinite legacy, also actively shaped its direction. Protection was especially important in that respect, with the "made to measure" tariff (and during the period from 1952 to 1960, generalised import licensing) stimulating widespread import-replacement, while a growing range of protective schemes shifted agricultural output towards the more labour-, land- and water-intensive parts of rural industry. The result was to distort allocation of resources towards activities that were uncompetitive internationally—and which, despite rapid productivity growth, remained so.

The Deakinite arbitration system was also preserved and, in some respects, entrenched. It retained all of its arcane features – for instance, the 1966 Metal Trades award recognised 330 classifications of work, and specified 53 different rates of pay with gradations of as little as one cent a day between them. Yet its impact during the period itself was weakened by the sheer size of the migrant inflow, as well as by the deep divisions within the union movement and, perhaps most of all, by the caution of generations scarred by depression and war. Together, those factors gave rise to years of wage moderation that underpinned the extraordinarily low rates of unemployment.

It is true that by the end of the Menzies era, expert opinion was starting to change. The Treasury had issued papers emphasising the importance of efficient resource allocation; and, increasingly, the McEwenite dogma was under attack, within the official family and outside it.[111]

Even so, change was slow and uneven, as the report of the Vernon Enquiry itself makes clear. Tasked to inquire into a long list of matters – while bearing in mind "that the objectives of the Government's economic policy are a high rate of economic and population growth with full employment, increasing productivity, rising standards of living, external viability, and stability of costs and prices" – the Enquiry argued there were limits to the capacity of Australia to absorb immigrants. It was also sceptical of foreign investment, fearing too great a degree of foreign control and that there might be insufficient foreign exchange earnings to service the debt or equity in the future.

These were hardly more outward-looking views than the Menzies Government had articulated; moreover, on protection, the report accepted most of the usual arguments in its favour: diversification of industry; redistribution towards urban workers, without depressing rural land values (13.59); stimulus to economic growth, especially nurturing "infant industries" that have, in Australia, by and large grown up (13.65); and a steady increase in capital investment. As for the future of tariff policy, it was cautious, rejecting all the proposed alternatives to made-to-measure protection, including unilateral liberalisation, currency devaluation and a move to a uniform tariff. Nor does it seem to have given any thought to reforming the industrial relations system. Despite the storm it provoked, the Vernon Enquiry largely endorsed the *status quo* – and would have been more restrictive than the Menzies Government ever was in setting migration levels and in regulating foreign investment.[112]

That suggests that if the Menzies Government was not ahead of expert opinion, nor was it behind it; it was largely a mirror of its age. That is unsurprising: great politicians, said Disraeli, must feel comfortable, both in themselves and in their times; and, when he was at the peak of his powers, Menzies was as great a politician as Australia has ever seen. Yet it would be wrong to think he merely channelled the popular mood; on the contrary, as a great politician, he formed the climate of opinion, positioning national development as not simply an over-riding economic goal but as a bulwark against the global threats to freedom.

The spirit of the age was also apparent in the approach the Menzies Government adopted to implementing its goals. As the American historian, Hugh Heclo, once put it, major epochs in public policy are defined "not by events, nor by ideas, but by ideas about events"[113] – the "ideas about events" which motivated the Menzies Government, along with many of its counterparts internationally, included an expansive view of government's role both in preventing depression from recurring and in promoting, sustaining and shaping economic growth.

But while far from *laissez-faire*, it pursued its objectives in a manner that emphasised the role of private initiative and gave considerable space to independent bodies, such as the Tariff Board, the Arbitration Commission, the Commonwealth Grants Commission and the Reserve Bank in the design of public policy. It could have been otherwise, as the examples of the UK and New Zealand[114] all too clearly show; the approach Menzies adopted, with its stress on the private sector, was the result of a conscious choice, made in the face of fierce and continuous criticism from his Labor opponents. Together with the outcomes, the fact that he made and stuck by that choice amply confirms his very high place in the pantheon of Australian prime ministers.

Endnotes

* We wish to thank William Coleman, Selwyn Cornish, Bob Gregory, David Kemp, John Nethercote, John Stone and Bob Wallace for their comments.

[1] The Commonwealth Court of Conciliation and Arbitration was separated in 1956 into an Industrial Court and a Conciliation and Arbitration Commission, following a High Court decision in the *Boilermakers'* case. However, references to the Arbitration Commission in this chapter should be read as covering both institutions, unless otherwise specified.

[2] Menzies' approach to these matters bears out his rejection of the label, "conservative," for himself and the Party. We hope to explore in subsequent work, we prefer the description of the policy package as "Deakinite", to Kelly's "the Australian Settlement" of "imperial benevolence", White Australia, "state paternalism", wage arbitration and protection against imports: Paul Kelly, *The End of Certainty: The Story of the 1980s*, St Leonards, NSW, Allen & Unwin, 1992.

³ See W.M. Corden, "Import restrictions and tariffs: A new look at Australian policy", *Economic Record*, 34(69), 1958, 331-46. Reprinted in H.W. Arndt and W.M. Corden, (eds), *The Australian Economy: A Volume of Readings*, Melbourne, F. W. Cheshire, 1963.

⁴ S. Richardson and P. Travers, *Living Decently: Material Well-being in Australia*, Melbourne, Oxford University Press, 1993.

⁵ P. Katic, and A. Leigh (2013), "Top Wealth Shares in Australia 1915-2012", Fig. 4. Available at <http://piketty.pse.ens.fr/files/KaticLeigh2013.pdf> [Accessed 5 Jan 2015]; A.B. Atkinson, and A. Leigh, "The distribution of top incomes in Australia", *Economic Record*, 83(262), 2007, 247-261; A. Leigh, *Deriving Long-Run Inequality Series from Tax Data*, Canberra, Centre for Economic Policy Research, Australian National University, 2004.

⁶ Parliament of Australia, 2009, *Social Security payments for people caring for children, 1912-2008: a chronology – Parliament of Australia*. [online] Available at: <http://www.aph.gov.au/About_Parliament/Parliamentary_Departments/Parliamentary_Library/pubs/BN/0809/children> [Accessed 29 Dec. 2015]; M. Gray, L. Qu, and R. Weston, *Fertility and Family Policy in Australia*, Melbourne, Australian Institute of Family Studies, 2008.

⁷ H. Wee, *Prosperity and Upheaval: the World Economy, 1945-1980*, Berkeley CA, University of California Press, 1986 (Table 14, column 5, 151). In his 1946 election policy speech, Menzies criticised Labor for having adopted "the view that immigration is undesirable so long as we have local problems of an industrial and economic kind to solve": http://electionspeeches.moadoph.gov.au/speeches/1946-robert-menzies

⁸ A. Goldbloom, J. Hawkins and S. Kennedy (2008), *"A quite unprecedented achievement'? Responding to the 1950s terms of trade boom"*, 7. Available at: <https,//www.researchgate.net/publication/242326775_'A_QUITE_UNPRECEDENTED_ACHIEVEMENT'_RESPONDING_TO_THE_1950S_TERMS_OF_TRADE_BOOM> [Accessed 29 Dec. 2015].

⁹ D. Pope and G. Withers, "Do migrants rob jobs? Lessons of Australian History, 1861-1991", *Journal of Economic History*, 53(04), 1993, 719-42.

¹⁰ W.A. Sinclair, *The Process of Economic Development in Australia*, Melbourne, Cheshire, 1976, 240.

¹¹ "Whatever justification there may be for applying such an adjustment system (to a wage assessed according to national economic capacity) in a closed economy, there can, so it seems to the Court, be none in an economy such as ours where so much of our productive effort depends for its value upon prices of exports and imports beyond the control of any Australian authority": Fair Work Commission (2015), *Basic Wage Inquiry (1952-1953)* 77 CAR 497 cited in *The post-war period: 1953–1965 basic wage inquiries* [online]. Available at: <https://www.fwc.gov.au/waltzing-matilda-and-the-sunshine-harvester-factory/documents/methods-wage-adjustment/the-post-war> [Accessed 29 Dec. 2015].

¹² Blanche D'Alpuget, *Mediator: A Biography of Sir Richard Kirby*, Melbourne University Press, 1977, 170.

¹³ However, it should be noted that, during the Korean wool boom, agriculture was temporarily close to its 20th century peak share (29 percent, against the 31 percent of 1917). These were therefore falls from a high level.

¹⁴ R.A. Foster and S.E. Stewart, *Australian Economic Statistics, 1949-50 to 1989-90*, Sydney, Reserve Bank of Australia, 1991, Table 5.13.

[15] This is the (somewhat caveated) view of Neville Cain, "Trade and economic structure at the periphery: The Australian balance of payments, 1890-1965", C. Forster, (ed), *Australian Economic Development in the Twentieth Century*, Sydney, George Allen & Unwin, 1971, 98.

[16] Commonwealth of Australia, *"The Australian balance of payments"*, supplement to the *Treasury Information Bulletin*, 1966, 23.

[17] A technical point is that the prices of protected manufacturing goods were inflated above world prices, by the tariff and, especially in the 1950s, by import quotas. For some of the automotive industry (for example), it is likely that protection allowed the value of Australian production to fall short of the value of the imported components *at world prices* (implying negative value added, again at world prices). The Australian Bureau of Statistics (and its predecessors) followed international practice, when estimating GDP and its components, and used Australian prices, not world prices. For our and other purposes, however, it would be better to re-price the components of GDP at world prices (duty-free import prices).

[18] M. Roser, "Sum of exports and imports and imports as share of GDP (%) 1950-2011", M. Nagdy and M. Roser, *International Trade — Our World in Data*, 2015. [online] Ourworldindata.org. Available at: <http://ourworldindata.org/data/global-interconnections/international-trade/> [Accessed 29 Dec. 2015].

[19] J. Crawford, N. Anderson and M.G.N. Morris, *Australian Trade Policy 1942-1966*, Canberra, Australian National University Press, 1968.

[20] R. Ewing and J. Hawkins, "Business cycles in Australia", for the Conference of Economists, 2006, Table 1, available at <https://www.academia.edu/16965511/Business_cycles_in_Australia> [Accessed 29 Dec. 2015].

[21] S. Furphy (ed), *The Seven Dwarfs and the Age of the Mandarins: Australian Government Administration in the Post-War Reconstruction Era*, Canberra, Australian National University Press, 2015. Available online at <http://press.anu.edu.au/titles/anu-lives-series-in-biography/the-seven-dwarfs-and-the-age-of-the-mandarins/>[Accessed 29 Dec. 2015].

[22] John Howard, *The Menzies Era: The Years That Shaped Australia*, Sydney, Harper Collins, 2014, 356-70.

[23] As well as Howard, 368, see A. Bell, "Master of codes and economics: Harold Bell, 1921-2008", *Sydney Morning Herald*, 24 June 2008, available online at http://www.smh.com.au/news/obituaries/master-of-codes-and-economics/2008/06/23/1214073145913.html [Accessed 25 Jan. 2016].

[24] Of the 23 authors, 19 held chairs or senior posts in university economics or allied departments in Australia, and two other were eminent foreign economists who visited Australia (J Meade and H Lundberg). The origins of these surveys, and the role of economists in the public policy debates of the time, are discussed in H.W. Arndt, *A Course Through Life: Memoirs of an Australian Economist*, Canberra, Australia, National Centre for Development Studies, Australian National University, 1985, at 26-2. Economic ideas also gained influence through the pattern of recruitment into the Commonwealth public service – see S. Encel, *Equality and Authority: A study of Class, Status and Power in Australia*. London, Tavistock Publications, 1970, 254-5.

[25] D. Lowe, *Menzies and the "Great World Struggle": Australia's Cold War 1948-1954*, Sydney, University of NSW Press, 1999, 47.

[26] Ibid., 131.

[27] H. Holt, *Advance Australia: inaugural lecture delivered by the Prime Minister, the Rt. Hon. Harold Holt at Monash University*, 11 September 1967, 3. Accessed 5 January 2015 at https://pmtranscripts.dpmc.gov.au/release/transcript-1659

[28] Canada, where policy-makers had had a strong commitment to a floating exchange rate regime since the 1930s, was the only country to demand and secure a special exemption from the articles of agreement that would allow it to retain a floating rate system. Even so, it pegged its currency to the US dollar until 1950 and then from 1962 to 1970.

[29] J.E. Meade, "The price mechanism and the Australian balance of payments", *Economic Record*, 32(2), 1956, 239-56; reprinted in Arndt and Corden, 396-415; see also P. Coleman, P. Drake and S. Cornish, *Arndt's Story: The Life of an Australian Economist*, Canberra, Australia, Australian National University Press (co-published with Asia Pacific Press), 2007, 179-80.

[30] Indeed, Meade criticised approaches that involved a crawling peg as an invitation to speculation (a "speculator's paradise"), especially in countries that lacked well developed futures markets in foreign exchange: Meade, 413.

[31] T.W. Swan, "Economic Control in a dependent economy", *Economic Record* 36 (73), 1960, 51-66; T.W. Swan, "Longer-run problems of the balance of payments", in 1963 and Corden, 384-95.

[32] M. Perlman, *Judges in Industry: A Study of Labour Arbitration in Australia*, with a foreword by R.M. Eggleston, Melbourne University Press, 1954, viii.

[33] W.M. Corden, *Australian Economic Policy Discussion: A Survey*, Melbourne University Press, 1968, 12.

[34] E. Lundberg and M. Hill, "Australia's long-term balance of payments problems", *Economic Record* 32(1), 1956, 28-49; reprinted in 1963 and Corden, 360-83. Lundberg and Hill projected a balance of payments corresponding to about 5 percent of GNP.

[35] Corden 1968, 19 and more generally, 18-21. In keeping with that assumption, Corden's own model (set out in W.M. Corden, "The geometric representation of policies to attain internal and external balance", *The Review of Economic Studies* 28(1), 1960, 1-22), assumed the supply of exports was completely inelastic.

[36] G. Haberler, R. Oliveira Campos, R. and J. Tinbergen, *Trends in International Trade*, Geneva, General Agreement on Tariffs and Trade, 1958, 6.

[37] F.H. Gruen, "Australian agriculture and the cost price squeeze", *Australian Journal of Agricultural Economics* 6 (September 1962), 1-20; reprinted in 1963 and Corden, 320-49.

[38] D. Lee, *Iron Country: Unlocking the Pilbara*, Minerals Council of Australia, 2015, 40.

[39] Commonwealth of Australia, *Report of the Committee of Economic Enquiry* [Vernon Report], Canberra, 1965, 2 vols, projections at Chapter 15, Appendix N.

[40] H. Lydall, "The Australian Economy, February 1962", *Economic Record* 38(81), 1962, 1-28; extracts reprinted in Arndt and Corden, 80-98 (at 96).

[41] See, for example, W.M. Corden, "The tariff", A. Hunter (ed.), *The Economics of Australian Industry: Studies in Environment and Structure*, Melbourne, Melbourne University Press, 1963, 174-214; W.M. Corden, "Protection", *Economic Record* 42 (1-4), 1966, 129-48. In

the early 1960s, C.R. "Bert" Kelly spoke in Parliament against the system of protection; and Maxwell Newton, in the *Australian Financial Review* and later *The Australian*, wrote similarly. However, they were very much in the minority.

[42] W.A. Sinclair, *The Process of Economic Development in Australia*, Melbourne, Cheshire, 1976, 14, 240.

[43] See, for example, Corden 1958, where it is noted (at 428) that because of the made-to-measure tariff, the "energies which might better go into competing on an economic basis are put into pressing for higher protection"; but where it is also suggested that these dangers can be dealt with by redirecting the Tariff Board to "do the job which Monopoly Investigating Commissions of various kinds do in other countries".

[44] Institute of Public Affairs (Australia), *Looking Forward: A Post-War Policy for Australian Industry*, Melbourne, Vic, Institute of Public Affairs, 1944, 25-6.

[45] R.G. Menzies, 'Address to the Liberal Party Federal Council' (6 Apr), G. Starr 1980, *The Liberal Party of Australia*, Richmond, Vic., Drummond/Heinemann, 1964, 217.

[46] J. Hicks, *The Crisis in Keynesian Economics*, Oxford, England, Blackwell, 1974, 1.

[47] F.H. Gruen in Arndt and Corden, 343.

[48] Particularly prominent was the social democratic reform package set out in R. Downing, H.W. Arndt, A. Boxer and R. Mathews, *Taxation in Australia*, Melbourne, Melbourne University Press, 1964.

[49] W.D. Borrie, *The Peopling of Australia*, G.J. Cohen Memorial Lecture, University of Sydney (8 October, 1958), reprinted in Arndt and Corden, 108-9.

[50] T. Sheridan, "Planners and the Australian Labour Market 1945-1949", *Labour History* 1987, 53.

[51] B. Chifley, *Election speech*, Melbourne, Vic., 28 March 1951. Available online at <http://electionspeeches.moadoph.gov.au/speeches/1951-ben-chifley> [Accessed 6 Jan 2016].

[52] A. Calwell, *Election speech*, Melbourne, Vic, 16 November 1961. Available online at <http://electionspeeches.moadoph.gov.au/speeches/1961-arthur-calwell

[53] Commonwealth of Australia 1965 [Vernon Report], (table 4.2, for 1945-6 to 1964-65).

[54] The contribution migration made to labour market flexibility in the advanced economies during the 1950s is stressed in Organisation for Economic Co-operation and Development, *Wages and Labour Mobility: A Report by a Group of Independent Experts*, Paris, 1965.

[55] These transfers of technology, and the resulting efficiency gains, were documented in D.T. Brash, *American Investment in Australian Industry*, Canberra, Australian National University Press, 1968.

[56] Sir Robert Menzies, *The Measure of the Years*, North Melbourne, Vic., Cassell, 1970, 99.

[57] A. Calwell, *Election speech*, Melbourne, Vic, 16 November 1961. Available online at <http://electionspeeches.moadoph.gov.au/speeches/1961-arthur-calwellhttp://electionspeeches.moadoph.gov.au/speeches/1961-arthur-calwell > [Accessed 6 Jan 2016].

[58] Commonwealth of Australia 1965 [Vernon Report], Vol. II, 980 and 995.

[59] D.T. Merrett, "Big Business and Foreign Firms", S.P. Ville and G. Withers (eds), *The Cambridge Economic History of Australia*, Port Melbourne, Vic, Cambridge University Press, 2015, 326.

[60] Derived from Foster and Stewart 1991, tables 1.2 and 1.15. Butlin estimates that capital imports accounted for 10 percent of gross domestic capital formation in the period 1951-1960 and for 12.2 percent in 1961-65: N.G. Butlin, "Some Perspectives of Australian Economic Development, 1890-1965", C. Forster (ed), *Australian Economic Development in the Twentieth Century*, Sydney, George Allen & Unwin, 1970, Table 6.8.

[61] D.T. Merrett, "Capital Markets and Capital Formation in Australia, 1945-1990", *Australian Economic History Review* 38(2), 1998, 142-3. Davis and Gallman argue that the underdevelopment of Australian financial markets in the 20th century was the long term consequence of the reaction to the financial crisis of the 1890s: see L. Davis and R. Gallman, *Evolving Financial Markets and International Capital Flows*, Cambridge, U.K., Cambridge University Press, 2001, 642-3.

[62] Selwyn Cornish, *The Evolution of Central Banking in Australia*, Sydney, Reserve Bank of Australia, 2010, 17.

[63] R.S. Gilbert, *The Australian Loan Council in Federal Fiscal Adjustments, 1890-1965*, Canberra, Australian National University Press, 1973, Table 16.2.

[64] K. Di Marco, P. Mitchell and W. Au-Yeng 2009, *A History of Public Debt in Australia*. [Treasury] Economic Roundup No. 1, 8. [online]. Available at: < http://archive.treasury. gov.au/documents/1496/PDF/01_Debt.pdf > [Accessed 4 Jan. 2016].

[65] M.J. Artis and R.H, Wallace, "A historical survey of Australian fiscal policy, 1945–66". N. Runcie, (ed), *Australian Monetary and Fiscal Policy: Selected Readings*, London, University of London Press, 1971, 403-81.

[66] A more recent judgment by Michael Keating is somewhat softer, but still condemnatory: "In practice, fiscal policy proved to be much less flexible than was anticipated in the 1945 White Paper on Full Employment, reflecting the unwillingness by government to vary both taxation and expenditure. Furthermore, Australia was much less inclined to use market instruments in prosecuting its monetary policy than other countries…Instead, the principal monetary instrument was variations in the amount of reserves that the private banks were required to lodge with the central bank." M. Keating, "The evolution of Australian macroeconomic strategy since World War 2", Ville and Withers 2015, 443-4.

[67] The White Paper specified that only "permanent" changes in export incomes should be met by changes in the exchange rate: Commonwealth of Australia, 1945, *Full Employment in Australia*, White Paper, [online] Canberra, Government Printer, paragraphs 89 and follows. Available at: <http://www.billmitchell.org/White_Paper_1945/index.html> [Accessed 5 Jan. 2016]. H.C. Coombs, who headed the group drafting the White Paper, subsequently related that he sent a memo to Fadden in mid-1950, advocating a long list of policy responses, including an appreciation of the exchange rate and a freeing up of the interest rate: Trial Balance. Issues of my working life, South Melbourne, Sun Books, 1983, 149-51.

[68] In 1954 Coombs remarked that there were limitations on the degree to which monetary policy measures could be employed in Australia, given that there was little day-to-day trade in government securities, and a lack of a market in short-term paper: *Other People's Money. Economic Essays*, Canberra, ANU Press, 1971, 14-15.

[69] Goldbloom, Hawkins and Kennedy, 2008.

[70] J.J. Pincus, *The Benefits of the Boom Revisited: A Response to John Edwards*. [online]

Minerals Council of Australia, 2014. Available at: <http://www.minerals.org.au/news/the_benefits_of_the_boom_revisited_a_response_to_john_edwards> [Accessed 5 Jan. 2016].

[71] G. Whitwell, *The Treasury Line*, Sydney, Allen & Unwin, 1986, 105-107. (Arguably, the first Australian "Keynesian" budget was Percy Spender's in 1940, using deficit financing and not taxation, in view of the existence of unemployed labour and other resources: see John Hawkins, "Percy Spender: an early Keynesian," *Economic Round-up*, no. 2, 2011.)

[72] C. Bowen, *The Money Men: Australia's 12 Most Notable Treasurers*, Melbourne University Press, 2015, chapter 6.

[73] R. Ewing and J. Hawkins, "Business cycles in Australia", *Paper for the Conference of Economists, 2006*, Table 1. Available at: <https://www.academia.edu/16965511/Business_cycles_in_Australia> [Accessed 29 Dec. 2015]. Foster and Stewart 1991, 151.

[74] J.C. Horsfall, *The Liberal Era: A Political and Economic Analysis*, Melbourne, Sun Books, 1974, 80-5. The proposal came not from the Treasury but from Salter, on secondment to Prime Minister's; it was repealed six months later.

[75] J. Hawkins, "Holt: an urbane treasurer", *Treasury Economic Roundup*, Canberra, 2012, 65-6.

[76] Excess demand not only threatened the balance of payments, but also led to domestic inflation. (The predominant explanation of inflation then was "demand push"; only later did the flawed concept of "cost-push inflation" gain currency.)

[77] Hawkins 2012, 67.

[78] Regarding the period to the early 1970s, McLean concluded that "The long period of prosperity Australia experienced after the Second World War is, therefore, no mystery. The international economy was flourishing and, like many other national economies that were highly integrated into the global trading system, it shared in the postwar boom", I.W. McLean, *Why Australia Prospered*, Princeton, Princeton University Press, 2012, 209. McLean emphasised convergence, a quasi-automatic tendency for laggards to catch up with leaders in living standards. What is not explained in his account is why convergence occurred during this period, but not after it, despite the persistence of productivity gaps compared to the United States, nor what explained the differences between countries in the extent to which convergence occurred.

[79] A. Kaspura and G. Weldon, *Productivity Trends in Australia*, Working Paper No. 9. Canberra, Department of Productivity, Research Branch, 1980. It is worth noting that there are significant uncertainties surrounding these estimates, particularly with respect to the size of the capital stock.

[80] See H. Wee, *Prosperity and Upheaval: The World Economy, 1945-1980*, Berkeley CA, University of California Press, 1986, Table 12. It is worth noting that the relativities for Canada and Australia during this period are very similar.

[81] See Butlin, 1970, Table 6.7.

[82] See J. Nevile, "How Productive Is Australian Capital?", *Economic Record* 43(3), 1967, Table II.

[83] W.A. Sinclair, "Capital Formation", in Forster 1970: 60-1.

[84] S. Broadberry and D.A. Irwin, "Lost exceptionalism? Comparative income and productivity in Australia and the UK, 1861-1948", *Economic Record* 83 (262), 2007,Tables 8 and 9.

[85] G. Bombach, *Post-war Economic Growth Revisited*, Amsterdam, North-Holland, 1985, 60. Some later evidence of the importance of these mechanisms for Australia is presented in H. Ergas and M. Wright, "Internationalisation, firm conduct and productivity", in P.W. Lowe and J. Dwyer (eds), *International Integration of the Australian Economy: proceedings of a conference held at the H.C. Coombs Centre for Financial Studies, Kirribilli on 11-12 July, 1994*. Reserve Bank of Australia, Sydney, 1994.

[86] Import licensing, during the period in which it was in operation, reinforced that effect of the tariff, as shown by G.G. Moffatt, *Import Control and Industrialization: A Study of the Australian Experience*, Melbourne, Melbourne University Press, 1970.

[87] In addition to its reliance on import protection and on financial repression, the economic framework differed from those of recent decades in its tolerance of anti-competitive behaviour by private firms. See A. Hunter, "Restrictive practices and monopolies in Australia", *Economic Record* 37(77), 1961, 25-49. Reprinted in Arndt and Corden, 268-301.

[88] N.G. Butlin, A. Barnard and J.J. Pincus, *Government and Capitalism*, Sydney, Allen & Unwin, 1982, 127-8, 278ff.

[89] J.McB. Grant, "The Petroleum Industry", in A. Hunter (ed.), *The Economics of Australian Industry: Studies in Environment and Structure*, Melbourne University Press, 1982, 283-4.

[90] C. Forster, "Economies of scale and Australian manufacturing", in C. Forster (ed), *Australian Economic Development in the Twentieth Century*, Sydney, George Allen & Unwin, 1970, 123-69 (at 164).

[91] L.B. Krause, and R.E. Caves (eds), *The Australian Economy: A View from the North*, Washington, D.C, Brookings Institution, 1984, 313-47. The regression results on page 337 imply a 48 percent productivity gap in manufacturing, compared with the US.

[92] See, for example, H.W. Arndt, *A Small Rich Industrial Country: Studies in Australian Development, Aid and Trade*, Melbourne, Canberra, Cheshire, 1968, 15ff.

[93] C. Massy 2011, *Breaking the Sheep's Back: The Shocking True Story of the Decline and Fall of the Australian Wool Industry*, St. Lucia, Qld., University of Queensland Press, 54.

[94] W.K. Hancock, *Australia*, London, Ernest Benn, 1930, 96.

[95] K.O. Campbell, "Current agricultural development and the utilisation of resources", in Arndt and Corden, at 306; reprinted from *Economic Record*, 32(1), 1956, 119-34.

[96] Gruen in Arndt and Corden, 345-6.

[97] Gruen, 340.

[98] See especially B. Davidson, *Australia Wet or Dry?: The Physical and Economic Limits to the Expansion of Irrigation*, Melbourne University Press, 1969.

[99] M. Rimmer, "Unions and Arbitration", in J. Isaac and S. Macintyre, (eds), The New Province for Law and Order: 100 years of Australian industrial conciliation and arbitration, Port Melbourne, Cambridge University Press, 2004, 294.

[100] B. Harley, "Managing Industrial Conflict", in Isaac and Macintyre 2004, 335.

[101] D'Alpuget 1977, 128-38; and S. Macintyre 2004, "Arbitration in Action", in Isaac and Macintyre, 81-6.

[102] *R. v. Kirby: Ex parte Boilermakers' Society of Australia* (1956) 94 CLR 254 (HC) and *Attorney-General (Commonwealth) v. The Queen* (1957) 95 CLR 529 (PC).

[103] J.R. Bray, "On the evolution of the minimum wage in Australia: options for the future", Canberra: Research School of Economics, College of Business and Economics, The Australian National University, 2013, Figure 1.

[104] Calculated from Table A.7 of M. Butlin, R. Dixon and P.J. Lloyd, "Statistical Appendix", in Ville and Withers 2014.

[105] See Butlin 1970, Table 6.7.

[106] An econometric analysis is set out in P.A. McGavin, *Wages & Whitlam: The Wages Policy of the Whitlam Government*, Melbourne, Oxford University Press, 1987.

[107] Hancock 1930, 193.

[108] McEwen, advised by Crawford, was a mercantilist: more wool exports to Japan, good; more textile imports from Japan, bad. But the first could not be had without the second.

[109] P.H. Lindert, *Growing Public: Social Spending and Economic Growth since the Eighteenth Century*, Cambridge, UK, Cambridge, 2004, Table 1.2.

[110] See, for example, Menzies' spirited defence of the Tariff Board's independence in 1962, reprinted in Crawford, Anderson and Morris 1968, 467.

[111] Whitwell 1986.

[112] A great deal more could be said about the Vernon report, including the background of its establishment, and the Treasury's role in the government's response: but not here.

[113] H. Heclo, M.J. Bane, M. Kazin and A. Wolfe, *Christianity and American Democracy: The Alexis de Tocqueville Lectures on American Politics*, Cambridge, Mass., Harvard University Press, 2007, 24.

[114] Michael Bassett, *The State in New Zealand 1840-1984: Socialism Without Doctrines?* Auckland University Press, Auckland, 1998.

8

The Condition of the People

Mikayla Novak

Most Australians spanning the generations have yearned for improvements in living standards, for themselves, their families and communities. Given that modern governments, for good or for ill, are extensively involved in enforcing institutional frameworks affecting economic, social and other manifestations of well-being, trends in living standards have, in turn, come to be regarded as a litmus test of the performance of modern government.

During his second period in office, from 1949 to 1966, the Prime Minister, Robert Menzies, recognised the central importance of improved living standards for his tenure of government. His last general election policy speech, delivered in November 1963, depicted a record of beneficial changes spanning well over a decade:

> a Liberal-Country Party government at Canberra has helped to create a revolutionary change in the economic climate, in production, in the growth of trade with the world, in living standards, in social services, in provisions for health, in the free choice of employment – and large and growing employment at that – in population growth, in large savings and large industrial investment, in increasing educational opportunities, in national development credit, and security.[1]

About six months later, in London, Menzies spoke about the sources of such improvements: "we know, and occasionally admit, that there is no uniformity among personalities, or talents, or energy. We have learned that true rising standards of living are the product of progressive enterprise, the acceptance of risks, the encouragement of adventure, the prospect of rewards. These are all individual matters. There is no government department which can create these things."[2]

To be certain, the Menzies Government castigated the doctrinaire socialism of its major political opponent, the Australian Labor Party, but it maintained a widespread measure of governmental intervention in national economic and social affairs. From time to time, Menzies himself credited his government's regulatory involvement in, say, industrial relations, or fiscal involvement in social welfare as another example, helping to uphold better living standards for Australians.

Did living standards improve during the Menzies era and, if so, to what extent? Furthermore, what roles did the Menzies Government play in shaping living standards during its period in office? Were those efforts constructive in shaping living standards enjoyed by Australians? This essay attempts to make a contribution toward answering these questions, which are essential to interpreting the relative performance of the long years of the Menzies prime ministership.

Assessing the condition of the people: measuring living standards during the Menzies era

While the term, "living standards," remains subject to varying interpretations, it is broadly depicted here to be construed as the level of wealth, comfort, material goods and necessities available to an individual person, a household, or a community, at least sufficient to ensure an adequate existence. Writing in the first half of the twentieth century, British-Australian economist Frederic Charles Benham expressed the desirability of living standards in the following terms:

> The man in the street and his wife want a better and more varied diet, better clothes and more of them, better housing, a better education for their children, more opportunities to travel and to enjoy themselves; in general, more of the necessities, comforts, amenities, and pleasures of life. The phrase which covers all these things is *standard of living*. They want a higher standard of living.[3]

With the formalisation of national income accounting standards from the early to mid-twentieth century, policy-makers tended to embrace the aggregate production by an economy, namely gross domestic product (GDP) or GDP per capita, as a representative or summary measure of living standards.

Since the 1960s, however, there has been growing criticism of the adequacy of GDP as a broad indicator of welfare, largely on account of either the exclusion, or inadequacy, of methodological treatment concerning various non-marketed activities and effects (for example, unpaid household production or environmental degradation).[4] Other matters, including the implications of accounting distinctions between flows and stocks, have also been raised in criticism of broad-ranging use of GDP indicators.

Despite the observation that GDP is correlated with an array of indicators for human welfare,[5] the perceived inadequacies surrounding GDP, or GDP per capita, as a singular measure capturing trends in living standards has led to efforts to present numerous indicators when attempting to quantify the level of, or the change in, living standards. The intention of such exercises is to obtain a better impression of the circumstances under which people live.

Statistical agencies such as the Australian Bureau of Statistics have adopted a "dashboard approach" toward presentation of indicators of living standards.[6] This approach presents a set of indicators alongside each other, with no judgments rendered as to their relative importance in the determination of living standards.

The dashboard methodology is by no means the perfect framework for presenting changes in living standards, not least since the selection of indicators may draw charges of *ad hocery* against those adopting such an approach.[7] By the same token, some argue this has the distinct advantage of avoiding a prospective loss of information arising from composing a single indicator of living standards, or weighting a set of indicators in certain, potentially contestable, ways. An emphasis upon a multi-dimensional, rather than mono-dimensional, approach to discerning trends in living standards is another characteristic favouring the presentation of numerous aspects of statistical information.

Living standards during the pre-Menzies period

In order to provide the context for the changes in living standards during the post-war Menzies Government, it is necessary to provide a brief account of the extraordinary economic and social circumstances which preceded it, namely the Second World War and the years immediately thereafter.

In the December 1942 edition of the *Economic Record*, J.S.G. Wilson characterised economic arrangements during the Second World War as akin to an "octopus of control" which "puts out its tentacles, reaching into hidden corners

– invading our private lives during these war years."[8] Those controls ranged from the acute micro-management of private consumption activities through to heavily centralised and regulated (public and private) financial settings.

Grounded in the objective of redirecting agricultural and manufacturing production from civil to military use (including by visiting American military personnel), and accounting for the depletion of global markets in tradeable commodities, government policies effectively transposed the austere economic conditions from the battlefields to the kitchens and dining tables of Australians through, for instance, a host of punitive rationing measures.

In October 1940, the first Menzies Government introduced petrol rationing, whose severity increased from 1941 until early 1946.[9] After the change of government in October 1941, when a Labor administration led by John Curtin took office, the Commonwealth introduced "rationing books" in 1942. The holder was permitted to buy limited amounts of essentials such as meat, butter, sugar and tea during a weekly period.

Specified textiles, clothing and footwear were also rationed from June 1942, subsequent to a rapid depletion of available retail stocks. According to one report, " 'Stampede buying' following recent ministerial announcements of an early short-age of woollen goods has so depleted stocks ... that blankets and other articles are now virtually unobtainable."[10] Meanwhile, a wide range of manufactures were prohibited for domestic production – including jewellery, evening dresses, coffee tables, standard lamps, dishwashers, carpet sweepers, musical instruments, theatre programs of more than one page, bath heaters, betting bags, billiard tables, cosmetics and school uniforms.[11]

In addition to government restrictions on consumption possibilities, households were encouraged to exude a modicum of self-sufficiency in their production habits. Advertising campaigns were waged to exhort the public to grow their own vegetables, and raise their own hens for egg laying. The latter call was partially in response to an egg shortage during the the Second World War period, precipitating a government "Egg Priority Scheme" in 1945 to redirect the retail supplies of scarce eggs in favour of families with young children and people with disabilities.[12]

During 1942 the Curtin Government also introduced a paternalistic campaign enjoining citizens to "save Australia" by smoking less, drinking less, recycling products such as clothing and other materials, eschewing the use of cosmetics, and consciously planning their meals.[13] This paternalism was informed by a desire by government for "people to save their money to invest in war loans to pay for all the weapons of war so badly needed."[14]

Under the directives of the federal Minister for War Organisation of Industry, John Dedman, and other senior ministers in the Curtin Government, the Commonwealth, often in concert with State and local government authorities, also issued personal identity cards; imposed direct price controls; reduced the Christmas-New Year holiday period to three days and restricted seasonal advertising; orchestrated electricity blackouts in cities; imposed daylight saving; curtailed weekday sporting events; banned political organisations that opposed the war effort; imprisoned conscientious objectors to the war; and detained certain residents originating from combatant nationalities.[15]

Another way in which public sector restrictions designed a war "home front" was through tightening of labour market regulations. For instance, "manpower" legislation was enacted to compel civilian men and women for war production activities, often entailing forced withdrawal of people from their previous civil occupations. From early 1942 government was empowered:

- to exempt a person from service or prohibit their enlistment;
- to prevent employers from engaging labour not authorised by the directorate;
- to restrict the right of employees to engage in the employment of their choice;
- to prevent employees from leaving their employment;
- to restrict the right of an employer to dismiss employees;
- to direct any person to leave particular employment and engage in another; and
- to compel individuals to register and provide information about themselves.[16]

The Commonwealth Government also actively engaged in a policy of financial repression, in addition to efforts to subordinate private savings and investment decisions to the broader wartime financial imperatives of the state.[17] Elements included limitations on company profits, imposition of uniform income taxation by taking over the income-taxing powers of the States, and a national savings campaign to raise additional sums for the Australian war campaign.

The extensive controls imposed by the Curtin Labor Government have been described in the following terms:

[Curtin's] government introduced controls and regulations into almost every area of life. Australians, accustomed to minimal interference from governments in their ordinary lives, now accepted an extraordinary growth in central government power. New federal departments organised and regulated every aspect of economic activity and myriad boards and commissions assumed oversight of almost every part of ordinary citizens' activities.[18]

It is often claimed that economic growth in Australia remained resilient during the Second World War, due in part to the contention that "[b]y 1939 the manufacturing sector was more important in the economy than it had been in 1914, but also more diversified into branches of industry vital to supplying both civilian and military needs. Consequently when the war broke out in Europe in 1939, Australia was much better placed than it had been in 1914."[19] The relatively greater contribution of women to the labour force has also been cited as a factor underpinning the claim of wartime growth.

As considered later in this essay, assessments of economic growth are complicated by the fact that public sector costs are included in gross domestic product (GDP). Indeed, conventional methods of measuring economic output are particularly dubious during periods of war, when the activities of government tend to predominate. When deducting public sector costs from GDP, and adjusting for price inflation that is usually elevated during wartime, real private GDP *fell* from about $1.9 billion in 1940 to about $1.7 billion in 1945, before recovering in subsequent years.[20]

Not only did inclusion of governmental costs in national accounting statistics mask the very real senses of hardship experienced by many civilian Australians during the Second World War, but the impairment of overall living standards during this period was affirmed by numerous primary and secondary accounts of how Australians lived during that period.

The American economists, Steven Horwitz and Michael McPhillips, recently suggested in the US context that "the greatest example of economic retrogression during the war was a return to self-sufficiency. Even with rationing, food supplies remained scarce, and many Americans were forced to grow their own food."[21] There were similar accounts expressed in Australia, with one presenter of the ABC's *Women Talking* radio series, for example, explaining she grew her own vegetables because "prices are prohibitive, and yet I must have some fresh vegetables to give my young baby".[22]

The mismanaged clothing rationing scheme of 1942 – in which the pre-announcement of rationing led to panic buying of articles of clothes from retailers – also hinted at the sense of hardship that Australians felt under the planned wartime economy.

At a store in Bourke Street, Melbourne, a salesperson remonstrated with a woman who purchased clothing items in bulk: "you'll have enough here to last you eight years," she said. "Well, supposing I have, I prefer to spend the money on myself instead of on Mr. Curtin."[23] Shop assistants reported that customers were indiscriminately purchasing items, without checking for price or fit. The restrictive effects of clothing rationing were also reflected, to some degree, in reported instances of thefts from clothes lines and from dry-cleaning and clothing stores.[24]

In response to the consequent clothing shortage, a so-called "Victory Suit," modelled by John Dedman himself, consisting of a two-button, single-breasted coat without a waistcoat, and trousers without cuffs and no more than nineteen inches wide at the bottom, was introduced.[25] Given the Government's eagerness to save on cloth and manufacturing, the "Victory Suit" also allowed only four pockets and disallowed buttons on the sleeves.

Other measures, such as prohibition of domestic manufacturing of evening wear, dinner gowns, swimming costumes, and so on, were also intended to reserve fibrous materials exclusively for military, rather than civilian, use. Australians also suffered from the prohibitions placed on producing non-essential clothing trimmings, whereas some people attempted to save their rationing coupons by converting tablecloths and tea towels into nightclothes and dresses.[26]

Maintenance of severe restrictions upon basic food consumption contributed toward deteriorating nutritional standards of average Australians. Whilst Australians enjoyed greater consumption of red meat, butter, and sugar than their counterparts in Britain and the United States, they lagged in dairy and vegetables. The pre-war daily average of 3 021 calories consumed by an Australian fell, in 1943, to 2 975 calories, and to 2 878 in 1944.[27]

There was some evidence to suggest that redirection of resources toward the military effort contributed to delays in improving the quality of Australian housing. The Melbourne University economist, Wilfred Prest, in a survey of housing, found a quarter of the kitchens investigated had no water supply, and half lacked a hot water service. Fewer than ten percent of homes had a refrigerator; about half used ice-chests; and the remainder relied on daily purchases of perishables which were constricted by supply controls.[28]

In addition, housing shortages almost trebled during the course of the war, partly a consequence of the regulated freezing of rents and property values. An estimated deficit of 120 000 dwellings at the start of the war rose to 350 000 by the end of the conflict.[29]

Official archival records suggest other features of Australia's wartime policy regime contributed to numerous hardships, with complaints that petrol rationing prevented people from attending church services, or visiting relatives or enjoying various leisure activities in which they might otherwise have participated.[30] This contributed to diminishing incentives for people to buy new motor cars, with, for example, the number of registered new vehicles falling in Victoria from about 17 400 in 1939-40 to about 2 000 in 1942-43.[31]

The intricate web of restrictions on availability of goods and services was conducive to development of an elaborate shadow economy "as the war progressed and some people cheated on the ration or evaded labour regulations".[32] Manifestations included clandestine sales of fresh produce, at inflated prices, in marketplaces; forgery and misappropriation of government-issued ration coupons and other documents, such as identification cards, travel cards, and military discharge certificates; and appearance of illicit goods in civilian homes.[33] As for alcohol, bottled beer became virtually unobtainable during the peak of the Second World War leaving "black market" operations as the "normal" method for the distribution of beer as well as spirits.[34]

Australian political discourse in the years immediately following the war also lends support to the proposition that the Second World War was characterised by an extreme diminution of living standards.

In the 1946 Federal election campaign, and the pivotal 1949 campaign, Robert Menzies, leader of the newly-formed Liberal Party, stressed the importance of "producing our way to prosperity" and warned of the dire consequences of mass electoral endorsement for the Labor program of extensive controls by government in economic affairs, including in the banking sector.

The pro-enterprise political messaging of Menzies seemed to resonate with the Australian public, in no small part due to the persistence of shortages of key commodities such as coal, electricity, petrol and steel, during the post-war years which also frustrated the attainment of full-employment macroeconomic objectives. In an interesting sociological perspective, John Howard, Prime Minister, 1996-2007, stated in his definitive account of the Menzies era that:

> Australia in 1949 was still smothered by wartime controls ... The perception that Australia was taking too long to shake off wartime austerity was reinforced whenever people went to the pictures, as the cinema was habitually referred to. Most of the movies shown were American, and they revealed an American way of life that was more modern and comfortable than that enjoyed by most Australians. In a subconscious way this irked many Australians. The Americans had been our allies in the war. That war was now over. Why should Americans appear so much better off than Australians? There were reasons for this, but they didn't alter the attitude. ... the portrayal of ordinary American life in Hollywood movies made many Australians impatient when such day-to-day comfort would also be available to them.[35]

The political victory of the Liberal-Country Party coalition led by Robert Menzies, in what has been described by some as "the most important election win in our history",[36] ensured that Australia avoided the near-certainty of a more deeply interventionist Commonwealth Government during the 1950s and 1960s, with significant implications for living standards in the longer term.

Living standards under Menzies: incomes and wages

As already mentioned, a commonly used measure of economic performance is GDP which indicates the market value of all final goods and services (including the costs of providing public sector services) produced in a country during a given year. Expressing GDP in per capita terms provides a gauge of the level of material living standards enjoyed, on average, by each resident person.

Adjusting the data to accommodate the effects of general price inflation, real GDP increased from about $5.2 billion in 1949 to about $11.1 billion in 1966 – an average annual increase of about five percent per annum. During this period, real GDP per capita rose from about $650 to about $1 000, equating to an increase of about two percent per annum.

Deducting the financial costs of governmental activities from GDP arguably provides an even more accurate representation of material living standards, since it is private sector activity which generates the incomes used to underwrite material improvement (and the revenues acquired by governments). Wolfgang Kasper has explained this in some detail:

[a] considerable component of gross national spending is based on the taxation of private production and wealth and constitutes a use of the nation's resources rather than a contribution to those resources. This component is made up of the costs of government administration, defence and community services, which form an integral part of national expenditure. If a government increases these outlays rapidly, as has been the case in recent years, national expenditure is bloated and this may easily create the impression of a more rapid growth of the economy than is actually taking place. The activities of these sectors do contribute to living standards, but since their output is generally not sold in the market place, the value of their contribution to economic well being is not accurately reflected in values attributed to them in the National Accounts. They are therefore best omitted when measuring national output.[37]

Figure 1 shows the trends in real "private gross domestic product" (PGDP) and real PGDP per capita in Australia during the Menzies era: Australians as a whole enjoyed significant increases in the value of private sector output, with real PGDP increasing by about five percent on average per annum whereas real PGDP per capita rose by about three percent each year. These trends provided a basis with which material standards of living improved for average Australians from the late 1940s to the late 1960s.

It should be noted that the Australian population rose considerably during the 1950s and 1960s, due to some extent to maintenance of assisted immigration programs by the Menzies Government which encouraged migrants predominantly from Great Britain as well as southern European countries. Indeed, as implied by Figure 5.1, growth in the monetary value of production by the private sector had consistently outpaced the growth in population (from 7.9 million in 1949 to 11.6 million in 1966).

General trends in material living standards are likely to understate the improvements in economic well-being enjoyed by migrants, since it can be presumed that their livelihoods would have been markedly improved in Australia than had they stayed in their home countries.[38]

On the other hand, it is often claimed that immigration induces economic costs for a destination country, for example, when migrants out-compete residents for jobs. What is ignored by such viewpoints is that migration, and population growth more generally, generates growth opportunities through augmenting labour supply and human capital stocks, and expanding local markets, and so

Figure 1: Real private gross product and real private gross product per capita, 1949 to 1966

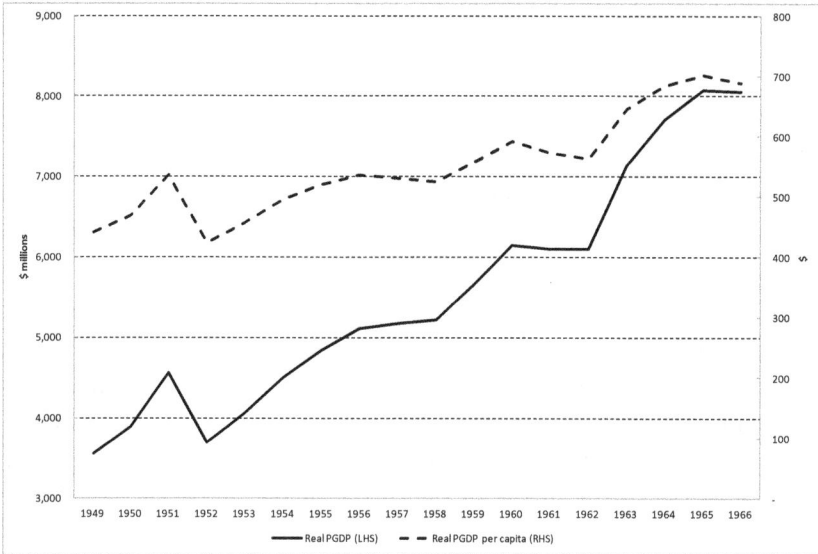

Private gross domestic product defined as gross domestic product less expenditure on goods and services by Commonwealth, State, and local governments.

Source: Measuring Worth, www.measuringworth.com; Alan Barnard, 1987, "Government Finance", in Wray Vamplew, ed., *Australians, Historical Statistics*, Fairfax, Syme and Weldon Associates, Sydney; R. A. Foster, 1996, "Australian Economic Statistics 1949-50 to 1994-95", Reserve Bank of Australia, Occasional Paper No. 8.

it was for Australia when post-war immigrants made significant contributions to development of, say, the building construction and infrastructure industries.

Furthermore, Australian residents have benefited substantially from improvements in the overall quality of life, through the infusion of new forms of artistic and cultural expression, cuisines, ethical and spiritual precepts, and a better appreciation of human diversity, induced by the exercise of "experiments in living" by immigrants in a liberal-democratic society. There was arguably no better display of this than the immensely beneficial contributions that immigrants from the Balkans and Italy have made to Australia after the Second World War and through the Menzies period.

A criticism of macroeconomic policy management under Menzies was the assumption of so-called "stop-go" discretionary fiscal and monetary policies, ironically inspired by the Keynesian dictum that governments should respond to changing economic circumstances so as to ensure economic stability. Reflecting the predilection for regular alteration of expenditure, taxation, interest rate and credit allocation settings, the annual growth rate of real PGDP fluctuated wildly during the 1950s and 1960s, from growth highs exceeding 15 percent in the early 1950s to lows of less than one percent in the early 1960s.

The proceeds of GDP or, in this case, PGDP, are in general terms distributed to the owners of capital and labour and, so, to obtain greater clarity with regard to how material living standards changed for individuals, it is necessary to examine trends in average wages.

The ability to earn an income enables an individual to purchase goods and services, including food, clothing, shelter, transport and entertainment, and to meet various financial commitments. It also staves off absolute poverty, and all the troubling economic and social consequences that they would entail. Trends in real average earnings are illustrated by Figure 2. They show that total average weekly earnings grew by an average of two percent per annum from 1949 to 1966.

Figure 2: Real average weekly earnings, 1949 to 1966

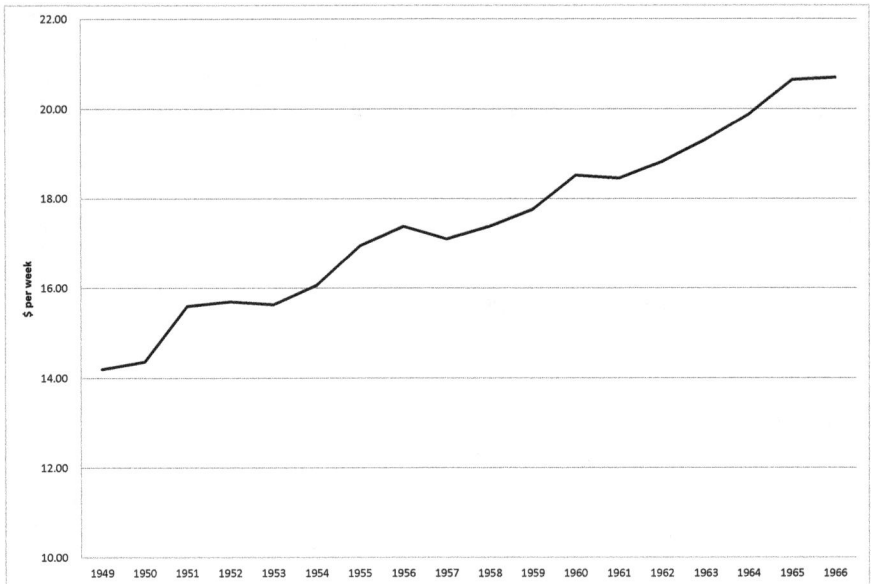

Source: Measuring Worth, www.measuringworth.com.

Although general price inflation had also risen significantly during the Menzies era, a worker on average earnings was getting ahead in real terms throughout the period, enabling them to enjoy more of the amenities provided through growing markets and broader economic development.

It has often been suggested in the Australian economic literature that the growth in real wages historically, especially within the manufacturing industries, had been facilitated by the maintenance of significant tariffs and other barriers against import penetration into the domestic economy.[39] This is because a larger manufacturing sector, as supported by trade protections, provided the means through which labourers could command relatively higher wages than working within agricultural industries whose returns would be largely enjoyed by land owners.[40]

It may well have been the case that the development of Australian manufacturing, and hence manufacturing employment and wage earnings, had been promoted by persistent tariff and non-tariff barriers against imports, at least to some extent. Given the labour intensity of Australian manufacturing it would appear that setting tariffs in a high-wage economy assisted most highly the most labour-intensive manufacturing industries, which were least suitable for the economic environment.[41] In addition, as discussed later in this essay, this policy came at a great economic cost to the living standards of Australians in their capacities as consumers.

Living standards under Menzies: health status

Changes in health status make a significant contribution to the living standards enjoyed by individuals, families and communities, by virtue of the facilitative role that improvements in health make to economic and social participation, and to quality of life more generally.

According to Figure 3, there had been considerable improvements in average life expectancy, at birth, enjoyed by Australians during the Menzies years. For Australians, average life expectancy rose from about 69 years to 71 years between 1949 and 1966, with stronger improvements in life expectancy enjoyed by females (two years over the period, compared with one year for males).

The incidence of mortality also fell during the Menzies period of government, with the total death rate per 100 000 people declining from about ten deaths in 1949 to about nine in 1966. An important aspect of the overall decline in mortality has been reduction in infant mortality, as a result of prenatal and postnatal care,

Figure 3: Life expectancy at birth, 1949 and 1966

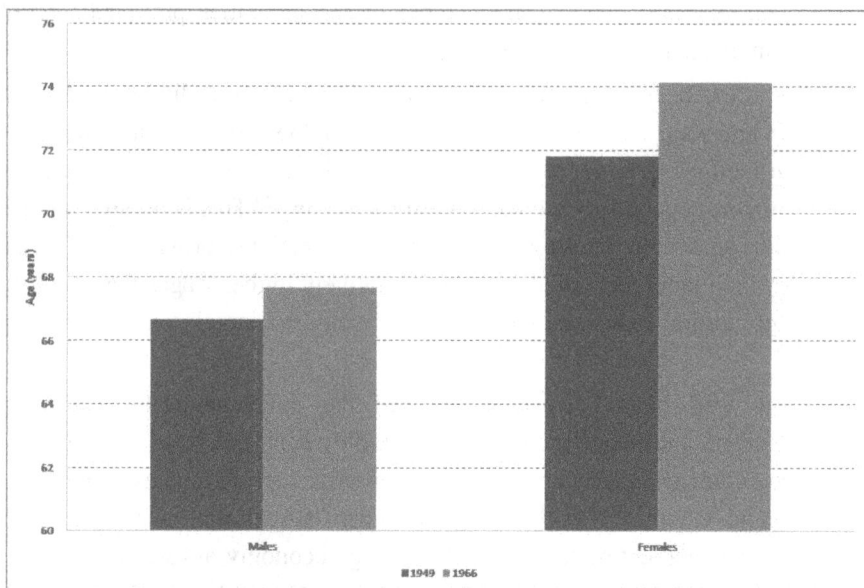

Source: Australian Bureau of Statistics, Australian Historical Population Statistics, cat. no. 3105.0.65.001; Human Mortality Database, www.mortality.org.

declines in infectious diseases, improved sanitation, new medicines, mass vaccinations, and improvements in birth conditions (Figure 4).

Another factor informing the trend decline in the overall mortality rate of Australians was the significant decline in the death rate attributable to infectious and parasitic diseases, such as cholera, typhoid fever, polio, smallpox and measles. As a result of vaccines, better public health measures and new medicines, the infectious diseases mortality rate fell from about 46 people per 1 000 to ten (Figure 5).

Despite generalised improvements in human health experienced during the Menzies period, cancer and circulatory diseases served as major contributors to mortality rates in Australia (Figure 6).

During the period from 1949 to 1966 death rates attributable to injuries and poisoning increased, and there was a relative increase in road fatalities nationally. In terms of the latter issue, the effect of legislation making wearing of seat belts compulsory, first introduced in Victoria in July 1971, remains a contentious issue, with other factors contributing to the gradual reduction in

Figure 4: Infant mortality rate, 1949 to 1966

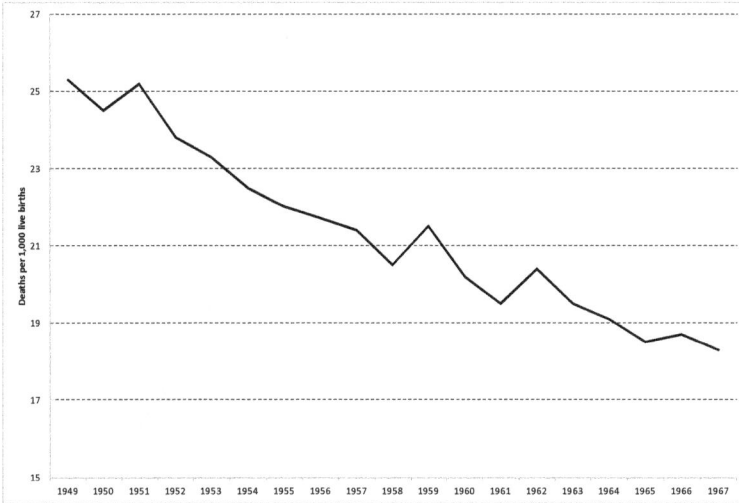

Number of deaths of babies under one year of age per 1,000 live births.

Source: Australian Bureau of Statistics, Australian Historical Population Statistics, cat. no. 3105.0.65.001.

Figure 5: Infectious diseases mortality rate, 1949 to 1966

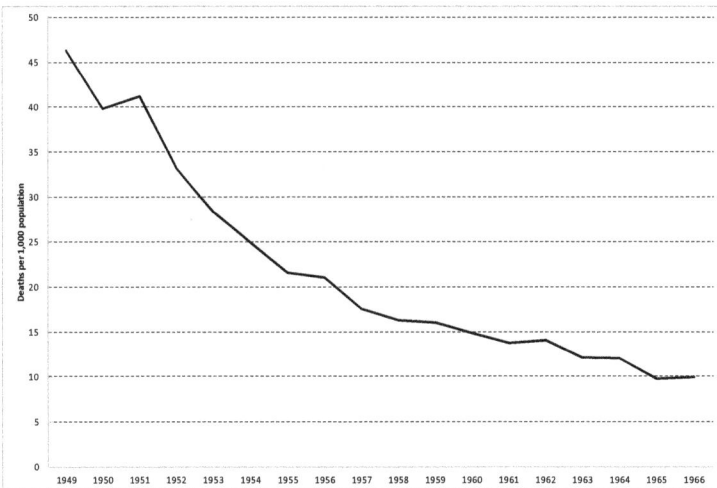

Number of deaths from intestinal and other bacterial diseases, sexually transmitted infections, viral infections, and other infectious and parasitic diseases, per 100,000 people.

Source: Australian Institute of Health and Welfare, 2008, "Mortality over the twentieth century in Australia: Trends and patterns in major causes of death", Mortality Surveillance Series No.

Figure 6: Cancer and circulatory diseases mortality rate, 1949 and 1966

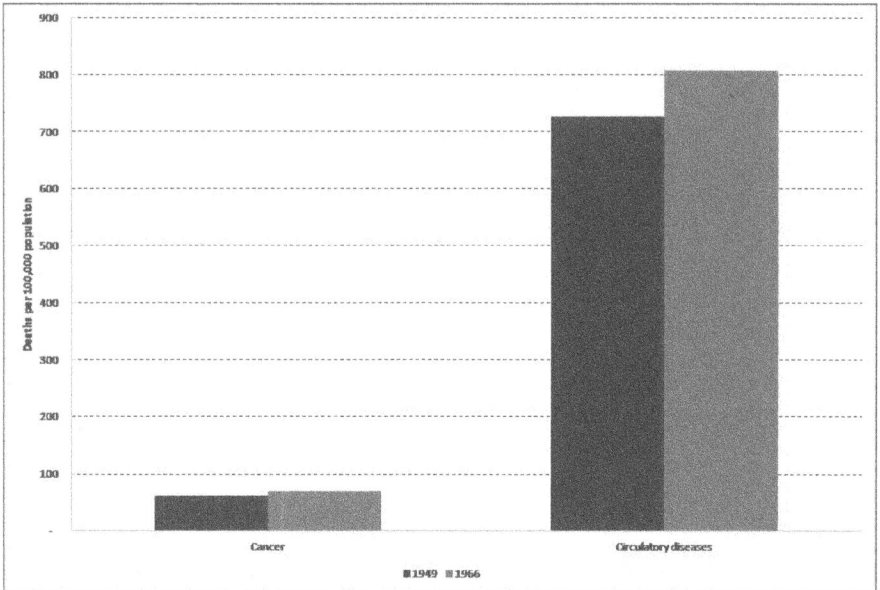

Cancer refers to deaths from all neoplasms (cancer) per 100,000 people (left-hand diagram). Circulatory diseases (right-hand diagram) refer to deaths from rheumatic fever and heart diseases, heart diseases, cerebrovascular diseases, and other circulatory system diseases, per 100,000 people.

Source: Australian Institute of Health and Welfare, 2008, "Mortality over the twentieth century in Australia: Trends and patterns in major causes of death", Mortality Surveillance Series No. 4.

road fatalities, post-Menzies, including improvements in vehicle manufacturing quality standards and road infrastructure safety enhancements.

Although some of the available evidence provides a mixed picture of varying aspects of health status, the data above present a picture of generally improving health status enjoyed by average Australians during the Menzies prime ministership.

Living standards under Menzies: educational attainment

The ability of people to secure potential gains from a growing economy and more harmonious society, with beneficial flow-on effects for living standards enjoyed over time, critically depends upon the level and quality of education attained both individually and throughout the community as a whole.

According to an international dataset of educational attainment, maintained by economists Barro and Lee, there were considerable improvements in the rates at which Australians completed schooling during the Menzies era (Table 1).

The share of the population aged 15 years to 64 years with no schooling qualifications declined steadily between 1950 and 1965. The extent to which the population maintained only primary school completions also steadily declined. The latter was attributable to the increasing propensity for students to remain in secondary schooling due, in no small part, to State government initiatives to raise the compulsory schooling age for children. These effects culminated in growth in the average years of schooling during the Menzies years.

Table 1: School education attainment, 15-64 years

	No schooling	Primary school completion only	Secondary school completion	Average years of schooling
	Percent	Percent	Percent	Years
1950	1.2	27.1	23.8	8.2
1955	1.0	22.6	27.4	8.5
1960	0.8	18.7	31.4	8.8
1965	0.7	15.4	36.2	9.2

Source: Barro-Lee Educational Attainment Dataset, http://www.barrolee.com/.

A hallmark of the Menzies era concerns the significant growth in the numbers of students enrolled in universities (Figure 7). In 1949 the total number enrolled in higher education institutions nationally was in the order of 32 000 people. By 1966 it was about 91 000 people. The number of women enrolled in Australian universities grew almost four-fold during the period, from about 7 000 to about 25 000, as young women with the encouragement of their parents sought to improve their human capital endowments to find their own independent sources of income.

Living standards under Menzies: affordability and availability of consumer goods

Vast improvements in availability of new goods for consumers, and the improved affordability of products formerly accessible only to those on higher incomes, was a feature of Australian life during the Menzies era.

Figure 7: Higher education institution enrolments, 1949 to 1966

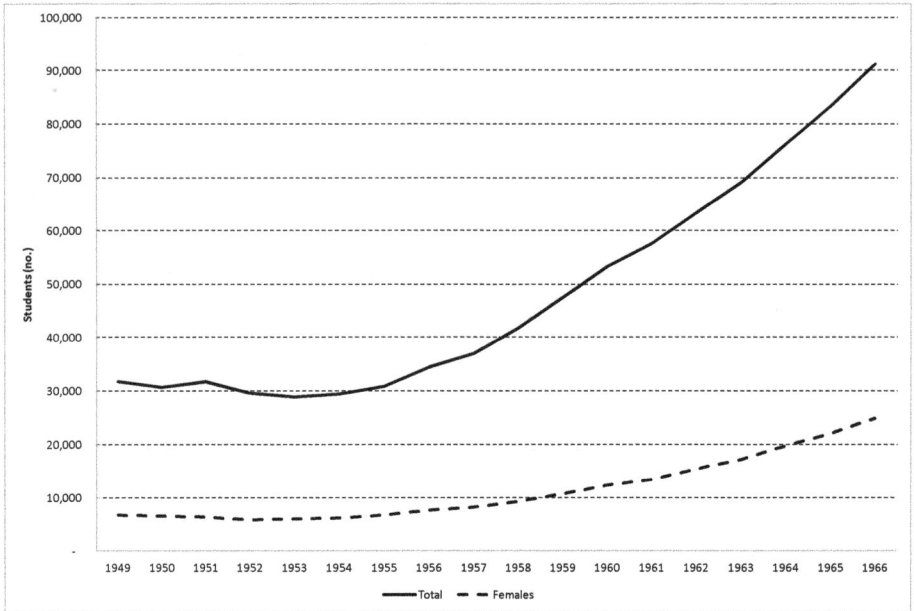

Number of students enrolled in higher education institutions.

Source: Brian R. Mitchell, 2003, *International Historical Statistics: Africa, Asia & Oceania, 1750-2000*, Palgrave Macmillan, Basingstoke.

It has been suggested by numerous economists that the level of consumption observed within an economy is an appropriate, direct measure of living standards, even if these are not without conceptual and empirical complications. Figure 8 presents estimates by Bryan Haig and Jennifer Anderssen of aggregate real consumption expenditures by Australians from the late 1940s to early 1970s,[42] broadly illustrating trend growth in spending both in aggregate and by each person on average.

Haig and Anderssen also provided information about the composition of real spending by Australian consumers over the long run (Table 2). Whilst additional information concerning the mix of consumption expenditures during additional years encompassing the Menzies era was not forthcoming from this source, the data presented in the Table suggest a relative decline in spending upon basic necessities, such as food and clothing, and a rise in the relative importance of durables, fuel, and services in the average consumption spending mix.

Figure 8: Real consumption expenditures, 1948-49 to 1970-71

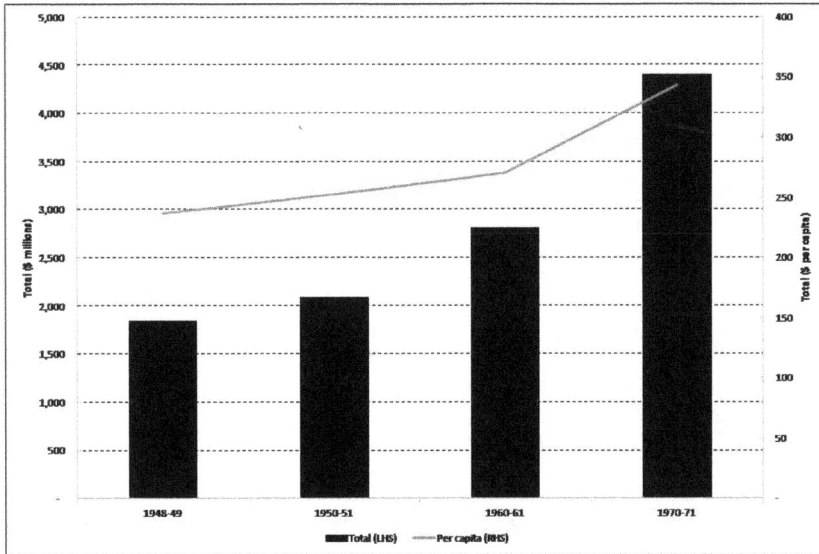

Source: Bryan Haig and Jennifer Anderssen, 2007, "Australian Consumption Expenditure and Real Income: 1900 to 2003-2004", *Economic Record* 83 (263): 416-431.

Table 2: Composition of real consumption expenditure per capita, percent , 1938-38 to 1980-81

	1938-39	1960-61	1980-81
Food	30.3	22.8	18.6
Cigarettes	3.0	5.1	2.7
Liquor	5.1	6.6	6.4
Clothing	11.1	8.8	5.9
Rent	12.1	10.3	12.3
Durable household goods	4.0	8.1	10.0
Fuel and light	2.0	5.1	5.5
Communication	1.0	0.7	1.4
Public transport	5.1	4.4	3.2
Private transport	11.1	11.0	12.3
Other goods and services[a]	19.2	21.3	24.5

Sum of category totals may not add to 100 due to rounding. (a) Including education, health, and recreation expenditures.

Source: Bryan Haig and Jennifer Anderssen, 2007, "Australian Consumption Expenditure and Real Income: 1900 to 2003-2004", *Economic Record* 83 (263): 416-31.

The growth in real consumption expenditures by Australians during the Menzies period was, on average, impressive. It needs to be recognised, nevertheless, that extensive price and non-price barriers against the infusion of cheaper imports into the Australian economy had a significant impact upon the ability of Australian consumers to improve their living standards upon those levels observed in the available data even modestly.

Customs duties (or "tariffs") were a longstanding policy instrument applied by successive governments to alter relative prices in favour of domestically produced goods, particularly by the manufacturing sector. The average nominal rate of assistance to manufacturing, proxied by the average duty payable on dutiable imports, remained at least 22 percent for much of the duration of the Menzies Government.[43]

In response to balance of payments problems induced by the Korean War wool boom, Australia introduced import licensing procedures in the early 1950s to ration foreign exchange and also restrict the entry of manufacturing imports. As a result of this policy the tariff was temporarily displaced as the chief means of ensuring trade protection, at least until 1960 when quantitative import controls were relaxed. Under the political influence of Country Party leader and Trade Minister, John "Black Jack" McEwen, industry assistance was increasingly extended to the agricultural sector in a "protection all round" strategy also to provide them with an array of benefits.[44]

By the 1960s there was growing recognition of the costs of import protections not only for trade-exposed industries relying on capital imports for their growth and development, but for consumers who were becoming increasingly accustomed to purchasing new household equipment and other conveniences from abroad.

With original contributions by the likes of the Australian economist, Max Corden,[45] it was shown that the "effective rate" of protection for manufacturing – taking account of the tariff structure on the value added produced in any given industry, that is, in relation to protection applied both to the final product and materials used by the industry – was much higher than that indicated by published average rates of protection.

According to estimates furnished by the former Industries Assistance Commission (IAC), now the Productivity Commission, the average effective rate of assistance for Australian manufacturing by the late 1960s had reached about 36 percent, with those rates significantly greater for the likes of automotive and clothing, textiles and footwear industries (Table 3). The predecessor to the IAC, the Tariff Board, estimated that tariffs and other forms of industry assistance to manufacturing imposed costs upon the broader Australian economy of the order of about $2.7 billion per annum in 1967, representing an implicit tax upon non-protected industries and consumers.[46]

Table 3: Average effective rates of assistance for manufacturing, 1968-69

Industry	Effective rate of assistance
Food, beverages and tobacco	16
Textiles	43
Clothing and footwear	97
Wood, wood products and furniture	26
Paper and paper products, printing	52
Chemical, petroleum and coal products	31
Non-metallic mineral products	15
Basic metal products	31
Fabricated metal products	61
Transport equipment	50
Motor vehicles	52
Other machinery and equipment	43
Miscellaneous manufacturing	34
Total manufacturing	36

Source: Industries Assistance Commission, 1976, *Assistance to Manufacturing Industries in Australia, 1968-69 to 1973-74*, AGPS, Canberra.

Of course, the costs associated with impeding the influx of abundant, cheap imports into Australia were well known even by the 1950s and 1960s. As the free trading economist, Frederic Benham, stated years prior to the election of the Menzies Government in 1949:

> [c]heap imports, whatever the reason for their cheapness, tend to raise, not to reduce, standards of living in the importing countries. Those concerned with a particular industry may urge that protection against competing imports would enable that industry to expand, or would prevent it from declining. Nobody disputes this. But is it desirable to penalize the whole consuming population for the benefit of the workers and shareholders in that industry? If it is, then why should not the same

argument be applied to every industry that faces foreign competition? Such all-round protection would no doubt enable money wages to be maintained, but it would lead to a substantial rise in the general cost of living, reducing real wages.[47]

Although the protectionist policy regime prevented Australians from accruing the full potential benefits of living standard improvements, they did secure improvements during the Menzies period in other ways. For example, Australians benefited substantially from growing production of electricity generated from the bountiful, and relatively cheap, coal deposits mainly located along the eastern seaboard, and rapid increases in the proportion of homes and businesses connected to electricity distribution networks.

Figure 9 shows national electricity generation per capita increased three-fold during the Menzies prime ministership, as aided by the growing productive capacity of existing generators and the commissioning of new generation works. The Snowy Mountains Hydro-Electric Scheme, presently providing almost a third of all renewable energy available to the eastern Australian electricity grid, was commissioned in 1949 and completed in 1974 at a total cost of about $820 million.[48]

Figure 9: Electricity generation, total and per capita

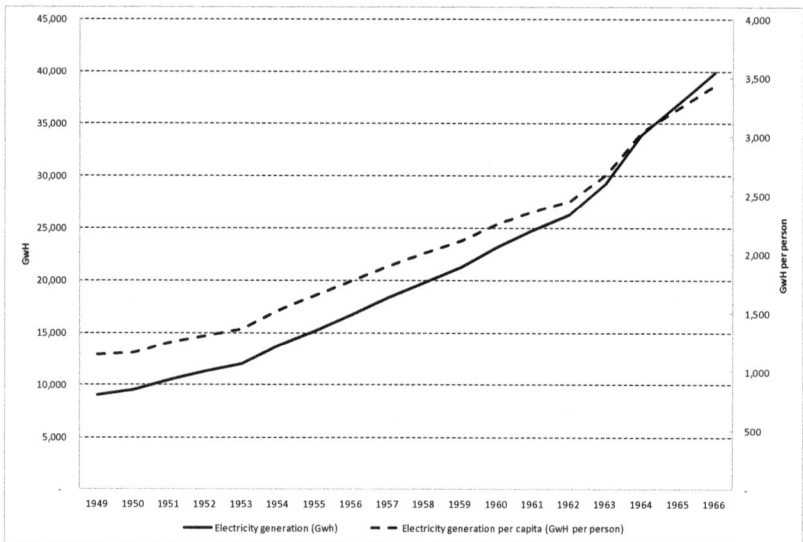

Source: Brian R. Mitchell, 2003, *International Historical Statistics: Africa, Asia & Oceania, 1750-2000*, Palgrave Macmillan, Basingstoke.

The extent of motor vehicle usage is another commonly used measure of living standards. It provides information about the capacity of individuals and families to attain a relatively expensive item (viz. a vehicle) for their own purposes. In 1949 there were about 655 000 vehicles in use in Australia. This had grown to more than three million vehicles by the year in which Robert Menzies retired (Figure 10). These included passenger and other motor vehicles produced domestically by the likes of General-Motors Holden, Ford, and Chrysler, albeit under the trade-distorting policies of tariffs and other protectionist measures.

Figure 10: Passenger motor vehicles in use, total and per 1,000 people

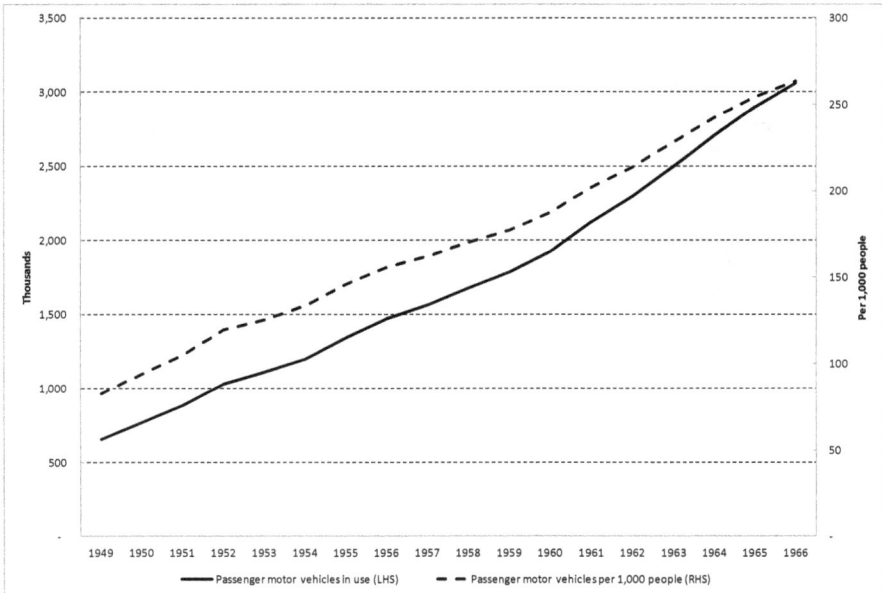

Source: Brian R. Mitchell, 2003, *International Historical Statistics: Africa, Asia & Oceania, 1750-2000*, Palgrave Macmillan, Basingstoke.

The ability of Australians to communicate with each other over long distances had been substantially enhanced by increasing uptake of telephones, which superseded unreliable and slow distribution of telegraph dispatches and postal letters commonly used during the late nineteenth and early twentieth centuries. The number of telephones in use in Australia grew from about one million in 1949 to almost three million by 1966 (Figure 11).

Figure 11: Telephones in use, total

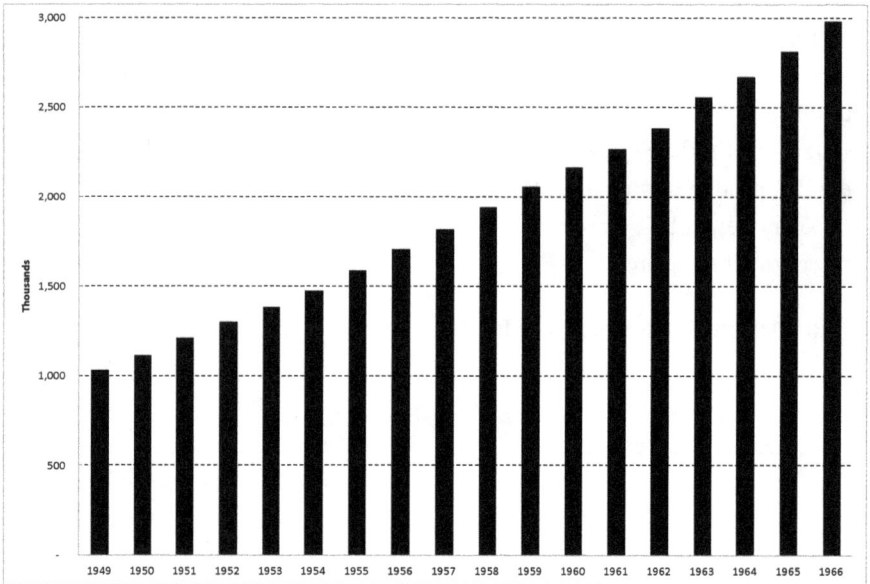

Source: Brian R. Mitchell, 2003, *International Historical Statistics: Africa, Asia & Oceania, 1750-2000*, Palgrave Macmillan, Basingstoke.

The extent of household ownership of selected appliances also illustrates the degree of improvement in living standards enjoyed by individuals and families during the Menzies period, embodying to some degree changing aspirations and expectations on the part of Australians for improved material circumstances.[49] These goods also played an important role in ameliorating the laborious intensity of home production, allowing women in particular to pursue work and other options with their time. As discussed by Snooks:

> The introduction of electrical household equipment does two things. First, it reduces the amount of time that household workers need to devote to housework, which provides more time for paid work and/or leisure ... Second, the introduction of household equipment reduces the energy demands of housework. This makes it possible to undertake market work in conjunction with household work, or to service larger houses without an increase in the time or energy spent on housework.[50]

In an analysis of consumer goods and time use in suburban homes, Tony Dingle found that about 40 percent of households owned a washing machine in 1955, whilst about 75 percent of homes in Sydney and Melbourne (about 50 percent in Brisbane) had a vacuum cleaner. In the same year, about 75 percent of all homes in Brisbane and Sydney had a fridge (about 66 percent in Melbourne). A few short years later, by the start of the 1960s, 60 percent of Australian homes had a washing machine, 73 percent a vacuum cleaner, and 94 percent had a refridgerator.[51]

Closely associated with infiltration of whitegoods and other electrical appliances in the Australian home was growing ownership of entertainment equipment, especially radios and televisions. It has been estimated that in 1956 only one percent of all Australian households owned at least one television. A decade later about 87 percent of households owned one or more television sets in their homes.[52]

Increasing prevalence of electrical appliances and entertainment goods in the Australian home has been credited, at least in part, to availability of "hire purchase" credit facilities, initially by the non-banking financial sector, during the 1950s and 1960s.

In essence, hire purchase entails an arrangement in which a borrower takes possession of a good and pays for that good in instalments, with the borrower owning the good outright once instalments are fully paid. Some have argued that the cultural effects of hire purchasing arrangements were significant:

> Motor cars and household equipment, which became available after the shortages of the war, were almost irresistible when they could be purchased out of current income rather than out of savings, by means of time payments. In recent years the television set, the motor boat, and the power lawn mower have exercised the same attraction. And in Australia, as in other countries, once the habit of using credit has been established, consumers finance not only their TV sets but also their home improvements and even their travels without saving beforehand.[53]

As shown by van der Eng, hire purchase and similar activities were facilitated by non-bank finance companies, with outstanding instalment credit advances from these entities increasing by a factor of thirty – from about $39 million in 1947 to about $1.1 billion in 1960 – making advances by finance companies accounting for one-third of all advances in Australia.[54]

Another factor conducive to proliferation of consumer goods was the increasing scale and sophistication of the Australian retailing sector. The first large, pre-planned mall or shopping centre opened in Chermside, Brisbane, in 1957, followed by Ryde, Sydney, later in the same year and Chadstone, Melbourne, in 1960.

Encouraged by growing usage of private motor vehicles and growth of housing in suburban areas, shopping centres expanded from capital-city central business districts into the suburbs. The retail outlets established within these large shopping centres provided new employment opportunities, including for women.[55]

The Productivity Commission also noted that, following developments in the United States during the 1950s, franchising retail ownership models became widespread throughout Australia from the late 1960s.[56]

Another feature of improving living standards observed during the 1950s and 1960s related to growing availability of aviation travel options for Australians, enabling them to engage more readily in business and leisure activities across long distances and share their experiences of journeys with family and friends at home (Figure 12).

Figure 12: Civil aviation travel

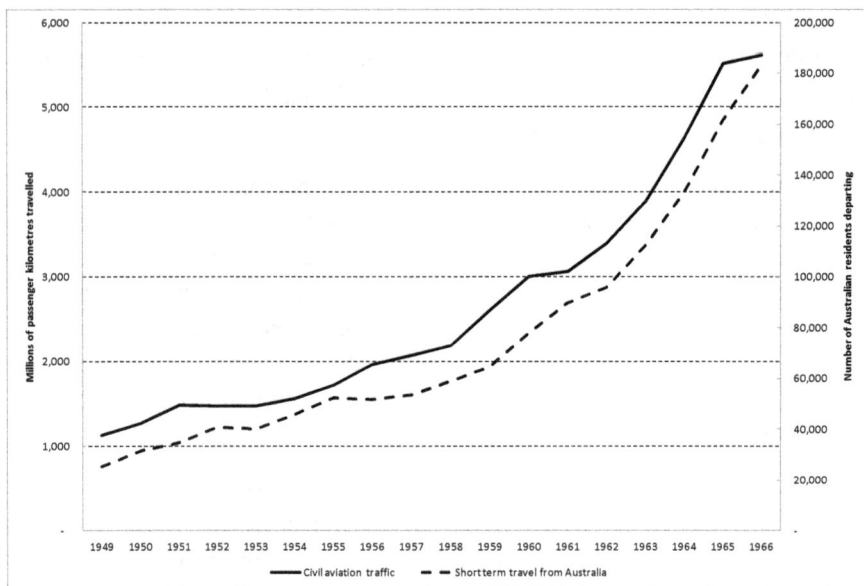

Source: Brian R. Mitchell, 2003, *International Historical Statistics: Africa, Asia & Oceania, 1750-2000*, Palgrave Macmillan, Basingstoke.

Table 4 illustrates affordability and flight time trends for the iconic "Kangaroo Route" between Sydney and London with a stopover in Asia or even

Europe. Affordability in this context refers to the numbers of weeks it would take for a person on average earnings to be able to purchase a return economy-class ticket for this flight. As indicated by the Table, the affordability of flying the "Kangaroo Route" improved significantly from the early 1950s as did the flying time between the two locations.

Table 4: Affordability and flying time on Sydney-London "Kangaroo Route"

Year	Affordability	Flying time
	Weeks on average earnings to afford a return economy-class ticket	Hours
1951	66.67	n/a
1954	50.49	51.30
1959	35.70	26.00
1971	19.32	22.00

Source: Airways Museum & Civil Aviation Historical Society, airwaysmuseum.com; Peter J. Rimmer, 2005, "Australia Through the Prism of Qantas: Distance Makes a Comeback", *The Otemon Journal of Australian Studies* 31: 135-157.

Housing

Special attention should be reserved to changes in affordability and quality of housing in Australia from the late 1940s to the late 1960s, given the prominence of housing within the broader policy framework of the Menzies Government. For Menzies himself such policies were of a politically totemic character, given the importance of "homes material, homes human, homes spiritual" as outlined in the famous "Forgotten People" speech of 1942.[57]

The considerable increase in homeownership throughout the country was an unquestionable hallmark of Australian experience during the mid-twentieth century.[58] According to Commonwealth Bureau of Census and Statistics (later Australian Bureau of Statistics) data, about 53 percent of all occupied private dwellings were owned by households (with or without a mortgage) in 1947. This figure steadily rose to about 63 percent in 1954, about 70 percent in 1961 and about 71 percent in 1966.[59] In a similar vein, the share of renters of private dwellings fell from about 44 percent in 1947 to about 27 percent by 1966.

The available statistics also indicate that as the average Australian household size declined, from 3.8 people per household in 1947 to 3.5 in 1966, the average size of new homes increased. In 1955 it was estimated that the average new house size in Australia was 115 metres squared, which rose to 130 metres squared by 1970.[60] These trends ensured that the number of rooms per dwelling, and rooms per occupant, increased from the late 1940s through to the late 1960s.[61]

Contrasting the experience of declining housing affordability during the late twentieth and early twenty-first centuries in Australia, the Menzies era was characterised by relatively stable affordability with the number of weeks for a person on average earnings to be able to purchase a median price capital-city house remaining relatively steady at 223 weeks since the early 1950s (Figure 13).

Figure 13: Housing affordability

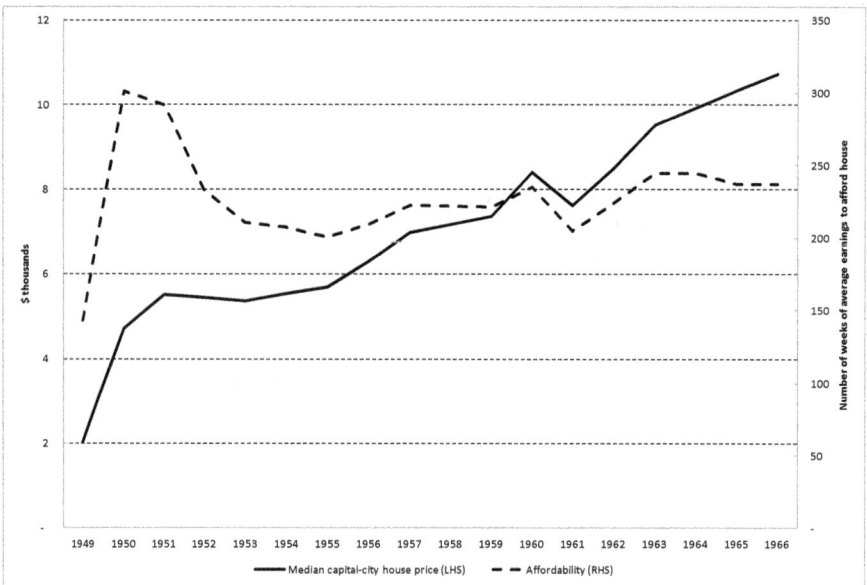

Median capital-city house price (LHS)   Affordability (RHS)

Source: Measuring Worth, www.measuringworth.com; Nigel David Stapledon, 2007, "Long Term Housing Prices in Australia and Some Economic Perspectives", University of New South Wales, Doctorate of Philosophy thesis.

Responding to the housing shortages evident through the period stretching from the Depression to the Second World War, and politically sensitive to accusations of neglect in housing policy which arose during the early 1950s, the Menzies Government devised several ways to stimulate the outright ownership of homes using the leverage of public funding and regulatory policies.

In an agreement with the State governments, the Menzies Government encouraged the States to sell their public housing stock to prospective private purchasers on credit terms, rather than maintaining these as public housing stock. Within four years of this arrangement being adopted, more than 75 percent of the houses being built each year under the Commonwealth-State Housing Agreement (CSHA) were sold. In 1956, the CSHA was renegotiated so that 20 percent (later 30 percent) of federal funding was passed on to building societies for lending to people either to buy or build housing.

The motivational underpinnings for these policies were outlined by the Minister for National Development, Senator W.H. (later Sir William) Spooner:

> [w]e take the view that people who have worked and saved to get enough money to put a deposit on their own homes are at least as entitled to receive some aid from the community's funds as is the person who seeks to solve his housing problem by going on a [State] Housing Commission waiting list.[62]

Other policies were enacted during the 1960s to promote the further acquisition of homes in the Australian property market. In 1964 the Government provided cash payments under a Home Savings Grants Scheme, easing the constraints experienced by young people seeking to purchase their first home. A year later, the Menzies Government created the Housing Loans Insurance Corporation, encouraging institutional lenders to advance additional loans to homebuyers by insuring loans of up to 95 percent of the value of a house worth up to $15 000.

Between 1947 and 1971 the total stock of dwellings in Australia increased from 1.92 million units to 4.01 million units. More than a third of the additional dwellings were built for government authorities or for buyers whose purchase loans were financed by Commonwealth funds. 365 000 dwellings alone were constructed under CSHA provisions, or through the initiative of State governments.

International comparisons

Although international comparisons across the entire range of living standards indicators presented in this essay are not directly available, it is nonetheless possible to use an admittedly highly selective array of indicators to assess Australia's living standards against other major countries during the Menzies period.

Trends in average life expectancy at birth of the total population for nine developed countries (including Australia) are depicted in Figure 14. Whilst Australia recorded a respectable improvement in life expectancy of 1.6 years from 1949 to 1966, other countries recorded relatively stronger increases partly on account of improvements in public health standards. These included Japan, which registered an average 13.3 years life expectancy improvement, France (6.6 years), Canada (4.3 years), and (West) Germany and Sweden (3.3 years).

Figure 14: Life expectancy at birth, selected countries, 1949 and 1966

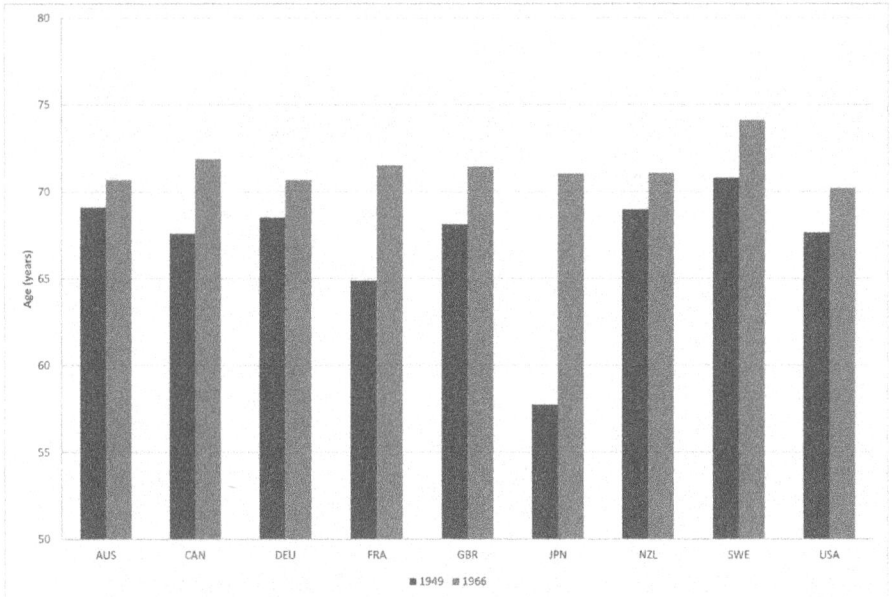

The countries represented in this Figure are Australia (AUS), Canada (CAN), (West) Germany (DEU), France (FRA), the United Kingdom (GBR), Japan (JPN), New Zealand (NZL), Sweden (SWE), and the United States (USA).

Source: Human Mortality Database, www.mortality.org.

As already discussed, the level of human capital accumulated within a country may be proxied by indicators of the average years of schooling recorded amongst the working-age population. Table 5 illustrates that by the mid-1960s Australians aged between 15 and 64 years on average had attained about nine years of school education, behind only the United States and New Zealand (ten years of schooling on average).

From 1950 to 1965, Australians on average attained an additional year of schooling, exceeding the increase in the average years of schooling attained by Japan (0.9 years), New Zealand (0.8 years), France (0.4 years) and Germany (0.3 years).

Table 5: School education attainment, selected countries, 15-64 years

	AUS	CAN	DEU	FRA	GBR	JPN	NZL	SWE	USA
1950	8.2	7.8	7.2	4.4	6.5	6.9	9.3	7.0	8.7
1955	8.5	8.1	7.5	4.6	6.7	7.4	9.7	7.3	9.1
1960	8.8	8.6	7.5	4.3	7.0	7.8	10.1	7.7	9.6
1965	9.2	8.9	7.5	4.8	7.7	7.8	10.2	8.1	10.4

The countries represented in this Table are Australia (AUS), Canada (CAN), (West) Germany (DEU), France (FRA), the United Kingdom (GBR), Japan (JPN), New Zealand (NZL), Sweden (SWE), and the United States (USA).

Source: Barro-Lee Educational Attainment Dataset, http://www.barrolee.com/

Using the "Penn World Table" historical time series estimates provided by the University of Groningen, Netherlands, it is possible to estimate the level of real per capita consumption expenditure by Australians relative to their counterparts in other countries (Figure 15).

Figure 15: Australian real consumption expenditures relative to other selected countries, 1950 to 1966

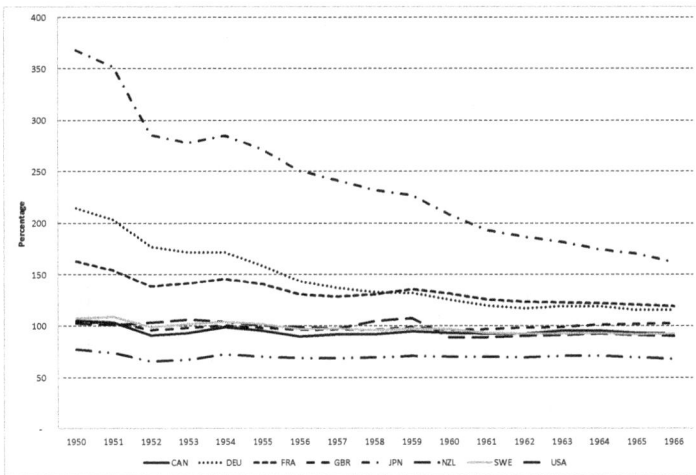

Real consumption expenditure per capita estimated in 2005 dollars and expressed in $ US millions. The countries represented in this Figure are Australia (AUS), Canada (CAN), (West) Germany (DEU), France (FRA), the United Kingdom (GBR), Japan (JPN), New Zealand (NZL), Sweden (SWE), and the United States (USA).

Source: Penn World Table Database, http://www.rug.nl/research/ggdc/data/pwt/?lang=en; Angus Maddison, "Statistics on World Population, GDP and Per Capita GDP, 1-2008 AD", http://www.ggdc.net/maddison/oriindex.htm.

During the Menzies era real per capita consumption spending in Australia was comparable to that of most countries selected in the sample, including Canada, New Zealand and the United Kingdom. Unsurprisingly, spending by consumers on a per capita basis in this country far exceeded those in France, Germany and Japan, partly on the basis of capital spending by these nations for reconstruction and general industrialisation purposes.

A notable feature of the data graphically presented in Figure 15 is the persistently lower levels of real per capita consumption expenditures by Australians compared with residents of the United States. The discrepancy in this direct measure of living standards between the two countries provides some affirmation of the anecdotal observations of John Howard, as noted above, concerning the aspirations of ordinary Australians to enjoy a level of material comforts commensurate with their American peers.

In a recent OECD publication the real wages of unskilled male labourers in the construction industry across a set of countries were compared, with nominal wages adjusted by the price of a subsistence basket of goods (based on a standard caloric and protein intake per day, as well as small quantities of clothing and fuel).[63] As shown in Table 6, the number of baskets a building labourer's daily wage purchased in Australia during the 1950s and 1960s largely exceeded that in Europe, but lagged behind North America. This information tends to corroborate the Australia-US discrepancy with respect to consumption expenditures.

Table 6: Real wages of building labourers, selected countries, 1940s to 1970s

	AUS	CAN	DEU	FRA	GBR	JPN	NZL	SWE	USA
1940s	58	52		15	41	8	n/a	42	76
1950s	68	76	23	12	36	7	n/a	23	103
1960s	59	85	41		49	13	n/a	80	153
1970s	97	192	72	31	62	27	n/a	100	179

Real wages expressed in terms of decadal averages. Real wage data proxied by the number of subsistence baskets purchased on a daily wage earned by a building labourer. The countries represented in this Table are Australia (AUS), Canada (CAN), (West) Germany (DEU), France (FRA), the United Kingdom (GBR), Japan (JPN), New Zealand (NZL), Sweden (SWE), and the United States (USA).

Source: Jan Luiten van Zanden, Joerg Baten, Marco Mira d'Ercole, Auke Rijpma, Conal Smith and Marcel Timmer, 2014, *How Was Life? Global Well-Being Since 1820*, OECD, Paris.

On the basis of this admittedly limited assessment, Australia largely provided its citizens with a reasonable standard of living compared to their counterparts in most other developed countries (with some notable exceptions such as the Indigenous population). On the basis of some key economic and social indicators, however, Australia lagged behind the United States during the Menzies period, although it is reasonable to suggest that such observations have persisted well after Menzies' retirement from political office.

Labour market and welfare policies under the Menzies Government: a critical assessment

Successive Australian governments at all levels have elected to intervene in economic and social affairs, simultaneously using a variety of policy instruments in an attempt to achieve certain outcomes. Several policy functions maintained by government have the capacity, at least in theory, to influence trends in living standards in the longer term.

Unsurprisingly, given its longevity in office, the Menzies Government certainly played a critical role in establishing new policies that guided the conduct of individuals, families, firms, community groups and others within Australian society. In other respects, the Commonwealth Government during the 1950s and 1960s maintained longstanding policy institutions, enacting somewhat marginal changes only, out of a concern to ensure political stability or retain electoral support.

It is not possible in this essay to recount every aspect of policy managed by the Menzies Government but, nonetheless, the following sections provide further details about two elements of policy with potentially significant implications for living standards attained by Australians.

During the colonial era in the nineteenth century, the public sector became actively involved in administering regulations designed to influence the nature of agreements between employees and employers about the terms and conditions of work, including the determination of wages (at least for those on lower incomes). The policy framework of the industrial regulatory regime quickly became entrenched during the first two decades of Federation and, despite periods of significant change, the basic policy settings and the political values which underpin them, have been preserved to this day.

Governments have also played a major role, in the fiscal context, of transferring cash payments to politically identified constituencies, on the basis of financial and other categories of need. These constituencies include people unable to find employment, those raising children and those retiring from the workforce on account of old age. The transfers to these and other groups have tended to grow in importance within the Commonwealth Government's overall expenditure mix since Federation.

Industrial relations

The Menzies Government essentially maintained the basic institutional structure of industrial relations, which enabled the Commonwealth to adjudicate inter-state industrial disputes, to interpret and enforce awards, and to set a minimum "basic wage" applicable to all workers.[64] For Menzies these activities, largely presided over by the Conciliation and Arbitration Court (later Commission), made "a powerful contribution to the living standards of unionists" and others involved in the system.[65]

Within the context of great policy esteem for discretionary macroeconomic stabilisation policies, aimed at maintaining full employment, there was a natural and obvious tension between providing adequate settings of wages and conditions for employees, and ensuring employment for all those who wished to work, whilst preserving a cost-competitive environment for domestic producers. These tensions were magnified during periods of elevated price inflation, which proved to be an occasional economic and political scourge for the Menzies Government.

During the Korean War of the early 1950s intense price-inflationary pressures, from external sources, accelerated increases in price-adjusted wages and encouraged the spread of over-award wage agreements. This led to the abandonment of quarterly cost-of-living adjustments (or the "needs" component) to the basic wage in September 1953, on grounds that a lack of change to wage determination principles would induce an unsustainable wage-price spiral as earnings moved ahead of formal awards.[66]

Cessation of regular cost-based adjustments was followed at intervals of one to three years by a series of decisions to adjust wage and pay margins (accounting for skills) across industries. For much of the remaining life of the Menzies Government, the principle of the "capacity of the economy to pay" higher wages tended to become a more important feature in federal wage determinations by the Commission, even if this principle was not clearly defined.[67]

Emergence of this principle as a criterion reflected, at least on the part of some presiding judges at the Commission, a begrudging acknowledgement of centralised wage determination arrangements rendering appropriate labour cost outcomes in the generalised economic interest. Even so, it had been noted that even with removal of cost-of-living adjustments in 1953, the real value of the basic wage remained virtually constant until the late 1960s.[68]

The effectiveness of centralised wage determination during the Menzies period was gradually undermined by the growing willingness of unions and employers to agree upon wage levels "over the award," or outside the regulatory confines of the Conciliation and Arbitration Commission. Direct negotiations became more widespread during the 1960s, threatening to erode the authority of governments in wage-setting processes.

Acceding to proposals put forward by employer groups during the 1960s, the Commission eventually adopted a "total wage" concept which amalgamated the basic wage and award margins. This offered some prospect for more effective governmental control over both total wage increases and wage differentials, but essentially unravelled, once again, in the late 1960s as industrial agitation grew in response to efforts to prevent wage rises awarded to workers in the metal trades "flowing on" to other industries.[69]

Gerard Henderson, in his 1983 essay depicting the prevailing "Industrial Relations Club," described how Sir Richard Kirby, in his capacity as President of the Commission, in fact applauded the inability of the body to enforce awards or orders emphasising the need for wages restraint:

> it is ... beyond controversy that the system works better when the arbitrating body has not the responsibility and distraction of enforcing awards. It is all to the good that the Commission's statutory aim of promoting goodwill in industry by conciliation and arbitration should not be made more difficult by the conflicting power of punishment.[70]

These developments contributed to rampant wage-price spirals. These soon degenerated into the "stagflation" of coincidentally high unemployment and high price-inflation rates, which contributed to the deteriorating living standards experienced by many Australians during the 1970s.

Development of the services sector of the economy, predominated by the roles played by the public sector, had implications for the ability of the regulated industrial relations systems to arbitrate wages disputes in such a way as to ensure effective management of labour costs within the Australian economy.

An interesting case study along these lines was the 1961 determination by the Commission to award substantial pay increases to people employed within the engineering professions on the basis of the "work value" they provided in (mainly public sector) workplaces. The increases in salaries awarded ranged from £100 to £600 per annum for employees within the Commonwealth public service, and up to £2 200 per annum in other places of employment.[71]

This later *Engineers' Case* ensured that engineering professional associations, on behalf of their members, succeeded in altering the methodology of wage determination away from the basic-wage-cum-margins approach for skills characteristic of most claims before arbitration tribunals by this occupation and employees in other industries, toward a broader, but more difficult to establish, notion of work value.[72]

Confirming the fears of public service and other employer groups, the Commission's decision in the case encouraged other professions to mobilise, forwarding claims for additional wages and salaries on a work value basis. For example, two months after the judgment was handed down, the Australian Council of Salaried and Professional Employees' Organisations sought pay increases of £300 per annum for 100 000 white-collar workers in New South Wales.[73]

As observed by Sol Encel at the time, award rulings for the emerging professional classes during the 1960s would affect financial relationships between levels of government:

> With the establishment of national professional standards, this problem will become more acute for State governments, which find that they are forced to provide salaries and conditions beyond the level at which they would prefer to operate. The consequence can only be to increase the financial dependence of the States on the Commonwealth, and thus to give the process of political centralization a further push. In this respect, Australia conforms to the general pattern of the modern industrial state, where the enforcement of national standards by professional and occupational groups has been the normal precursor of the acceptance of responsibility by the central government for the maintenance of these standards.[74]

There seems little doubt that with relatively low unemployment rates throughout the country, the Menzies Government attained, by and large, its stated objective to maintain full employment. It could also be said the improvements in living standards enjoyed by those working during the post-war "long boom" masked problems in the institutional design of the framework for Australian industrial relations, presided over by the Menzies Government but which, nonetheless, did not become so apparent until well after Robert Menzies' retirement.

Henderson observed significant increases in average weekly earnings during the Menzies era were often followed by peaks in aggregate employment, with obviously adverse implications for the living standards of those not employed – particularly people with fewer skills – as a result of the wage hikes. This casual observation appears to have been affirmed by more rigorous economic analysis with, for example, John Freebairn and Glenn Withers suggesting relative wages were unresponsive to labour market imbalances:

> [c]ertainly there is no evidence that the Arbitration system reflects market forces in its relative award determination. There is little evidence that changes in relative award wages and changes in relative unemployment/vacancies act jointly to clear occupation markets after exogenous supply and demand shifts.[75]

Aggregate statistical measures confirming low unemployment at the national level also tended to mask issues concerning the effect of industrial relations system rulings upon people on the fringes of formal labour markets. It has been claimed, for example, that the provision of full award wages to Indigenous people working in cattle stations in the Northern Territory led to a loss in employment for these workers and, in some instances, forcing Indigenous Australians off their traditional lands for resettlement in townships on welfare payments.[76]

Although some have disputed the contribution of the Commission's decision in inducing unemployment among the cattle stations, citing such matters as drought conditions, increasing capital utilisation, and a decline in the relative economic importance of the livestock industries.[77] Whilst certainly race-based distinctions in relation to wages and conditions are intolerable, this case nonetheless highlighted the potential risks surrounding the divorce between centralised wage determination and economic and financial circumstances at the firm level.

It should be unsurprising that the Australian industrial relations system may have operated in ways detrimental to the interests of some workers given the conflicting objectives embedded within the Australian industrial relations system, arguably from its very inception.

Ideally, the purpose of industrial relations regulation should be to facilitate the process by which employees and employers reach mutually advantageous agreements concerning the terms and conditions of employment.[78] In practice, the framework has invariably been influenced by a "quite ostensibly social policy criterion" of ensuring wages for workers so they may live in reasonable comfort:

> the legacy of federal arbitration was … an ambivalent one, since, to the extent that the 'living wage' succeeded in raising the wages floor, and, thereby, compressing the overall distribution of incomes, it was doing things that in other climes and later times were to be functions of advanced social security systems.[79]

More generally, even as early as the 1960s, academic economists, business managers and political figures expressed growing disquiet about poor labour productivity and underperformance, especially from an internationally comparative perspective, even if the loudest concerns had passed by Menzies' political career.

To the extent that the industrial relations regime of the Menzies period ensured that wages were loosely set, if at all, in reference to productivity performances in the business establishments, individual workers at least in some industries or occupations may have been deprived of potentially greater wage gains (conditional upon improving production per effective hours worked) than would have been otherwise the case. Worse still, some workers may have even been priced out of the labour market as a result of the centralised industrial relations regulatory framework.

Social welfare transfers

After the defeat of the Labor Government in 1949, the Menzies Government played an active role in maintaining and, indeed, extending, the welfare state by identifying new areas of need amongst those in the electorate already in the receipt of benefits, and by identifying groups similar to those already in receipt of transfers.

In 1950, for example, the Menzies Government extended child endowment (a scheme introduced by the first Menzies Government in 1941) to the first (or only) child. Increases in the rates of endowment, in 1964 and 1967, were intended to diminish poverty among large families, whilst student children between 16 and 21 years of age were rendered eligible to receive benefits under the scheme in 1964.[80] These measures effectively rendered the endowment scheme as a universal benefit.

Individuals in receipt of various pension payments also received increases in assistance during the life of the Menzies Government. For example, in 1956, pensionable widows were awarded higher pensions if they had more than one dependent child under the age of sixteen. By 1963 this criterion was relaxed by the making of a payment in respect of first (or only) children and a separate mother's allowance, in addition to the pension.

Widows and single age and invalid pensioners, who paid rent and were wholly dependent on pensions, were provided discretionary supplemental assistance from 1958. Age pensions, in particular, received a wide variety of supplementary benefits including the medical scheme, as noted above, and funeral benefits, concessions from public sector trading enterprises in the form of reduced telephone rental rates, transport fares, radio and television licence fees, and reduced local government rates.[81]

During the Menzies era the financial position of welfare beneficiaries had improved. Payment rates for age, invalid and widows' pensions were frequently adjusted upwards and, since the 1950s, they had increased more rapidly than living costs generally.

With respect to the age pension, more Australians were able to access this payment as the Menzies Government gradually relaxed means testing provisions. In 1954, income from property was excluded from means testing arrangements; and, in 1961, a significant reform was enacted to treat income and property as interdependent under a merged means test.

These policies effectively signalled the end of previous proposals by liberal-conservative governments in Australia to introduce a European-style contributory scheme as a way of helping to contain the overall costs of welfare provision whilst eliminating the need for means testing that posed as a penalty upon thriftiness amongst eligible recipients.[82]

In this regard, Graeme Starr has noted the irony that Menzies' political detractors admonished him for not abolishing the means test on age pensions altogether, but that the legacy of his government is now criticised for providing "middle class welfare" to those not necessarily in the most financially pressing circumstances.[83]

Whilst it is true that the unique political circumstances in Australia of the mid-twentieth century need to be accorded due consideration when assessing the Menzies era, the inertia of political change means that actions undertaken by governments decades ago can exert powerful economic, financial and social pressures many years, if not decades, later. In addition, actions undertaken at any given time serve as precedents for future governments, setting a certain element of "path dependency" with regard to the course of policy development.

Although it should be clear that the Menzies Government continued to preside over a welfare system which, on an internationally comparative basis, emphasised the provision of means-tested benefits, there were policy developments, at least at the margin, which partially eroded this distinctive feature of Australian welfarism.

Gwen Gray and John Murphy, in their assessments of social policies in the Menzies period, note that the Commonwealth gradually extended the coverage of cash and in-kind welfare programs to a larger proportion of the population.[84] With regard to the age pension, for example, relaxation of means testing and increases in payment rates meant the eligible (full or part) pension population rose from about 38 percent in 1947 to about 53 percent in 1966.

Ironically, such developments were instigated by the Menzies Government to promote reward for "thrift" of whichever means were available to families, as well as to facilitate a sense of "self-reliance" by way of personal consumption activity. These developments, on their own basis, induced a greater sense of dependency by the so-called "independent" middle classes upon government, and in so doing diminished the extent to which welfare remained closely targeted to those in need.

Successive governments have tended to adjust welfare policies at the margins in efforts to effect modest changes to the extent to which payments and services are targeted to those on lower incomes. The basic policy "infrastructure" of subsidies and transfers to individuals and families who can afford to look after their own needs was, however, maintained under Menzies and, indeed, expanded, so as to placate important political constituencies.

In budgetary terms, this process was reflected in the growth of Commonwealth social welfare spending from about four percent of GDP in 1949 to about nine percent in 2013, although it has also been argued that large-scale immigration, full employment and high economic growth combined, at least to some extent, to contain growth in cash transfers.[85]

Countering the notion that criticism of the Menzies record can only be gleaned through a modern perspective, it should be stressed that alteration in welfare policy stance towards those better-off fostered a set of political difficulties for

214

the Liberal-Country Party Coalition Government, particularly the Gorton and McMahon governments of the late 1960s and early 1970s.

The available statistical evidence indicates that overall inequality in Australian society declined during the Menzies period, as indicated by the reduction in the Gini coefficient from 0.38 in 1950 to 0.35 in 1960 and 0.32 in 1970,[86] and that the progressive income tax system worked to suppress income inequalities further. The transfer of cash from higher income to lower income earners also would have had the desired effect, even if non-cash benefits such as education and health care were largely not subjected to means testing arrangements.

Despite these beneficial outcomes from an equity standpoint, critics of the Coalition increasingly pointed to the presence of absolute poverty in various locations and the enactment of certain policies, such as housing subsidies and other elements of middle class welfare, in drawing attention to perceived inadequacies of the Menzies legacy in managing redistributionist programs.

Academic researchers, most notably Ronald F. Henderson, and non-government welfare organisations pointed to a proportion of the population deemed to be living in "chronic poverty," whereas the journalist John Stubbs wrote in his book, *The Hidden People*, about the poor, including pensioners, the unemployed, Indigenous people, widowed women, and homeless men, who "have been hidden by the increasing affluence of the rest of our society, and buried in the statistics."[87]

These issues were evocatively exploited in a political sense by the Labor Party in opposition under Gough Whitlam. The eventual election of a government led by Whitlam in 1972 facilitated a rapid expansion of welfare state programs to overcome the alleged neglect by its political predecessors that substantially elevated the overall size of government in the process.

Conclusion

Notwithstanding a strain in modern Australian party political and quasi-party political rhetoric that the Menzies era was marked by economic and social mediocrity and underachievement, most Australians enjoyed substantial economic and social improvements.

Living standards for the average Australian, and even for certain groupings often portrayed as disproportionately suffering from disadvantage, were improving during Menzies' prime ministership. Incomes and wages for people were rising; health outcomes improved; women and men enjoyed greater educational opportunity and attainment; and consumers had ready access to more affordable goods and services, with a wider array of conveniences within reach of the ordinary Australian.

Very great care must be taken when attributing the causes of these developments to specific factors, particularly public policy actions by governments. This stems, in no small part, from a complex "entangled political economy" of fiscal and regulatory interventions interwoven with action undertaken by civil societal actors, both domestically and abroad.[88]

The fortuitous material circumstances enjoyed by many Australians were doubtlessly the product of many developments, many of which were beyond the direct influence of public policies. The revival of post-war private sector economies, in Australia and the OECD countries, and the "Golden Age" of technological innovation from 1945 to 1971,[89] were, for instance, among the key determinants of improving living standards in Australia during the Menzies era.

In a large part, the policies of the Menzies period also reflected continuation of a long-term consensus on the basics of Australian economic policy, popularly labelled "The Australian Settlement."[90] This included industry protection, centralised wage setting and arbitration, state paternalism, and selective migration, all of which in various ways constrained the long run economic and social potential of inhabitants situated on this continent. To this could be added the activist role of the Menzies Government in formalising the post-war welfare state, the hazardous economic and fiscal consequences of which loom as most pressing in the years and decades to come.

Regardless of which causes of living standards improvements predominated during the 1950s and 1960s, an enduring feature of the electoral successes of the Menzies Government was, surely, its capacity to point to improvements in generalised living standards under its watch, even if its direct contribution to such outcomes was marginal at best; or perverse, in some instances, at their worst.

Even as researchers in economics, political science and other social science disciplines continue to debate the extent to which policies enacted by Menzies and his government shaped living standards during the 1950s and 1960s, this does not overshadow the fact that, on the basis of numerous measurements, the "condition of the people" was, clearly, generally much improved during the Menzies years.

Endnotes

[1] Sir Robert Gordon Menzies, 1963, Federal Election 1963 Policy Speech, http://australianpolitics.com/downloads/1963/63-11-12_menzies-election-policy-speech.pdf

[2] Sir Robert Gordon Menzies, *Afternoon Light: Some Memories of Men and Events*, Penguin Books, Cassell Australia, 1967, 282.

[3] F.C. Benham, *Benham's Economics: A General Introduction*, edited by F.W. Paish, seventh edition, Pitman, London, 1964, 24.

[4] Ian W. McLean, 1987, "Economic wellbeing", in Rodney Maddock and Ian W. McLean, eds., *The Australian Economy in the Long Run*, Cambridge University Press, Cambridge; Tom Kryger, 2000, "Living Standards", Parliament of Australia, Parliamentary Library Current Issues Brief No. 4; Joseph E. Stiglitz, Amartya Sen and Jean-Paul Fitoussi, 2009, *Report by the Commission on the Measurement of Economic Performance and Social Progress*, http://www.stiglitzsen-fitoussi.fr/en/index.htm; Jan Luiten van Zanden, Joerg Baten, Marco Mira d'Ercole, Auke Rijpma, Conal Smith and Marcel Timmer, 2014, *How Was Life? Global Well-Being Since 1820*, OECD, Paris.

[5] Mikayla Novak, 2010, "A partial defence of GDP", ABC Drum Online, 6 October; Diane Coyle, 2014, *GDP: A Brief But Affectionate History*, Princeton University Press, Princeton.

[6] Australian Bureau of Statistics, "What approach did the ABS take in presenting progress data?", Measures of Australia's Progress, 2010, cat. no. 1370.0.

[7] For example, Jonathan Pincus, 2014, "The Wellbeing of the Australian People: Comments on the Treasury's Framework", in Andrew Podger and Dennis Trewin, eds., *Measuring and Promoting Wellbeing: How Important is Economic Growth?: Essays in Honour of Ian Castles AO and a Selection of Castles' Papers*, ANU Press, Canberra.

[8] J.S.G. Wilson, 1942, "The Octopus of Control (Australia's War Economy – May to October, 1942)", *The Economic Record* 18 (2): 192-208, 208.

[9] Commonwealth Bureau of Census and Statistics, 1944, *Official Year Book of the Commonwealth of Australia, 1944 and 1945*, No. 36.

[10] "Rush to buy clothes. Melbourne 'Orgy of Spending.' Blankets Gone.", *Sydney Morning Herald*, 7 June 1941.

[11] Stuart Macintyre, 2015, *Australia's Boldest Experiment: War and Reconstruction in the 1940s*, NewSouth Publishing, Sydney, 101.

[12] Kate Darian-Smith, 2009, *On the Home Front – Melbourne in Wartime: 1939-1945*, Melbourne University Press, Carlton.

[13] Kate Darian-Smith, Ibid.; Michael McKernan, 1995, *All In! Fighting the War at Home*, Allen & Unwin, St. Leonards; Mark L. Wahlqvist, ed., 1981, *Food and Nutrition in Australia*, Cassell Australia, North Ryde.

[14] McKernan, op.cit., 147.

[15] Robert Lewis, "The Home Front – World War 2", http://www.anzacday.org.au/history/ww2/homefront/overview.html; Kate Darian-Smith, 1996, "War and Australian Society", in Joan Beaumont, ed., *Australia's War, 1939-45*, Allen & Unwin, St. Leonards.

[16] Australian War Memorial, "Reserved Occupations, Second World War", https://www.awm.gov.au/encyclopedia/homefront/reserved_occupations/

[17] Macintyre, op. cit.

[18] Ibid., 136.

[19] Ian W. McLean, *Why Australia Prospered: The Shifting Sources of Economic Growth*, Princeton University Press, Princeton, 2013, 178. Similar suggestions were made in John Howard, *The Menzies Era*, HarperCollins Publishers, Sydney, 2014, 371.

[20] Measuring Worth, www.measuringworth.com; Alan Barnard, 1987, "Government Finance", in Wray Vamplew, ed., *Australians, Historical Statistics*, Fairfax, Syme and Weldon Associates, Sydney.

[21] Steven Horwitz and Michael J. McPhillips, 2013, "The Reality of the Wartime Economy: More Historical Evidence on Whether World War II Ended the Great Depression", *The Independent Review* 17 (3): 325-347.

[22] National Archives of Australia, 2008, Memento Magazine, no. 34, http://www.naa.gov.au/naaresources/publications/memento/pdf/memento34.pdf

[23] McKernan, op. cit., 149.

[24] Kate Darian-Smith, op. cit., 34.

[25] McKernan, op. cit., 155-6.

[26] Kate Darian-Smith, op. cit., 35.

[27] Macintyre, op. cit., 167.

[28] Ibid., 177.

[29] Kate Darian-Smith, op. cit., 84.

[30] Lorna Froude, "Petrol rationing in Australia during the Second World War", *Journal of the Australian War Memorial* 36 (May), https://www.awm.gov.au/journal/j36/petrol.asp#88

[31] Kate Darian-Smith, op. cit., 45.

[32] McKernan, op. cit., 142.

[33] Kate Darian-Smith, op. cit.

[34] Timothy Blum, 2011, "Profits Over Patriotism: Black Market Crime in World War II Sydney", University of Sydney, Bachelor of Arts (Honours) Thesis manuscript; McKernan, op. cit., 162.

[35] Howard, op. cit., 8-9.

[36] Senator Hon. Scott Ryan, 2009, "Menzies: The most important election win in our history", http://scottryan.com.au/media/article/menzies-the-most-important-election-win-in-our-history

[37] Wolfgang Kasper, 1986, "Australia's Negative Growth Rate", *IPA Review* 40 (1): 35-7.

[38] Glenn Withers, 2002, "The economics of immigration", The Australian National University, Graduate Program in Public Policy, Discussion Paper No. 95.

[39] J.B. Brigden, D.B. Copland, E.C. Dyason, L.F. Giblin and C.H. Wickens, *The Australian Tariff: An Economic Inquiry*, Melbourne University Press, Melbourne, 1929.

[40] However, it could be argued immigration induced by the prospect of higher wages in tariff-protected manufacturing might have acted, to some extent, to ameliorate the increase in real wages.

[41] Anderson, op. cit.

[42] Bryan Haig and Jennifer Anderssen, 2007, "Australian Consumption Expenditure and Real Income: 1900 to 2003-2004", *The Economic Record* 83 (263): 416-31.

[43] Matthew Butlin, Robert Dixon and Peter J. Lloyd, 2015, "Statistical Appendix: selected data series, 1800-2010", in Simon Ville and Glenn Withers, eds., *The Cambridge Economic History of Australia*, Cambridge University Press, Cambridge.

[44] For a critique of industry assistance to agriculture, see E. Sieper, 1982, *Rationalising Rustic Regulation*, The Centre for Independent Studies, Research Studies in Government Regulation No. 2, St. Leonards.

[45] W.M. Corden, "The tariff", in A. Hunter, ed., *The Economics of Australian Industry*, Melbourne University Press, Melbourne, 1963; W.M. Corden, 1966, "The Structure of a Tariff System and the Effective Protection Rate", *Journal of Political Economy* 74: 221-37; Max Corden, 2005, "Effective Protection and I", *History of Economics Review* 42: 1-11.

[46] Alf Rattigan, *Industry Assistance: The Inside Story*, Melbourne University Press, Melbourne, 1986.

[47] Benham, op. cit., 490-1.

[48] Snowy Hydro, "The History", http://www.snowyhydro.com.au/energy/hydro/the-history/

[49] Greg Whitwell, *Making The Market: The Rise of Consumer Society*, McPhee Gribble, Fitzroy, 1989.

[50] Graeme Donald Snooks, *Portrait of the Family within the Total Economy: A Study in Longrun Dynamics, Australia 1788-1990*, Cambridge University Press, Cambridge, 1994, 58.

[51] Tony Dingle, "Consumer Goods, Housewives and Time Use in the Suburban Home from the 1920s to the 1980s", in Robert Crawford, Judith Smart and Kim Humphrey, eds., *Consumer Australia: Historical Perspectives*, Cambridge Scholars Publishing, Newcastle, 2010.

[52] Bureau of Transport and Communication Economics, 1994, "Statistical summary of the communications, entertainment and information industries", Communications Futures Project, Work in Progress Paper No. 1, Canberra.

[53] Margaret G. Myers, 1961, "The Control of Consumer Credit in Australia", *Journal of Finance* 16 (3): 409-22, 412-3.

[54] Pierre van der Eng, 2008, "Consumer Credit in Australia During the 20th Century", Australian National University, School of Management, Marketing and International Business, Working Paper No. 489.

[55] Matt Bailey, "Inside Suburban 'Persian Bazaars': The Reception of Regional Shopping Centres in Sydney during the 1960s", in Crawford, Smart and Humphrey, op. cit., 2010.

[56] Productivity Commission, 2011, *Economic Structure and Performance of the Australian Retail Industry*, Report No. 56, Canberra, 14.

[57] Robert Menzies, *The Forgotten People: And Other Studies in Democracy*, with introductory essay by David Kemp, Liberal Party of Australia (Victorian Division), Melbourne, 2011.

[58] Matters of changing homeownership rates, and the development of Australian suburban areas, are discussed in greater detail in the essay by Lionel Frost in this volume.

[59] Tony Kryger, 2009, "Home ownership in Australia – data and trends", Parliament of Australia, Department of Parliamentary Services, Parliamentary Library, Research Paper No. 21.

[60] Clive Hamilton and Richard Denniss, *Affluenza: When Too Much is Never Enough*, Allen & Unwin, Crows Nest, 2005.

[61] McLean, op. cit., 328.

[62] Cited in Graeme Starr, "Menzies and Post-War Prosperity", in J.R. Nethercote, ed., *Liberalism and the Australian Federation*, The Federation Press, Annandale, 2001, 190.

[63] van Zanden, et. al., op. cit., Ch. 4.

[64] Consistent with the previously decentralised nature of industrial relations regulation in Australia, state governments during the Menzies period also played a major role in settling disputes and setting minimum wages within the confines of their respective jurisdictions.

[65] Hon. Sir Robert Gordon Menzies, 1955, Federal Election 1955 Policy Speech, http://electionspeeches.moadoph.gov.au/speeches/1955-robert-menzies

[66] J. Rob Bray, *Reflections on the Evolution of the Minimum Wage in Australia: Options for the Future*, Australian National University, Research School of Economics, 2013; N.G. Butlin, A. Barnard and J.J. Pincus, *Government and Capitalism: Public and Private Choice in Twentieth Century Australia*, George Allen & Union, Sydney, 1982; Glenn Withers, "Labour", in Rodney Maddock and Ian W. McLean, eds., *The Australian Economy in the Long Run*, Cambridge University Press, Cambridge, 1987.

[67] Albert George Kenwood, *Australian Economic Institutions since Federation: An Introduction*, Oxford University Press, Melbourne, 1995, 126.

[68] Flora Gill, 1987, "Determination of Wage Relativities Under the Federal Tribunal: 1953-1974", Australian National University, Department of Economics, Working Paper in Economic History No. 88.

[69] Ibid., 126-7.

[70] Gerard Henderson, 1983, "The Industrial Relations Club", *Quadrant* 27 (9): 21-9.

[71] P.C. Molhuysen, 1962, "The Professional Engineers' Case", *Australian Economic Papers* 1 (1): 57-78.

[72] S. Encel, 1964, "Social Implications of the Engineers' Cases", *Journal of Industrial Relations* 6: 61-6.

[73] Molhuysen, op. cit., 65.

[74] Encel, op. cit. 66.

[75] John Freebairn and Glenn Withers, 1977, "The Performance of Manpower Forecasting Techniques in Australian Labour Markets", 4 (1): 13-31.

[76] Gerard Henderson, "How to create unemployment: the Arbitration Commission and the Aborigines", in John Hyde and John Nurick, eds., *Wages Wasteland: A Radical Examination of the Australian Wage Fixing System*, Hale & Iremonger, Sydney, 1985; Sir John Kerr, "Reflections on the Northern Territory Cattle Station Industry Award Case of 1965 and the O'Shea Case of 1969", in H.R. Nicholls Society, *Arbitration in Contempt: The Proceedings of the Inaugural Seminar of the H.R. Nicholls Society*, H.R. Nicholls Society, Melbourne, 1986.

[77] Joe Isaac and Stuart Macintyre, *The New Province of Law and Order: 100 Years of Australian*

Industrial Conciliation and Arbitration, Cambridge University Press, Cambridge, 2004; Fiona Skyring, "Low Wages, Low Rents, and Pension Cheques: The Introduction of Equal Wages in the Kimberley, 1968-1969", in Natasha Fijn, ed., *Indigenous Participation in Australian Economies II: Historical Engagements and Cultural Enterprises*, ANU Press, Canberra, 2012.

[78] Henry Ergas, 2015, "IR Report: Productivity Commission falls short of the mark", *The Australian*, 9 August.

[79] Francis G. Castles and John Uhr, 2002, "Federalism and the Welfare State: Australia", The Australian National University, Research School of Social Sciences, 14.

[80] Dale Daniels, 2009, "Social security payments for people caring for children, 1912 to 2008: a chronology", Parliament of Australia, Parliamentary Library Background Note.

[81] Ronald Mendelsohn, *The Condition of The People: Social Welfare in Australia, 1900-1975*, George Allen & Unwin, Sydney, 1979.

[82] Thomas Henry Kewley, *Social Security in Australia, 1900-72*, Sydney University Press, Sydney, 1973.

[83] Graeme Starr, op. cit., 191.

[84] Gwen Gray, "Social Policy", in Scott Prasser, J.R. Nethercote and John Warhurst, eds., *The Menzies Era: A Reappraisal of Government, Politics and Policy*, Hale & Iremonger, Sydney, 1995; John Murphy, "Social Policy and the Family", in Scott Prasser, J. R. Nethercote and John Warhurst, eds., *The Menzies Era: A Reappraisal of Government, Politics and Policy*, Hale & Iremonger, Sydney, 1995.

[85] Mikayla Novak, "The welfare state grows and grows", in Gary Johns, ed., *Right Social Justice: Better Ways to Help the Poor*, Connor Court Publishing, Ballan, 2012. Francis G. Castles and John Uhr, op. cit.

[86] van Zanden, et. al., 2014, op. cit., 206; Andrew Leigh, 2005, "Deriving Long-Run Inequality Series from Tax Data", *The Economic Record* 81 (255): S58-S70. The Gini coefficient is an indicator of the degree of income distribution within society ranging between zero and one, with a value of zero corresponds with perfect equality of income distribution (all people earn the same income) and one corresponds with perfect inequality (one person earns all income).

[87] John Stubbs, *The Hidden People: Poverty in Australia*, Cheshire-Lansdowne, Melbourne, 1966; Peter Hollingworth, *The Powerless Poor: A Comprehensive Guide to Poverty in Australia*, Stockland Press, North Melbourne, 1973.

[88] Richard E. Wagner, 2014, "Politics as a Peculiar Business: Additive vs. Entangled Political Economy", George Mason University, Department of Economics, Working Paper No. 14-23.

[89] Michael Hanlon, 2014, "The golden quarter", *Aeon magazine*, 3 December, http://aeon.co/magazine/science/why-has-human-progress-ground-to-a-halt/

[90] Paul Kelly, *The End of Certainty: Power, Politics and Business in Australia*, Allen & Unwin, St. Leonards, 1994.

Menzies with the Prime Minister of Japan, Nobusuke Kishi, at the signing of the historic Australian Japan Commerce Agreement of 1957

Menzies greeted by villagers in Papua New Guinea

Menzies in talks with Indonesian President, Dr Sukarno, in Jakarta 1959. Menzies was the first Australian prime minister to visit Indonesia

Meeting with John F. Kennedy in the White House, 1962

Menzies meets the Press Gallery in his office, Parliament House, Canberra

Menzies in talks with US President Lyndon B. Johnson at the White House, 1964

Menzies outside the Lodge in Canberra with the family dog, Pie, 1962

Menzies, a keen photographer, in action

Menzies with Athol Townley, Minister for Immigration and later Minister for Defence

Political adversaries Robert Menzies and Arthur Calwell share a light-hearted moment at the opening of the R.G. Menzies Library at the Australian National University. The two men enjoyed an amicable relationship outside the parliamentary chamber. Seated to the other side of Menzies is ANU Chancellor, H.C. "Nugget" Coombs.

Portrait of Sir Robert Menzies in his robes as a Knight of the Most
Ancient and Most Noble Order of the Thistle, 1963

Dame Pattie and Sir Robert Menzies, 1968, portrait by Godfrey Argent

9

Town and Country in the Menzies Years

Lionel Frost

James Menzies, born in Ballarat in 1862 to parents who had migrated from Scotland, was a skilled coach-painter. He decorated carriages, railway engines and farm machinery. James married Kate Sampson (born in 1866), the daughter of a Cornish miner who had migrated to Ballarat during the gold rush.[1] In 1893 James and Kate moved with their three children to a new Mallee township, Jeparit, where Kate's brother was the proprietor and editor of the local newspaper. Jeparit had been founded in 1889, when the area's pastoral leases expired and the Victorian Lands Department made 320-acre blocks available for selection. The land was attractive because the light soil could be cultivated easily and was suited to wheat-growing. The tough, dense mallee scrub could be cleared cheaply by rolling and burning. Jeparit had only a few shops in 1893. The Menzies operated a general store, providing credit to farming families until harvest time. Their fourth child, Robert, was born in one of the rooms at the back of the store, where the family lived, in 1894.

Robert Menzies recalled: "Life for my parents was, in a financial sense, difficult and even grim."[2] The prosperity of firms in rural towns was linked to the prosperity of local farmers who relied on town products and services for inputs and access to external markets. The spending of farming families and their capacity to repay debts was dependent on the value of the annual harvest. Rainfall in the Mallee region is low and unpredictable, the topsoil is light and fragile, and hot winds can shrivel crops before they are harvested. The flow of farm income virtually ceased during the "Federation Drought" of 1895-1902. In 1898 an *Argus* reporter estimated that 80 percent of the Mallee population was dependent on store credit for food.[3] Farmers were able to clear their debts after the drought broke in 1903-4.[4] The use of seed drills to apply superphosphate and the keeping of sheep on fallowed ground allowed farmers to cash in on a run of good seasons before the Great War.[5] The State government built storages and distribution channels running from rivers and creeks to supply farmers with water for stock and domestic use. As in other regions, settlers and townspeople organised community activities that took the rough edges off pioneer life. James Menzies was a trustee of Jeparit's Methodist Church and a member of the Shire Council, and secured land for the town's showgrounds and memorial hall.

By 1910, demand for Mallee land was booming in Victoria, New South Wales and South Australia. Many farmers owned multiple properties which helped them to defray the fixed costs of farm equipment and provide land for sons and daughters who wished to continue farming. The average farm size in the Mallee was 1044 acres in 1910-11.[6] When they arrived in Jeparit, James and Kate Menzies selected 640 acres of land and let it out on a share-farming basis (with a tenant providing all of the labour and retaining half of the harvest proceeds). The land, which cost £200, was sold for £2080 in 1910. The Menzies children initially attended school at Jeparit, continuing their schooling in Ballarat, where they boarded with their paternal grandmother. After selling their business and farm the Menzies moved to Melbourne, to the middle-class suburb of Kew. Robert took up a scholarship at Wesley College; his father would represent Lowan (a large electoral district extending from Horsham to the South Australian border, which included Jeparit) in the Victorian Legislative Assembly from 1911 to 1920.[7]

Judith Brett has observed that given Robert Menzies' rural background it might be expected that as a politician he would be committed to advancing the interests of rural people. "Menzies, however, did not become the supreme political representative of rural Australia but of the comfortable urban middle class, and he was frequently out of sympathy with the Country Party which did represent the sort of people among whom he grew up."[8] While this interpretation posits an incongruity between Menzies' background and political values, the apparent divide between urban and rural concerns during his lifetime is often overstated. Town and country were linked symbiotically as part of a complex spatial system that connected primary producers to external markets, creating issues of national rather than sectoral importance.[9] Before the Great War, rural-based pressure groups that called for a reduction in the size of the public sector to ease the burden of taxes and railway freight charges enjoyed a broad base of support that reflected the common interests of households and business groups across town and country.[10]

The formation of the Country Party before the Great War resulted in farmers being elected to Commonwealth and State parliaments. Country Party strategies to advance the specific economic interests of farmers created discord with liberal and conservative groups that persisted through the interwar years.[11] In the 1930s centralised and regulated marketing of primary products was supported by the Country Party and its leader, Earle Page, as a means of extending protectionist policies to the primary sector. This was consistent with the objectives of the Labor Party, the Country Party's initial enemy, and was opposed by the Nationalists and then the United Australia Party.[12] Menzies was skeptical of rural socialists and their advancement of sectoral rather than national issues. His relations with Page were difficult. After Menzies became prime minister in 1939, Page refused to serve in the ministry and, in the House of Representatives, "tried to destroy Menzies ... in a carefully prepared philippic".[13]

In his second term as prime minister, Menzies articulated the natural constituency of the Liberal Party as "The Forgotten People," the title of a 1942 radio speech, a middle class of "salary-earners, shopkeepers, skilled artisans, professional men and women, farmers, and so on" that "are for the most part un-organized" and "are not rich enough to have individual power. They are taken for granted by each political party in turn."[14] A pragmatic and effective coalition with the Country Party allowed Menzies to span this constituency and act as broker for national interests. Menzies maintained good working and personal relations with Country Party leaders Arthur Fadden and John McEwen (it was Menzies who coined the latter's "Black Jack" nickname). The success of the coalition, together with Menzies' support, allowed McEwen, as Minister for Commerce and Agriculture, then Trade, to maintain high levels of protection for manufacturing and agriculture and continue a policy of assisted immigration.[15]

During the post-war economic boom, when employment levels were high and locally-manufactured consumer goods became cheaper and more freely available, Australian cities were able to cope with population growth despite initial shortages of housing. Between the censuses of 1947 and 1966, the total population of Australia's five largest cities increased by 71 percent. Sydney and Melbourne alone added close to two million inhabitants.[16] In contrast to Britain, where post-war resources were directed to the public sector and building land was zoned and expensive to build on, house-building in Australia remained a largely private sector activity based on a comparative advantage in cheap land. This was a product of the value that Menzies placed on the suburban home at the centre of his vision for the nation.

"One of the best instincts in us is that which induces us to have one little piece of earth with a house and garden which is ours, to which we can withdraw, in which we can be amongst our friends, into which no stranger can come against our will". For Menzies, homeownership was a way of giving people a "stake in the country", making them less susceptible to "foreign" ideologies, more committed to their community, and less likely to engage in social and industrial activities that would threaten security of their investment.[17] Menzies' housing policy included incentives that were intended to encourage home ownership. The proportion of the Australian housing stock that was owner-occupied rose from 53 percent in 1947 to 70 percent in 1961; only 41 percent of UK houses were owner-occupied in 1961.[18] The post-war sprawl of suburban housing that the Menzies Government encouraged has been criticised for its aesthetic blandness and lack of planned infrastructure provision. However, care needs to be taken to place the Menzies achievement in the context of structural economic changes and a shifting balance in population between metropolitan and non-metropolitan Australia. A different policy response may have led to housing shortages that would have undermined living standards, and created a housing stock that was incompatible with the way of living for which most people revealed a preference.

Town and country before the Second World War

When Menzies moved to Melbourne in 1910, almost two out of every three Australians (62 percent) lived outside the capital cities. One in five lived in other towns with at least 2 500 inhabitants.[19] A significant redistribution of the Australian population between its metropolitan and non-metropolitan components took place during and between the two world wars. By 1947, half of the population lived in the capital cities. A further 18 percent lived in other towns. Between 1911 and 1947 the share of the population living in rural areas fell from 44 percent to 31 percent. When Menzies retired in 1966 the capital cities (including Canberra) housed 58 percent of the population. Other urban areas increased their share to 25 percent. Rural Australia's population declined in absolute terms, from 2.4

million to 1.9 million, and its share of total population shrunk from 31 percent to 17 percent.

Before the Great War, most Australians regarded development of pastoral, agricultural and mining industries as central to the nation's economic future. As in many parts of the world, there was a strong association in most peoples' minds between ownership of land and wealth, security and freedom. The demand for land that was suitable for farming was consistently high until the Second World War. This demand generally exceeded supply, but the supply of land was inelastic (the amount of land that was available tended not to increase in response to increases in its price). When changes in technology or runs of good seasons raised expectations about whether land could be developed and used profitably, the new land that was offered was taken up quickly. Colonial and State governments responded by working actively to increase the supply of farmland. Public land was made available for sale at less than the market price and on credit terms. Infrastructure such as railways and irrigation works, which were seen as essential to successful farming, was provided.

On the eve of the Great War, Australian country towns and provincial cities were enjoying a golden age of economic activity and civic amenity, built on links between the urban and rural sectors of the economy. Australian pastoralists and farmers were not self-sufficient peasants, but specialist, market-minded producers who needed frequent access to urban goods manufactured locally and services consumed on the spot, at the same time and location as they were produced. In small towns, rural producers dealt with merchants and stock and station agents to arrange the sale and transport of their products to wider markets.[20] Surplus land workers lived in local towns and worked as casual shearers and farm labourers. When the land in a particular area was settled more closely there was an immediate boost to business in the nearest town. Primary producers operated within dense networks of small towns, within easy reach when travelling by horse and cart, over rough roads.

Larger provincial towns and cities usually developed at river crossing points or where main roads and railway routes that linked small towns to the capital cities intersected. They provided a wider range of sophisticated products and did business over a wider area than small towns did. In the capital cities, firms that sought to take advantage of economies of scale and needed access to wider markets found the workforce and transport facilities that they needed. The economy of the capital cities was a simple one that depended largely on provisioning and servicing the rural sector and the needs of the city's own inhabitants.[21]

After the Great War, technological and global forces that were beyond the control of governments weakened the economic base of small towns. Local manufacturing, which had thrived when technologies were simple and transport costs were high, struggled to survive. Technological change in the flour milling and brewing industries made it difficult for small town firms to compete with metropolitan ones. Motor cars and better roads made it possible for farming families to shop and do business in larger centres, where a wider range of professional services, especially health care, was available. The changing demands of the farming sector, in particular for technologically complex purchased inputs, shifted farm spending from small town firms to those in more diverse regional centres. Servicing of these inputs was also less likely to be done in small towns. The use of non-local sources of finance and farm labour meant that a proportion of farm income leaked from the local region in the form of interest payments and wages.

By the 1930s, further increases in export income derived from the wool industry depended on favourable seasonal and market conditions and technological improvements, rather than investment in bringing land into production, as had been the case in the past. Commodity prices declined after the Great War as more land was brought into production worldwide. Virtually all of the land that was suitable for farming was now occupied. Falling prices and rising costs squeezed farm incomes, and dust storms attested to the long-term environmental damage that had been brought about by intensive working of low-quality soil.

In the inter-war period the Australian economy was re-shaped by a series of supply- and demand-side changes that shifted resources from rural and mining activity to manufacturing. The tertiary sector maintained its position, providing just over half of jobs and GDP. Changes in the relative profitability of industries, rather than tariffs and subsidies, account for this structural change.[22] Large-scale public investment in electricity generation and transmission expanded production possibilities in manufacturing, offices and retail trade. Manufacturing prospered in clusters of industries that grew rapidly around new technologies of electricity and the internal combustion engine. These clusters tended to form in metropolitan locations, which offered economies of scale and proximity to customers and labour supplies. Firms responded to price signals and changing cost functions by increasing the supply of time-saving products, such as cars and washing-machines, and time-using products, such as radios and cinemas. These were normal goods, the demand for which was increased by rising incomes. Demonstration effects and advertising also increased demand. Public capital formation, in urban roads, bridges and sewerage systems was also to the advantage of large cities.[23]

The population of the capital cities had been growing rapidly prior to the Great War. Public transport improvements in Sydney and Brisbane resulted in new suburbs being developed; Melbourne, Adelaide and Perth had large areas of subdivided land along existing rail and tram lines available for building. The Great War cut short a boom in these cities by disrupting migration flows and diverting resources from residential construction. After that War, demand for urban house building was increasingly fed by a drift of population from country areas. In-migration of people born in Australia accounted for 51 percent of the population growth of capital cities' between 1911 and 1947 (natural increase accounted for a further 44 percent).[24] Builders embraced the informal Californian Bungalow, which offered larger rooms while economising on expensive building materials. Set on square rather than narrow rectangular blocks, with space for a driveway and garage, this became the predominant housing style of the inter-war suburb. Sydney's suburban building boom was sustained throughout the 1920s, but conservative lending and high interest rates checked housing demand.[25] House-building was interrupted by the Great Depression. Construction virtually ceased during the Second World War and, in 1945, the nation faced a housing shortage that some experts estimated was as high as 480 000 dwellings.[26] An estimated 10 percent of Melbourne's population in 1943 was sharing housing or living in boarding houses.[27] At the 1947 national census there were only 877 dwellings for every thousand households.[28]

The post-war boom

The Second World War boosted Australia's domestic industrial base. Latent resources were released to meet the needs of the military and develop domestic substitutes for products hitherto imported. By 1943, aggregate GDP was 41 percent higher than in 1939.[29] Metals processing, machine tools and engineering industries used in aeroplane and armaments production retained an expanded role, with motor vehicles and metal fabrication expanding as war production slowed. The labour and capital directed to the war effort, when converted to peacetime activity, helped overcome housing shortages and supplied markets that boomed with the release of pent-up demand for family formation. Some war-related industry was established in Adelaide and non-metropolitan towns for strategic regions, to avoid a concentration of industry in Sydney and Melbourne.[30] In contrast to the post-Great War era, rural producers enjoyed a boom in export prices – they rose by 343 percent between 1946 and 1951, compared to 38 percent from 1919 to 1925 – and a sharp improvement in the terms of trade.[31] There was a spike in wool prices during the Korean War boom, created by the demand for wool by the US Government and the inelasticity of supply. As farm incomes increased, ageing equipment was replaced and prosperity returned to provincial towns. Some towns attracted new industries that were seeking cheap land, creating jobs that stimulated housing investment and civic improvement.[32]

For many farming families, a gap had opened up between the amenities that were available to them, and those that were generally in use in the cities. On the farms themselves, houses in the early 1940s were generally poorly equipped in terms of kitchen facilities, hot water services and telephones.[33] In 1950, 95 percent of households in Melbourne had mains electricity, compared to just over half in the Mallee and the Wimmera.[34] Now, country people who remembered the droughts and economic depression of the 1930s and 1940s saw science and technology, embodied in agricultural research, the car and truck, electricity and the telephone as key contributors to a "golden age" in which rural Australia had matured and its way of life stabilised.[35]

The technologies that made country life easier and less isolated were also to the advantage of the capital cities and coastal industrial centres such as Geelong, Newcastle and Wollongong. The consensus that Australia was underpopulated, reinforced by the threat of invasion, prompted the Chifley Government to begin a program of assisted immigration. As both workers and consumers, migrants underpinned the expansion of manufacturing and these effects were strongest in the capital cities where most manufacturing employment was located (immigrants accounted for 38 percent of the capital cities' population growth from 1947 to 1961, compared to 5 percent from 1911 to 1947).[36] Further industrial development required sites with large amounts of cheap land with space for large, single-storey factories and warehouses, easy access to main roads, and affordable worker housing, preferably close by. The old, inner-suburban industrial areas of the capital cities had none of these advantages: land prices were high, traffic was congested, and much of the housing stock had been judged by government inquiries to be unfit for habitation. Sydney, Melbourne and Adelaide already had large industrial bases and offered economies of scale for new industrial investment at outer suburban Dandenong and Broadmeadows

(Melbourne), Parramatta and Bankstown (Sydney), and Elizabeth and Clovelly Park (Adelaide).[37] Vacant land between railway lines was filled in with factories and suburbs as trucks and car ownerships gave firms and people more flexibility in distribution and commuting. Despite the prosperity of country towns in the 1950s, Australia's five largest cities added almost two million inhabitants between 1949 and 1961, which accounted for two-thirds of the nation's population growth, and increased their share of total population from 50 to 54 percent.

The commitment of the Commonwealth Labor Government to planned post-war reconstruction, centred on the goal of decentralisation of economic activity, placed regional development firmly on the policy agenda. Decentralisation was embraced widely as a solution to the problems of both urban congestion and the decline of rural communities. As Nicholas Brown has observed, the principle appealed to a wide range of interest groups, from workers who felt alienated by production processes in metropolitan factories to the upholders of conservative values about traditional family units and social duty.[38]

The Department of Post-War Reconstruction, established in 1942, was headed by an enthusiastic Keynesian economist, H.C. Coombs. Coombs and his staff, made up of a new generation of young, academically trained public servants, approached their work with the conviction that "a better balanced distribution of population can be achieved by first concentrating development in a small number of selected centres and basing this development on secondary industries as the prime mover."[39] The Commonwealth Housing Commission, established in 1943 to increase the supply of affordable housing, recommended that the Commonwealth use the powers that it had acquired during the war to ensure that new industry was not to be concentrated in only a few regions (that is, the major cities) and that public and private decisions about housing and land use would be better coordinated. Most of the States compiled surveys on the human, physical, and economic resources of their major regions to assist the Department of Post-War Reconstruction in formulation of plans for decentralisation and regional development. In a 1949 report, the department recommended that "developed towns" be created around places such as Albury that would be large enough to generate economic advantages, and yet be small enough to enable problems of urban congestion to be managed effectively.

This era of Commonwealth land use planning yielded two successes: the Snowy River scheme and the creation of a Department of Immigration.

The grander promise of planned economic development, balanced between metropolitan and regional locations, remained unfulfilled. There were several reasons for this. The referendum in 1944 to allow the Commonwealth to use its wartime planning powers in peacetime was defeated. The projects undertaken had long lead times (for example, the Snowy River scheme, which started in 1949, was not completed fully until the early 1970s). The Menzies Government was much less disposed to the philosophy of planning. The watchwords were now private investment, individual home-ownership, and limited government intervention. When war-time restrictions were released there was a boom in private investment and a groundswell of conservative opposition to the Labor Government's plans.

It was the States that were left with the job of attempting to promote decentralisation. Early in the 1950s, Queensland's Bureau of Industry, under the direction of Colin Clark, sought to encourage diversification through the promotion of small regional economies, each built around a prosperous and dynamic city. Clark opposed tariffs and subsidies to support inefficient industries and favoured the expansion of manufacturing industries, such as food processing, which enjoyed natural protection, and tertiary industries, such as retailing and tourism, which were not subject to import competition.[40] Clark's recommendation that income taxation powers be returned to the States to provide the States with funds for regional development and to counter the concentration of authority in Canberra was not implemented. This was at odds with the desire of Commonwealth governments to retain their ability to vary rates of income taxation as a tool of the emerging science of macroeconomic management.

New South Wales and Victoria set up regional development committees. Early in the 1950s the Queensland and Tasmanian governments began to provide financial assistance for regional development. By the 1960s, New South Wales, Victoria and South Australia had also implemented regional development schemes. These schemes consisted of loans to encourage firms to move to decentralised locations, subsidised rail freight rates to non-metropolitan areas, power subsidies and, in some cases, payroll tax rebates. Although most State governments tried to encourage a decentralised pattern of industrial location within their own States, they nevertheless competed with each other to attract large firms that sought the economies of scale available in major cities.[41] Because governments pursued policies of decentralisation that were "scattergun" in nature, spreading assistance unselectively over wide areas, much government assistance was ineffective and fewer resources were left for regional areas that had real growth potential.[42]

Suburban pioneers

In 1940, Australian real per capita consumption was almost exactly the same as it was in 1910. Three decades later, the figure had doubled. Total population had increased by 80 percent. In other words, after the "Long Boom" of the post-war era, there were almost twice as many Australians and they were, on average, twice as wealthy.[43] As in many countries, Australia entered the post-war period facing a backlog of demand for housing and consumer goods due to deferred consumption and investment. Australia's capital cities continued to act as magnets for jobs and people, but they did so within a greater enlarged set of production possibilities. As accumulated war-time savings were released, with household expenditure sustained by almost continuous full employment, more Australians were able to purchase capital assets and consumer durables. Increased aspirations and household purchasing power were fuelled by advertising and the availability of credit, and an expanding range of products that were hitherto seen as luxuries were now considered to be necessities. As Greg Whitwell has written, the Australian economy was transformed into a modern consumer society, with spending behaviour driven by a "suburban imperative" – "the need to buy a house in the suburbs, to fill the house with a range of appliances, and to acquire a car".[44]

A global investment-led upturn in the business cycle was inevitable in the post-war years. From the early 1950s, prosperity was maintained for a further 15 to 20 years by greater international mobility of capital and technology in search of profit opportunities, the rapid growth of world trade and the acceptance of stable currency values. There were, however, distinctive features of the Australian experience.[45] Like the United States, Australia entered the boom during the War itself and was largely spared the destruction of capital that characterised much of Europe and Asia. The growth of the labour supply after the War, though boosted by migrants born overseas, was not as large as that of the capital stock. This was not a period of rapid growth in the public sector, as was the case in many other countries, and the growth of the capital stock was a product of the development of the private sector. A rise in the marginal propensity to invest was reinforced by the private capital inflows that more than offset reduced levels of overseas borrowing by public sector. International trade did not play a major role in the Australian boom. Domestic production was stimulated by full employment and the growth of national income, which increased the volume of bank deposits available for lending, and provided security for borrowers and lenders. To encourage home ownership, the Menzies Government directed lending funds to housing at concessional interest rates.

During the inter-war years, the major influence on the location of residential areas and jobs in Australian capital cities was the networks of rail lines linking suburbs to central business districts and dockside areas. At stations, junctions, and termini, shopping strips developed, some of them with department and other stores to rival those of city centres. These suburbs were built in a way that people could get around them on foot, or by taking public transport. Beyond easy walking distance of public transport, the land generally remained undeveloped. By the post-war period, trucks were freeing factories and other workplaces from the need to locate close to railway lines. Motor cars, which became increasingly affordable as incomes rose and production costs fell, allowed workers to follow the factories to the semi-rural fringe, where cheap land once considered too remote from public transport to be developed was available. In 1945 there was one car for every 11 Melbourne residents; by 1965 there was one for every three.[46] The old inner industrial areas and middle-class residential suburbs were by now largely filled and their populations had stopped growing, or declined.

There were other supply-side obstacles to addressing the demand for housing. Shortages of coal restricted production of bricks and tiles, and timber, nails, hinges, cement and other building materials were scarce. A building material price index with a 1929 base shows values of 186 in 1946, rising to 426 by 1953.[47] There was also a shortage of qualified building tradespeople. Commonwealth legislation of 1940 controlled rents and eviction provisions. Rent control powers were transferred to the States in 1948, and subsequent legislation effectively mirrored that of the Commonwealth. Rent control was intended to prevent landlords from exploiting the housing shortage, but reduced rates of return had the effect of discouraging investment and properties tended to fall into disrepair. The number of units of housing available for rental declined in absolute terms. The legislation advantaged sitting tenants who could buy at low prices when landlords chose to sell.

In 1954 the Menzies Government, having identified the lifting of home ownership rates as a policy objective, began selling off public housing, allowing tenants to buy their own homes on concessional terms. As a result, the stock of public housing was predominantly in the form of flats, which reduced the housing choices available for subsequent generations of low income applicants for public housing. State housing authorities offset the lack of Commonwealth activity to some extent by building new housing estates in growing industrial areas.[48] Patrick Troy has argued that with these changes in access to public housing the Menzies Government effectively abandoned the principle, expressed by the Curtin Government in 1941, that decent housing was the right of every citizen. In the absence of a public housing policy that integrated Commonwealth and State-run housing bodies, resources that might have been used to provide a minimum standard of housing for all Australians were diverted to the private housing market.[49]

In the 1949 policy speech, Menzies declared: "The best people in the world are not those who 'leave it to the other fellow,' but those who by thrift and self-sacrifice establish homes and bring up families and add to the national pool of savings and hope one day to sit down under their own vine and fig tree, owing nothing to anybody".[50] The philosophy was embraced by families who responded to the gap between cost of buying an established house and their own budgets by providing the labour required to build.[51] Rather than rent privately or live with parents until they had saved enough to buy, or until public housing became available, people typically bought a block of land with the intention of building a house on it. In doing so, they tended to move outwards along an axis from older suburbs, to a ring of new suburbs that became "the city's main breeding zone and the main residential building site".[52]

Between 1947 and 1966, 67 percent of Melbourne's population growth took place in outer suburbs that were developed after the Second World War.[53] The most rapidly-growing included the Shire of Mulgrave (later the City of Waverley), a former market garden area to the east that grew from 5 000 inhabitants in 1947 to 69 000 by 1966.[54] Nearby Nunawading, and Broadmeadows and Keilor to the north and north-west of Melbourne, also grew fast. Municipalities such as Moorabbin and Preston, which had been developed as suburbs in the 1920s, grew at a more moderate rate, but more than doubled in population during the post-war boom. A ring of outer suburbs, some first developed during the 1920s building boom, accounted for all of Sydney's metropolitan population growth from 1947 to 1966.[55] Half of all building permits issued in Sydney in the late '40s and early '50s were for houses with fibre cement sheeting walls, and the growth of Bankstown, Fairfield, Holroyd, and Liverpool from a total of 49 000 inhabitants in 1947 to 384 000 in 1966 created a western suburbs "fibro belt'" of modest, often self-built houses.[56]

Land prices were low on the suburban frontier because abundant lots were available due to previous subdivision activity and few services beyond electricity and piped water were provided. The common lot size of quarter of an acre (approximately 1 000 square metres) was large enough to conform to health regulations regarding the use of septic tanks and pan toilets. These lots provided room for garages and makeshift bungalows in which families could live while the main house was being built. Local governments required road reservations that were wide enough for "nature strips", but roads were generally not graded, let alone metalled or paved, and footpaths, gutters and stormwater drains were not provided.[57]

The self-building household had three options. The first was for the owner to do all of the construction, using family labour and/or that of friends and neighbours. This could be a stressful process if materials were in short supply. Co-operative building societies who lent to owner-builders required each stage of construction to be checked and signed off by a qualified builder. The second was for the owner to act as site manager, coordinating the various sub-contractors in the construction process. Thirdly, the owner could hire a builder and reduce costs by providing "sweat equity" in the form of unskilled labour. Timber, which was easier for amateurs to work with and less expensive than bricks, was the material used for exterior walls in three out of every five new houses built in Victoria in 1953-54. More than 40 percent of Australian houses completed in 1954 were owner-built; the proportion remained at around one-third throughout the 1950s.[58] Cheap substitute building materials, such as concrete roof tiles, plasterboard, fibro, plywood, compressed fibre board and metal-framed windows reduced costs, as did brick veneer construction.[59] By the end of the decade, half of Victoria's new house completions were built in brick veneer.[60]

After 1956, population growth eased, housing supply increased and construction costs declined.[61] Alistair Greig has argued that by 1961 the immediate post-war housing challenge had been met and the housing market took on different characteristics.[62] The owner-builder gave way to the private contract builder: by the mid-1960s the latter accounted for 70 percent of new houses, with less than 15 percent built by owners.[63] The proportion of the housing stock made up of flats increased, most constructed by small speculative builders. As the

1960s progressed, homebuyers could afford bigger and better-equipped houses such as the project homes built by large construction firms.[64] The transformation of Australia into a nation of home-owners was most pronounced in the capital cities. In 1961, when the national rate of home-ownership was 70 percent, the rate in Melbourne was 82 percent. In Clayton, a new Melbourne working-class suburb, the rate was 94 percent in 1968.[65] In Sydney, the rate of home-ownership in 1961 was 71 percent , but this was a large increase on the 1947 figure of less than 40 percent.[66]

In *Australia's Home*, architect Robin Boyd observed that post-war material shortages engendered austere housing styles. "The traditional plan and structure remained unaltered, but one by one the decorations and embellishments went."[67] "With all this pruning and saving," another architect, Max Freeland, observed that "the average standard house of the immediate post-war years was an unlovely thing."[68] The critique was more than aesthetic. Once people began to use their cars for commuting and new suburbs began to develop away from public transport routes, a fresh set of urban problems emerged quickly. A contemporary economist, Max Neutze, argued persuasively that the ability of large cities to sustain growth by building more road space and creating new outer suburbs imposed substantial costs in the form of traffic congestion, lengthening journeys to work, pollution, and rising housing costs. Because these costs were imposed on society as a whole rather than on individual firms and households, Neutze argued that they were not taken into account in the making of location decisions.[69] As Boyd put it, the ordinary person had to pay "the price of privacy" by building in suburbs "beyond the reach of the pipes and wires which conveyed twentieth century comfort, and ... so remote from his work that at least one-eighth of his waking hours would be taken in travel".[70]

New post-war suburbs were an "unplanned mess" of poorly drained streets and mostly unsewered houses.[71] In Sydney, the Cumberland County Council, a new authority sitting between local councils and the State government, completed a master plan in 1948 that was based on the provision of sewerage, street paving and drainage, schools and other infrastructure in new suburbs. Implementation of the Plan was, however, delayed until 1951, by which time the metropolitan population was growing at twice the projected rate and much unplanned suburban development had taken place.[72] The Metropolitan Water Sewerage and Drainage Board and the Department of Main Roads failed to keep up with suburban expansion. In 1950-51, 29 percent of houses in metropolitan Sydney were not connected to sewerage and their occupants used septic tanks or relied on pan collectors; by 1960-61 the proportion of unsewered houses increased to 37 percent.[73] In 1957 a journalist reported that in Sutherland Shire, where the population increased from 29 000 in 1947 to 132 000 in 1966, the lack of road paving and drainage would "shame an outback town".[74]

Critiques of post-war suburbia are not unfounded. But the suburban block and the scope it offered for self-building was attractive, and even necessary, under post-war conditions. The couples forming households in new suburbs were fulfilling aspirations that were deeply rooted in the Australian experience.[75] Before the Great War property and land ownership was equated world-wide with independence, security and the potential for wealth creation. Home ownership was more feasible in the settler societies of the Americas and Australasia than it was in Europe, due to higher disposable incomes, a more active building sector and cheaper land. In Australian cities, home-ownership rates in 1890 ranged from an average of 30 percent in Sydney to 41 percent in Melbourne.[76] Working-class people could afford to buy houses, and the average house size increased as new, progressively larger houses were built for owner-occupation.

For people who had migrated from Britain, owning a house in Australia was "shaped by pressures of both emulation and avoidance: a desire, on the one hand, to reproduce loved and familiar styles and patterns of life; and, on the other, to escape the crowding and poverty of houses which were no longer home-like".[77] Only the wealthiest British households could afford to buy a house outright: the national home-ownership rate in 1914 was 10 percent. Workers tended to live in small terrace houses, often shared with lodgers. In the twentieth century, the most likely route to home ownership for working-class households was to buy the house they previously rented. Lending was tighter in Australia during the inter-war years, and the ability to buy a house was a mark of respectability, as it depended on a person's ability to save and hold a steady job. In the post-war period, home-ownership once again became more democratic, with opportunities broadly available across social classes. Self-builders who had migrated from the UK told of the sense of pride they felt in doing something that was not possible in their homeland.[78]

Barbara and Graeme Davison similarly detect a pioneer spirit amongst post-war suburbanites who "did battle with the elements, creating little oases of domestic safety and comfort in a dangerous world".[79] In the winter of 1955, Melbourne's *Sun* newspaper ran a series of reports on the state of the "heartbreak streets" – hundreds of miles of unmade roads in each new suburb.[80] A reporter found that "Young couples who have built their homes on the city's fringes step out of their front gates into mud," and supported the argument with photos and interviews:

> Life, the ordinary housewifely shopping outing, which is a pleasure to most women, becomes drudgery. Back home from the shops means … not a cup of tea, but half-an-hour of scraping and washing off mud [from] her pram before she can take it into her house.

In response, citizen groups, drawing on stocks of social capital, held working bees to improve road surfaces, build footpaths and nature strips, and form drains. Women took a leading role in this work, and were active in lobbying local councils and State governments to improve conditions. In Oakleigh, a "neighbourly gang" of housewives built their own roads, wheeling barrows and laying bricks, with their husbands doing the heavier work on the weekends.[81] Volunteer groups established churches and sports clubs, built community halls, and raised money to support local schools. The post-war couples who built homes and communities in new suburbs embodied the civic-minded, nation-building meanings that Menzies ascribed to home ownership.[82]

Endnotes

1 Fred Raven, *History of the Menzies Family in Jeparit*, Jeparit Chamber of Commerce, 1966; Robert Menzies, *Afternoon Light: Some Memories of Men and Events*, Cassell Australia, 1967, 5-12.

2 Sir Robert Menzies, *Afternoon Light: Some Memories of Men and Events,* Melbourne, Cassell, 1967, 8.

3 "The Thirsty Mallee," *Argus* (Melbourne), 8, 10, 12, 15 March 1898.

4 *Leader* (Melbourne), 16, 30 January, 5 March 1904.

5 Lionel Frost, "The Correll Family and Technological Change in Australian Agriculture", *Agricultural History*, 75 (2), 2001, 217-41.

6 Statistical Register of Victoria.

7 James Menzies (1862-1945), *Argus*, 2 November 1945. Obituaries Australia. http://oa.anu. edu.au/obituary/menzies-james-16803. Accessed on 16 July 2015.

8 Judith Brett, *Robert Menzies' Forgotten People*, revised edition, Melbourne University Press, 2007, 130.

9 Lionel Frost, "Across the Great Divide: The Economic History of the Inland Corridor", Alan Mayne (ed), *Beyond the Black Stump: Histories of Outback Australia*, Wakefield Press, 2008, 57-84.

[10] In 1902, James Menzies, then a Dimboola Shire councilor, was a delegate of the Kyabram Reform League, an important reform group that endorsed candidates in most seats at the Victorian state election that year. H. L. Nielson, *The Voice of the People, Or, the History of the Kyabram Reform Movement*, Arbuckle, Waddell & Fawckner, 1902; *Age* (Melbourne), 10 April 1902; John Rickard, *Class and Politics: New South Wales, Victoria and the Early Commonwealth, 1890-1910*, Australian National University Press, 1976, 178-179.

[11] D.B. Graham, *The Formation of the Australian Country Parties*, Australian National University Press, 1966.

[12] Greg Whitwell and Diane Sydenham, *A Shared Harvest: The Australian Wheat Industry, 1939-1989*, Macmillan, 1991, 50-65.

[13] Carl Bridge, "Page, Sir Earle Christmas (1880–1961)", *Australian Dictionary of Biography*, National Centre of Biography, Australian National University, http://adb.anu.edu.au/biography/page-sir-earle-christmas-7941/text13821, published first in hardcopy 1988, accessed online 28 September 2015.

[14] R.G. Menzies, *The Forgotten People* (1942). Reprinted in Brett, *Robert Menzies' Forgotten People*, 21-8.

[15] Peter Golding, *Black Jack McEwen: Political Gladiator*, Melbourne University Press, 1996.

[16] Lionel Frost, "Urbanisation", Simon Ville and Glenn Withers (eds), *The Cambridge Economic History of Australia*, Cambridge University Press, 2015, 249.

[17] Patrick Troy, "Suburbs of Acquiescence, Suburbs of protest", *Housing Studies, 15* (5), 2000, 717-38.

[18] Colin G. Pooley, "Patterns on the Ground: Urban Form, Residential Structure and the Social Construction of Space", Martin Daunton (ed), *The Cambridge Urban History of Britain: Volume III 1840-1950*, Cambridge University Press, 2000, 444-5.

[19] The figures in this paragraph are calculated from Census data and Wray Vamplew (ed.), *Australians: Historical Statistics*, Fairfax, Syme & Weldon, 1987, 41. The 1911 census understates the proportion of the population living in non-metropolitan towns, as several country towns had less than 2500 inhabitants but still performed urban functions.

[20] Simon Ville, *The Rural Entrepreneurs: A History of the Stock and Station Agent Industry in Australia and New Zealand*, Cambridge University Press, 2000.

[21] Frost, "Urbanisation", 248-59.

[22] David Merrett and Simon Ville, "Tariffs, Subsidies and Profits: A Re-assessment of Structural Change in Australia 1901-39", *Australian Economic History Review, 51* (1), 2011, 46-70.

[23] W.A. Sinclair, "Capital Formation", Colin Forster (ed), *Australian Economic Development in the Twentieth Century*, George Allen and Unwin, 1970, 37-40.

[24] David Merrett, "Australian Capital Cities in the Twentieth Century", J.W. McCarty and C.B. Schedvin (eds), *Australian Capital Cities: Historical Essays*, Sydney University Press, 1978, 191.

[25] Sinclair, "Capital Formation", 31-33; Nigel Stapledon, "Trends and Cycles in Sydney and Melbourne House Prices from 1880 to 2011", *Australian Economic History Review, 52* (3), 2012, 308.

[26] F. Oswald Barnett, W.O. Burt and Frank Heath, *We Must Go On: A Study in Planned Reconstruction and Housing*, Wilke and Co., 1944, 34. The various estimates of the housing shortage were based on the decline in rates of house building relative to rates of marriage compared to the pre-war period, or on estimates of the number of heads of households that were sharing houses or flats with other families. They also included estimates of the number of families living in old housing that was no longer fit for habitation.

[27] Graeme Davison and Tony Dingle, "Introduction: The View from the Ming Wing", Graeme Davison et al (eds), *The Cream Brick Frontier: Histories of Australian Suburbia*, Monash Publications in History No. 19, 1995, 9.

[28] Tony Dingle, "Necessity the Mother of Invention, or Do-It-Yourself", Patrick Troy (ed), *A History of European Housing in Australia*, Cambridge University Press, 2000, 66.

[29] Ian McLean, *Why Australia Prospered: The Shifting Sources of Economic Growth*, Princeton University Press, 2013, 178.

[30] Carol Fort, (2015) "Militarisation and Urbanisation: The Second World War, Public Housing and the Shaping of Metropolitan Adelaide", *Australian Economic History Review*, 55 (1), 42-61.

[31] McLean, op. cit., 187-9.

[32] See, for example, D.M. Whittaker, *Wangaratta*, Wangaratta City Council, 1963, 172-3; Keith Swan, *A History of Wagga Wagga*, City of Wagga Wagga, 1970, 171.

[33] Alan Holt, *Wheat Farms of Victoria: A Sociological Survey*, Melbourne University Press, 1947, 100.

[34] Graeme Davison, "Fatal Attraction? The Lure of Technology and the Decline of Rural Australia 1890-2000", *Tasmanian Historical Studies*, Vol. 9, 2003, 49-50.

[35] Joy McCann, "History and Memory in Australia's Wheatlands", in G. Davison and M. Brodie (eds.), *Struggle Country: The Rural Ideal in Twentieth Century Australia* (Clayton: Monash University ePress, 2005), 03.5.

[36] Merrett, "Australian Capital Cities in the Twentieth Century", 191.

[37] Lionel Frost and Tony Dingle, "Sustaining Suburbia: An Historical Perspective on Australia's Growth", Patrick Troy (ed), *Australian Cities: Issues, Strategies and Policies for Urban Australia in the 1990s*, Cambridge University Press, 1995, 33.

[38] Nicholas Brown, *Governing Prosperity: Social Change and Social Analysis in Australia in the 1950s*, Cambridge University Press, 1995, 127.

[39] Quoted by C.J. Lloyd and Patrick N. Troy, *Innovation and Reaction: The Life and Death of the Federal Department of Urban and Regional Development*, George Allen & Unwin, 1981, 11.

[40] Chilla Bulbeck, "Colin Clark and the Greening of Queensland: The Influence of a Senior Public Servant on Queensland Economic Development 1938 to 1952", *Australian Journal of Politics and History*, 33 (1), 1987, 7-18.

[41] Brian Head, "Economic Development in State and Federal Politics", Brian Head (ed), *The Politics of Development in Australia*, Allen & Unwin, 1986, 39-41.

[42] Peter Self, "Alternative Urban Policies: The Case for Regional Development", Patrick Troy (ed), *Australian Cities: Issues, Strategies and Policies for Urban Australia in the 1990s*, Cambridge University Press, 1995, 248.

[43] Rodney Maddock, "The Long Boom 1940-1970", Rodney Maddock and Ian McLean (eds), *The Australian Economy in the Long Run*, Cambridge University Press, 1987, 79.

[44] Greg Whitwell, *Making the Market: The Rise of Consumer Society*, McPhee Gribble, 1989, 38.

[45] Maddock, "The Long Boom 1940-1970".

[46] Davison and Dingle, "Introduction", 14. A new Holden car cost the equivalent of 78 week's work on average weekly earnings in the early 1950s; by the early 1970s the cost was equivalent to 30 weeks of earnings.

[47] Richard Harris (2000), "To Market! To Market! The Changing Role of the Australian Timber Merchant, 1945-c.1965", *Australian Economic History Review*, *40* (1), 31.

[48] See for example Renate Howe (ed), *New Houses for Old: Fifty Years of Public Housing in Victoria, 1938-1988*, Ministry of Housing and Construction, 1988; Lois Bryson and Faith Thompson, *An Australian Newtown: Life and Leadership in a Working Class Suburb*, Kibble Books, 1972; Mark Peel, *Good Times, Hard Times: The Past and Future in Elizabeth*, Melbourne University Press, 1995.

[49] Patrick Troy, *Accommodating Australians: Commonwealth Government Involvement in Housing*, Federation Press, 2012, 3, 107.

[50] Quoted by Davison and Dingle, "Introduction", 5.

[51] Troy, op. cit.; Dingle, "Necessity the Mother of Invention".

[52] Tony Dingle, "People and Places in Post-War Melbourne", Graeme Davison et al (eds), *The Cream Brick Frontier: Histories of Australian Suburbia*, Monash Publications in History No. 19, 1995, 30.

[53] Commonwealth of Australia, *Census of Population and Housing*, 1947, 1966.

[54] Dingle, op. cit., 30-9.

[55] Commonwealth of Australia, *Census of Population and Housing*, 1947, 1966; Graeme Aplin, "The Rise of Suburban Sydney", Max Kelly (ed), *Sydney: City of Suburbs*, New South Wales University Press, 1987. The population growth of the outer suburbs was equivalent to more than 100 percent of metropolitan growth, as the population of the City of Sydney and its inner suburbs declined in absolute terms.

[56] Peter Spearritt, *Sydney Since the Twenties*, Hale & Iremonger, 1978, 99-105; Charles Pickett, *The Fibro Frontier: A Different History of Australian Architecture*, Powerhouse Publishing, 1997.

[57] Tony Dingle and Carolyn Rasmussen, *Vital Connections: Melbourne and its Board of Works 1891-1991*, McPhee Gribble, 1991, 127.

[58] Dingle, "Necessity the Mother of Invention", 68.

[59] Harris, "To Market! To Market!", 31-3.

[60] Davison and Dingle, "Introduction", 10-11.

[61] Stapledon, "Trends and Cycles in Sydney and Melbourne House Prices", 310.

[62] Alistair Greig, *The Stuff Dreams Are Made Of: Housing Provision in Australia 1945-1960*, Melbourne University Press, 1995, 188-93.

[63] Dingle, "Necessity the Mother of Invention", 67.

64 Don Garden, "Type 15, *Glengarry* and *Catalina*: The Changing Space of the A.V. Jennings Home in the 1960s", Davison et al (eds), *The Cream Brick Frontier*, 140-53; Ann Garnter, "Death of the Project House? Reflections on the History of Merchant Builders", Davison et al (eds), *The Cream Brick Frontier*, 108-39.

65 Judith Brett, *Australian Liberals and the Moral Middle Class: From Alfred Deakin to John Howard*, Cambridge University Press, 2003, 123. In Sydney

66 Spearritt, op. cit., 105.

67 Robin Boyd, *Australia's Home: Why Australians Built the Way They Did*, second edition, Penguin, 1978, 118.

68 J.M. Freeland, *Architecture in Australia: A History*, Penguin, 1972, 280-1.

69 Max Neutze, *Economic Policy and the Size of Cities*, Australian National University Press, 1965, 60.

70 Boyd, op. cit., 129.

71 Dingle and Rasmussen, *Vital Connections*, 217.

72 Robert Freestone, *Urban Nation: Australia's Planning Heritage*, CSIRO Publishing, 2010, 145-8.

73 Spearritt, op. cit., 100.

74 Quoted by Paul Ashton, Jennifer Cornwall and Annette Salt, *Sutherland Shire: A History*, University of New South Wales Press, 2006, 157.

75 Brett, op. cit.

76 Lionel Frost, *The New Urban Frontier: Urbanisation and City Building in Australasia and the American West*, New South Wales University Press, 1991, 124.

77 Graeme Davison, "Colonial Origins of the Australian Home", Patrick Troy (ed), *A History of European Housing in Australia*, Cambridge University Press, 2000, 6.

78 Lionel Frost, "An Outer Suburban House of the 1950s", Susan Marsden (ed), *Our House: Histories of Australian Homes*, Australian Heritage Commission, 2001. http://www.environment.gov.au/resource/our-house-histories-australian-homes-41. Accessed 24 July 2015.

79 Barbara Davison and Graeme Davison, "Suburban Pioneers", Davison et al (eds), *The Cream Brick Frontier*, 43.

80 Barry McCrea, "Heartbreak streets", *Sun* (Melbourne), 9-13, 15 August 1955.

81 John Murphy, *Imagining the Fifties: Private Sentiment and Political Culture in Menzies' Australia*, UNSW Press, 2000, 24.

82 Brett, op. cit., 123-5.

Select Bibliography

Aplin, Graeme, "The Rise of Suburban Sydney," Max Kelly (ed), *Sydney: City of Suburbs*, New South Wales University Press, 1987, 192-209.

Ashton, Paul, Jennifer Cornwall and Annette Salt, *Sutherland Shire: A History*, University of New South Wales Press, 2006.

Boyd, Robin, *Australia's Home: Why Australians Built the Way They Did*, second edition, Penguin, 1978.

Brett, Judith, *Australian Liberals and the Moral Middle Class: From Alfred Deakin to John Howard*, Cambridge University Press, 2003.

_____ *Robert Menzies' Forgotten People*, revised edition, Melbourne University Press, 2007.

_____ "The Menzies Era, 1950-66," Alison Bashford and Stuart Macintyre (eds), *The Cambridge History of Australia: Volume 2 The Commonwealth of Australia*, Cambridge University Press, 2013, 112-34.

Bridge, Carl. "Page, Sir Earle Christmas (1880–1961)," *Australian Dictionary of Biography*, National Centre of Biography, Australian National University, http://adb.anu.edu.au/biography/page-sir-earle-christmas-7941/text13821, published first in hardcopy 1988, accessed online 28 September 2015.

Brown, Nicholas, *Governing Prosperity: Social Change and Social Analysis in Australia in the 1950s*, Cambridge University Press, 1995.

Bryson, Lois and Faith Thompson, *An Australian Newtown: Life and Leadership in a Working Class Suburb*, Kibble Books, 1972.

Bulbeck, Chilla, "Colin Clark and the Greening of Queensland: The Influence of a Senior Public Servant on Queensland Economic Development 1938 to 1952," *Australian Journal of Politics and History*, 33 (1), 1987, 7-18.

Darian-Smith, Kate, "World War 2 and Post-War Reconstruction, 1939-49," Alison Bashford and Stuart Macintyre (eds), *The Cambridge History of Australia: Volume 2 The Commonwealth of Australia*, Cambridge University Press, 2013, 88-111.

Davison, Barbara and Graeme Davison, "Suburban Pioneers," Graeme Davison et al (eds), *The Cream Brick Frontier: Histories of Australian Suburbia*, Monash Publications in History No. 19, 1995, 41-50.

Davison, Graeme, "Colonial Origins of the Australian Home," Patrick Troy (ed), *A History of European Housing in Australia*, Cambridge University Press, 2000, 6-25.

_____ *Car Wars: How the Car Won Our Hearts and Conquered Our Cities*, Allen & Unwin, 2004.

Davison, Graeme and Tony Dingle, "Introduction: The View from the Ming Wing," Graeme Davison et al (eds), *The Cream Brick Frontier: Histories of Australian Suburbia*, Monash Publications in History No. 19, 1995, 2-17.

Dingle, Tony, "People and Places in Post-War Melbourne," Graeme Davison et al (eds), *The Cream Brick Frontier: Histories of Australian Suburbia*, Monash Publications in History No. 19, 1995, 27-40.

_____ "Necessity the Mother of Invention, or Do-It-Yourself," Patrick Troy (ed), *A History of European Housing in Australia*, Cambridge University Press, 2000, 57-76.

Dingle, Tony and Carolyn Rasmussen, *Vital Connections: Melbourne and its Board of Works 1891-1991*, McPhee Gribble, 1991.

Fort, Carol, "Militarisation and Urbanisation: The Second World War, Public Housing and the Shaping of Metropolitan Adelaide," *Australian Economic History Review*, 55 (1), 42-61.

Freeland, J.M., *Architecture in Australia: A History*, Penguin, 1972.

Freestone, Robert, *Urban Nation: Australia's Planning Heritage*, CSIRO Publishing, 2010.

Frost, Lionel, *The New Urban Frontier: Urbanisation and City Building in Australasia and the American West*, New South Wales University Press, 1991.

_____ "The Contribution of the Urban Sector to Australian Economic Development Before 1914," *Australian Economic History Review*, 38 (1), 1998, 42-73.

_____ "An Outer Suburban House of the 1950s," Susan Marsden (ed), *Our House: Histories of Australian Homes*, Australian Heritage Commission, 2001. http://www.environment.gov.au/resource/our-house-histories-australian-homes-41. Accessed 24 July 2015.

_____ "Across the Great Divide: The Economic History of the Inland Corridor," Alan Mayne (ed), *Beyond the Black Stump: Histories of Outback Australia*, Wakefield Press, 2008, 57-84.

_____ "Urbanisation," Simon Ville and Glenn Withers (eds), *The Cambridge Economic History of Australia*, Cambridge University Press, 2015, 245-263.

Frost, Lionel and Tony Dingle, "Sustaining Suburbia: An Historical Perspective on Australia's Growth," Patrick Troy (ed), *Australian Cities: Issues, Strategies and Policies for Urban Australia in the 1990s*, Cambridge University Press, 1995, 20-38.

Garden, Don, "Type 15, *Glengarry* and *Catalina*: The Changing Space of the A.V. Jennings Home in the 1960s," Graeme Davison et al (eds), *The Cream Brick Frontier: Histories of Australian Suburbia*, Monash Publications in History No. 19, 1995, 140-53.

Garnter, Ann, "Death of the Project House? Reflections on the History of Merchant Builders," Graeme Davison et al (eds), *The Cream Brick Frontier: Histories of Australian Suburbia*, Monash Publications in History No. 19, 1995, 108-39.

Golding, Peter, *Black Jack McEwen: Political Gladiator*, Melbourne University Press, 1996.

Graham, D.B., *The Formation of the Australian Country Parties*, Australian National University Press, 1966.

Greig, Alistair, *The Stuff Dreams Are Made Of: Housing Provision in Australia 1945-1960*, Melbourne University Press, 1995.

Harris, Richard, "To Market! To Market! The Changing Role of the Australian Timber Merchant, 1945–c. 1965," *Australian Economic History Review*, *40* (1), 22-50.

Head, Brian, "Economic Development in State and Federal Politics," Brian Head (ed), *The Politics of Development in Australia*, Allen & Unwin, 1986, 1-55.

Howe, Renate (ed), *New Houses for Old: Fifty Years of Public Housing in Victoria, 1938-1988*, Ministry of Housing and Construction, 1988.

Lloyd, C.J. and Patrick N. Troy, *Innovation and Reaction: The Life and Death of the Federal Department of Urban and Regional Development*, George Allen & Unwin, 1981.

Macintyre, Stuart, *Australia's Boldest Experiment: War and Reconstruction in the 1940s*, NewSouth, 2015.

McLean, Ian, *Why Australia Prospered: The Shifting Sources of Economic Growth*, Princeton University Press, 2013.

Maddock, Rodney, "The Long Boom 1940-1970," Rodney Maddock and Ian McLean (eds), *The Australian Economy in the Long Run*, Cambridge University Press, 1987, 79-105.

Merrett, David, "Australian Capital Cities in the Twentieth Century," J. W. McCarty and C. B. Schedvin (eds), *Australian Capital Cities: Historical Essays*, Sydney University Press, 1978, 171-98.

Merrett, David and Simon Ville, "Tariffs, Subsidies and Profits: A Re-assessment of Structural Change in Australia 1901-39," *Australian Economic History Review*, *51* (1), 2011, 46-70.

Murphy, John, *Imagining the Fifties: Private Sentiment and Political Culture in Menzies' Australia*, UNSW Press, 2000.

Neutze, Max, *Economic Policy and the Size of Cities*, Australian National University Press, 1965.

Nielson, H.L., *The Voice of the People, Or, the History of the Kyabram Reform Movement*, Arbuckle, Waddell & Fawckner, 1902.

Peel, Mark, *Good Times, Hard Times: The Past and Future in Elizabeth*, Melbourne University Press, 1995.

Pickett, Charles, *The Fibro Frontier: A Different History of Australian Architecture*, Powerhouse Publishing, 1997.

Pooley, Colin G., "Patterns on the Ground: Urban Form, Residential Structure and the Social Construction of Space," Martin Daunton (ed), *The Cambridge Urban History of Britain: Volume III 1840-1950*, Cambridge University Press, 2000, 429-65.

Rickard, John, *Class and Politics: New South Wales, Victoria and the Early Commonwealth, 1890-1910*, Australian National University Press, 1976.

Rowse, Tim, *Nugget Coombs: A Reforming Life*, Cambridge University Press, 2002.

Self, Peter, "Alternative Urban Policies: The Case for Regional Development," Patrick Troy (ed), *Australian Cities: Issues, Strategies and Policies for Urban Australia in the 1990s*, Cambridge University Press, 1995, 246-64.

Spearritt, Peter, *Sydney since the Twenties*, Hale & Iremonger, 1978.

Stapledon, Nigel, "Trends and Cycles in Sydney and Melbourne House Prices from 1880 to 2011," *Australian Economic History Review*, 52 (3), 2012, 293-317.

Swan, Keith, *A History of Wagga Wagga*, City of Wagga Wagga, 1970.

Troy, Patrick, "Suburbs of Acquiescence, Suburbs of protest," *Housing Studies*, 15 (5), 2000, 717-38.

_____ *Accommodating Australians: Commonwealth Government Involvement in Housing*, Federation Press, 2012.

Whitwell, Greg, *Making the Market: The Rise of Consumer Society*, McPhee Gribble, 1989.

Whitwell, Greg, and Diane Sydenham, *A Shared Harvest: The Australian Wheat Industry, 1939-1989*, Macmillan, 1991.

10

Sir Robert Menzies and Australian Education

Greg Melleuish

There are two key periods in the history of the role of the government in development of education in Australia. The first ranges from the early 1860s to the early 1880s and was concerned with establishment of a system of state schools at an elementary, or primary, level in each of the colonies.[1] Schools were to be run by the government, attendance was made compulsory and the instruction secular; what was meant by secular varied from colony to colony. Most important, government funding was withdrawn from all denominational schools. Those denominations which sought to provide an education which included religion had to find the means to support those schools. This meant the Catholic Church in particular. It refused to countenance secular education as it was defined in state schools. It was aided in its efforts by a large number of vocations by young men, and especially young women, who joined the various teaching orders thereby making the Catholic school system viable.

Introduction of secular state education in the mother colony, New South Wales, is especially associated with the name of Sir Henry Parkes, and his public service adviser, William Wilkins.[2] It can be said that creation of a set of state schools in each of the colonies was one of the great achievements of colonial Australia, matched only by the building of the railways in each colony. Establishment of a school system was one of the first major administrative achievements of Australia. The one great failing was its inability to accommodate Catholic Australians.

If the 1860s through to the 1880s was the first heroic age of Australian education, then it must be said that the 1950s and 1960s was the second.[3] If it was Henry Parkes who placed his stamp on the first period, then it was Sir Robert Menzies who did the same for the second. The system inaugurated in the 1880s of a government education system which had primary education as its principal focus, a large private sector of which schools run by the Catholic Church formed the majority and a small number of universities, primarily devoted to professional education, including teacher training, continued, with some modifications, for the next seventy years. What became of those who simply pursued what is best described as a liberal education was left very much to the fates. Many went on to become lawyers. As to the rest, it should be remembered that the Commonwealth Public Service did not have any provisions for recruiting generalist graduates until the 1930s.[4] University positions were few and far between. University-educated Australians of an intellectual disposition often ended up as expatriates.

Nineteenth century university teachers, of whom Charles Badham is the most prominent example,[5] planted civic humanist principles in their students and the consequence was the extraordinary generation who wrote the Commonwealth Constitution. Even Sir 'Enry Parkes was a great advocate of the belief that university graduates would provide leadership in a democratic society.[6] There has been a long tradition of what is best described as aristocratic liberalism in Australian democracy, the belief that the elected representatives in a democracy should constitute an aristocracy, in the sense of the rule of the best. The trustee theory of representation encouraged such a view.[7]

A belief in the power of education to effect progress has been a crucial element of liberalism since the nineteenth century in Australia. It rests on a faith that, just as it is possible to improve the material conditions of humanity, so human beings can also be improved in a moral, intellectual and spiritual manner. By the late nineteenth century liberalism in Australia, as in other parts of the English-speaking world, had come to possess strong links with philosophical Idealism and its belief in the development of "personality" as the product of the evolution of both the individual and the collective. In Australia the most coherent expression of this philosophical liberalism was F. W. Eggleston's *Search for a Social Philosophy* published in 1941.[8]

Menzies was clearly influenced by Idealism and does occasionally invoke the idea of personality. For Menzies, as for most adherents of Liberalism, the power of education lay in its capacity to improve individuals thereby allowing them to be the motor of social progress. Education gave individuals the capacity to bring a better world into being. Moreover, for Idealist liberals, progress would lead to creation of a world in which autonomous individuals would develop a strong sense of social cooperation thereby enabling them to work together willingly for the common good. Eggleston referred to this as the Christian ethic.[9]

Liberalism based on Idealism and with a considerable emphasis on education emphasises a quite different type of individual to one which focuses on entrepreneurial and business activity. Liberal Idealism was attractive to professionals as it emphasised duty and cooperation. It remained the dominant form of philosophy in Australia until the Second World War with the one exception of the Sydney Andersonians.[10]

Education is not mentioned in the Commonwealth Constitution as a field in which the Commonwealth had power to legislate and was therefore left to the States as their responsibility. As already mentioned, there was much vigorous educational reform conducted in the States in the first decade of the twentieth century. What then happened is open to speculation but it is clear that Australia after the Great War was not the same place it had been in 1914.[11] It is possible to argue that, just as there was no longer a Liberal Party on the political stage, so much of the dynamic which liberalism had provided for Australian national development for the seventy years until 1914, had dissipated as the country enjoyed Commonwealth governments led either by Labor or ex-Labor politicians for 22 of the 30 years between 1919 and 1949. Menzies was the first prime minister of Australia after Deakin to be a graduate of an Australian university.

In the early twentieth century the State governments had been active in the educational sphere. One thinks in this regard of a figure such as Peter Board who instituted reforms in New South Wales education in the early twentieth century, or Frank Tate in Victoria.[12] By the 1940s the various States equally were not the engines of liberal dynamism which they had once been. The *Engineers' Case* encouraged the growth of Commonwealth power while the power of the purse moved inexorably in favour of the Commonwealth.

When R. G. Menzies re-established the Liberal Party in 1944 he was also, in a very real sense, re-establishing Liberalism in Australia. Of greatest significance is the fact that he was doing so at the national level. The key issue is what sort of liberalism and, more importantly, what sort of individual, did he have in mind? Two things stand out. The first is that Menzies' liberalism and his understanding of the individual had been informed by Idealism; his ideal individual combined a sense of independence with strong notions of duty and responsibility.

Secondly, Menzies' liberalism was closely tied to his educational ideals and his understanding that education was a primary means through which an individual developed his or her individuality, or personality. Menzies published a considerable amount on education, as well as delivering many speeches on the topic throughout the whole of his political career. He had what might be described as a well-developed philosophy of education which had strong roots in his Idealist liberalism.

Menzies' liberalism was closely tied to his views about education and the belief that education was a means of ensuring that human beings progressed and developed, and were able to transcend their failings and weaknesses. Menzies argued on a number of occasions that material progress by itself can lead to barbarism and all the terrible events of the twentieth century. It needed to be complemented by some sort of moral and spiritual progress. A key factor in that progress was to be a humanities education. Menzies was perfectly aware of the human capacity to perform evil acts but, as a good liberal, he did not subscribe to the idea of a fallen human nature which could not be saved without the (unearned) gift of God's grace. In this regard he stood with David Hume and the Anglophiles of the Scottish Enlightenment, not the dour and miserable Calvinists. Menzies was essentially an optimist unlike the pessimistic atheist Calvinist, John Anderson, who stood in opposition to the whole basis of Menzies' philosophy of education.[13]

A humanities education would ensure that democracy in Australia maintained a form rooted in moderation and decency and was not corrupted by the possible vices which material progress could bring into being. It would perform the following tasks:

- Create good democratic citizens who would not be trapped by their narrow or provincial concerns.
- Ensure that material progress did not again lead to the sorts of barbarism which had marked the twentieth century.
- Provide the appropriate leadership required by a democracy, a leadership which would be marked by intelligence and moral responsibility.

It can be argued that, after the Second World War, Australia re-dedicated itself to progress, in a similar fashion to the Australia of the 1860s and 1870s which had inaugurated the first educational revolution. It was Menzies' great achievement to provide a refurbished liberal understanding of what progress meant in contrast to the social democratic vision provided by his Labor opponents. Australia would become a country engaged in secondary manufacturing industry, which required an educated population and a scientific infrastructure. This entailed expanding both secondary education and the universities. This idea of progress as national development established itself firmly as the core public philosophy of Australia. It was Menzies' role to ensure that this ideal was rooted in liberalism, not socialism, and that it moved in the direction of civilisation, not barbarism.

This idea of progress was widely, but not universally, held. It was an idea held in contempt by John Anderson and his small band of followers. Colin Clark was highly critical of the emphasis on the development of manufacturing industry, arguing that it failed to gain export markets even if it provided so much employment.[14]

Menzies was an enthusiastic advocate of education as an essential liberal element of any attempt to create a progressive Australia founded on the energy and activities of its individual citizens. The humanities were central to this vision. But that did not mean that he wanted to rush out and use the power of the Commonwealth to impose his educational vision on the country. Menzies was a constitutionalist and was well aware of the value of the separation of powers in a federation, quoting Montesquieu in support of that principle:

> Montesquieu, who had such an influence upon organic political science, had no respect for uniformity. He looked for a system (which the United States and Australia to a degree adopted) where there is a division of power, where power checks power.[15]

Nor, at any stage, did he seek to intervene in curriculum matters. Menzies did not express any interest in what schools and universities should teach. He deliberately stayed out of such matters on the ground that educational institutions knew how to behave properly. Menzies' interest was primarily in funding.

Menzies' understanding of the humanities was somewhat ill-defined. He did not seek to revive the classics, perhaps because, unlike his mentor, Owen Dixon, he appears not to have been an enthusiastic classicist; at university he needed two attempts to pass first-year Latin.[16] His speeches illustrate the way in which the Bible had formed the "furniture of his mind," but there is very little to suggest that he had much in the way of knowledge of the classical world or classical authors. His view of the humanities seems to have been coloured by his Idealism and its accompanying values of a vague spirituality and citizenship as well as by his understanding of what it meant to be British. Menzies' conception of the humanities was founded largely upon a combination of his love for English literature and a somewhat woolly Idealism; it stood at the opposite extreme to John Anderson's tough-minded view of classicism as relentless criticism. Menzies stood for all those notions of democracy, the state, citizenship and the universities which Anderson spent his career criticising.

The most important question to address in understanding Menzies and the actions which his Government took in relation to education is the connection between his philosophy of education and the policies which were adopted. In the twenty-first century it is too often assumed that Commonwealth involvement in educational matters, both universities and schools, was both inevitable and something positive. But Canada, for obvious reasons, does not have a federal department of education. Menzies believed in both progress and the efficacy of education as a motor of progress but that did not mean that this would automatically translate into Commonwealth money to support education.

As has been argued, Menzies was an Anglophile Scot who idealised what he saw as "Englishness" as a set of cultural attributes. This can be seen clearly in his essay on "The English Tradition."

> The travelling Englishman, the writing Englishman, the politically vocal Englishman, the governing Englishman in scattered colonies and protectorates has, so far, been broadly the educated Englishman. Education in England has a long and, if you like, conservative tradition behind it. The educated Englishman, therefore, has certain inherited and acquired mental habits which deserve study. He cannot be explained in a sentence, or disposed of by a single epigram. He is probably the most civilized of human beings; he is certainly one of the most complex.[17]

It would not be unfair to say that Menzies was very much concerned with the "educated Australian" and the possible means of creating a collection of such individuals who would become the leadership group of a democratic society. Menzies was an aristocratic liberal who understood that, if democracy was to grow and prosper, it required an educated elite who were devoted to the public good, who ruled on behalf of those who had elected them. Note the following comment from *Forgotten People*:

To discourage ambition, to envy success, to have achieved superiority, to distrust independent thought, to sneer at and impute false motives to public service—these are the maladies of modern democracy, and of Australian democracy in particular.[18]

A healthy democracy would appreciate, and make good use of, the ambitions of those who sought recognition and who entered public service to benefit the public good. A harmony between the ambitious few and the democratic citizenry was to be central to democracy.

Hence, during his career, Menzies' educational focus was primarily on the Australian university because it embodied what was best about England and the English, an institution which would produce the educated leaders of the future. This can be seen clearly in the seven features which he attributes to a university in a **modern** community in a pamphlet written in 1939:

First, the University must be a home of pure culture and learning.

Secondly, the University must serve as a training school for the professions.

Third, the University must serve as a liaison between the academician and the "good practical man."

Fourth, the University must be the home of research.

Fifth, the University must be a trainer of character.

Sixth, the University must be a training ground for leaders.

Seventh, the University must be the custodian of mental liberty, and the unfettered search for truth.[19]

The whole of the pamphlet is bathed in a glow of calm, peace and the spiritual which Menzies idealises as The University:

there can be no bounds to set to the flight of thought. There is an infinite value in the individual human soul; there is something infinitely moving in the spectacle of the human soul struggling towards the light.[20]

It reads a little like an English equivalent of Hermann Hesse's Glass Bead Game except that Menzies is adamant that the world of practice and the world of the University are inextricably connected. He clearly believed that an organic relationship should exist between the University and the society of which it was part. The contemplative life of the University enriches the soul but, for Menzies, the active life is to be preferred over the contemplative one. Perhaps the most important aspect of Menzies' comments are those on leadership, which indicate the way in which he understood the relationship between the educated leaders and the rest in a democracy:

> Democracy demands leaders and leadership. It demands leaders who will not be afraid to tell the people that they are wrong and to persuade and guide them. I do not deny, on the contrary I uphold, the right of the people to censure freely, to criticize, to elect, to reject.[21]

Menzies' view of the relationship between the University and the wider society in a democracy is a classical expression of aristocratic liberalism. There is an assumption underpinning it that independent individuals who follow their ambition and take up the mantle of leadership will somehow have a harmony of interests with those whom they lead.

There is a consistency in Menzies' writings on education, from decade to decade, from the 1930s to the 1960s, with a concentration on the need for a balance between material advancement and the ethical and the spiritual, the need to create good citizens and the problems of leadership in a democratic society. In a major speech on education delivered in the House of Representatives in 1945 Menzies:

> The broad problem, of which all these matters that I have mentioned are merely aspects, is the problem of education for citizenship ... The greatest failure in the world in my lifetime ... has not been the failure in mechanical capacity or manual capacity half as much as it has been the failure of the human spirit. War after war is the result of a failure of the human spirit, not of some superficial elements but of the fatal instability of man to adjust himself to other men in a social world. With all of our scientific development of this century, it still remains true that "the proper study of man is man", and that the real "peace-maker" is human understanding. The closer the countries of the world have come to each other in point of time, the more they have tended, unhappily, to develop a narrow spirit of self-sufficiency. The more absorbed the people become in the technique of material living, the more they have neglected their moral responsibilities, and the more, unhappily, they have neglected the problems of popular government.[22]

Now consider this extract from a radio broadcast Menzies made in 1954:

> But what do we mean by education. I have known men with University degrees who remained basically stupid and unperceptive and selfish. I have known men who had no schooling after they were thirteen, who

spoke what we would call bad English, but who had character, wisdom, reflection, and a warm understanding of their fellow-men.

Education does not simply mean the compulsory getting of a stock of knowledge. Knowledge is good; but wisdom is better. It is the way a man's mind works that matters. To be educated is to have learned how to think; to have acquired self-discipline; to have understood duty and the rights of others.

These tasks are not merely scientific or mechanical. A man may be a great scientist, and be uncivilised. He may have mastered the technique of the law but have no real understanding of its spirit. Education must produce a sense of values, high ethical standards, and a spirit of tolerance, or it fails.[23]

Again, this address, delivered to the 1961 conference, The Challenges to Australian Education, Menzies provides his definition of the purpose of education:

Once we get above the rudiments, education is the business, I repeat, of producing an educated personality. The work of organising a community educational service is therefore a complex one, requiring great skill, devotion, and understanding. What is to be aimed at is a general system, producing individuals of great variety.[24]

Education in Australia, he argued, has two great tasks. First there is the need

to train as many students as possible in bodies of knowledge which will make them more competent to deal with the practical affairs of life. We must train and equip more competent workers in every branch of every industry; more and better scientists and technologists, more and better administrators, engineers, doctors and lawyers …[25]

But, as always, Menzies is fully aware of both the limitations of modern science and the need to find a remedy to the human propensity for evil:

Modern advances in applied science [are sometimes mistaken for] the proof of advancing civilisation. These are among the mere mechanical aids to civilisation. Civilisation is in the hearts and minds of men. It will advance or fall back according to the use we make of knowledge and of skill. In spite of all we have had to our hands, the twentieth century has seen more of hatred and envy and malice, than any of us could have foreseen when we were young and hopeful.

We must recapture our desire to know more, and feel more, about our fellowmen; to have a philosophy of living; to elevate the dignity of man, a dignity which, in our Christian concept, arises from our belief that he is made in the image of his Maker.[26]

These statements across three decades express a consistent educational philosophy by Menzies. At its core stood the need to produce an "educated personality" who would be a good citizen, a desire to embrace science as the basis of modern progress, and the need for proper moral development so that human beings will be able to keep up with the advancement of science and the relevance of education for democracy. It is a liberal vision of progress. The horrors of the first half of the twentieth century were no doubt at the back of Menzies' mind. He was determined that liberal progress was not only desirable but also, in the face of human weakness, an achievable goal. Nor was he alone in his task of creating an educated personality. James Darling, the headmaster of Geelong Grammar, for instance, argued that "The civilized man, sensitive, wide in his interests, tolerant and yet courageous, intellectual and strong in principle, is our ideal, and it is by our education that we must pursue it."[27]

Menzies' writings on the University and education exhibit a well thought out position on the place of education in a modern, liberal progressive social order. Education is a motor of progress which, if properly conducted, will enable human beings to advance materially and technologically and create a more civilised world. Universities will produce the educated elite of this progressive social order; this elite will be composed of genuine individuals and this variegated group will be able work together for the public good and be able, and willing, to take decisions to benefit the public good even if such decisions were unpopular.

The main problem was that education was not a Commonwealth matter, and Menzies was a good constitutionalist. There was little he could do in the educational realm unless opportunities presented themselves.

In this regard, the key factor seems to have been the inability, or unwillingness, of the State governments to fund their increasing educational needs at a time when financial power was moving towards the Commonwealth. The old educational order was the creation of the first educational revolution of the nineteenth century. It had seen only a fraction of students complete much in the way of secondary education, and an even smaller proportion attend university. Moreover, the States did not have the burden of educating that significant proportion of students who attended Catholic and other private schools. Older style teaching methods allowed for large classes and the amount of technology required was not high. Nevertheless, educational standards at the elite high schools, both public and private, were very high because they only educated students of a high quality. Given Australia's occupational profile there was little need, or desire, to expand the education system significantly. Furthermore, the birth rate declined during the 1930s.

This had begun to change by the late 1940s with an increase in the birth rate and an enlarged intake of migrants. The cost of education began to rise. To give an example, although there was a small decline in the number of secondary students in New South Wales between 1945 and 1950, between 1950 and 1960 the number of secondary schools and students doubled.[28] There was also a significant increase in the number of university students. The scheme to provide university education for ex-servicemen also increased the number of university students in the short term. Put simply, education had again become an important public policy issue in Australia, just as it had been in the 1860s and 1870s.

What then did Australian universities look like during the 1950s?[29] The first thing is that they still looked to Britain and, in particular, Oxford and Cambridge, as their spiritual home and source of inspiration. This was not surprising given that the 1950s was the last decade in which strong ties between Australia and Britain seemed to be natural to both parties. Australian universities were small provincial institutions which dreamed of Oxford and Cambridge but exhibited clearly that the Scottish universities had been their founding model. There was little interest in American education and even less in that of continental Europe.

P. H. Partridge pointed out, early in the 1950s, that there was an attitude in the wider Australian community that the universities themselves were to blame for some of their problems.[30] It can be argued that they had not put down deep roots in their communities and were regarded as somewhat exotic institutions, a view with roots in the nineteenth century. They trained professionals and teachers but they were not looked upon with enormous affection by large numbers of Australians.

There appears to have been a disjuncture between universities' somewhat inflated and romantic view of themselves and the reality of university life in Australia. Menzies clearly shared that romantic view, along with an ideal of the humanities which had a powerful religious or spiritual dimension. But it could be said that Menzies hoped to make that ideal a reality.

Some Commonwealth funding for universities had commenced under Menzies' predecessor but it is Menzies who took the major steps towards Commonwealth funding of universities when he accepted the recommendations of the Murray Report. There was a slow and elaborate courtship ritual between the Commonwealth and the universities, as represented by the Australian Vice-Chancellors Committee (AVCC), before they embraced each other in what would become a very peculiar union.

Some of the features of that courtship are as follows:

- The universities and the AVCC clearly wanted funding from some source. The Commonwealth looked like the best bet as it had become financially dominant within the Australian system of government. The universities did not receive large amounts of money from bequests or from their alumni (this may say something about Australian culture; my great-grandfather left money in his will to the American college which he had attended in the 1880s). According to the Murray Report, by the 1950s only 15.6 percent of their income came from fees.[31]

- The universities had expanded in the post-war period; they probably needed to expand physically. But, if that was the case, why was so little income being earned from fees?

- The universities launched a campaign emphasising how they were in crisis and in need of an injection of funds.

- Menzies did not move precipitously as he had other concerns and appears to have been wary of extending Commonwealth responsibilities. He was guided by the course of events, not ideology.

From 1951 onwards the Commonwealth made some grants to the universities under section 96 of the Constitution but which required that universities supply three times the grant from State governments and fees.[32] As Menzies himself later stated, this funding, embodied in the States Grants (Universities) Bill, was not paid directly to the universities but was made possible by the constitutional amendments of 1946 which inserted "benefits to students" into the Constitution.[33]

From the early 1950s the Menzies Government inaugurated a scheme of undergraduate university scholarships.[34]

Finally, in 1956, he established the Prime Minister's Committee on Australian Universities which was composed of two British academics, including the chairman, Sir Keith Murray, the Australian head of the CSIRO who was a fervent advocate of Commonwealth funding for universities, and two senior businessmen. Surprisingly, no-one on the panel raised the question of the financial implications of the expansion of the universities: no-one asked how much this might cost the Commonwealth in the longer term. This was a very British way of doing things; when higher education was expanded in Britain it was done on the haziest of notions of economic growth (which turned out to be wrong) and with little consideration of how it was going to be funded. As Noel Annan pointed out, in Britain where the same Murray was in charge of universities as he who gave advice to the Commonwealth Government, "the wave of expansion gathered such momentum that when it broke it left devastation behind it."[35]

The Murray Committee, it could be said, let the children loose in the lolly shop. The lobby group was allowed to decide what should be done. Moreover, Menzies accepted the recommendations of the report.

Looking at the Murray Report a number of things stand out:

- It is framed within a doctrine of national progress and development in which the growth of manufacturing industry is given prominence along with the idea that science is now crucial for any country wishing to prosper.

- The educational philosophy mirrored that of Menzies with a humanistic rationale combined with arguments in favour of science. There was no real scrutiny of what the place of universities was/should be in Australia. No attempt was made to look beyond an accepted British ideal of a university. A certain model of the university was assumed. In particular, the report supported the idea of academic autonomy and of the academic being left free to follow their inquiries wherever they might lead.

- There appears to have been no discussion regarding the issue of raising fees or of exploring other means of funding universities.

- It advocated a £500 per annum increase for professors.[36] (In 1955 the minimum annual pay for adult males was £764). In 2015 terms, that would be about $20,000 pa.

- The Treasury had been side-lined from the process and there appears to have been no estimates of what Commonwealth funding for universities might entail in future decades.[37]

This was Menzies' great triumph; or was it? Certainly, historians who have written on the topic, such as A.W. Martin and Cameron Hazlehurst, have tended to hail Menzies as the great saviour of Australian universities.[38] More recently, Hannah Forsyth has disagreed, seeing Menzies' funding of the universities as a Commonwealth grab for control, citing a 1959 cabinet document which states that "Money is the weapon by which oversight of universities will be secured."[39]

There is another possibility, which is that the AVCC hoodwinked Menzies into giving them what they wanted. The only problem with that interpretation is that, in appointing Murray as the chair of the committee, Menzies seems to have been conniving at giving the universities what they sought.

In some ways, given who could afford to go to universities in the 1950s, it looks suspiciously like a case of middle class welfare. Why, for example, did Menzies not canvass the issue of increased fees for students? Surely, given the values which Menzies had espoused since *The Forgotten People*, of the self-reliant individualism of the Middle Class, he should have supported the possibility of some sort of increased contribution by those who received the benefits of such an education. Martin suggested that the funding of the universities was motivated by a desire to counter the idea Labor was more friendly to universities and education than the Liberal Party.[40] If so, it must be said that the move was a miserable failure.

Menzies had a somewhat old fashioned view of universities based on his idealisation of Oxford and Cambridge and his student years at the University of Melbourne. I think that he saw them as being a sort of gentlemen's club and that those running them could be trusted to behave properly (he never had the benefit of seeing the episodes of *Yes, Minister* and *Yes, Prime Minister* involving universities). He had a great faith in British culture and its civilising capacities. Reading his writings on universities and education, it is possible to argue that Menzies saw the opportunity to create "educated men" who would become the leaders of Australian democracy. It was a noble and generous vision as it would consummate the ideals of aristocratic liberalism. It would produce an educated elite who were imbibed with such values that they would rule in the best interests of the people as a whole. In any case, the Commonwealth now had control of the purse strings in case the universities did not live up to what was expected of them.

But Menzies' vision was not to be. Menzies would be, I think, genuinely shocked by the way in which Australian universities subsequently evolved. An objective assessment of the behaviour of the AVCC and the academic world generally at the time would have awoken Menzies out of his dream. Universities were not special; they were just another interest group in search of money.

The major implication of the Murray Report was that the intervention by the Commonwealth completed the process whereby universities in Australia became rent-seekers of the Australian taxpayer rather than independent entities. It also raised the spectre of increasing Commonwealth control of universities in terms of setting their priorities and directing what they would do. It was quite a price to pay for a £500 pay rise.

In the short term, the triumph of the universities as embodied by implementation of the Murray Report served to increase academic hubris, and perhaps to increase the distance separating the universities from the wider Australian community. As it seemed to confirm the "aura" which universities placed around themselves, it encouraged academics to think that they had a "special place," including a privileged right to criticism. Interestingly, Menzies made an observation on this matter in a speech delivered at the University of New South Wales in the course of which he defended free speech: "Freedom is to be seen as a faculty enjoyed by all citizens, not because they are academic or because they conduct a newspaper, but because they are citizens."[41]

The ultimate outcome of the Murray Report was expansion of Australian universities who believed that they stood in some way aloof from the society which they served, and who now developed the notion that they had a special right to Commonwealth funding. This came up against a government which came to appreciate that, because they held the purse strings, they could impose controls on the universities.

Menzies had hoped to ensure that the State governments paid their proper share of the funding of the universities, but he also boasts in his memoirs that, at the time of his retirement, his Government had spent some $249 million dollars on universities.[42] Bob Besant notes that student numbers more than doubled in the next decade while full-time staff numbers increased by 100 percent. After 1960 the rule that, for £1 allocated by the Commonwealth, there had to be a matching £3 from the State, was dropped to a ratio of 1:1.85.[43] The crazy world of the contemporary Australian university was beginning to emerge.

The key aspect of Menzies' actions in commissioning the Murray Report and then adopting its recommendations, is acceptance that the management of universities required some sort of national framework; universities were central to the project of national development and progress. They were to be public universities, and they would be funded primarily by the Commonwealth. They would ensure that progress would possess both a material and a moral/spiritual dimension. The principle of national development comes to override both a belief in the sturdy independence of the individual and the desire to preserve a federal system based on a proper allocation of government responsibilities as set out by the Constitution.

Ironically, Menzies' great fear was that Commonwealth involvement in university matters would lead to uniformity and homogeneity and a lack of variety. Yet there was already a uniformity about Australian universities, and Australian education generally, prior to the Murray Report. Commonwealth involvement only aggravated that situation, even if, as a result of the subsequent Martin Report, it set out to establish colleges of advanced education.[44] There was little incentive for establishment of private universities or specialist universities, especially ones focusing on technical and/or technological matters. Nor was any consideration given to liberal arts colleges on the American model or to highly specialised technological institutes. There was only one model up for consideration, and that was the British.

It has to be recognised that the Australian tradition of public education, based on its State government bureaucracies, has never been friendly to variety or diversity. It is little wonder that universities evolved in a similar fashion. That uniformity had been the product of the first education revolution of the 1860s and 1870s when the various colonies had inaugurated their different, but similar, systems of secular public education. Now the second education revolution launched by Menzies would seek individuality and variety but end up by, yet again, confirming the Australian talent for uniformity and homogeneity.

This is also the case with Menzies' other significant contribution to the second education revolution in Australia, the beginning of the funding of non-government schools. It is clear that Menzies had a soft spot for what he termed, "church schools", and his educational philosophy approved of the religious education which they provided for their students. Speaking at Mt Scopus in 1960, he said:

> I want to tell you, not for the first time, that I am a tremendous believer, an enthusiastic believer, in schools which have the background of religion; I think it is a marvellous thing that the boys and girls who are at this school, and who will be at it in future, should be able to grow up adhering to their faith, knowing the foundations of their faith, and keeping in contact with the great literary and religious tradition which serves to decorate that faith.[45]

Religious education, of whatever kind, helped to create good Australian citizens. The first Australian educational revolution had created a secular state system of education which failed, however, because it left Catholics outside of the tent. This exclusion, and the fact that Catholics had to pay both fees for their own schools and taxes to support state schools, was a significant continuing sore in Australian public life. The Labor Party may have had many Catholic members of Parliament (State as well as Commonwealth), and supporters, but it failed to do anything to remedy what many saw as an injustice. On the other hand, one could argue that not receiving government largesse provided non-government schools with a certain independence.

State governments were not going to remedy this situation. It was Menzies who took the first steps to provide financial assistance for non-government schools by the Commonwealth Government. Menzies always emphasised that he was not, despite his background, a sectarian creature, and believed that religious differences should not be part of Australian public life.[46]

The measures were announced as part of the policies for the 1963 House of Representatives election, the last which Menzies would fight.[47] They included the funding of science blocks for all schools and provision of Commonwealth scholarships for senior students at high school regardless of the type of school. As Graeme Starr pointed out in his biography of Sir John Carrick, state aid for non-government schools was an issue which could both attract voters and repel them,[48] a not unimportant consideration given the wafer thin majority of the Government in the House of Representatives in 1963. It was an opportunity to put to rest, once and for all, the idea that the Liberal Party was a Protestant party, and to attract Catholics into the party. Menzies and Carrick worked together to achieve state aid because it was both good public policy and a means to end the running sore of sectarianism in Australian life.[49]

These measures fitted easily into the Menzies vision of an educated Commonwealth. Funding science was a way of securing progress and national development in the material sense while scholarships for senior students was a way of ensuring that there would be an educated elite, based on merit, who would come to run the country. Again, it meshed well with Menzies' vision of the role education had to play in ensuring that Australian democracy had the leadership it required.

Looking back from the vantage point of the twenty-first century it is easy to point to where Commonwealth funding of schools has led and, anachronistically, to ask why Menzies ever bothered. But that would be unfair. Menzies had a noble educational vision. It was a liberal vision and not narrowly Australian:

> The challenge to us as a nation is to play our part in increasing the

world's resources. And, in essence, that is a challenge to us to improve our education; for it is only by constantly improving education and skills that we discharge our world duty.[50]

He was, as this essay has argued, in many ways an old-fashioned liberal with a philosophy grounded in Idealism and the need to build a harmonious international order. I believe that it is true to say that Menzies had a similar vision of a harmonious organic society for Australia. A harmonious society was one composed of autonomous individuals who could come together and cooperate, recognising the benefits of being good citizens. They would elect leaders who equally worked for the public good; a good democracy required an educated and ethical elite to lead it.

He understood the role which education, and, in particular, the universities had to play in ensuring that this type of modern democratic society worked as it should, for the benefit of the country, and ultimately for the benefit of the world. Education was crucial to ensuring the project of Australian national development and progress. To this end Menzies helped to inaugurate what was essentially the second educational revolution in Australia by providing funding for both public universities and independent schools in Australia. Both measures were guided by the desire to create a more harmonious Australia; the former by creating a leadership class which was both technically capable and ethically motivated, the latter by seeking to put an end to a period of sectarian conflict which was one of the more unpleasant aspects of Australian life until the 1960s.

Menzies cannot be blamed for where the educational revolution he helped to inaugurate ultimately led except insofar as he failed to consider the financial implications of government funding of the universities. But then, the British fell into exactly the same trap. What one can say is that his educational policies were motivated by a generous vision about the future of Australia. One only wishes that his generosity had been matched by those who were the beneficiaries of the changes which he brought into being.

Endnotes

[1] A.G. Austin, *Australian Education 1788-1900: Church, State and Public Education in Colonial Australia*, Sir Isaac Pitman & Sons, Melbourne, 1961.

[2] D. Morris, "Henry Parkes – Publicist and Legislator" and C. Turney, "William Wilkins – Australia's Kay-Shuttleworth", in C. Turney (ed.), *Pioneers of Australian Education: A Study of the Development of Education in New South Wales in the Nineteenth Century*, Sydney University Press, Sydney, 1969, 155-245.

[3] The major secondary sources for Menzies part in the second education revolution are Bob Besant, "Robert Gordon Menzies and Education in Australia", *Melbourne Studies in Education*, Vol. 47, Nos 1 & 2, November, 2006, 163-187; A.W. Martin, "R.G. Menzies and the Murray Committee", in A W Martin, *The 'Whig' view of Australian history and other essays*, ed. J.R. Nethercote, Melbourne University Press, Melbourne, 2007, 176-205, Hannah Forsyth, *A History of the Modern Australian University*, NewSouth, Sydney, 2014, Grant Harman, "Development of Higher Education", in Scott Prasser, J. R. Nethercote & John Warhurst (eds.) *The Menzies Era: A Reappraisal of Government, Politics and Policy*, Hale & Iremonger, Sydney, 1995. For Menzies own account of his educational policy see Sir Robert Menzies, *The Measure of the Years*, Cassell, London, 1970, 81-97.

[4] William Coleman, Selwyn Cornish, & Alf Hagger, *Giblin's Platoon: The Trials and Triumph of the Economist in Australian Public Life*. ANU E-Press, Canberra, 2006, 162.

[5] See, for example, Michael Hogan (ed.), *A Lifetime in Conservative Politics: Political memoirs of Sir Joseph Carruthers*, UNSW Press, Sydney, 2005, 37-42.

[6] Sir Henry Parkes, *Fifty years in the Making of Australian history*, Longmans, Green & Co, London, 1892, 297

[7] See Greg Melleuish, *Despotic State or Free Individual: Two Traditions of Democracy in Australia*, Australian Scholarly Press, 2014, especially Chs 3 & 4.

[8] F.W. Eggleston, *Search for a Social Philosophy*, Melbourne University Press, Melbourne, 1941.

[9] Eggleston, op. cit., 320-30.

[10] S.A. Grave, *A History of Philosophy in Australia*, University of Queensland Press, St Lucia, 1984, especially Ch. 2.

[11] Michael Roe, *Nine Australian Progressives: Vitalism in Bourgeois Social Thought 1890–1960*, University of Queensland Press, St. Lucia, 1984, 315-20.

[12] A.R. Crane and W.G. Walker, *Peter Board: His Contribution to the Development of Education in New South Wales*, ACER, Melbourne, 1957; R.J.W. Selleck, *Frank Tate: a Biography*, Melbourne University Press, Melbourne, 1982.

[13] On Anderson's educational ideas, see John Anderson, *Education and Inquiry*. D.Z. Phillips (ed.), Blackwell Oxford, 1980. On Anderson's views on liberal education, see Greg Melleuish, "Democracy, Utilitarianism and the Ideal of Liberal Education in Australia", *Knowledge Cultures*, Vol. 3, No. 3, 2015, 136-40.

[14] Colin Clark, *Australian Hopes and Fears*, Hollis & Carter, London, 1958, Ch. XI.

[15] R.G. Menzies, "The Challenge to Education", in R.G. Menzies et al, *The Challenge to Australian Education*, F.W. Cheshire, Melbourne, 1961, 5.

[16] Cameron Hazlehurst, *Menzies Observed*, Allen & Unwin, Sydney, 1979, 20.

[17] Robert Gordon Menzies, *Speech is of Time: Selected Speeches and Writings*, Cassell, London, 1958, 34.

[18] Robert Menzies, *The Forgotten People and Other Studies in Democracy*, Liberal Party of Australia, Melbourne, 2011, 36.

[19] R.G .Menzies, *The Place of a University in a Modern Community*, Melbourne University Press, Melbourne, 1939, 11, 19, 20, 25, 26, 27, 30.

[20] Ibid., 31.

[21] Ibid., 30.

[22] Speech by the Rt Hon R.G. Menzies, KC, MP, on Education, 30 July 1945, Sir Robert Menzies Papers, Ms 4936/6/15, 1415-6.

[23] R.G. Menzies, Australia Today – Man to Man Series – No 26 Wednesday 17 March 1954, Menzies Papers, Ms 4936/6/45 Various Broadcasts 1953-4, Box 257, 4.

[24] R.G. Menzies, "The Challenge to Education", 4.

[25] Ibid., 11-12.

[26] Ibid., 12.

[27] James Ralph Darling, *The Education of a Civilized Man*, F. W. Cheshire, Melbourne, 1962, 28.

[28] Craig Campbell & Geoffrey Sherington, *The Comprehensive High School: Historical Perspectives*, Palgrave Macmillan, New York, 2006, 74.

[29] James B. Conant, "Confidential report to the Carnegie Corporation James B. Conant on the University situation in Australia in the year 1951", *History of Education Review*, Vol. 39, No. 1, 2010, 8-22; Hannah Forsyth, "Academic Work in Australian universities in the 1940s and 1950s", *History of Education Review*, Vol. 39, No. 1, 2010, 44-52

[30] P.H. Partridge, "The Australian Universities," W.V. Aughterson, *Taking Stock: Aspects of Mid-Century Life in Australia*, F. W. Cheshire, Melbourne, 1953, 52.

[31] Report of the Committee on Australian Universities (Chair: Sir Keith Murray), September, 1957, Commonwealth Government Printer, Canberra, 24.

[32] Besant, 'Robert Gordon Menzies and Education in Australia", 178

[33] Menzies (1970), 85.

[34] Grant Harman, "Development of Higher Education", in Scott Prasser, J.R. Nethercote and John Warhurst (eds) *The Menzies Era; A Reappraisal of Government, Politics and Policy*, Hale & Iremonger, Sydney, 1995, 244.

[35] Noel Annan, *Our Age: Portrait of a Generation*, Weidenfeld and Nicolson, London, 1990, 382.

[36] Report of the Committee on Australian Universities, 122.

[37] Martin, "R.G. Menzies and the Murray Committee", 198-9.

[38] Martin, op. cit., 203; Cameron Hazlehurst, *Menzies Observed*, 379.

[39] Forsyth, *A History of the Modern Australian University*, 59.

[40] Martin, op. cit., 203.

[41] Sir Robert Menzies, *The Universities – Some Queries*, Wallace Wurth Memorial Lecture, University of NSW, Sydney, 1964, 14.

[42] Menzies (1970), 90.

[43] Besant, "Robert Gordon Menzies and Education in Australia", 180.

[44] Menzies (1970), 91.

[45] Sir Robert Menzies, Official Opening and Dedication at the Senior School Building Mount Scopus Memorial College,16 September, 1960, Ms 4936 Folders 131-136, Speeches July-September 1960, Box 210, 12–13.

[46] Menzies, *The Forgotten People,* 51-2.

[47] Federal Election 1963: Policy Speech of the Prime Minister (the Right Hon. Sir Robert Menzies, K.T., Q.C., M.P.), delivered in Melbourne on 12 November 1963, 21-2.

[48] Graeme Starr, *Carrick: Principles, Politics and Policy*, Connor Court, Ballan, 2012, 172.

[49] Ibid., 171.

[50] R.G. Menzies, "The Challenge to Education", 2.

11

Menzies, the Constitution and the High Court

Anne Twomey

Young Menzies and the Constitution

Robert Menzies achieved his most profound impact upon the Constitution and his greatest legal success[1] at the tender age of 25 in the famous (or infamous) *Engineers' Case*.[2] It was a radical start to a conservative career. He was acting for a union, overturning precedent and successfully advocating centralism over federalism.[3] The result was described by Menzies as "revolutionary."[4]

The first High Court, comprised of justices who had been deeply involved in drafting the Constitution, treated the Constitution as a political compact for a federation, rather than a legal text, and interpreted it as giving effect to implied doctrines. These included the doctrine of reserved State powers, which treated certain legislative areas as reserved for State parliaments, and the doctrine of immunity of State instrumentalities, which made the agencies of each level of government immune from the acts of the other.

By the time Menzies faced the High Court in the *Engineers' Case* in 1920, the composition of the bench had changed. It was now dominated by a new breed of legalists who were prepared to read the Constitution as a statute rather than a political compact.[5] Menzies persuaded them to overturn the precedents of the Court and to establish a new, legalistic way of interpreting the Constitution, which enhanced central Commonwealth power at the expense of the States.[6] This method of interpretation has dominated in High Court jurisprudence ever since. It must have been a salient experience for the young Menzies – to see the Constitution change so profoundly, simply by an alteration in the composition of the Court and an opportunistic argument by an ambitious counsel.[7] Formal constitutional change would never be so easy.

His experience as a barrister also gave Menzies a deeper understanding of the Constitution and an appreciation of its relationship to politics. As Sir Paul Hasluck noted, Menzies was not like the "many noisy amateurs who can recite a text without knowing its meaning or can use terms such as 'sovereignty' and 'rights' as though they are sticks and stones to beat a dog and not concepts to enlighten the mind of man." Hasluck saw Menzies as a "constitutionalist in philosophy as well as debate," who was respectful of his constitutional advisers and fully understood and appreciated their advice.[8]

The politics of constitutional reform

While understanding the law is important, so, too, is the politics when it comes to constitutional reform. It is an inherently political exercise – sometimes grubby and often dispiriting. To succeed, constitutional reform requires strategy, political nous, leadership and commitment. It also requires moderation and a good dose of common sense. These elements, however, are more often than not missing from referendum campaigns, bolstering their failure rates.

Although Menzies is renowned for only putting one constitutional amendment to referendum, during his long tenure as prime minister,[9] he had significant experience in referendum campaigns, on both the proposing and opposing sides. Menzies, looking back on his career, observed that:

> [C]onstitutional development is much more than a lawyer's exercise. It is the product of a fascinating mixture of legalism, politics, public psychology, sociology, whatever label you care to put on these exercises ….
>
> Now in my years at the Bar, and in constitutional cases, I thought and spoke as a lawyer, viewing the structure of government from the outside, as it were. As a political minister, and particularly as a Prime Minister, I learned that things look different from the inside. This is what you might call the 'seamy side' of constitutionalism.[10]

Menzies noted that, as a politician, he became more conscious of the need for Commonwealth power in order to ensure that great policies are effective. He admitted to chafing against the legalism of the federal system[11] – a legalism that he had helped bring about through the *Engineers' Case*. But he also recognised that there were ways that the Constitution could change without any formal amendment. They included changes in methods of interpretation by the courts and the reinterpretation of old powers in new ways that would not have been anticipated by the drafters of the Constitution.[12] Menzies may have been conservative but he was not an originalist – he accepted the need for the Constitution to change by interpretation to meet the practical demands of the day.

Referenda as turning points in Menzies' political career

By 1926, Menzies was well known as an accomplished junior barrister, but his first foray into politics came in response to the Bruce-Page Government's 1926 referendum to give the Commonwealth greater power over corporations, trade unions and industrial disputes. Menzies joined a committee supporting the "No" case and was allocated the task of speaking at meetings throughout Victoria. Hence, Menzies' first political speeches were given in a campaign to oppose formal constitutional change.[13] As with most referenda, it failed at the ballot-box. Having gained a taste for public speaking and politics, Menzies sought election to the Victorian Parliament the following year,[14] later becoming Attorney-General and Deputy Premier, before moving to the Commonwealth Parliament in 1934.

In 1937, as Commonwealth Attorney-General, Menzies found himself on the side proposing referendum questions. He failed, however, to convince the Australian people to give the Commonwealth legislative control over "air navigation and aircraft" to exempt marketing schemes from section 92 of the Constitution. As he later observed, "if ever there was a matter that called for national treatment rather than local, it was civil aviation."[15] Nonetheless, both referendum questions were defeated, failing to achieve an overall majority.[16] Menzies attributed the near loss of his electorate of Kooyong at the next election to the unpopularity of his referendum proposal. His normal buffer of a majority of 15 000 votes was reduced to 1 500, causing him to fear losing his seat.[17] This no doubt made him wary about the potential political cost of a failed referendum campaign. He proposed no constitutional reform during his first period as prime minister from 1939-1941, but this was unsurprising given the outbreak of war.

It was, however, Menzies' successful campaign against Labor's 1944 referendum about giving the Commonwealth post-war legislative power, which had even broader political ramifications for him. It gave him the support and the authority he needed to draw the non-Labor parties together to form the new Liberal Party.[18] Undaunted by the referendum's loss, Labor went to a referendum again in 1946, with three questions on social services, marketing schemes and industrial relations powers. The Liberal Party, under Menzies, was given a free vote on the issues. Menzies supported the social services amendment,[19] which was successful. The other two referendum questions failed. Labor submitted a further referendum to the people in May 1948 on giving the Commonwealth power to control rents and prices. This, too, failed. Thus, by the time Menzies returned to power in 1949, he had had substantial personal experience of the failure of formal constitutional reform.

When it comes to constitutional reform, Menzies' second period of government can be broken into three distinct periods. The first period, from 1949 to 1951, commenced with the development of two referendum proposals concerning double dissolutions and anti-nationalisation measures, which were overtaken by the failed referendum to give the Commonwealth Parliament power to deal with communism. The second period was one where consensus was sought through a major parliamentary review of constitutional reform. The third period, at the end of Menzies' premiership, involved the passage of legislation to hold a referendum on the issues of breaking the nexus between the Senate and the House of Representatives (section 24) and the repeal of section 127 of the Constitution. However, the holding of a referendum was aborted upon Menzies' retirement and not revived until 1967.

Formal constitutional reform proposals, 1949-1951

Proposed reform of double dissolution procedure

Upon election in 1949, Menzies faced a problem that was to be the scourge of later prime ministers – a hostile Senate. As half the Senate is elected every three years, he faced a lag which gave Labor a majority in the Senate during his first term.[20] Menzies wanted a double dissolution to clear out the Senate and give him a chance at control. The position had been complicated, however, by legislation passed in 1948 that provided for an increase in the number of Senators and introduction of the system of proportional representation. Ten Senators were elected from each State, so that five were to be elected every three years. This uneven number was important, because it gave the more popular party the opportunity to achieve a majority in the Senate by winning three out of the five seats. A double dissolution, requiring the election of ten Senators, made it most likely, however, that the main parties would win five seats each, perpetuating any deadlock. This was confirmed by modelling by the Chief Electoral Officer.[21]

In May 1950 Menzies introduced the *Constitution Alteration (Avoidance of Double Dissolution Deadlocks) Bill* 1950 into Parliament.[22] Its effect would have been to amend section 57 of the Constitution to split a double dissolution into two simultaneous half-Senate elections. Each elector in a State would vote for five Senators to be elected for a six-year term in one ballot and for another five Senators to be elected for a three-year term in the other ballot. This would have increased the chances that the more popular major party would win a majority and ensured that the Senate returned to its normal cycle of half-Senate elections every three years.

If successful, this amendment would also have removed the other main disincentive for governments to hold a double dissolution – the drop in the quota which permits independents and small parties to be elected with a smaller percentage of the vote. Menzies' proposal would have maintained the same quota as in an ordinary half-Senate election due to the operation of the two separate ballots.[23]

The referendum bill contained a further provision that would have amended the Constitution so that the total number of Senators for a State had to be divisible by two, but not by four, in order for there always to be an uneven number of Senators elected in half-Senate elections and thus also in the two Senate ballots at a double dissolution.[24] Chifley wryly observed that perhaps Menzies should go into the "crossword puzzle business," [25] but Menzies graciously attributed this oblique formula to the greater wisdom of the draftsman who added a "slight touch of humour into an otherwise somewhat matter-of-fact proposal."[26]

The Opposition objected to the Bill. It argued that it was designed to give governments majorities in the Senate so as to avoid the effective review of government legislation in the Senate.[27] The Labor Party, in the Senate, referred the Bill to a select committee.[28] The committee, comprising only Opposition senators, reported in November 1950 that the Bill should be dropped and the Constitution should be instead amended so that joint sittings would be used as the means to resolve deadlocks between the Houses.[29]

It is not clear why the Menzies Government ceased to pursue this proposal. It is likely that Menzies did not wish to divert attention from the primary issue of communism at the double dissolution election (in which he achieved his sought-after majority in the Senate without a constitutional amendment) or at the subsequent referendum on dissolution of the Communist Party. After the defeat of that referendum, the prospect of further constitutional reform was abandoned for some time. When asked in 1953 whether he would pursue a referendum on deadlocks at the forthcoming half-Senate election, Menzies responded with a curt, "No." [30] It was one of the labours of Hercules that he no longer needed to undertake. The *Sydney Morning Herald* suggested in 1961 that this was because a government that had been in office for a long time did not have any contentious measures that it needed to push through Parliament, unlike an incoming government.[31]

Proposed referendum on nationalisation

In Menzies' campaign speech for the 1949 election he promised to repeal the *Bank Nationalisation Act* and amend the Constitution to make it impossible for governments to nationalise businesses or industries by creating government monopolies without the approval of the people first being given in a referendum.[32] Menzies noted that voters in the past had been asked to give extra powers to the Commonwealth Parliament, but on this occasion they would be asked to hand back powers to themselves."[33]

It was originally intended that this proposal proceed to referendum at the same time as the deadlocks referendum. A draft bill was approved by Cabinet in April 1950.[34] The Government intended to introduce the referendum bill in May 1950,[35] but it proved too difficult to draft the amendment in such a way that would not result in constant challenges to Commonwealth legislation. There were too many areas in which the Commonwealth currently held a monopoly or might wish to do so for legitimate reasons, resulting in a shopping list of exceptions to the proposed amendment, including postal, telegraphic, telephonic or other like services (apart from broadcasting or television services), defence, marketing schemes and currency and coinage. Laws made with respect to the territories were also exempted as were laws with respect to the licensing of businesses such as banks, ships, aircraft operators or exporters of primary products. Even with this extensive list of exceptions, concerns were raised by government departments about its potential application during circumstances such as war, rendering it increasingly complex and raising dangers about its future interpretation.[36] The proposal was dropped.

In 1953, Menzies explained in a radio broadcast that "it has not proved possible to devise a constitutional amendment which will adequately protect banking and other industry, and yet not cripple the Commonwealth in times of national emergency."[37] He did not wish to leave it to the High Court to decide when an emergency justified action by the Parliament in taking over an existing factory or plant for public purposes, as the Court "cannot have either the information or the responsibility."[38]

Communist Party Case, *election and referendum*

In his first term of government, Menzies had secured the dissolution of the Communist Party on 15 June 1940 under the *National Security (Subversive Associations) Regulations* 1940 (Cth). These regulations were later held to be invalid by the High Court after they had also been used against the Jehovah's Witnesses.[39] Starke J described the regulations as "arbitrary, capricious and oppressive" because they put bodies "out of existence and divested [them] of their rights and their property on the mere declaration of the Executive Government."[40] By the time the regulations were struck down, however, the ban on the Communist Party had been lifted by the Curtin Labor Government in December 1942, as the Communist Party had declared its support for Australia's war effort after the Soviet Union had become an ally following its invasion by Germany in 1941.[41]

In 1948, as the Cold War intensified, the Liberal Party adopted as policy a proposal to ban the Communist Party again. It formed an important part of Menzies' policy speech in the 1949 election campaign.[42] Once elected, Menzies' *Communist Party Dissolution Bill* was introduced in Parliament. The recitals in the preamble to the Bill declared that the Australian Communist Party engages in actions "designed to bring about the overthrow or dislocation of the established system of government of Australia and the attainment of economic, industrial or political ends by force, violence, intimidation or fraudulent practices." The core of the proposed Act empowered the Governor-General to declare certain bodies associated with communism to be unlawful if he was satisfied they were prejudicial to the security and defence of Australia. The Governor-General could also declare that a person was a member of the Communist Party and likely to engage in acts prejudicial to the security of the Commonwealth or the execution of its laws. Once a person had been so declared, he or she was prohibited from being a Commonwealth public servant or holding an office in a union.

There was a power to obtain judicial review of a declaration, but only as to whether or not a person or body in fact fell within the relevant category of being a communist – not the judgment about whether or not their activities were likely to be prejudicial to the security of the Commonwealth. The burden of proof was also reversed so that unless the person declared to be a communist gave evidence in person, he or she had the burden of proving that he or she was not a communist.

Academics, such as Julius Stone,[43] and even prominent Liberals, such as Norman Cowper, criticised the repressive tactics adopted by the Bill, urging that people be prosecuted through the courts for offences rather than being "declared" by the Governor-General. Cowper put the Liberal position against the Bill best when he said:

> Every community has the right and duty to take steps to protect itself against forces which threaten its destruction. But, in choosing the steps to take, it must, I suggest, avoid any which are likely also to destroy those rights and liberties which are the justification for its existence. The rule of law, the principle that no man shall be punished unless he be convicted by due process of an offence established by law, the right freely to utter and publish criticism of authorities and institutions, the right to associate in trade unions, political parties, and other groups – surely these are the essentials of human progress? What shall it profit a nation if it gain complete relief from the Communist or any other menace and lose these fundamental rights? The thing that we find most detestable in Communism is its denial of these rights. Why oppose Satan if we are going to adopt his ways? ...
>
> The test of an unlawful association should be, not the opinions and prejudices of voters and legislators regarding it, but legal proof of unlawful acts and purposes – that is to say, of acts and purposes which are unlawful whether they are done or held by communists or Calathumpians, by members of the Miners' Federation or the Melbourne Club.[44]

The Labor Party took the view that while Menzies had a mandate for banning the Communist Party, his mandate did not extend so far as the provisions that prevented a right of appeal in relation to the assessment of the prejudicial nature of the organisation or persons subject to a declaration or other provisions that undermined civil liberties, such as the reversal of the burden of proof. It therefore substantially amended the Bill in the Senate, in a manner that the Government was not prepared to accept. Menzies promised to bring the Bill back in three months and that, if it was not passed, a double dissolution election would follow.[45] In the face of this threat, the Labor Opposition collapsed and the Bill passed the Senate on its second outing on 19 October 1950. The Act came into force after receiving royal assent the following day.[46]

It was immediately challenged by the Australian Communist Party and a number of unions in the High Court. Dr H.V. Evatt, Deputy Leader of the Opposition, took up the brief to argue that the law was invalid. On 9 March 1951, by a majority of 6 to 1 (with only Chief Justice Latham dissenting), the High Court struck down the validity of the *Communist Party Dissolution Act.* The majority held that the Parliament could not recite itself into power, by simply stating in the recitals that the Communist Party was subversive and threatened the defence of Australia.[47] Nor could the validity of an Act depend upon the opinion of the decision-maker that it is within constitutional power. As Justice Fullagar observed, a "power to make laws with respect to lighthouses does not authorize the making of a law with respect to anything which is, in the opinion of the law-maker, a lighthouse."[48] The connection with the defence power had to be established as a matter of fact, not Government opinion, and in this the Government failed.

Justice Dixon also expressed concern about the effect of the law upon civil liberties. He concluded that only the supreme emergency of war itself could extend the defence power to affect the status, property and civil rights of persons specifically named or otherwise identified.[49] Australia's participation in the Korean War was not enough to trigger such an expanded reading of the defence power as would be needed to support such an extreme law.

Menzies declined to make any legal criticism of the High Court's judgment, although he later told Dixon that he was "shocked" on reading his judgment in the case.[50] In the House of Representatives, Menzies went out of his way to note the "great learning" and "unquestioned integrity" of the judges and pointed out that the Court had simply declared the law of the Constitution rather than cast judgment on the merits of the law.[51] He also, however, declared that the Court's judgment "discloses grievous limitations upon the powers of the Commonwealth Parliament." Menzies argued that "many facts which those responsible for executive government and therefore for the safety of the country know only too well are not susceptible of legal proof, or alternatively could be proved only by the most dangerous disclosure of the personnel and operations of our Security Service."[52] In discussing alternative ways of dealing with the problem, he raised the prospect of a reference of power by the States under section 51(xxxvii) of the Constitution or a constitutional amendment.[53]

Menzies' first priority, however, was a double dissolution election so that he could gain control of the Senate. He had hoped for one from the very commencement of his term, but he wanted a "lively issue" to base it on.[54] In the end, the lively issue was communism, but he still needed a trigger to activate the double dissolution provisions, as the Senate had ultimately passed his *Communist Party Dissolution Act*. Menzies ordered that the *Commonwealth Bank Bill,* which had already been rejected once by the Senate, be moved to the head of the Senate's notice paper so that it could be rejected a second time in order to allow a double dissolution to be held.[55] In his ministerial statement on the High Court's judgment in the *Australian Communist Party Case,* Menzies taunted Chifley to reject the *Commonwealth Bank Bill* so that the constitutional machinery could operate and they could go to their "masters, the Australian people" to seek their verdict on "the Communist conspiracy."[56]

Concerned about the risk of a double dissolution election, Evatt advised that instead of rejecting the Bill, it should be sent to a parliamentary committee. He considered that such a referral would not amount to a "failure to pass" the Bill as required in order to trigger a double dissolution election.[57] The Senate referred the Bill to a select committee for consideration. Menzies, however, argued that this deferral of consideration *did* amount to a failure to pass it. He sought a double dissolution from the Governor-General, William McKell. While Labor supporters argued that McKell should seek the advice of the Chief Justice as to whether or not the conditions for a double dissolution had been met,[58] McKell granted Menzies his double dissolution – the first since 1914.[59] Chifley was shocked, having been advised that referral to a parliamentary committee was a normal parliamentary event and could not be regarded as a failure to pass the Bill.[60] On this occasion, Labor's parliamentary tactics had failed.

The election was held on 28 April 1951. The Liberal-Country Party Coalition won, losing only five seats to the Labor Party in the House of Representatives. Crucially, in the Senate, the Coalition picked up six seats from Labor, giving it a majority of 32 seats to Labor's 28.

Menzies then held a special Premiers' Conference in June 1951 at which he requested the States to refer the matter of communism to the Commonwealth under section 51(xxxvii) of the Constitution. Predictably, the States with Labor governments – New South Wales and Queensland – refused. This was the catalyst for Menzies announcing a referendum on the issue.

Despite starting with considerable public support,[61] the referendum held on 22

September 1951 failed, winning in only three States and losing the overall vote. Percy (later Sir Percy) Joske, a Liberal Member of the House of Representatives from 1951 to 1960, later observed that Menzies had shown "a failure to understand the Australian people and their appreciation both of freedom and of the rule of law."[62] He noted that the opinion quickly developed in the populace that "while proper steps should be taken to protect freedom and justice, justice was not to be denied to the law-breaker, and that he was entitled to a proper trial in a court of law." In addition, he noted that many people who opposed communism were still concerned that the power sought could be used "for dictatorial purposes" and that people could be declared to be communists even though they were not at all.[63]

Menzies attributed the loss, in part, to the complicated nature of the question. He concluded that if the Government had only sought the power to make laws with respect to communism, the referendum would have passed. However, Menzies was concerned that this would not be enough. It was difficult for the Government to prove in a court that a person or association had communist beliefs, especially without revealing its sources of intelligence. Hence, it wanted the power to "declare" persons or organisations to be communist, without having to prove it in court. It therefore sought authorisation for the enactment of an Act in the terms previously struck down by the High Court. This, according to Menzies, took the debate away from communism and focused it upon the "contentious details of the Act."[64] Menzies concluded that not only is the electorate reluctant to confer new powers on the Commonwealth but it is also "unwilling to modify in any way the old principle that 'a man is innocent until he is *proved* guilty'."[65]

Menzies concluded from his bruising experience that:

> The truth of the matter is that to get an affirmative vote from the Australian people on a referendum proposal is one of the labours of Hercules.... I don't think you will recall a single instance of a 'Yes' vote on constitutional change except a change designed to increase the amount of money being paid by the Commonwealth to someone else.[66]

Menzies attributed one of the impediments to constitutional change to the fact that these changes have to be put into statutory form. He thought that this "technical appearance" raises deep suspicion and distrust in the mind of the layman 'and when in doubt he votes 'No'."[67]

While Menzies may have been frustrated by his loss, others have argued that it was to his benefit in the long-term and ultimately saved his reputation from being marked with a McCarthyist taint.[68]

Joint Committee on Constitutional Review

Instead of engaging in partisan referendum battles, Menzies changed tack by seeking to achieve bipartisan agreement on constitutional reform. A parliamentary Joint Committee on Constitutional Reform, originally promised in Menzies' 1954 campaign speech,[69] was finally established by resolution of the both Houses on 24 May 1956.[70] It was constituted by both Labor and Coalition members.

The committee issued an interim report in 1958 before Parliament was dissolved and was revived in the next Parliament to present a final report in 1959. It primarily focused on parliamentary matters, such as the number of Members and Senators and the nexus between the Houses, disagreements between the Houses and the reckoning of the population for the purposes of distributing seats. In relation to the latter issue, the committee recommended the repeal of section 127 of the Constitution, which excluded Aboriginal people from the population count for the purposes of the allocation of seats amongst the States. It also considered the Commonwealth's legislative and economic powers as well as the method for altering the Constitution.

Despite its report having bipartisan support, at least at the committee level, the Menzies Government did not pursue the wide-ranging recommendations of the committee. Many have pointed to the hostility of the new Attorney-General, Sir Garfield Barwick, to the work of the committee as one reason for the Government's failure to adopt, or even to respond formally to, its recommendations.[71] Sawer suggested that the bipartisan recommendations of the committee were "probably somewhat to the left of the average opinion of this Parliament"[72] and the view was generally taken that the Opposition members had out-manoeuvred the Government members on the committee in getting their way.[73] This was because Government members on the committee were backbenchers, whereas the Opposition had "weightier" representation through more senior members, such as Arthur Calwell and Senator Nick McKenna, aided by the ambitious backbencher, Gough Whitlam.[74]

The Opposition moved a motion in the House of Representatives in 1961 that the recommendations of the committee "should be submitted to the people for their approval."[75] Calwell pledged the Opposition's support to all the proposed amendments, not just the ones that suited Labor best.[76] Barwick regarded such a proposal as "utter folly" as it would involve the people voting on a long list of complicated proposals.[77] Barwick also objected that the States had not been consulted. He argued that it was more practical to work with the States to achieve reform through cooperative legislation.[78] The debate on Calwell's motion was adjourned and never resumed. While the committee's report went on to gather dust, it has been suggested that it may have had an effect through influencing Justices of the High Court in the way that they have since interpreted constitutional powers.[79]

Formal Constitutional Reform Proposals – 1965-1966

Menzies returned to formal constitutional reform in 1965 with proposals to repeal section 127 of the Constitution and to break the nexus between the Senate and the House of Representatives. Both of these matters had been raised by the Joint Committee, but had been neglected until towards the end of Menzies' premiership.

Repeal of section 127 of the Constitution

Aboriginal voting issues came to prominence in 1961. While the right to vote in Commonwealth elections was restored in 1949 to Aboriginal people living in New South Wales, Victoria, South Australia and Tasmania as well as to Aboriginal people who had served or were currently serving in the armed forces, voting rights continued to be denied to Aboriginal people living in Queensland and Western Australia. In October 1961, the Select Committee on Voting Rights of Aborigines recommended that all Aboriginal people have the right to vote in Commonwealth elections.[80] This recommendation was implemented in 1962.[81]

Around the same time, in 1961, the Federal Conference of the Labor Party resolved that the exclusion of Aboriginal people from the race power in section 51(xxvi) of the Constitution should be removed.[82] The Leader of the Opposition, Arthur Calwell, introduced the *Constitution Alteration (Aborigines) 1964* into the Commonwealth Parliament on 14 May 1964.[83] It would have repealed section 127 and removed the exclusion of Aboriginal people from the race power in section 51(xxvi) of the Constitution. Calwell noted that the exclusion of Aboriginal people from this provision was originally intended to protect them from discriminatory legislation.[84] He considered, however, that its meaning had become distorted and it had become an excuse for excluding Aboriginal people from pensions and welfare, although this had since been corrected. Calwell also objected to the specific mention of a race in the Constitution. He said: "We do not mention Scottish, Irish, Welsh, English or German descent in the Constitution, and aboriginal descent should not be singled out for comment, either."[85]

In relation to section 127, Calwell argued that the only reason for excluding Aboriginal people from the reckoning of the population of a State for constitutional purposes was because it was considered impossible to take an accurate census of the whole Aboriginal population in 1901. As such a complete census had since become possible, it was appropriate to repeal section 127 as it no longer served a purpose and could be regarded as insulting.[86] The Minister for Territories, Charles Barnes, pointed out that, in practice, Aboriginal people were counted in the census.[87] Indeed, they had been counted in the census (to the extent practicable) from its beginning in the Commonwealth. In practice, they were only excluded for the purposes of allocating seats in the House of Representatives amongst the States.

Calwell also expressed his hope that a referendum to this effect would be held at the same time as one amending section 24 of the Constitution to break the nexus between the sizes of the two Houses. He guaranteed Opposition support to both referendum proposals and concluded that it was highly desirable that they be held.[88]

Billy Snedden, the Attorney-General, responded on behalf of the Government. He accepted that section 127 should be repealed, although he rejected any urgency in doing so. When it came to section 51(xxvi), however, he rejected the proposal to delete the exclusion of Aboriginal people from its terms. He argued that their removal would simply add to discrimination, be it adverse or beneficial discrimination. He stated that his party wanted to "move to the stage where there is no special legislation, whether it is beneficial or disadvantageous." He saw the proposed alteration of section 51(xxvi) as "turning back the clock."[89] He was also concerned that laws under this power would have to apply to all Aboriginal people, wherever situated, and that it would be impossible to apply one law to Aboriginal people who live in starkly different circumstances in different parts of the country.[90]

On 1 April 1965, Calwell again moved in the House of Representatives that the recommendations of the Joint Committee on Constitutional Review be submitted to the people.[91] Menzies replied that it would not be wise to put all the recommendations of the committee to the people at a referendum because "experience indicates that if that were to be done the whole lot would be lost."

He noted that putting a great mass of proposals for constitutional change to the people had been tried before and failed. He observed:

> The whole problem of constitutional change in our country is bedevilled by the fact that the disposition of the people is to say: 'When in doubt, vote "No".' The change suggested needs to be crystal clear. It needs to be one which does not lend itself to misinterpretation or to absurd fears which are occasionally promoted. These requirements are not easy to attain, but simplicity on a matter which really engages the public attention and to which the people will direct their minds thoughtfully is essential.[92]

Menzies announced instead that two recommendations of the Joint Committee on Constitutional Review would be pursued – the repeal of section 127 of the Constitution and the breaking of the nexus between the size of the two Houses.[93] He accepted that section 127 was "completely out of harmony with experience and modern thinking" and should be repealed. He rejected, however, the suggestion that the exclusory words in section 51(xxvi) should be repealed, noting that it was a power to make discriminatory laws in relation to the people of any race and that the preferred position was that Aboriginal citizens would stand equal with every other citizen before the law, enjoying its benefits and sharing its burdens.[94] Menzies also raised the concern that if the exclusion of Aboriginal people from section 51(xxvi) were struck out, the Commonwealth Parliament could set up separate bodies of law with respect to Aboriginal people, such as separate industrial laws, health laws or quarantine laws. He noted that such a matter would require a good deal of thought.[95]

Whitlam responded that he had previously taken the same view about the amendment of section 51(xxvi), but that he had since changed his mind for two reasons. First, he noted that there were still some "obnoxious" State laws and it was desirable that the Commonwealth be able to legislate to render them inconsistent and therefore invalid. Secondly, he noted the lack of social capital of Aboriginal people and the need for additional positive measures in relation to matters such as housing and education.[96]

On 6 August 1965, the Attorney-General, Billy Snedden, wrote to Menzies providing drafts of the two proposed referendum bills and a draft paper concerning section 51(xxvi) containing proposals for its alteration.[97] Menzies asked Snedden to put these views to the Cabinet.[98] Snedden argued that section 51(xxvi) should be amended, in a separate referendum question, to delete the words "other than the aboriginal race in any State." He noted that there was a strong body of opinion in support of this proposal.[99] Some, he observed, considered that any reference to Aboriginal people in the Constitution amounted to discrimination as it suggested that they were different to other citizens. Others wanted the change so that the Commonwealth could legislate specifically with respect to Aboriginal people. Snedden noted that it was illogical to argue for both views, as they were contradictory, but that a great many people in favour of the change had probably not identified its true purpose and would therefore probably embrace both arguments.[100]

Snedden also discussed the repeal altogether of section 51(xxvi). He rejected this idea, as it would deprive the Commonwealth of a head of power that might be needed (such as for the resettlement of the Nauruans) and prevent the Commonwealth from legislating in such a way as to render inoperative State laws that imposed racial discrimination.[101] Snedden also rejected inserting an anti-racial discrimination clause in the Constitution, as it would give rise to a great deal of litigation, in a similar league to that produced by section 92 of the Constitution.[102]

The Cabinet, however, decided that section 51(xxvi) should not be amended and that section 127 should be repealed.[103]

On 11 November 1965, Menzies introduced the *Constitution Alteration (Repeal of Section 127) 1965*. As the title made clear, it only addressed the repeal of section 127. Menzies noted that section 127 was no longer relevant and should be removed. He pointed out that it was not related to the right to vote. He observed that section 41 of the Constitution "has always guaranteed an Aboriginal the right to vote at Commonwealth elections if he had a right to vote at elections for the more numerous House of the Parliament of a State."[104] This is a curious statement because while it may certainly be argued that this was what was intended by section 41,[105] it was not interpreted that way by Commonwealth officials in the first half of the twentieth century,[106] leading to the disenfranchisement until 1949 of Aboriginal people whose rights ought to have been constitutionally protected.

The referendum bill did not include any alteration to section 51(xxvi). Menzies again argued that the exclusion of Aboriginal people from that power in fact protected them from discrimination, rather than facilitating it. He stated that it was the Government's view that such a power would "not be in the best interests of the Aboriginal people."[107] He then discussed the case for repealing section 51(xxvi) altogether, noting that it had its attractions, especially as it had never been used. He was concerned, however, that one day it might conceivably be needed. He picked up Snedden's example of the possible need to legislate with respect to the people of the Nauruan race if it was necessary to help them to be re-established somewhere out of Nauru.[108] Finally, Menzies addressed the inclusion of an anti-racial discrimination provision in the Constitution. He pointed to the Bill of Rights in the United States and criticised the constitutionalising of rights on the basis that it would "produce a crop of litigation." He noted that such a provision "could readily invalidate laws which, while designed to protect the special interests of Aborigines, could be held technically to discriminate either for or against them".[109]

The Opposition supported the repeal of section 127, regarding it as a blot on the Constitution, but expressed disappointment that the proposal did not extend to removing the exclusory words in section 51(xxvi).[110] W. C. Wentworth, a Liberal member, proposed that the referendum bill should go further by repealing section 51(xxvi) and replacing it with a power to make laws with respect to the advancement of the Aboriginal natives of the Commonwealth of Australia. He also proposed adding a new section to the Constitution that would prohibit the Commonwealth and the States from making or maintaining any law that discriminated against Australians on the basis of race, although it would not preclude the making of laws "for the special benefit of the aboriginal natives of the Commonwealth of Australia." As Wentworth was unable to move these proposals as an amendment to the referendum bill, for procedural reasons, he stated that he would include them in a private Member's Bill that he would submit to the House for its approval.[111]

The Government's referendum bill passed in December 1965 and was set to head to a referendum in the new year on 28 May 1966.[112]

Breaking the nexus between the Houses

In April 1965 Menzies also proposed a referendum to break the nexus between the two Houses. Section 24 of the Constitution provides that the number of Members of the House of Representatives shall be, as nearly as practicable, twice the number of Senators. Menzies wished to increase the size of the House of Representatives so that there would be approximately one Member for 80 000 electors. If the nexus remained, this would have required the expansion of the Senate so that it continued to be half the size of the House. The Senate is normally expanded in multiples of 12, as each of the six States must be equally represented and half the Senators must be able to be elected every three years.[113] Menzies pointed out that in order to make the Senate workable, it was necessary that an odd number of Senators be elected at periodical elections for half the Senate, as this would avoid the major parties winning equal numbers of seats. Hence, it would be necessary to increase the Senate by 24 Senators and the House of Representatives by 48 Members, if the nexus were to remain. That would be too much.[114] He concluded that the nexus between the Houses needed to be broken.

The nexus reform involved not only the redrafting of section 24 of the Constitution, but also the repeal of sections 25, 26 and 27 of the Constitution.[115] Section 25 reduces the representation of a State in the House of Representatives if the State limits its franchise on the basis of race. Snedden noted that section 25 "should be repealed as being of an apparently discriminatory character," noting that it had not ever had any practical application and could be easily avoided by a State if it so desired. By including its repeal in the referendum question on the nexus, he hoped to attract support for that referendum from those opposed to discriminatory provisions.[116] In October 1965 it was also decided to amend section 7 of the Constitution to guarantee that Original States would have at least 10 Senators each, in order to allay concerns that, once the nexus was broken, the House of Representatives would be expanded and the Senate reduced in size.[117]

Deferral of referendum on s 127 and the nexus

It was intended that the two referenda on the repeal of section 127 and the breaking of the nexus would be held on 28 May 1966. In the meantime, however, on 20 January 1966, Menzies surprised his party by retiring as prime minister.

In February, just as the five million Yes/No cases had been printed and were about to be distributed for the referendum, the Cabinet, under the new prime minister, Harold Holt, decided to defer the referendum.[118] The main impetus for doing so was a desire to put off the nexus referendum question. It was considered wasteful to hold a separate referendum on section 127, so it, too, was deferred.[119] An alternative rationale was claimed in the "No" case to the subsequent referendum on the nexus in 1967. It alleged that Holt had cancelled the referendum in 1966 "when a public opinion poll revealed that only 23 percent of the electors intended to vote Yes, 47 percent intended to vote No and the remainder were undecided."[120]

Holt's public justification for deferring the referenda was that his was a new government and while it continued to support the referendum proposals, it had too many other "important and pressing matters" to deal with and was not able to commit itself to a referendum campaign at this stage.[121] He observed that the delay would not have any practical impact because Aboriginal people were already counted in the census and section 127 did not prevent Aboriginal people from voting.[122]

There was some debate as to whether the referendum could be halted after the bills had been passed by the Parliament, but the Cabinet received legal advice that it could do so.[123] When both proposals were finally brought back for a referendum in 1967, Cabinet had been persuaded by its two successive Attorneys-General to alter section 51(xxvi) by removing the exclusion of Aboriginal people from its application.[124]

On 28 February 1967 the Cabinet agreed that both the repeal of section 127 and the alteration of section 51(xxvi) should be included in the one referendum question.[125] As is well known, the referendum proposal concerning this question passed with an overwhelming majority, but the other referendum question seeking to repeal section 25 and break the nexus between the two Houses failed.

Menzies and the High Court

Appointments and interaction with Justices of the High Court

Menzies' career in federal politics started as a consequence of a series of for-tuitous or contrived manoeuvres concerning judicial appointments. When Menzies was Attorney-General in the Victorian Government and seeking a seat to move into federal politics, Sir John Latham was the Commonwealth Attorney-General and wished to leave politics to become Chief Justice of the High Court. This would free up the federal seat of Kooyong for Menzies, who could then also take office as Commonwealth Attorney-General.[126] The only spanner in the works was the incumbent Chief Justice, Sir Frank Gavan Duffy, who, according to Fricke, imposed a number of conditions before he would consider resigning, including the appointment of his son, Charles, as a Justice of the Supreme Court of Victoria.[127]

In May 1933, Menzies secured the appointment of Charles Gavan Duffy as a Supreme Court judge.[128] Sir Frank then wanted a portrait to be painted of him. According to Fricke, Menzies organised for the Victorian Bar to commission a portrait of Gavan Duffy,[129] yet he still did not resign. Latham, fed up with the delay, announced his retirement at the forthcoming election in September 1934. Menzies resigned from the Victorian Parliament and was elected in Kooyong at the September election. He was immediately appointed Commonwealth Attorney-General. Gavan Duffy finally resigned in October 1935, being replaced as Chief Justice by Sir John Latham, upon the recommendation of Menzies as Commonwealth Attorney-General. The game of musical chairs then ceased.

Menzies and Latham maintained a close political relationship after Latham's elevation to the High Court, with Latham continuing to provide legal and political advice to the Government. For example, in June 1940, Latham advised Menzies to sever ties with the United Kingdom if it was defeated in the war, and that, as Chief Justice, he should be involved in the relevant Cabinet decision. Menzies agreed.[130] Latham, who was the only dissentient in the *Communist Party Case,* also advised Menzies upon how to formulate an amendment to the Constitution to overturn the judgment and secure the banning of the Communist Party.[131]

Menzies had served as pupil to Owen Dixon in 1918 and remained in awe of Dixon's powers. When the opportunity arose to appoint a new Chief Justice of the High Court in 1952 to replace Latham, Menzies himself asked Dixon, noting that he could not forego the pleasure of doing so, despite the fact that it was really the Attorney-General's role.[132] Dixon's appointment left a vacancy on the Court. Menzies and Dixon discussed possible appointees. Dixon noted that the Court was already carrying two "passengers" (meaning judges he regarded as lazy or incompetent) and that it could not cope with more.[133] Dixon raised five possible candidates, Taylor and Owen from New South Wales and Scholl, Smith and Douglas Menzies (Menzies' cousin) from Victoria.[134] Menzies queried whether consideration should be given to a balance between New South Wales and Victoria, but Dixon rejected such a notion.[135] In the end, Menzies chose Alan Taylor for the appointment, even though Dixon preferred William Owen.[136] To offload the "passengers" on the Court, Justices McTiernan and Webb were offered diplomatic appointments, but each refused.[137] Menzies continued to consult Dixon about appointments to the High Court,[138] along with other political and legal matters.[139]

Dixon even encouraged Menzies to become his successor as Chief Justice when he retired. Menzies, however, was having none of it, writing to his daughter that when he had finished his political career, he wanted to live the rest of his life in his own way, having "no ambition to knock off work to carry bricks!"[140] It was Barwick that Menzies had in mind for the job of Chief Justice. In a conversation between the two of them, Barwick suggested to Menzies that they were the two most suitable candidates for appointment to the Court, and that Barwick was more dispensable from the Government than Menzies.[141] Barwick had already been removed from his coveted office as Attorney-General, after unsettling the business community over trade practices legislation,[142] and was causing trouble as Minister for External Affairs, upsetting the Americans by pushing the limits of their ANZUS treaty obligations to protect Australian troops if they were attacked in Borneo.[143] There was, therefore, political advantage in his removal from ministerial office and appointment to the High Court.[144]

Under pressure from Menzies, Barwick agreed to put his name forward as a replacement for Dixon as Chief Justice. Barwick was about to depart upon a major overseas tour to Moscow and Europe to meet foreign leaders and assumed that any appointment would be delayed until his pressing work in external affairs was completed. The Cabinet, however, decided that the appointment should be made immediately and the foreign tour would not go ahead.[145] Barwick was informed by phone in Sydney airport that his appointment had been approved and that he had to resign with immediate effect. He had no opportunity for a farewell from colleagues or to speak in the House of Representatives again. He later referred to the "almost unceremonious and hasty way in which the appointment was made."[146] Barwick apparently later told friends: "The old man kicked me out ... I don't know what else I could have done about it."[147] While Barwick's appointment was accepted as suitable by both sides of Parliament,[148] Dixon was appalled by it. At first he contended that Menzies must have been against it but had been overruled by others. He later recognised Menzies' complicity in the appointment, feeling deeply betrayed by it.[149]

Significant constitutional cases determined by the High Court

The most vexing High Court judgment during Menzies' second period of government was undoubtedly the *Communist Party Case*,[150] which not only prevented Menzies from dissolving the Communist Party, but imposed limits on the Commonwealth's legislative powers that continue to have effect, although they have been watered down in recent years.[151]

During Menzies' second term as prime minister, the High Court continued its process of re-shaping the Constitution, achieving major constitutional reform through "interpretation" rather than amendment. The separation of powers was further delineated and entrenched through the High Court's judgment in the *Boilermaker's Case*.[152] The power of the States to bind the Commonwealth was confined to a limited, but unclear, category of circumstances in the *Cigamatic Case*.[153] The paralysis of Commonwealth-State financial relations for future decades was ensured by the *Second Uniform Tax Case*,[154] while the ability of the States to impose business franchise fees as a way of getting around the prohibition on them imposing excises, was facilitated by the *Dennis Hotels Case*.[155] While the Dixon Court, 1952-64, which covered most of the Menzies era, has universally been praised for the quality of its jurisprudence, none of these constitutional judgments was particularly well-reasoned and most have been qualified or required significant reinterpretation by the High Court in the decades since.[156]

Conclusion

Menzies had a sophisticated relationship with the Constitution, experiencing it through both the law and politics. He found formal constitutional reform dispiriting and ineffective and recognised that necessary reform could be achieved more effectively through constitutional interpretation by the High Court. While he had a close relationship with some members of the Court, he nonetheless remained wary of giving it too much power to decide matters that were essentially political in nature. In that sense, he sought to maintain the separation of powers, leaving legal matters for the judiciary and political and policy matters for the representatives of the people in the Parliament.

Constitutional reform, which combines both legal and political matters, is allocated by the Constitution ultimately to the decision of the people. Despite being a master of politics and the art of winning elections, not even Menzies could overcome the scepticism of the Australian people and their reluctance to amend the Constitution at referendum. The consequence is a more active High Court that sees constitutional reform by interpretation as part of its mandate due to the failure to achieve it through formal democratic means.[157]

Endnotes

[1] Philip Ayres, *Owen Dixon,* The Miegunyah Press, 2003, 30.

[2] *Amalgamated Society of Engineers v. Adelaide Steamship Co Ltd* (1920) 28 CLR 129.

[3] Note that Menzies later described himself as a federalist – but on the basis that individual freedom is protected by the division of power between the Commonwealth and the States: Robert Menzies, *Central Power in the Australian Commonwealth,* Cassell, 1967, 24.

[4] Menzies op. cit., 48.

[5] See further: Anne Twomey, "The Knox Court", Rosalind Dixon and George Williams (eds), *The High Court, the Constitution and Australian Politics,* Cambridge University Press, 2015, 98, 101-7.

[6] Menzies, op. cit., 38-9.

[7] Note that Menzies' forays as counsel for the States were not always as successful. His efforts to confine the type of conditions that may be placed on section 96 grants to financial conditions failed miserably in the *Federal Roads Case:* Percy Joske, *Sir Robert Menzies 1894-1978 – A New, Informal Memoir,* Angus & Robertson Publishers, 1978, 41-2.

[8] Paul Hasluck, *Sir Robert Menzies,* Melbourne University Press, 1980, 5.

[9] George Williams and David Hume, *People Power – The History and Future of the Referendum in Australia,* UNSW Press, 2010, 92.

[10] Menzies, op. cit., 7, 9.

[11] Ibid., 9.

[12] Ibid.

[13] A.W. Martin, *Robert Menzies – A Life,* Vol. 1 1894-1943, Melbourne University Press, 1993, 48-50.

[14] Menzies nominated for election to the Legislative Council in 1927 and ran in the election in 1928, losing to George Swinburne. Swinburne died in the Chamber three months later and Menzies won his seat in a by-election: A. W. Martin, *Robert Menzies – A Life,* Vol. 1 1894-1943, Melbourne University Press, 1993, 61-6.

[15] Menzies, op. cit., 16.

[16] The aviation question was approved in only two States. The marketing question was rejected in all States.

[17] Menzies, op. cit., 17

[18] Letter by Menzies to his son Ken, 5 September 1944, quoted in: A.W. Martin, *Robert Menzies – A Life,* Vol. 2 1944-1978, Melbourne University Press, 1999, 7-8.

[19] Martin (1993), 56.

[20] While the Liberal-Country Party Coalition in 1949 won 23 Senate seats, as opposed to Labor's 19, Labor retained a majority due to its success in the previous half-Senate election (it won 15 of the 18 seats contested). The Coalition was in a minority, holding 26 seats to Labor's 34.

[21] Memorandum by Chief Electoral Officer to Secretary, Attorney-General's Department, 4 May 1950: National Archives of Australia (NAA) A406 E1964/258.

[22] CPD (HR) 4 May 1950, 2217.

[23] Memorandum by R. R. Garran, 26 April 1950: NAA A406 E1964/258.

[24] CPD (HR) 4 May 1950, 2223. If this proposal had gone ahead, then the current number

of 12 Senators per State with six elected at half-Senate elections, would not have been permitted.

25 "Referendum to Avoid Senate Deadlock", *Canberra Times,* 5 May 1950, 4.

26 CPD (HR) 4 May 1950, 2223.

27 CPD (Senate) 21 June 1950, 4606 (Senator Cooke).

28 CPD (Senate) 21 June 1950, 4612 and 4617.

29 Report of the Select Committee of the Senate on the Constitution Alteration (Avoidance of Double Dissolution Deadlocks) 1950, Australia, *Parliamentary Papers,* 1950-51, Vol. 1, 233. See also: "Senators Propose Counter-plan To Deadlocks Bill", *Sydney Morning Herald,* 29 November 1950, 5.

30 CPD (HR) 10 March 1953, 709. Recommendations for reform of section 57 made by the Joint Committee on Constitutional Review were also ignored.

31 "Hard Thinking Faces Govt. Over Drift in Employment", *Sydney Morning Herald,* 18 April 1961, 2.

32 It was proposed that unlike a referendum under section 128, the nationalisation referendum would only need the approval of a majority of voters overall – not a majority of voters in a majority of States.

33 Robert Menzies, Election Campaign Speech, 10 November 1949: http://electionspeeches. moadoph.gov.au/speeches/1949-robert-menzies

34 Letter by K.H. Bailey, Solicitor-General, to J.G. Crawford, Secretary, Department of Commerce and Agriculture, 28 April 1950: NAA A4931 D46A.

35 "Nationalisation Referendum Bill Next Week", *Sydney Morning Herald,* 17 May 1950, 5.

36 See detailed departmental comments, May 1950: NAA A4931 D46A.

37 "Legal Obstacles to Safeguards Against Socialism", *Sydney Morning Herald,* 12 March 1953, 1. See also: "Referendum Mooted to Prevent Nationalisation", *Canberra Times,* 11 March 1953, 1.

38 "Legal Obstacles to Safeguards Against Socialism", *Sydney Morning Herald,* 12 March 1953, 1.

39 *Adelaide Company of Jehovah's Witnesses Inc v. Commonwealth* (1943) 67 CLR 116.

40 Ibid., 154 (Starke J).

41 See further: George Winterton, "The *Communist Party* Case", H.P. Lee and G. Winterton (eds), *Australian Constitutional Landmarks,* Cambridge University Press, 2003, 108, 110.

42 Robert Menzies, Election Campaign Speech, 10 November 1949: http://electionspeeches. moadoph.gov.au/speeches/1949-robert-menzies.

43 Julius Stone, "Anti-Red Bill – The Onus of Proof", *Sydney Morning Herald,* 18 May 1950, 2.

44 Norman Cowper, "Action Against Communism", *Australian Quarterly* 22(1) (1950) 5-6.

45 "Double Dissolution if Red Bill Unpassed Says Mr Menzies", *Canberra Times,* 24 June 1950, 1.

46 See further: George Winterton, "The *Communist Party* Case", H.P. Lee and G. Winterton (eds), *Australian Constitutional Landmarks,* Cambridge University Press, 2003, 108, 123-4.

47 *Australian Communist Party v. Commonwealth* (1951) 83 CLR 1, 263 (Fullagar J).

48 Ibid., 258 (Fullagar J).

49 Ibid., 197-8 (Dixon J).

50 Philip Ayres, op. cit., 224.

51 CPD (HR) Vol. 212, 13 March 1951, 365.

52 Ibid., 366.

53 Ibid., 367.

54 Robert Menzies, *The Measure of the Years,* Coronet Books, 1972, 43.

55 A.W. Martin (1999), 183.

56 CPD (HR) Vol. 212, 13 March 1951, 368.

57 Joske, op. cit., 203.

58 "Responsibility of Decision on Mr McKell", *Canberra Times,* 14 March 1951, 1; "Dissolution seen as certain", *Sydney Morning Herald,* 16 March 1951, 1; and "Menzies Will Seek Double Dissolution this Morning", *The Mercury,* 15 March 1951, 1. See also: Zelman Cowen, "Introduction to Second Edition", in H. V. Evatt, *The King and His Dominion Governors,* Frank Cass & Co, 1967, xxv.

59 Menzies had sought the views of Garfield Barwick and provided the Governor-General with opinions by the Attorney-General and the Solicitor-General, which McKell accepted: Christopher Cunneen, *William John McKell,* UNSW Press, 2000, 207; and John Howard, *The Menzies Era,* Harper Collins, 2014, 116-7. Menzies took the view that McKell was not obliged to accept his advice, as McKell had to be satisfied, on his own judgment, that the conditions of section 57 of the Constitution were met: Robert Menzies, *The Measure of the Years,* Coronet Books, 1972, 45.

60 L.F. Crisp, *Ben Chifley: A Political Biography,* Longmans, 1961, 406. See also: Kylie Tennant, *Evatt: Politics and Justice,* Angus & Robertson, 1970, 269.

61 The opinion polls were 80 percent in favour of a Yes vote at the beginning of the campaign: Kylie Tennant, *Evatt: Politics and Justice,* Angus & Robertson, 1970, 285.

62 Joske, op. cit., 205.

63 Ibid.

64 Menzies (1967), 18-20. See also: A.W. Martin, *Robert Menzies – A Life,* Vol. 2 1944-1978, Melbourne University Press, 1999, 190-3.

65 Menzies (1967), 20.

66 Robert Menzies, Speech to Federal Council of the Liberal Party, 19 November 1951. See: "National Convention on Constitution is Liberal Plan", *Canberra Times,* 20 November 1951, 4; and L.F. Crisp, *Australian National Government,* Longmans, 3rd ed, 1967, 40.

67 Menzies (1967), 21.

68 L.F. Crisp, op. cit., 404, fn 3; Kylie Tennant, *Evatt: Politics and Justice,* Angus & Robertson, 1970, 260; George Winterton, "The *Communist Party* Case", H.P. Lee and G. Winterton (eds), *Australian Constitutional Landmarks,* Cambridge University Press, 2003, 108, 131.

69 R.G. Menzies, Campaign Speech, 5 May 1954: http://electionspeeches.moadoph.gov. au/speeches/1954-robert-menzies. Note that a constitutional convention had also been requested by the NSW Opposition in 1953 to review Commonwealth-State financial relations: "Request for Convention," *Sydney Morning Herald,* 29 June 1953, 3.

70 CPD (HR), 24 May 1956, 2453; (Senate), 24 May 1956, 980.

71 J.E. Richardson, "Reform of the Constitution: the Referendums and Constitutional Convention" in Gareth Evans (ed), *Labor and the Constitution 1972-1975,* Heinemann, 1977, 89; L.F. Crisp, *Australian National Government,* Longmans, 3rd ed, 1967, 54; CPD (HR) Vol. 30, 13 April 1961, 820 (Gough Whitlam); Cheryl Saunders, "The Parliament as Partner: A Century of Constitutional Review", G. Lindell and R. Bennett (eds), *Parliament – The Vision in Hindsight,* Federation Press, 2001, 454, 476-7.

72 Geoffrey Sawer, "Reforming the Federal Constitution", *Australian Quarterly,* 32(1) (1960) 29.

73 Richardson, op. cit., 89.

[74] Sawer, op. cit.; and Geoff Turner, "Consensus Betrayed: Lessons from the 1959 Joint Committee on Constitutional Review", *Australian Journal of Politics and History* 39(2) (1993) 184, 191-2.

[75] CPD (HR) Vol. 30, 13 April 1961, 806.

[76] Ibid., 808.

[77] Ibid., 809-10.

[78] Ibid., 811. Note that the Liberal State Premiers had expressed their objections already at a meeting in June 1960: Geoff Turner, "Consensus Betrayed: Lessons from the 1959 Joint Committee on Constitutional Review", *Australian Journal of Politics and History,* 39(2) (1993) 184, 190.

[79] E.G. Whitlam, *On Australia's Constitution,* Widescope, 1977, 194; Geoff Turner, "Consensus Betrayed: Lessons from the 1959 Joint Committee on Constitutional Review", *Australian Journal of Politics and History,* 39(2) (1993) 184, 194.

[80] *Report of the House of Representatives Select Committee on Voting Rights of Aborigines,* 19 October 1961, Australia, *Parliamentary Papers,* 1961 Vol. II, 1391, 1404 [77].

[81] *Commonwealth Electoral Act 1962* (Cth).

[82] At the time, section 51(xxvi) gave the Commonwealth Parliament power to make laws with respect to "the people of any race, other than the aboriginal race in any State, for whom it is deemed necessary to make special laws". It was proposed to delete the words "other than the aboriginal race in any State".

[83] See also the *Constitution Alteration (Number of Senators and Members of the House of Representatives)* 1964 introduced by Labor in the Senate on 24 September 1964. It also failed to pass.

[84] CPD (HR), 14 May 1964, 1902-3 (Mr Calwell).

[85] Ibid., 1903 (Mr Calwell). Snedden took the same view at 1906.

[86] Ibid., 1904 (Mr Calwell).

[87] Ibid., 1913 (Mr Barnes).

[88] Ibid., 1905 (Mr Calwell).

[89] Ibid., 1907 (Mr Snedden).

[90] Ibid., 1908 (Mr Snedden).

[91] CPD (HR) 1 April 1965, 528 (Mr Calwell).

[92] Ibid., 533 (Sir Robert Menzies).

[93] Ibid., 533-5 (Sir Robert Menzies).

[94] Ibid., 533 (Sir Robert Menzies).

[95] Ibid., 534 (Sir Robert Menzies).

[96] Ibid., 537 (Mr Whitlam).

[97] Letter by B.M. Snedden, Attorney-General, to Sir Robert Menzies, Prime Minister, 6 August 1965: NAA A4940 C4257.

[98] Letter by E.J. Bunting, Secretary to the Cabinet, to B.M. Snedden, Attorney-General, 19 August 1965: NAA A432 1965/3174.

[99] Cabinet Submission No 1009 by the Attorney-General, B.M. Snedden, 23 August 1965, 5: NAA A4940 C4257.

[100] Cabinet Submission No 1009 by the Attorney-General, B.M. Snedden, 23 August 1965, 7: NAA A4940 C4257.

[101] Cabinet Submission No 1009 by the Attorney-General, B.M. Snedden, 23 August 1965, 8: NAA A4940 C4257.

[102] Cabinet Submission No 1009 by the Attorney-General, B.M. Snedden, 23 August 1965, 9: NAA A4940 C4257.

[103] Cabinet Decision No 1175, 30 August 1965: NAA A4940 C4257.

[104] CPD (HR) 11 November 1965, 2638 (Sir Robert Menzies).

[105] Note, however, that the High Court later neutered section 41 by interpreting it as only applying to persons who had the right to vote in State elections before the uniform franchise came into effect in 1902: *R. v. Pearson; Ex Parte Sipka* (1983) 152 CLR 254. For the history of the application of s 41, see: Anne Twomey, "The Federal Constitutional Right to Vote in Australia," *Federal Law Review* 28(1) (2000) 125.

[106] See, e.g., Opinion by R.R. Garran, Solicitor-General, 2 January 1925 in: Benson and A. Kirk (eds), *Opinions of the Attorneys-General of the Commonwealth of Australia*, Vol. 3: 1923-1945, Commonwealth of Australia, 2013, Opinion No. 1367, 76.

[107] CPD (HR) 11 November 1965, 2639 (Sir Robert Menzies).

[108] Ibid. Note that such an example had originally been provided in an opinion by Geoffrey Sawer. However, it was later excluded from the draft second reading speech on the referendum bill on the basis that there was "considerable doubt whether the Nauruans do in fact constitute a 'race' for the purposes of placitum (xxvi) of section 51": Memorandum by P.H. Bailey, Prime Minister's Department, to Senator Henty, 26 November 1965: NAA A463 1965/5445.

[109] CPD (HR) 11 November 1965, 2640 (Sir Robert Menzies).

[110] CPD (HR) 23 November 1965, 3068 (Mr Calwell).

[111] CPD (HR) 23 November 1965, 3070 (Mr Wentworth).

[112] Cabinet Decision No 1352, 27 October 1965: NAA A4940 C4257.

[113] Note, however, the observation by Quick and Garran that section 13 of the Constitution was drafted to include the possible contingency of an odd number of senators in each State: John Quick and Robert Garran, *The Annotated Constitution of the Australian Commonwealth,* Angus and Robertson, 1901, 432. Nonetheless, the draft YES case for the 1965 referendum asserted that the election of five Senators at one half-Senate election and six at the next "would produce curious results" and frequent periods of a deadlocked Senate: NAA A4940 C4257.

[114] CPD (HR) 1 April 1965, 535 (Sir Robert Menzies).

[115] Cabinet Decision No 1175, 30 August 1965: NAA A4940 C4257.

[116] B.M. Snedden, "Constitutional Amendments: Sections 24-27 and 51(xxvi)": NAA A4940 C4257.

[117] Cabinet Decision No 1308, 20 October 1965: NAA A4940 C4257.

[118] Cabinet Decision No 24, 15 February 1966: NAA A4940 C4257. See also: "Referendums put off until after elections", *Canberra Times,* 16 February 1966, 1.

[119] "Suggested Answer to Question re Statement by the Prime Minister on the Referendum," undated: NAA A432 1965/3174.

[120] "Referendums to be held on Saturday, 27th May, 1967 – The Arguments FOR and AGAINST", 6 April 1967, 9: NAA A463 1965/5445. See also on lack of public support for the nexus referendum: "Referendum to be major decision by new Cabinet", *Canberra Times,* 27 January 1966, 3.

[121] CPD (HR) 8 March 1966, 23 (Mr Holt).

[122] Ibid.

123 Letter by J.Q. Ewens, Acting Secretary, Attorney-General's Department, 9 February 1966: NAA A432 1965/3174. Compare Gair's view that only Parliament could stop the referendum: "Statement by Senator V.C. Gair on the Postponement of the Referendum", 16 February 1966: NAA A432 1965/3174.

124 Cabinet Submission No 397, 1966, by B.M. Snedden, Attorney-General, 12 August 1966; Cabinet Submission No 46, 1967, by the Attorney-General, Nigel Bowen, January 1967; and Cabinet Decision No 79, 22 February 1967: NAA A4940 C4257. For a discussion of the history to this change see: Anne Twomey, "The Race Power – Its Replacement and Interpretation", *Federal Law Review* 40 (2012) 413, 419-22.

125 Cabinet Decision No 102 (HOC), 28 February 1967: NAA A4940 C4257.

126 Joske, op. cit., 68.

127 Graham Fricke, "Gavan Duffy, Frank," A. Blackshield, M. Coper and G. Williams, *The Oxford Companion to the High Court of Australia,* Oxford University Press, 2001, 296-7.

128 "Supreme Court Judge – Appointment Announced", *Argus,* 31 May 1933, 7. Note that the choice was a popular one and Charles Gavan Duffy was well-qualified and respected. There is no suggestion the appointment was unmerited.

129 Fricke, op. cit., 296-7.

130 Fiona Wheeler, "Sir John Latham's Extra-Judicial Advising," *Melbourne University Law Review* 35 (2011) 651, 660-1, quoting from letters dated 20 and 22 June 1940.

131 Clem Lloyd, "Not Peace but a Sword! – The High Court under J.G. Latham", *Adelaide Law Review,* 11 (1987) 175, 202; Fiona Wheeler, "Sir John Latham's Extra-Judicial Advising", *Melbourne University Law Review* 35 (2011) 651, 671.

132 Philip Ayres, *Owen Dixon,* The Miegunyah Press, 2003, 229.

133 Ibid.

134 Ibid., 229-30.

135 Note that Barwick, too, in advising Gough Whitlam on High Court appointments, would later reject the relevance of State representation on the Court. He also preferred appointment direct from the Bar than from a Supreme Court: Letter by Sir Garfield Barwick to Gough Whitlam, Prime Minister, 14 September 1973: NAA M514/3.

136 Ayres, op. cit., 234.

137 Ibid., fn 10, 355.

138 Re the replacement of Fullagar J, see: Robert Menzies, Letter to Heather Henderson, 31 July 1961, Heather Henderson (ed), *Letters to My Daughter – Robert Menzies, Letters 1955-1975,* Pier 9, 2011, 63.

139 Fiona Wheeler, "Sir John Latham's Extra-Judicial Advising", *Melbourne University Law Review* 35 (2011) 651, 661-2.

140 Robert Menzies, Letter to Heather Henderson, 31 July 1961, Heather Henderson (ed), *Letters to My Daughter – Robert Menzies, Letters 1955-1975,* Pier 9, 2011, 63-4. See also: Percy Joske, *Sir Robert Menzies 1894-1978 – A New, Informal Memoir,* Angus & Robertson Publishers, 1978, 38. Compare Barwick's speculation that Menzies might have preferred the office of Chief Justice to that of Prime Minister: Garfield Barwick, *A Radical Tory,* The Federation Press, 1995, 214.

141 Garfield Barwick, *A Radical Tory,* The Federation Press, 1995, 209.

142 Brian Galligan, "The Barwick Court", Rosalind Dixon and George Williams (eds), *The High Court, the Constitution and Australian Politics,* Cambridge University Press, 2015, 203.

[143] David Marr, *Barwick,* Allen & Unwin, 1992, 206-8.

[144] Note, for example, the allegation by Allan Fraser that the Prime Minister "chopped [Barwick's] head off" in response to American protests against Barwick's actions as Minister for External Affairs: CPD (HR) 23 April 1964, 1471.

[145] Marr, op. cit., 208.

[146] Barwick, op. cit., 213. Calwell added that Barwick had been ruthlessly despatched by the Prime Minister for political reasons: CPD (HR) 23 April 1964, 1465-6.

[147] Marr, op. cit., 209.

[148] CPD (HR) 23 April 1964, 1463-4 (Menzies and Calwell).

[149] Ayres, op. cit., 2p. 86.

[150] *Australian Communist Party v. Commonwealth* (1951) 83 CLR 1.

[151] See *Thomas v. Mowbray* (2007) 233 CLR 307.

[152] *R. v. Kirby; Ex parte Boilermakers' Society of Australia* (1956) 94 CLR 254. For a discussion of this case and other significant constitutional cases of the Dixon Court, see: Helen Irving, "The Dixon Court", Rosalind Dixon and George Williams (eds), *The High Court, the Constitution and Australian Politics,* Cambridge University Press, 2015, 179.

[153] *Commonwealth v. Cigamatic Pty Ltd* (1962) 108 CLR 372.

[154] *Victoria v. Commonwealth* (1957) 99 CLR 575.

[155] *Dennis Hotels Pty Ltd v. Victoria* (1960) 104 CLR 529.

[156] *Dennis Hotels,* while not formally reversed, was effectively overridden in *Ha v. New South Wales* (1997) 189 CLR 465. The doctrine in the *Cigamatic Case* was subject to major reform in *Re Residential Tenancies Tribunal (NSW) ex parte Defence House Authority* (1997) 190 CLR 410. The authority of the *Boilermakers Case* has been cut down by a series of exceptions, such as the doctrine of *persona designata.*

[157] *New South Wales v. Commonwealth* (2006) 229 CLR 1, [132]-[134] (Gleeson CJ, Gummow, Hayne, Heydon and Crennan JJ).

12

Federalism in the Menzies Years

J.J. Pincus

Menzies is a transitional figure who presided over consolidation of Commonwealth financial dominance, but did not exploit to the full the political influence that this dominance entailed.[1]

Menzies as theorist

A true adherent of federalism prefers a federal polity to a unitary one – like that of New Zealand – and to the constitutional arrangements in the Australian colonies prior to 1901, with its six independent polities. On this weak test, Menzies was, indeed, a federalist. Menzies never showed any interest in the abolition of either the States or the central government.

A strong adherent of federalism as a system of government would articulate strong arguments in favour: it is a bulwark for freedom from tyrannical government; it respects local autonomy and encourages local responsibility. On this test, Menzies earns a bare pass mark.

Along with most Liberal leaders, when Menzies defended federalism in principle, it was not so much for itself, but rather as an important constitutional tradition that, unfortunately, had to be compromised when it hampered the pursuit of "the national interest."[2] Menzies, however, also recognised that federalism contributed to the establishment of a balance between freedom and power.

> I am a Federalist myself. I believe as I am sure most of you do, that in the division of powers between a Central Government and the State governments, there resides one of the true protections of individual freedom.[3]

Any protestation of adherence to federalism, it should be said, went against the bulk of academic writing. Most intellectuals who wrote on the subject saw it as a pity that Labor failed in the 1940s to obtain a vast extension of central powers, especially in view of the presiding belief in the potency of Keynesian macro-economic management: with a few exceptions, the leading textbooks in Australian political science adopted a "Westminster" view of Australian government and ignored federalism and the States; those that gave federalism some attention mostly concluded that the States were doomed, and that was a good thing, despite the obvious fact that Australians, other than in the Australian Capital Territroty, depended on the States for the public provision of a wide range of services – hospitals, schools, universities, railways, urban transit, electricity, gas, water, for example.[4]

In his Virginia lectures, Menzies offered a limited and conventional account of the advantages of federal arrangements:

> I am, particularly for a large continent with widely scattered communities with great regional or local problems and understandable local prides and patriotisms, a Federalist. At our present stage of development, and for a long time to come, State Parliaments and Governments are and will be essential. The Constitution itself contemplates their continued existence and respects the powers "reserved" for them.[5]

At best, this is a nod towards the idea of subsidiarity – decisions should be entrusted to the most decentralised level of government that is competent to make them.

The emphasis on the dignity and autonomy of individuals and of small voluntary associations that characterised the Catholic social doctrine of subsidiarity is echoed in the more secular versions. Support of the federal system fitted comfortably with Menzies' and the Liberal Party's emphasis on the individual and the family and on small and medium enterprise. Thus, it is not surprising that the 1945-46 platform of the nascent Liberal Party endorsed the federalist principle, putting it in sharp contrast with the Labor Party. Within his party, Menzies endorsed this aspect of the platform; however, he seems to have made few public statements about federalism as a constitutional principle.

Menzies' position was that the States would continue to exist and to attract considerable political support – and, indeed, some premiers were formidable foes during his years as prime minister.[6] Nonetheless, he speculated that, had a Constitution been passed in 1950, it might well have been a unitary one.

In addition, he endorsed the idea, associated with A.V. Dicey and James Bryce, that power inevitably shifts in federations either towards the centre at the expense of the States or provinces (as in the Australian case), or the reverse. A federal division of power or responsibility was, at best, a temporary state. The High Court of Australia, from the *Engineers' Case* of 1920 – which Menzies led for the union – proved to be a powerful centralising force, interpreting the Constitution in a way that the equivalent Canadian courts have not done.[7]

Menzies by and large approved this centralisation, as is shown by the continuation of the previous quotation (about how the division of powers protects freedom):

> And yet how true it is that as the world grows, as the world becomes more complex, as international affairs engage our attention more and more, it is frequently ludicrous that the National Parliament, the National Government, should be without power to do things which are really needed for the national security and advancement.[8]

Menzies' position was not with those "States' righters" who prefer a weak and limited central government, with the strong, sovereign States.

At this point, it is important to distinguish constitutional powers from their exercise: if government "power" is measured by public spending, tax revenues, public employment or by what could be called the "presence" of government in everyday lives, then the "powers" of the Commonwealth and the States both increased markedly during Menzies' regime.

With the exception of the foreign affairs powers ceded by the British government, however, the enhanced constitutional power of the central government came at the expense of those of the States: there was no boost to the collective constitutional power of Australian governments. The transferred powers were, nonetheless, more effective in the hands of the Commonwealth. For this essay, most important was that the 1942 transfer of the Income Tax not only made the Commonwealth financially much stronger than the States, but it also boosted the taxing capacity of the Australian governments collectively: that was its purpose and its effect.

To return to theory: many who support federalism as a system do so in the belief that it constrains the power and scope of government generally, compared with a unitary arrangement. There is some empirical support for this belief,[9] and it is reflected in the Labor Party's antagonism towards federalism.

Because federalism enhances the opportunities for inter-governmental competition for the political affiliation of citizens, it can, however, lead to more public spending or regulation. In a federation, a person is a member of two polities. These polities overlap geographically: State and Commonwealth. If the State does not satisfy some citizens' desire for, say, government assistance to private schools, then they can look to the central government to provide, and vice versa. The Menzies Government did in fact make incursions into areas that formerly were exclusively occupied by the States – but without the kind of anti-federalist pronouncement made by a later Liberal Prime Minister, the Honorable John Howard, to the effect that citizens do not care which government does the job, so long as the job is done.

In practice

Menzies was a pragmatic, centralising federalist, who generally welcomed the extensions of central powers, and made use of them.

Clearly, Menzies was comfortable with those accretions of central power, at the expense of the States, that gave the Commonwealth the strength and range necessary to carry out tasks he considered were of national significance – in particular, national development – or were being neglected by the States – with the proviso that the powers, if not obtained through amendment to the Constitution, relied on judicial interpretations of which he approved. Thus, he happily made use of the enhanced financial powers of the Commonwealth to fund forays into territory previously occupied solely or largely by the States. These incursions were financed by income tax, the 1942 transfer of which left the States too little by way of own-source revenue and, therefore, vulnerable not only to such incursions but also to becoming increasingly dependent on Commonwealth recurrent grants and on Commonwealth subscriptions to the States' loan raisings.

In various writings on his record and his political philosophy, Menzies frequently alluded to that fact that the States were hard pressed financially (owing not only to the loss of the income tax but also to increases in demands made on the States), and claimed that this made it appropriate for the Commonwealth to step into fields formerly considered exclusively State matters; indeed, in 1970 he pointed with some pride to the large Commonwealth subventions required to meet the "needs" of, for example, aged and young persons for homes, of capital works for accommodation of mental health patients, and of universities.[10]

Despite denying that the States were "sovereign" entities, Menzies in his post-war governments was, however, somewhat abstemious in depriving the States of their autonomy in decision-making, especially on spending and taxing: "The *Engineers' Case* notwithstanding, Menzies disliked Commonwealth inroads on State powers."[11] In particular, the States were left to decide how to use their loan monies, even though in the early 1950s the Commonwealth's subscription amounted to more than half the total (to be substituted later by central bank credits); and he ensured that there was no Commonwealth bureaucracy to impinge on the autonomy of the State universities in the spending of Commonwealth grants.

In this context, it is worth noting that a federal structure was then the norm for non-government organisations: for political parties (not least the Australian Labor Party), trade unions, professional bodies (of lawyers, doctors and so on), business lobbies, benevolent societies, the RSL, and the Country Women's Associations, to list a few. When these had a "national" office, it was often a coordinating body, with little or no power over the State-based organisations. Civic life in Australia was then deeply federated. But, as with the constitutional division of powers, these arrangements generally proved to be temporary, and not immune to the forces of centralisation.

In the 1950s, the strength of the Liberal Party was in State-oriented elites who operated in State-regulated professions, such as accountancy and law, with Menzies himself and John Howard being important examples of the kind. Once those professions became national, as they now are, with all the State-based professional services firms now national (if not international) in focus, so did the geographical orientation of elites. And the same happened with the unions, with the reforms driven by Bill Kelty and consolidation making that trend even stronger.

The other practical consideration was that the Liberals were in coalition with the Country Party (now the National Party), necessary to pass legislation in the House of Representatives. That party successfully advocated policies that furthered the interests of rural and regional voters. Some of these fields of policy – most notably in foreign trade – were clearly the prerogative of the central government, and did not depend on the Commonwealth's having deep pockets. But the constant focus of the Country Party was on securing, for rural and regional Australia, a range of services (and their infrastructure), including transport, communications, health, education, water (especially for irrigation) and electricity; and securing them on terms of availability, quality and especially price equal or close to those on which they were being provided in the cities. Some, like the services of the Postmaster-General's Department, were exclusively Commonwealth; others involved policy areas occupied by the States, if not formerly exclusively, then at least predominantly; all required increased budget subventions, which the Commonwealth could make more easily than could the States.

Fiscal federalism

On the question of what kind of federalist Menzies was or became, not only his words but also the actions of his governments from 1949 need to be examined. These reinforce the judgment that he was a pragmatic, centralising federalist: the Commonwealth made inroads into what were largely State matters, and actively used central banking and fiscal powers to manage the economy. Thus, although Menzies professed himself committed to ensure that the States retained a significant degree of autonomy, nonetheless his government saw the States increasingly dependent on Commonwealth grants, and those grants increasingly came with conditions.

The States themselves were caught in a fiscal squeeze. On the demand side, rapid population growth – natural and immigrant – put pressure on the States' budgets for a range of services and for attendant capital works, especially education and health. On the funding side, the States' own recurrent revenues were insufficient – in 1948-49, State tax revenues amounted to a mere 1.9 percent of GNP, compared with 5.7 percent in 1938-39 – and tax reimbursement grants from the Commonwealth did not bridge the recurrent gap.[12] Moreover, the Commonwealth effectively set the ceiling on State public works spending, through its control of the Loan Council and through its and the Commonwealth Bank's subscriptions to State loans.[13]

During Menzies' post-war governments, the High Court (in the *Second Uniform Tax Case*, 1957) reaffirmed the validity of the scheme whereby the Commonwealth induced the States not to impose an income tax. Moreover, in 1949, the High Court, by three to two, determined that a State levy on retail sales of milk was an excise duty, on the grounds that its ultimate economic incidence was on the milk producers. This was the beginning of the end of most indirect taxation by the States. The fiscal superiority of the Commonwealth was thus consolidated.

The Menzies governments, however, made some efforts at boosting the own-tax resources of the States. The States, by contrast, generally found it politically more attractive to seek additional Commonwealth funding than to impose new taxes or to increase their own taxes and charges. In 1952 the Commonwealth initiated talks with the States about their re-entering the income tax field. The subsequent report by Treasury officers was discussed at the 1953 Premiers' Conferences, but nothing came of it. The Commonwealth vacated the land tax in 1952-53, but the States did not raise their rates by as much as the previous Commonwealth rate, and later shrank the tax base through thresholds and exemptions. When the Commonwealth withdrew its entertainment tax, only three States re-imposed theirs. In the 1950s, the only new State tax was that levied by New South Wales in the form of licence fees on poker machines.[14]

Thus, the central feature of federalism during the Menzies era was (those dreaded words) vertical fiscal imbalance: the Commonwealth had more tax revenue than it spent or wanted to spend on its own purposes. Taxes are rarely popular with those who pay them, and everyone knew that the income tax, the most productive of all the taxes, was a Commonwealth impost. Thus, the Commonwealth, having suffered the obloquy, wanted some political return, which it obtained in two ways.

First, it increased its own spending: presumably, the ideological and political pay-off was greater than that from the alternative, which was a reduction in the tax burden. In particular, Menzies opened up new avenues of Commonwealth spending on objects previously exclusively matters for the States, or novel for the Commonwealth, or in competition with State provision – scholarships for university students; science laboratories in private schools; private health insurance (1953-54, after the invalidation of the *Pharmaceuticals Benefits Act 1944*, on the grounds that it involved civil conscription).

Second, from the remaining substantial excess of tax revenue, the Commonwealth made large grants to the States, which the States spent: between the 1949 and 1964 budgets, the States became considerably more reliant on Commonwealth grants, which grew from 41 percent of State fiscal resources to 54 percent. Again, the Commonwealth wanted something in return, sufficient to overbalance the opprobrium of being the taxing agency. It being impolitic to starve the States too much, too quickly, the grants to the States increasingly came with conditions. The most benign was what could be called "branding" – "this national highway cost $Xm and was funded by the Commonwealth of Australia."

More serious were conditions that interfered with the spending decisions or autonomy of the States: what to spend on, when and how.

By the end of the era, the Commonwealth mandated the "specific purposes" on which 29 percent of the grants were to be spent, up from 22 percent in 1949.[15] Many of the grants required "matching" by the States, the most important being for roads and universities (the latter with advice from the Australian Universities Commission, 1959 – 1977).[16]

In addition, the Menzies Government in 1959 made a fundamental and lasting change to the system of State grants. The new Financial Assistance Grants (FAGs) substantially redistributed monies from the more populous New South Wales and Victoria, towards the two remaining "claimant" States, Western Australia and Tasmania, but also towards South Australia: during the previous decade, these three States had received increasing amounts of "Special Grants," the evidentiary basis for which was opaque. The Commonwealth rejected the advice of its own Treasury that the "claimant" States should make above average revenue efforts and accept below average expenditure outcomes; and that Tasmania's low population density and higher *per capita* overhead costs of government were insufficient justification for a continued special subsidy to that State. In effect, this was the start of the extremely equalising grants system of the Commonwealth Grants Commission.[17]

Horizontal fiscal equalisation is an effort to erase any intrinsic differences in the fiscal capacities and responsibilities of the States; that is, to homogenise the States, thereby countering the principal defence that Menzies himself gave for the existence of the States as political entities.[18]

Other aspects of central control

Economically, the years of the Menzies governments—indeed, up until the early 1970s—were rightly considered a "golden era": rapid economic development (housing and automobiles, especially) and high population growth (baby boomers and immigration); trivial unemployment; low inflation, apart from during the Korean War; generally mild and short economic fluctuations. To a greater or less extent, many other "developed" countries similarly enjoyed good times. It was only towards the end of the period that unfavorable comments started to be made about the decline in Australia's ranking in the league table of living standards.

After the Second World War, great effort was put into achieving central control of the overall or macro economy. This was unlikely to be effective unless it was coordinated across Australian governments or, as happened, became the responsibility of the central government. Menzies correctly saw that the post-war macroeconomic problem was managing excessive (not deficient) demand for consumption goods and services, including housing and automobiles and associated infrastructure, as well as for private and public capital investment driven by rapid population growth, boosted by an active immigration program. For this more pleasant problem, fiscal policy was supplemented with tight, centralised financial regulation as well as quantitative control over imports, through an elaborate and extensive system of licensing. Very helpful for macroeconomic management were the operations of the increasingly centralised industrial relations system;[19] Menzies had "no doubt that the system has justified itself in terms of industrial peace and productivity"; and he supported the system through legislation.[20]

Adherence to the Bretton Woods principle of fixed exchange rates meant that the period was marked by concern about the balance of payments, which acted as a constraint on macroeconomic policy generally and, more particularly, a constraint on the drive for more rapid population and economic growth—important and linked objectives for Menzies. In order to relax this constraint somewhat, the Menzies governments negotiated loans from the International Bank of Reconstruction and Development (IBRD), and in London, Canada and Switzerland. Under the conditions of the IBRD loan, Australia was required to show that the monies would be directed to projects that should improve the balance of payments.[21] Nonetheless, as already mentioned, this condition did not lead the Menzies governments to interfere with the States' decisions on how to spend their Loan Council allocations. Menzies' respect for the status of the States is not, however, sufficient to explain this self-denying ordinance: Menzies also had an ideological objection to central planning.[22]

When the Bruce-Page Government borrowed £34m from the UK Government in 1925, it set up the Development and Migration Commission (D&M Commission) with two purposes: to investigate impediments to the establishment of new industries and the expansion of existing ones; and, more importantly for present purposes, to examine and advise the Commonwealth about schemes devised under the Migration Agreement with the UK, whether by the States or by the Commonwealth. Bruce favoured the coordination of Commonwealth and States' plans for large-scale investments. In contrast,

Menzies rubbished the report in 1965 of the Economic Enquiry committee (the Vernon Committee),[23] which had advocated two new "national planning" bodies, one for special projects (like the D&M Commission), the other being the Advisory Council on Economic Growth. Presumably, Menzies did not regard the use of conditional or "special purpose" grants as "planning," but merely as ensuring that the Commonwealth's policy objectives were met.

Presumably, also, a similar rationale can be used for the creation of the Australian Atomic Energy Commission in 1953, replacing committees that came into being in 1949 and 1952.[24]

There was a major extension of the powers of the Commonwealth in 1946, to provide allowances and services to individuals, including students, and to families. Menzies had supported the "Yes" case in the referendum.[25] In the field of health, Sir Earle Page, Minister for Health, 1949-1956, significantly influenced the exercise of these powers. Page, while endeavouring to prevent the "socialisation of medicine," had long been a proponent of national insurance schemes. He had failed to introduce such schemes in 1928 and 1938; and he was acutely aware of the victory of the medical profession over the Chifley Government on the bureaucracy of prescriptions. Page, according to Bridge, "exercised his genius for finding a workable compromise": free essential drugs to the community; free medical services for the poor; subsidies to contributions to private health funds; increases in Commonwealth grants to hospitals.[26]

Within Menzies governments' health policies were some implications for the States. Firstly, initially the Pharmaceutical Benefits scheme used Labor legislation, but in a way that restricted the rights of hospitals to prescribe subsidised drugs (from a short list of "essential and life-saving" pharmaceuticals, which was made more comprehensive in 1960). Secondly, grants to hospitals were conditional on there being a charge for accommodation in public wards. All States but Queensland accepted these grants. (Queensland used the proceeds of a lottery, "the Golden Casket," to fund public hospitals.) This requirement for a charge should not be seen as an anti-State action, but motivated by the belief in encouraging individual responsibility – as was the system of subsidies to private health insurance (introduced in 1953), also designed not to interfere with the relationship between doctor and patient.

Similarly, the housing policies of the Menzies Government impinged on the autonomy of the States.[27] Home ownership was a central plank of the Liberal Party, much stressed in Menzies' famous "Forgotten People" speech of 1942.

Until 1955, Labor's Commonwealth and State Housing Agreement of 1945, with its emphasis on low-cost rental accommodation, hamstrung his governments. Senator W.H. Spooner, Minister for National Development, 1951-64, obtained a revised housing agreement, one that ensured that most of the money would be available for people to buy or build their own houses. By 1971, the share of owner-occupied housing rose above three-quarters (from below 60 percent in 1947). Similarly, the Home Savings Grants Scheme (1964) and Home Loans Insurance Corporation (1965) would have reduced the pressure on State governments to provide rental housing.

The last matter to examine is transport. All the States restricted road-transport in order to protect their own railways. In Victoria, in 1932, the Minister of Railways, Robert Menzies, had introduced legislation to amend and extend earlier restrictions. In the *Hughes* and *Vale Cases* (1954, 1955), however, the High Court declared that restrictions by New South Wales on interstate road transport were invalid, as contrary to section 92 (which mandated that interstate trade, commerce and intercourse should be "absolutely free"). What is of interest here is the lack of Commonwealth reaction. The few powers in section 51 that mention transport or its facilitation deal with lighthouses and the like; control of railways for naval and military purposes; and the consensual acquisition of State railways and the building of railways within a State. Under section 96, however, the Commonwealth had long made grants to the States for roads: the grants were never conditional upon deregulating road transport.[28] Moreover, through international treaties, the Commonwealth did gain some control over aviation in the 1920s, and used its powers not only to subsidise commercial airlines, but also to regulate them. Labor, having failed to nationalise Australian National Airways (ANA), established Trans-Australia Airlines (TAA) in 1946, intending that it become the monopoly: the High Court invalidated the inter-State side of that plan. When Ansett took over Australian National Airways, the Menzies Government set the resultant duopoly in statutory stone, so that only two airlines could service routes between major airports (including capital cities).[29]

This had the effect of sheltering both major airlines from competitive entry and, therefore, had the potential to protect the Commonwealth's equity in TAA—except that, at the time, Ansett-ANA was struggling to compete profitably against TAA, so the two-airline policy has often been interpreted as a means of shoring up Ansett-ANA. But the policy may also have slowed the progress of air-transport in general, inter-State as well as intra-State, thus, indirectly, slightly protecting the States' equity in railways.

Conclusion

The Commonwealth Government loomed larger in the consciousness of citizens at the end of the Menzies era, than at the beginning. Although the Menzies governments dismantled much of what remained of wartime controls—beginning notably with the abolition of petrol rationing—more generally the trajectory of impact of the Commonwealth on everyday life was appreciably upwards. The Commonwealth had the revenue to make use of its added powers over social security and student payments, including Commonwealth Scholarships for university students. In addition, the Commonwealth was involved with the States in various fields of service delivery, either through its own spending, or *via* Specific Purpose grants to the States: schools, hospitals, law enforcement, justice and correctional services, national parks, environmental management, personal welfare assistance, the regulation of workplaces and retail trade, electricity, ports, the support of mineral exploration, roads, water supply, prefabricated houses, migrant hostels, uniform gauge.

The former Commonwealth Bank was now four. From 1960, central banking was entrusted to the newly-created Reserve Bank. Other functions were assigned to a trading bank, a savings bank, and a development bank (for the Country Party).

The national capital grew in population and importance, although the program to transfer the Federal public service from Melbourne to Canberra was little implemented until the early 1960s.[30] More Commonwealth departments were created, including Trade in 1956. Demand for telephone and telegraph services supplied by the Postmaster-General's Department (and, behind the scenes, radio and television transmission) increasingly rose;[31] and the intensified "two airlines" policy was a matter of considerable public attention.

Moreover, the financial system was increasingly heavily regulated through the Commonwealth Bank (later, Reserve Bank of Australia), acting as the central bank and directed by the Treasury, attempting to regulate not only traditional bank loans, but also the burgeoning hire purchase arrangements; and the Commonwealth used tax law to increase the investment in government securities by private sector superannuation funds.[32] National wage cases grew in prominence and significance, given that the effective regulation of unit wage cost was crucial to the Commonwealth's macroeconomic management.[33]

Menzies was committed to federalism as a principle that accorded with his broader philosophical and political ideas. It was a principle, however, to be abrogated when it interfered with national development, broadly conceived.

320

Endnotes

1 Campbell Sharman, "Federalism and Commonwealth-State Relations" in S. Prasser, J.R. Nethercote and J. Warhurst, eds., *The Menzies Era*, Sydney, 1995, 45; see also Campbell Sharman, "Federalism and the Liberal Party", in J.R. Nethercote, ed., *Liberalism and the Australian Federation*, Annandale, N.S.W. , 2001, 297.

2 Wayne Errington, "Federalism and Liberal thinking", in Peter van Onselen, ed., *Liberals and Power: The Road Ahead*, Carlton, Vic., 2008, 261.

3 R.G. Menzies, *Central Power in the Australian Commonwealth: an examination of the growth of Commonwealth power in the Australian federation*, London, 1967, 24. See also Peter G. Tiver, *The Liberal Party: Principles and Performance*, Milton, Qld., 1978, 130, citing Menzies' 1945 attack on Labor's proposed Constitutional amendments.

4 Andrew Parkin, "The States, Federalism and Political Science: A Fifty-Year Appraisal", *Australian Journal of Public Administration*, Vol. 62, Issue 2, 2003, 101-12.

5 Menzies, op. cit., 3.

6 Thomas Playford was Premier of South Australia for over 26 years (1938 to 1965); Henry Bolte was Premier of Victoria from 1955 to 1972.

7 C.D. Gilbert, *Australian and Canadian Federalism Australian and Canadian Federalism 1867-1984: a study of judicial techniques*, Melbourne, 1986.

8 Menzies, op. cit., 24.

9 Anne Twomey and Glenn Withers, *Australia's Federal Future: Delivering Growth and Prosperity: a Report for the Council for the Australian Federation*, Canberra, 2007.

10 R.G. Menzies, *The Measure of the Years*, North Melbourne, 1970

11 A.W. Martin, "Menzies, Sir Robert Gordon (Bob) (1894-1978)", *Australian Dictionary of Biography*, 15, Melbourne, 1970.

12 R.L. Mathews, W.R.C. Jay, *Federal Finance: Intergovernmental Financial Relations in Australia since Federation*, Melbourne, 1972, 192.

13 The Commonwealth's share of the national tax revenues fell during the Menzies governments, from over 80 percent to about 60, in part because it ceased to divert so much income tax revenue to State loan raisings.

14 Matthews and Jay, *Federal Finance*, 192.

15 Sharman, *Menzies Era*, 140

16 Mathews and Jay, *Federal Finance*, 221-9, has the details of grants for roads, railway standardization, harbours, TB, mental health, Red Cross, emergency housekeeping, natural disasters, rural industries, water resources (in W.A.), immigrant hostels. For some grants, the States had to 'match' the Commonwealth's contribution, sometimes (e.g., housing grants) £3 to £1.

17 Mathews and Jay, op. cit., 240-52.

18 The modern justification of horizontal fiscal equalisation includes the argument that, if there were significant differences in the fiscal capacities and responsibilities of the states – so that, for example, if Tasmania became the Australian equivalent of Appalachia – then the Commonwealth would step in with its own nationally-uniform programs that

would displace the States from the relevant fields of spending or taxing: thus, HFE 'saves' federalism by abolishing one of its rationales.

[19] See Henry Ergas, this volume.

[20] *Measure*, 133. Menzies, who had opposed S.M. Bruce's attempt to centralize the power over workplace relations, responded to the High Court 1965 ruling against the exercise of judicial power by the Commonwealth Court of Conciliation and Arbitration, by creating the Commonwealth Conciliations and Arbitration Commission and a separate Commonwealth Industrial Court: A.W. Martin, *Robert Menzies: A Life 1894-1943*, Melbourne, 1993, 48.

[21] R.S. Gilbert, *The Australian Loan Council in Federal Fiscal Adjustments, 1890-1965*, Canberra, 1973, 270-80.

[22] However, he expected that the Australian Universities Commission would prevent "needless duplication"; and the "Two Airlines" policy had elements of central planning: Menzies, *Measure*, 85, 138.

[23] *Report of the Committee of Economic Enquiry* (Chairman: Sir James Vernon), Commonwealth of Australia, Canberra, 1965.

[24] nga.gov.au, "Australian Atomic Energy Commission – Fact sheet 253," accessed 10 August 2015.

[25] A.W. Martin, *Robert Menzies. Volume 2, 1944-1978: A Life*, Melbourne, 1999, 56.

[26] Carl Bridge, "Page, Sir Earle Christmas (1880–1961)", *Australian Dictionary of Biography*, 11, Melbourne, 1988.

[27] This discussion draws heavily on Graeme Starr, "Menzies and post-war prosperity", in J.R. Nethercote, ed., *Liberalism and the Australian Federation*, Annandale, NSW, 2001.

[28] One effect of the State regulation was the formation of Ansett Airlines—when refused a permit to operate a coaching service within Victoria, Reginald Ansett bought a plane: Charles Fahey, "Ansett, Sir Reginald Myles (Reg) (1909–1981)", *Australian Dictionary of Biography*, 17, Melbourne, 2007.

[29] In his 1954 election speech, Menzies said that the Government intended to sell the Commonwealth Shipping Line, conditional on securing the right price. http://electionspeeches.moadoph.gov.au/speeches/1954-robert-menzies. Instead, in 1957, his Government created the Australian National Line. In 1952, the Government sold its share of the Commonwealth Oil Refinery to the Anglo-Iranian Oil Company (later, British Petroleum).

[30] Bob Minns, *A History in Three Acts: Evolution of the Public Service Act 1999*, 2004, accessed at http://www.apsc.gov.au/publications-and-media/archive/publications-archive

[31] In 1947, the Postmaster-General's department employed over half of the Commonwealth's public servants: Minns, *History*.

[32] See *Fairfax v. Federal Commissioner of Taxation* 1965, discussed in Gilbert, *Federalism*, 23-4.

[33] Ergas, this volume.

13

Menzies and the Institutions of Government and Parliament

J. R. Nethercote

By education and experience Robert Menzies was steeped in the traditions of responsible parliamentary government mainly as developed at Westminster. The twin pillars of government as he came to understand it were ministerial (executive) responsibility to Parliament, and the rule of law, entrusted to an independent, impartial judiciary. His appreciation of such government was neither simply academic nor abstract, however.

It owed much to personal observation of Victorian politics in the first decade and a half of the Federation and embraced public meetings and the advocacy and debate of ideas, political campaigning, and the role of newspapers in the political life of the community. His father, James, was active in local government and public interest campaigns, not least that of the conservative, small government movement based on Kyabram in northern Victoria. From 1911 to 1920, he was a member of the Legislative Assembly of Victoria. One of his mother's brothers, Sydney Sampson, was member for Wimmera in the House of Representatives from 1906 until 1919, as an Independent Protectionist, Liberal and then Nationalist. He was, among other things, proprietor of a local newspaper where, as a boy, Menzies performed various chores.

As Menzies grew older he increasingly participated in the public affairs of the Victorian community. At university he was a leading figure in what are now known as student politics, as president of the Student Representative Council and editor of the student newspaper. During the Great War he was an advocate of conscription in debates during the plebiscites of 1916 and 1917. And it was his campaigning against the Bruce-Page referendum of 1926 that effectively led to his progressive shift from the bar to parliament.

Before election to the House of Representatives in 1934 he had six years in the Victorian Parliament, initially in the Legislative Council. For a time he was a Minister without Portfolio from which he resigned in protest against proposed government assistance to a regional business. From 1929 until 1934 he was a member of the Legislative Assembly; from 1932 until 1934 he was Attorney-General and Minister for Railways. It was in these years that he first showed his considerable skills as a party builder. Throughout his career he was keenly conscious (unlike, for example, Alfred Deakin) that advancement of worthy ideas required supporting organisation and that parties were a vital link between the public and parliament. In 1931, he was a major participant in attracting Joseph Lyons, Postmaster-General in the Scullin Government, to leave Labor and join the newly-formed United Australia Party. Within Victoria, he was instrumental in formation of the Young Nationalists who played a major role in the 1932 election which brought the Argyle Government to office.

It was not until 1935 that Menzies, then aged 40, first visited England and saw Westminster first-hand. He was a member of the Australian delegation to the Jubilee celebrations for King George V. By this time his admiration for British institutions and traditions was well-formed, but the mould was that of Australia and, in particular, Victoria. It carried the stamp of Spring Street as well as Big Ben.

He understood, in a Burkean way, that institutions, however entrenched, were neither static nor inanimate. Their operation was contingent on circumstances and upon the people on whose participation they depended.

During his four decades as a central and generally pre-eminent figure in Australia's political life, all the major institutions – the Crown (monarchy and governor-general), the Parliament (Senate and the House of Representatives), the Executive Government (ministers and Cabinet), and the administration – underwent major development. He left his mark upon them all even if his views did not necessarily prevail or endure.

By the time he retired, the practices of government were very different from when he entered public life during the mid-1920s. Earlier essays in this volume demonstrate his insight into the nature and role of political parties in the workings of parliamentary democracy; and his developing approaches to, for example, the Federation and the universities. Campaigning, at which he was exceptionally accomplished, was, in his earliest years, covered by newspapers; travel was most frequently undertaken by rail. In his final years, wireless was the major medium of communication but television was of such increasing importance that he used it to open his last House of Representatives campaign. The aeroplane was the main means of inter-state travel.

The Monarchy

Menzies was a strong believer in constitutional monarchy. His faith in the Crown was not simply formal and professional; it was deeply personal as well. He was perhaps the only Prime Minister of Australia, and one of the few in the Empire/Commonwealth, to enjoy a close relationship with the Royal Family which dated from his first visit to London in 1935, for King George V's jubilee celebrations, and lasted until the jubilee celebrations of Queen Elizabeth II. It was epitomised, as his prime ministership drew to a close, by his appointments as a Knight of the Thistle in 1963 and as Lord Warden of the Cinque Ports in 1965.

His attitude to monarchy was very much part of his faith in the government Australia had inherited from Britain. As he wrote:

> Those of us who have, in the nineteenth and twentieth centuries, inherited, first, a system of Responsible Government, and then a Constitutional Monarchy in the true sense, have not been forced into revolution. Our inheritance and our instincts are continuous.
>
> A democracy needs a focal point; otherwise it is 'without form and void'. There must be a powerful centripetal force in any nation if it is to be cohesive and strong. . . .

In a monarchy, that focal point is the Crown. "[N]o amount of cold analysis can destroy the basic fact that the Crown remains the centre of our democracy; a fixed point in the whirl of circumstance."[1]

In the course of his long service in government and politics Menzies, on several occasions, had to address questions concerning the monarchy. Throughout his term as Attorney-General he had carriage of adoption by Australia of the Statute of Westminster, a matter he publicly deemed important but not urgent; in a *Forgotten People* address after the debate in the House in 1942 about its adoption, he declared the relevant legislation was of "relatively minor importance". One of his concerns was the indivisibility of the Crown, which he strongly supported. Another was his ambivalence about trying to put the Imperial relationship into "written form. . . . There was a living spirit, and we endeavoured to imprison it within the four corners of a legal formula."[2]

Early in his time in Commonwealth Government, the matter of King Edward VIII's proposed marriage to Mrs Wallis Simpson arose. Menzies, as Attorney-General, was immediately involved. He and the Prime Minister, Joseph Lyons, found themselves "on common ground." Menzies drafted the critical cable Lyons sent to his UK counterpart, Stanley Baldwin. As Lyons reported to the House of Representatives at a special sitting on 11 December 1936:

> . . . the proposed marriage, if it led to Mrs Simpson becoming Queen, would invoke widespread condemnation, and that the alternative proposal or something in the nature of a specially sanctioned morganatic marriage would run counter to the best popular conception of the Royal Family.

When, three decades later, Menzies reflected upon the abdication, he laid great stress upon the nature of monarchy in modern times: "all institutions have come under scrutiny and even challenge. It has, in my time, been one of the strengths of the Monarchy that succeeding Monarchs have enjoyed the personal respect of the people." The King, he emphasised, was "not his own master; not an absolute Monarch, but a constitutional one with far more duties than rights."[3]

Different questions arose when, in 1949, the prime ministers of the time approved that India, although it had become a republic on independence, could remain a member of what was now to be called the Commonwealth of Nations. Menzies, advocating the indivisibility of the Crown, disliked the decision and much that followed as a consequence: "in one stroke, the common allegiance to the Crown ceased to be the bond of union . . . When we were all related by a common allegiance, our relationship was organic and internal; it still is for most of the older members. But for the Republicans, the relationship is in a sense functional and certainly external."[4]

He lamented: "however a monarchist might regret these events, I, for one, learned to live with them. After all, there were some elements in the association which could and should survive." He presciently concluded: "Our association could still be a special one, with a special sense of relationship which could be unique in the modern world."[5]

A consequence of these innovations within the Commonwealth of Nations was new legislation concerning the Queen's style and titles in those nations retaining the monarchy. In 1953, Australia adopted a *Royal Style and Titles Act* which declared Her Majesty to be "Elizabeth the Second, by the grace of God, of the United Kingdom, Australia and her other Realms and Territories Queen, Head of the Commonwealth, Defender of the Faith." The *Royal Powers Act* 1953 clarified the powers of the monarch when personally present in Australia, stating in particular that:

> At any time when the Queen is personally present in Australia, any power under an Act exercisable by the Governor-General may be exercised by the Queen. (section 2 (1))

Royal visits to Australia

Under the post-war Menzies Government royal visits were more frequent than before the war. The monarchy thus became more personal and less distant.

Hitherto, there had been a number of visits usually associated with significant parliamentary events, the opening of the first Commonwealth Parliament in May 1901 by the Duke of Cornwall and York (later King George V) and the opening of Parliament House, Canberra, in May 1927 by the Duke of York (later King George VI).

Two of the King's other sons also visited. The Prince of Wales was in Australia for several months in 1920. The Duke of Gloucester came in 1934; he came again in 1945 for a two-year term as governor-general.

Following the war a visit by King George VI was planned – he had gone to Canada, and the United States as well, before the war, and South Africa shortly after it ended. For reasons of health the trip to the Antipodes was eventually cancelled, replaced by an intended visit by Princess Elizabeth and the Duke of Edinburgh in 1952. The King died while they were in Kenya en route to Australia. They returned to England immediately.

Australia was well-represented at the Coronation of the new Queen the following year, the delegation, led by Menzies, including Harold Holt and John McEwen, Dr Evatt, the Leader of the Opposition, and several other parliamentary figures.

Early in 1954, the Queen, accompanied by the Duke of Edinburgh, became the first reigning monarch to visit Australia. They stayed for two months but had to depart promptly at the end of March so that Australia could hold a general election scheduled for 29 May. It was estimated that three-quarters of the population saw her. Among other activities she opened sessions of both the Commonwealth Parliament and the New South Wales Parliament.

There had been questions even in 1901 about whether, under the Constitution, anyone but the Governor-General could open a session of a parliament of the Commonwealth.[6] In 1934, it was proposed that the Duke of Gloucester open a session of the Commonwealth Parliament. The Governor-General, Sir Isaac Isaacs, a former justice and Chief Justice of the High Court (1905-31; 1930-31), vetoed the proposal as unconstitutional.[7]

In 1953, the matter was dealt with by means of a new Senate standing order:

14A. In respect of any occasion upon which Her Majesty the Queen is personally present in Australia and intends to signify in person the cause of the calling together of Parliament, references in Chapter 1 of these Standing Orders to His Excellency the Governor-General shall be read as references to Her Majesty the Queen, unless otherwise ordered.[8]

Other important change were made in succeeding years. In 1955 the Queen, advised by Menzies, issued a warrant for the Great Seal of Australia. Three years later, the Letters Patent issued to the Governor-General since Queen Victoria's time were amended, again on Menzies' advice. They had hitherto provided that Australian constitutional documents were signed by the monarch and counter-signed by a UK minister of state. Thereafter, such documents were counter-signed by the Prime Minister of Australia.

After the 1954 royal visits became more frequent. The Duke of Edinburgh made several visits including one in 1956 to open the Olympic Games in Melbourne and another to open the Royal Australian Mint. Queen Elizabeth the Queen Mother came for nearly a month in 1958 followed, the next year, by Princess Alexandra of Kent. Her brother, the Duke of Kent, came in 1964. In 1965 the former Governor-General, the Duke of Gloucester, made a third visit. And at the end of Menzies' prime ministership arrangements were made for the Prince of Wales to spend a term at Geelong Grammar's Timbertop campus.

The Queen herself came once more during Menzies' prime ministership, in 1963, a visit coinciding with the 50th anniversary of the foundation of Canberra. It was during this visit that Menzies was made a Knight of the Thistle.

For all his enjoyment of the pomp and ceremony of monarchy, and his profound attachment to Australia's British legacy, Menzies was nevertheless circumspect about royal visits: "The press are always howling for a Royal Visit. I have some reservations about having too many of them."[9] He was shrewd enough to understand that, to maintain interest and enthusiasm without provoking boredom or cynicism, the preferred course would be periodical but relatively infrequent visits.

He was also sparing in his public and semi-public appearances with royal visitors, something which was not difficult because, as he put it, the State premiers "are so parochial about their own rights that in their own areas they almost deny the existence of any Federal Ministers."[10] This both ensured that the royal visitors met without excessive inhibition a broad cross-section of Australian society, and reduced the prospect that royal sentiment in the nation would be unduly identified with himself and his government.

The Governor-Generalship

The place of the monarchy in Australia's public life intersected early in Menzies' time in federal politics with the governor-generalship. Under the Constitution the Governor-General is the monarch's "representative in the Commonwealth" (section 2) and the officer charged with "the execution and maintenance of the Constitution and of the laws of the Commonwealth" (section 61).

In 1938 the need arose to find a new governor-general to replace Lord Gowrie who had spent a decade in Australia as governor in South Australia and New South Wales and finally as Governor-General. Under the Statute of Westminster it now fell to the Prime Minister (Lyons) to make a recommendation to the King. In 1938 it was announced that Gowrie would be succeeded towards the end of 1939 by the Duke of Kent, the only one of King George V's surviving sons who had not visited Australia.

Menzies may have been involved in these decisions. He was certainly involved in the decision announced a year later that, because of the outbreak of war, the Duke of Kent would not be coming to Australia and Lord Gowrie would continue in the post, which he did until 1944. Gowrie, holder of the Victoria Cross and a veteran of Gallipoli, was a very suitable occupant of the post during war-time.

Though the Duke of Kent was killed in an air crash in 1942, Gowrie nevertheless had a royal successor, the Duke of Gloucester. Gloucester was an unusual choice for a Labor Government and may have arisen from "the instinctive understanding of the place of Parliament and of the place of the Crown in the Commonwealth" which Menzies discerned in Curtin, the Prime Minister at the time.[11] Gloucester came for two years. After he departed, there was plenty of controversy about his successor.

Ben Chifley had been prime minister since the death of Curtin in 1945. A veteran of the fight against Jack Lang within the New South Wales Branch of the Labor Party, his choice fell upon another engaged in those battles, the Premier of New South Wales since 1941, W.J. McKell. The appointment was attacked on party political and "jobs for the boys" grounds. Several Opposition front-benchers, in the words of A. W. Martin, "ostentatiously boycotted the event," but Menzies and the Country Party leader, Fadden, observed the courtesies.[12]

Menzies' view was cogently expressed in the House of Representatives:

> The real essence of our attack lies in this: that McKell was, at the moment when his appointment was announced, Premier of an Australian State, and actively engaged as a partisan leader in Australian political affairs. That is a grave disqualification. It strikes at the very foundation of the office of the Governor-Generalship, because that office in Australia should be as far removed from party politics as is the Crown itself in Great Britain.[13]

He recorded in his memoirs that he advised his colleagues that "we should treat the new Governor-General with all the respect due to his office, and that we should not allow our constitutional views to colour our relations with him."[14] With the passage of time Menzies developed a warm regard for McKell and, as prime minister, recommended an extension of his term, a knighthood and appointment to the Privy Council.

The Government attacked critics of the appointment on nationalist grounds, that the post should go to an Australian. Menzies, in the House, asserted that "the immediate point at issue is not whether an Australian should be eligible . . ., but whether an active party political leader should be transferred by his own party to a post which should, by tradition, and, indeed, necessity, be completely free of party politics."[15]

Pointing out that the governor-generalship was held at pleasure, he observed that occupancy could "fluctuate with every change of the constitution of the Commonwealth Parliament? This is degrading the Governor-Generalship by making it the direct product of the party politics of the country."[16]

Menzies' views on this matter remained unaltered. When, in 1969, the Minister for External Affairs, Paul Hasluck, for whom he had a very high regard, was appointed to the post, he wrote thus to Heather Henderson:

> But I must say that the greatest shock I have received was the appointment

of Paul Hasluck to the Governor-Generalship. Not that Paul won't do it very well, but that it violates every principle which I stated quite clearly at the time of the McKell appointment.[17]

He also wrote personally to Hasluck to explain his public reticence about the appointment, reiterating the views he had expressed twenty years earlier whilst expressing his confidence that Hasluck would "succeed famously" in the post.[18]

McKell's immediate successors were Field Marshal Sir William Slim, the victor of the Burma campaign during the war, and subsequently Chief of the Imperial General Staff; Lord Dunrossil, a retired Speaker of the House of Commons; and Lord De L'Isle, another holder of the Victoria Cross, a former Cabinet minister (briefly) and a businessman. All met a criterion Menzies considered essential for the appointment: the Queen knew them.

When Lord De L'Isle's term came to an end prematurely (at his own request) controversy again arose about another British appointment. There was scuttlebutt that the Duke of Gloucester, visiting Australia at the time, was being tested for another run. But this time there was concern even within the Cabinet at very high levels.

Canada had been appointing Canadian citizens as governor-general since 1952, and New Zealand since 1962. Likewise, state Labor governments had usually appointed Australians since the war (most of them, distinguished servicemen).

A sign of shifting opinion came in 1966 when a newly-elected Coalition government in New South Wales chose an Australian diplomat who had won a Victoria Cross during the war for the vice-regal office. Moreover, other institutions such as universities and the Anglican Church which had historically looked for British appointees to higher level posts were steadily if slowly now seeking distinguished locally-born contenders.

When De L'Isle departed John McEwen, the Deputy Prime Minister, certainly thought the time had come for an Australian-born appointment to Yarralumla. He privately arranged for Sir Owen Dixon, who had recently retired as Chief Justice of the High Court, to be sounded out. Dixon pleaded that his health precluded him from appointment.[19]

Menzies, as it happens, seems to have reached a similar view. His first choice fell upon Vice-Admiral Sir John Collins who had subsequently been Australian High Commissioner in Wellington. But he, too, declined interest.[20]

The choice, therefore, fell upon Lord Casey who, in addition to his long parliamentary and ministerial experience, had previously been Governor of Bengal in the last years of the Raj. Aged 75, Australian-born and a notable Gallipoli veteran, Casey had extensive associations with both Britain and the United States. He was unusually well-fitted for the transitional role of bringing an Australian disposition to the governor-generalship without breaking too sharply with its British background.

An interesting sidelight to Casey's appointment may be found in some views Menzies expressed at the time of De L'Isle's appointment at the age of 52 following Dunrossil who had died in office after only a year. "The office of Governor-General," he wrote to Heather Henderson in Geneva, "is one which should not be filled by a man in the sixties. De L'Isle at fifty-two should be able to stand up to the travel, and the meals, and the boredom, and the isolation, and the bowing and scraping of ambitious parasites quite comfortably."[21]

It is a mark of Menzies' appreciation of public opinion that his approach to royal involvement in Australian life has lasted many decades after he left office. The evidence suggests that he skilfully judged the timing of change of governor-general appointees from British recruits to Australian citizens. His emphasis, however, on the Governor-General's role as representative of the Queen very soon declined in relevance. The big quality sought seems to be that the appointee should be an eminent Australian.

Cabinet and Ministers[22]

Menzies first became a minister in 1928. He was an Honorary Minister. He did not head a department and a major function was to handle legislation in the Legislative Council. This phase of his career did not last long for he, along with others, soon resigned from the ministry because of opposition to a proposed subsidy to a rural abbatoir.[23]

His resignation had both a political as well as doctrinal dimension. Reflecting his father's political philosophies, he was opposed to subsidising rural activity. Doctrinally, he understood the basic rule of Cabinet government: a minister unwilling to support government policy or decision should resign.

His next period in a ministry came a few years later when, now a member of the Legislative Assembly, he was appointed to the Argyle Coalition Government on 19 May 1932. Third in precedence, he was, among other things, Attorney-General and Minister for Railways. These appointments marked the beginning of three-and-a-half decades as a front-bench parliamentarian, broken only, after a fashion, by two years as a backbencher from October 1941. In that time he was a minister, in total, for more than a quarter of a century, and a party leader for a similar period which included six years as Leader of the Opposition in the House of Representatives.

Menzies' experience as a front-bench parliamentarian is virtually unrivalled in Australia (John Howard's experience, almost uninterrupted, exceeds three decades). Menzies' experience embraced the maturing of Cabinet government in Australia from a late semi-formal stage during the 1930s to an eventual maturity which bears close affinity to the institution as it exists early in the twenty-first century. When he first became a minister Cabinet business was largely transacted at plenary meetings of all ministers. By the time he retired Cabinet was the top group of ministers meeting usually weekly (especially if parliament was sitting); but an increasing amount of business was being handled in committees. The organisation and paperwork of Cabinet business was by then substantially handled by a secretariat located in the Prime Minister's Department.

Cabinet government in Australia broadly follows practice in Westminster and Whitehall. But there are distinctive features. When Menzies first entered the ministerial ranks of executive government it was often the case that the head of government held another portfolio, frequently doubling as Treasurer. And there were an assortment of others, not all paid, as honorary ministers, ministers without portfolio and assistant ministers. Apart from the head of government, it was not unusual for ministers to hold two or even three portfolios (as was the case with Menzies himself in both Victoria and the Commonwealth).

In Menzies' last government, sworn in on 18 December 1963, the basic pattern was for each minister to have one department within his portfolio jurisdiction. The main reminder of earlier arrangements took the form of non-Cabinet ministers simultaneously appointed as, in the case of Senator John Gorton, for instance, "Minister assisting the Prime Minister in Commonwealth activities relating to research and education which fall within the Prime Minister's Department."

A big difference between the first ministry in Victoria and his last government was size. The McPherson ministry he joined in 1928 had a dozen members. His last government had 25; 12 of them constituted the Cabinet.

There are two other significant characteristics of the ministries to which Menzies belonged and, after 1939, headed except for the few weeks of the Fadden Government. Nearly all were coalitions with the Country Party. In the first 15 years these were not always happy alliances either in Victoria or the

Commonwealth. Those formed after 1949 endured relatively harmoniously notwithstanding periodical tensions. Menzies throughout insisted on choosing all ministers with the proviso that he would consult with the Country Party leader about invitations to members of that party.

A second characteristic singular to Australian national government is the practice of drawing a significant proportion of the ministry from the second chamber. In 1928, Menzies himself was one of four members of the Legislative Council appointed as ministers. When he formed his first government in April 1939, four of the 16 members came from the Senate. (In Canada, by contrast, it is rare for more than two ministers to be drawn from its appointed Senate.)

Menzies' second prime ministership itself marked a significant stage in evolution of that office. He took no other portfolio (except in 1960-61 when he was also Minister for External Affairs). In 1951 he vested the role of organising the business of the House in another minister, designated the Leader of the House. From the beginning he devoted much time to Australia's international interests, both in the usual centres of London and Washington, and in progressively visiting other countries of importance to Australia, often being the first Prime Minister of Australia to do so: among them, the Netherlands; France; Thailand; India; Japan; Malaya; Singapore; South Africa; Canada. And he established his home in Canberra, at the Prime Minister's Lodge.

Menzies' great ascendancy in Australian government coincided with growth in national functions, first, owing to the war; and, second, a consequence of post-war reconstruction and subsequent prosperity. The result, with the passage of time, was not only more ministers but also greater formality and structure in the conduct of collective ministerial business. These developments all occurred without any change to the basic elements of Cabinet government. The Cabinet itself, which in Australia has remained an operational institution, is both the apex of politics and the point at which politics and administration intersect. It is an institution in which unity is essential and almost invariably observed formally.

In Menzies' time, the main occasion when Cabinet responsibility was suspended was in 1940. Prior to restoration of coalition between the United Australia Party and the Country Party in March 1940, the latter party had announced its opposition to the Motor Vehicles Agreement Bill.[24] When the legislation came before the Parliament in May, the Country Party opposed it and it passed with the support of the Labor Party. (This situation has precedent at

Westminster; there have been various occasions when Cabinet responsibility has been suspended there, for example, over tariff matters during the early 1930s; or the European Union at various times.)

The force of Cabinet responsibility was clearly on display in July 1962. Leslie Bury, Minister Assisting the Treasurer, delivered a speech in which he differed publicly with the known views of the Prime Minister and John McEwen, the Country Party leader, Deputy Prime Minister and Minister for Trade, concerning the consequences for Australia of British membership of the European Economic Community (the Common Market). Menzies sought and received his resignation.[25]

During the Menzies years there was only one case of a ministerial resignation stemming from what is now known as conflict of interest. In February 1940, J. N. Lawson, the Minister for Trade and Customs, resigned after winning stakes with a racehorse rented from a leading industrialist who had just gained a potentially lucrative motorcar-manufacturing monopoly from the Government.[26]

During the inter-war years there were various attempts to place Cabinet operations on a more regular basis. At different times visitors to London sought advice from Sir Maurice Hankey, Secretary to the Cabinet in Whitehall until 1938; Hankey himself visited Australia in 1934, mainly for discussions about defence but his views about Cabinet operations were obtained.[27]

The onset of war shortly after Menzies first became prime minister brought matters to a head. Menzies spent much of his first prime ministership seeking to bring order and despatch to the generally relaxed ways of handling Cabinet business. The most durable innovation was the small War Cabinet to which the head of Defence, Frederick Shedden, was appointed secretary and usually attended meetings. It lasted throughout the war and met frequently.[28]

A counterpart, the Economic Cabinet, was appointed in November 1939 and included, from the War Cabinet, the Prime Minister, the Treasurer and the Minister for Supply and Development. Sir Ernest Fisk, managing director of a radio and communications manufacturing firm in which the Commonwealth Government had a part interest, was appointed Director of Economic Co-ordination and Secretary to the Economic Cabinet. It was, according to Menzies, "in effect . . . a business committee of the Full Cabinet, entrusted with the duty of carrying out the business side of the war." It hardly prospered at all and it soon fell into disuse after the coalition was reconstituted in March 1940.[29]

In June 1941 Menzies tried again, establishing an Economic and Industrial Committee of Cabinet, to be chaired by the Treasurer, Arthur Fadden, "to expedite the handling of business on the economic side of the war and to promote better co-ordination in the economic policy of the Government," insisting that it was "not merely a committee of report but one of action like the War Cabinet." Its short life came to an end with the fall of the Fadden Government in October 1941, replaced to some extent by the Production Executive after the Curtin Government took office; it survived until 1946.[30]

A related body, the Advisory War Council (AWC), established in October 1940, had its origins in the Government's precarious position in the House of Representatives, and the Labor Party's refusal to participate in a national government. It was composed of leading Government and Opposition figures. Serviced by the War Cabinet Secretariat, its decisions, where supported by ministers present, were immediately adopted.

Early in 1944, following the 1943 election, Menzies, having resumed leadership of the United Australia Party and successfully claimed leadership of the Opposition, withdrew his party from the AWC, although Percy Spender remained a member and Billy Hughes was subsequently reappointed.

The Curtin and Chifley governments undertook important rationalisation of the Cabinet. Henceforward all ministers headed a department. Administrative support for Cabinet grew although officials did not often attend meetings.

When Menzies returned to the prime ministership in 1949, the Cabinet had 19 ministers. All but one minister headed a department and three headed a couple; the exception was the Vice-President of the Executive Council, Dame Enid Lyons. As with the predecessor Chifley Government, the Cabinet and the ministry were co-terminous; Casey, in particular, urged him to create a Cabinet of senior ministers. But Menzies, for six years, sought initially to deal with the growing agenda by means of 19 standing committees. This framework proved "unrealistic and unwieldy." After the 1951 election, a four-committee structure was created to support the Cabinet: defence preparations; economic policy; legislation; and general administration. The Legislation Committee oversaw preparation, content and timing of the legislative program for Parliament. The General Administration Committee was chaired by the Vice-President of the Executive Council (who was also Deputy Leader of the Liberal Party) and was, according to Professor L. F. Crisp, "especially successful in relieving the full Cabinet of a miscellany of lesser but inescapable Cabinet business."[31]

Following the 1954 election, there was further consolidation: the Prime Minister's Committee, concerned with important policy issues, especially in the economic field; and the Vice-President's Committee for second order and administrative issues. There were still specialist committees for other matters such as defence and legislation and, from time to time, ad hoc committees on particular matters.

It was only after the 1955 election that the enduring Cabinet structure was established; it has formed the foundation for all subsequent development. The Government was divided into a Cabinet (the 12 senior ministers) and an outer ministry (10 ministers). The division was flexible. Outer ministers attended Cabinet whenever they had a submission being discussed. And the Attorney-General, if not in the Cabinet, was often in attendance. All ministers, whether or not in the Cabinet, were bound by all decisions.[32]

This structure has survived for six decades; only during the Whitlam Government was there an unsuccessful reversion to a Cabinet composed of all ministers.

It was in 1949-50 that Cabinet was placed on firm institutional and administrative foundations. This step was signalled by Allen Brown's appointment as Secretary, Prime Minister's Department (he had previously been Director-General of Post-War Reconstruction). In October 1949 he wrote to the Public Service Board:

> The Prime Minister has instructed me to provide a more complete service in relation to Cabinet and its sub-committees and has indicated that he realises this will necessitate the introduction into the Department of some new officers appropriately qualified.[33]

This development was not affected by the change of government two months later. When the Menzies Government took office a *Handbook of Cabinet and Cabinet Committees* was issued incorporating a two-page statement of Cabinet procedure. This statement encouraged departments to discuss submissions with the Treasury beforehand, and any other department with "a particular interest in the subject."[34] It also made clear that the Prime Minister's approval was required before any subject could be listed for Cabinet consideration.[35]

In the case of the Treasury it would seem that the injunction was more honoured in the breach than the observance for, in October 1951, a Cabinet officer directed that the Treasury be given a copy of every Cabinet or committee decision. "Since dept consultation with them may not take place, it is imp[ortant] that they receive their copy as soon as possible after a decision has been authorised."

The *Handbook* also stated:

> The Secretary to Cabinet attends Cabinet meetings and records the time and place of meetings, names of Ministers present, and the decisions of Cabinet. No mention is made in Cabinet minutes of the views of individual Ministers.
>
> The Secretary communicates decisions of Cabinet in duplicate to Ministers who are themselves responsible for taking action thereon. The Minister concerned instructs his Department as to action to be taken to give effect to the decision.[36]

So far as Cabinet committees were concerned, Menzies proposed that senior officers might attend "on appropriate occasions." Officials very occasionally attended meetings of Cabinet itself.[37]

Time continued to be a problem in Cabinet proceedings. In May 1951 Menzies "asked Ministers to help him shorten Cabinet meetings by making themselves familiar with Cabinet papers before the meeting and by speaking briefly."[38]

Decision-making in the Menzies Cabinets was largely by agreement. Votes were rarely taken.[39]

For various reasons all Menzies' governments were composed of people – all men except for Dame Enid Lyons – with considerable ministerial experience. Although he himself had reached ministerial rank within months of his election to parliament he generally believed that people should have about five years' experience before moving to the front bench. But there were exceptions. Percy Spender was a member of the first Menzies Government, a little more than 18 months after his election to the House. Likewise, following the 1949 election, Senator William Spooner immediately became a minister and was, indeed, a minister for his entire 14 years in the Senate. Others who rose to ministerial rank relatively quickly included Paul Hasluck, William McMahon and Sir Garfield Barwick. Most other new ministers in post-war Menzies governments waited 8-9 years, essentially three parliaments. None of the large cohort of Coalition entrants in 1949 entered the Menzies ministry after the 1958 election. Likewise, subsequent newcomers to the ministry were mainly drawn from new entrants to Parliament elected in 1955 or shortly thereafter.

Most Menzies governments included a minister from each State of the Commonwealth, but sometimes the representation was only one. South Australia had two members from 1949 to 1955 and, thereafter, only one. Contrariwise, it was only after 1956 that there were two Tasmanians in the ministry.

Ministers mainly had relatively safe seats. In 1961, however, three ministers lost seats, two of them in Queensland. And, in the post-war period, only two ministers died in office; another, Athol Townley, died a week after announcement that he would be going to Washington, DC, as Ambassador. Senator Sir William Spooner, however, retired from the Senate immediately following diagnosis of a terminal illness; and Senator Sir Shane Paltridge died within a couple of days of resigning.

Most ministers, when they left the ministry, also left Parliament, immediately or soon after. Only five went to the backbench and one of them simply saw out his term as a senator.

The remainder, upon leaving the government, took other public appointments. Two, Sir Garfield Barwick and Senator Sir John Spicer, accepted judicial appointments; in Barwick's case, as Chief Justice of the High Court. Quite a number went abroad as high commissioners or ambassadors. The most usual destinations were London and Washington, DC. A Country Party minister, Scottish-born Hugh Roberton, opened Australia's embassy in Dublin in 1965.

Only two ministers were obviously dropped from the post-war governments: Wilfrid Kent Hughes after the 1955 election, reportedly owing to his habit of continually commenting on foreign policy matters; and Allen Fairhall after the 1958 election (perhaps a consequence of the need for a New South Welshman to make a place for Barwick). Fairhall won back his frontbench place after the 1961 election). Leslie Bury, who resigned over Government policy concerning British entry into Europe, was appointed Minister for Housing after the 1963 election.

It was a period when conspicuous public service was often recognised with a knighthood and many ministers in the post-war Menzies governments, especially those appointed between 1949 and 1958, were so honoured. The real mark of distinction in these years was appointment to the Privy Council. Such appointment was largely reserved for party and deputy party leaders. John McEwen and Harold Holt were so honoured in the Coronation Honours List. Exceptional appointments were those of Sir William Spooner, Leader of the Government in the Senate, 1958-64, and Paul Hasluck, in 1966.

During the 1950s there were periodical rumblings about electing ministries as the Labor Party did, or a more modest version as practised by the Liberal Party in Victoria where two ministers were elected by the party room. On a couple of occasions there was some formal consideration of the question but it never went any further.[40]

Public Administration[41]

In both Victoria and later the Commonwealth Menzies had respectful relationships with the public service and the senior officials with whom he dealt. He was Attorney-General in both jurisdictions and thus worked with one of the few parts of the public service where the staff had professional training and qualifications, often in the form of a university degree. Elsewhere, the administrative grades of public services were staffed by men with matriculation level education; returned servicemen of the Great War had preference.

There is some evidence that Menzies was certainly conscious of a need to build up the competence of the public service. Certainly, when war came, he, as prime minister, oversaw extensive recruitment of academics, often accompanied by recent graduates, and businessmen to government posts for the purposes of policy-making and higher direction of the war. As had happened during the Depression, the economists, L.F. Giblin and Douglas Copland, were immediately involved in economic matters; among the more famous, Dr H.C. Coombs, then on the staff of the Commonwealth Bank, was seconded to the Treasury and subsequently took a range of public service posts culminating in appointment as Director-General of Post-War Reconstruction in 1943. Another immediately involved was Professor Leslie Melville, Coombs' superior at the Bank. Some officials were also reassigned from their usual work to activities more directly related to the war; Dr Roland Wilson, for example, left his post of Statistician and became Secretary of the newly-formed Department of Labour and National Service. The businessmen included Sir Keith Murdoch as Director-General of Information (an inspired appointment given Murdoch's famous intervention during the Great War concerning the Gallipoli campaign) and Essington Lewis, General Manager of BHP, as Director-General of Munitions with a status comparable to that of the Chiefs of Staff.[42]

The central machinery of government was, at the time,rudimentary. So it was that provision of high level administrative support for Cabinet was assumed by Frederick Shedden, Secretary, Department of Defence, who was, throughout, Secretary of the War Cabinet. Shedden's earlier experience embraced several periods in London where he learnt about coordination in government from Sir Maurice Hankey, Secretary of the British Cabinet and previously Secretary to the Committee of Imperial Defence.[43]

In the ensuing years there was a major reorientation of administration towards the changing requirements of the war. Menzies, in his first Government, included a Department of Supply and Development which mainly took over functions of equipment and other support activities from the Defence Department. The new ministry also included a new Department of Social Services carved out of the Treasury.

A Department of Information was created immediately upon declaration of war, as foreshadowed in the War Book. In November, Defence was reorganised with the creation of separate service departments under a Department of Defence Coordination. The following year saw establishment of a Department of Munitions in June and the Department of Labour and National Service in October.

Menzies, following his visit to London early in 1941, made major additions to the departmental machinery of government in June 1941, additions designed with the assistance of Shedden, Secretary to the War Cabinet, who had accompanied him to London. These departments were: Aircraft Production; External Territories; Home Security; Transport; and War Organization of Industry.[44]

The only major change later made was creation of the Department of Post-War Reconstruction in December 1942, excised from the Department of Labour and National Service.[45] Thus, the departmental machinery of government was virtually entirely in place before Menzies lost the prime ministership in August 1941 and before Japan entered the war.

In addition to the organisation and staffing of administration for war purposes, there were various other attempts to expedite the war effort. Among the more important were endeavours to establish machinery for consultation with what are now called "stakeholders." Those concerning business and industrialists worked well enough but, from the beginning, there were difficulties in developing comparable mechanisms with organised labour, the Australasian Council of Trades Unions often being simply unresponsive. Menzies himself took a personal interest in encouraging cooperation with labour but even his overtures did not meet with any apparent success.

Hasluck provided an important appraisal of the achievement of the Menzies Government between 1939 and 1941. After reviewing the record, and taking account of various criticisms, he concluded:

> Considering first the weakness and inexperience of the administrative services when the war began and, second, the political difficulties of the whole period of his office, the administrative labours of Menzies command respect, even when they are criticised in points of detail. The accomplishment in organising the nation for war was considerable.

Furthermore, after he had corrected most of his own errors while in office, the groundwork of his administration proved sound enough to enable the rapid intensification of the war effort in 1942 and 1943 without any substantial change in principle or method.[46]

On leaving office, the Coalition, a dispirited body which in the case of the UAP hardly even bothered to have party meetings, had little to say about administrative questions though it still had, through the Advisory War Council, opportunities to observe government more closely than would have been possible under usual arrangements. In February 1944, as already noted, Menzies, having resumed leadership of the UAP and claimed Leadership of the Opposition, removed the UAP from the Council although Percy Spender continued to participate, as did the Country Party.

Especially after the end of hostilities, however, the public service increasingly became a target of Opposition criticism on grounds of size and alleged political partisanship. The Chifley Government's general disposition in favour of public service administration of programs meant that there was no sustained effort to reduce staffing levels of government. Increasing prominence of some top officials, notably Dr H.C. Coombs, the Director-General of Post-War Reconstruction, and, from 1949, Governor of the Commonwealth Bank, seemed to exemplify the rise and power of bureaucracy as it had evolved during the war years.[47]

Dr Evatt, Deputy Prime Minister, Attorney-General and Minister for External Affairs, was a particular object of attention, an attention which sharpened when Paul Hasluck, after leaving the Department of External Affairs, made some pointed observations in a public lecture delivered in the University of Western Australia to which he had returned in order to write the civil history of Australia during the war. Criticism reached its peak when the head of External Affairs, Dr J.W. Burton, unsuccessfully contested Labor preselection for the newly-created seat of the ACT. Burton's elevation itself had been a source of considerable controversy and very much a factor in Hasluck's departure from the Department.[48]

Once back in office neither Menzies nor most of his colleagues evinced any serious worries about the top officials inherited from their Labor predecessors although there were some persistent backbench mutterings. In *The Measure of the Years* he recorded:

> When I came in . . . for my long second term as Prime Minister, there was a feeling around that Labour had attached significance to the political

342

views of senior public servants; that the service was becoming somewhat political.

Whether this was true I have always taken leave to doubt. But the very existence of the rumour made me quite determined that my own administration's record should be clear. At the very outset I was told by people in my party organization that certain men in the Prime Minister's Department were or had been officers or members of the Labour Party. I recall my reply with some satisfaction. 'So long as they are competent and honest men, what of it. Kissing will not go by political favour in my department!'

At least two of the officers my party official had referred to were relatively senior, and in a position in which they might be required to offer advice. Each in turn did so on occasion, and always with complete objectivity and integrity.[49]

One head of a small department whose post was abolished was reassigned to the growing Department of Social Services as deputy head. Dr Burton continued as secretary to the Department of External Affairs until June 1950 when, at his own request, he took six months' leave to write a book. Upon return to duty he was appointed High Commissioner in Ceylon (now Sri Lanka). Very soon after arrival in Columbo he returned to Australia and won Labor endorsement for the NSW seat of Lowe at the May 1951 double dissolution election; William McMahon, who had won the seat for the Liberals in 1949, retained it and was shortly appointed to the ministry.

Menzies was a strong advocate of the impartiality of the public service. It was one of the reasons he was opposed to having officials appearing before parliamentary committees on policy matters. But he recognised they had political views and did not raise any objection to them standing for parliament and their reinstatement if not successful.[50]

He had warm relations especially with senior officials, tempered by a measure of reserve and distance. He called them "the boys". According to Sir John Bunting:

'The boys' were very much companions, and especially if he got to know them well, he enjoyed their company as much as he appreciated their official ministrations. He developed a personal though not undue official friendship . . . it is right and necessary for both sides that there should be an arm's length or reasonably aloof position as between ministers and senior departmental officers.[51]

On taking office, the new government made only limited alterations to departmental arrangements, basically adopting changes planned by the Chifley Government. The Department of Post-War Reconstruction was abolished, its functions being dispersed among another agencies, the most important being assignment of the Economic Division to the Prime Minister's Department. Works and Housing was also abolished, works functions being incorporated into Interior while housing became part of the new Department of National Development. Otherwise there were a few amalgamations.

For the rest of his time in office, Menzies was circumspect about departmental change. The most significant restructuring was in the field of international trade, customs administration and primary industry as a consequence of which two departments, Commerce and Agriculture, and Trade and Customs, were reorganised into three: Trade (Trade and Industry from 1963); Primary Industry; and Customs and Excise.[52]

A less successful attempt at departmental rationalisation centred upon Defence. Initially all three service departments (Navy, Army, Air) had been retained notwithstanding some vigorous criticism by Menzies from the Opposition benches. In 1957, a high level committee under Lieutenant-General Sir Leslie Morshead, a prominent Sydney businessman who had landed at Gallipoli on 25 April 1915, recommended abolition of the service departments and replacement by a unified Defence administration headed by a Minister and an associate minister. The three services, supported by various ex-service bodies, resolutely fought for the status quo; and the proposed ministerial arrangements fell foul of the then widely held view that departments should have one, and only one, minister. The committee had a modest success with a proposal that two departments, Supply and Defence Production, concerned with equipping the defence services, should be amalgamated. Various less formal attempts to bring greater cohesion to Defence administration met with limited success.[53]

Outside the public service, the Government had a major success in reform of banking, especially central banking. Shortly after winning office, the Government presented legislation to replace a single governor of the Commonwealth Bank, then the central bank, with a board. This legislation was resisted by the Opposition which was able, because of its majority in the Senate, to defeat it. The bill eventually formed the basis for the double dissolution in 1951. Afterwards, with majorities in both houses, the Government achieved its purpose.

Following the 1955 election, fresh legislation was introduced to separate central from trading banking. This legislation was also defeated in the Senate when, unusually, the Opposition combined with the newly-formed breakaway Democratic Labor Party. But, after the 1958 election, the Government recovered a majority in the Senate and secured passage of the legislation. The Reserve Bank of Australia came into existence on 1 January 1960, as did the new Commonwealth Bank, composed of trading, savings and development banks. This basic structure of banking has proven very durable.[54]

The Government eventually succeeded in containing the size of the public service. From peak of 161 031 in mid-1951, it fell by nearly ten thousand in the following year and by nearly 3 000 the next year. Thereafter it climbed slowly and by mid-1961 it had reached 165 214. Most of the reductions in the 1950s came from temporary employees; a number came from transfer of Commonwealth Hostels from the public service to a government-owned company.

Throughout the entire 15 years of the post-war Menzies Government, the number of permanent staff continued to grow, from 55 852 in mid-1949 to 123 122 in mid-1965. In the same period, the numbers in the ACT grew from 6 507 (1949) to 13 418 (1965).

The public service in this era was still divided between Canberra and Melbourne. Departments in Canberra included Prime Minister's, Treasury, External Affairs, Attorney-General's, Commerce and Agriculture, Immigration, National Development, Interior and Health. Among the more significant agencies located in Canberra were the Tax Office, the Bureau of Census and Statistics, the Audit Office, the Public Service Board and the Commonwealth Office of Education.

All the Defence group of departments were located in Melbourne together with Civil Aviation, Shipping and Transport, Postmaster-General's, Labour and National Service, Social Services, Repatriation and the Tariff Board. Once development of Canberra recommenced in the late 1950s, departments were progressively moved from Melbourne. The most conspicuous was the Defence group, located first in the Administration Building (now the John Gorton Building) and later at Russell Hill; by the end of the 1960s Social Services and Repatriation were moving north.

During the 1950s internal efforts to improve the efficiency of departments and agencies were limited. The division of administration between Melbourne and Canberra was viewed as an impediment, an impediment compounded by dispersal of Commonwealth locations within Melbourne itself. Relocation of administration in the national capital was seen as an important step towards improved administration.

In addition to the locational factor, the rationalisation and restructuring of departments and agencies was inhibited by various arbitration rulings and determinations. Within these restraints and inflexibilities the Public Service Board strove to improve efficiency of performance by application of organisation and methods techniques of analysis to staff deployments and operational procedures. Staff development and training was also greatly enhanced from pre-war practice, an approach to administrative improvement that derived from methods used by the armed services during the war. Another way in which war-time approaches were applied to staffing came in replacement of academic by psychological (aptitude) tests in recruitment, combined with interviews in both recruitment and promotion.

The innovation which in time had the greatest impact on administration was the early use of automatic data processing (ADP) and other forms of mechanisation. The first applications occurred during the early 1950s; the Commonwealth was among the first organisations in Australia to see the potential of mechanisation for enhancing efficiency. It was perhaps three decades before the impact was pervasively felt but the seeds were sown very early.

It was at the end of the 1950s that public service staffing arrangements eventually opened the way to lifting the quality of administration. The first came as a consequence of an important initiative by Menzies himself, namely the establishment of a committee to advise on public service recruitment. The committee was headed by Sir Richard Boyer, Chairman of the Australian Broadcasting Commission. Among its more significant recommendations were proposals that the public service should be recruiting more graduates for the general ranks of administration, what was known as the Third Division (which also included specialists, such as lawyers, doctors and engineers as well). These ideas were adopted, if not quite in the form advocated by the committee. Menzies himself introduced the necessary amendments to the Public Service Act into the House of Representatives in 1960. Like application of ADP to administrative tasks, this would in time prove to be a critical change to the character of the public service.[55] It also dovetailed neatly with another of Menzies' important initiatives, expansion of the universities, addressed in essays by John Howard and Greg Melleuish.

The second change was also concerned with the relationship of educational

346

qualifications to staffing, this time in the form of pay rates. An arbitral decision known as the Engineers' case (but not to be confused with the High Court case of 1920), and based upon an earlier decision concerning scientific staff in the CSIRO, it opened the way to recognising educational qualifications in determining the remuneration of staff. This provided the basis for extensive overhaul and rationalisation of all staffing in the APS (and elsewhere), with a flexibility simply not previously available. Apart from consequences in terms of streamlining staff structures, it provided the opportunity to place remuneration practice in the public service on a much more competitive and discriminating basis in which market rates became a key guide in fixing levels of remuneration.

To oversee public service development in these new circumstances the Government selected F.H. (later Sir Frederick) Wheeler as chairman of the Public Service Board, at that time the central pay, management and staffing authority of the service. A commerce graduate of the University of Melbourne, Wheeler had effectively been second in command at the Treasury for five years when, at the beginning of 1953, he took up the post of Treasurer of the International Labour Organization in Geneva. From the late 1950s various efforts were made to persuade him to return to Australia, which he was keen to do. A decision was finally taken in mid-1959 that he would succeed Sir William Dunk as chairman of the Public Service Board at the beginning of 1961.

It was very unusual to make or announce such an important appointment so far in advance. Also unusual was the great resistance to the appointment from the Treasury itself, and the enthusiasm of H.A. (later Sir Henry) Bland, secretary to the Department of Labour and National Service, to get the job. Bland was a son of Australia's first professor of public administration, Professor F.A. Bland of the University of Sydney, by this time a Liberal member of the House of Representatives and chairman of the Joint Committee of Public Accounts. Harold Holt, now the Treasurer, had worked with Bland for many years as Minister for Labour. Encouraged by Sir Roland Wilson, Secretary to the Treasury, he took up Bland's cause when the matter was considered by a ministerial committee composed of Menzies, McEwen and Holt. After nearly an hour's discussion, they decided in favour of Wheeler.

Wheeler brought great technical and analytical competence to his new role. It was combined with a deep sense of public service professionalism and vocation. Armed with the Boyer recommendations and the flexibilities flowing from the Engineers' decision, he was able to guide the public service through a rigorous overhaul of its staffing and organisational structures, combining active recruitment programs with a competitive pay policy.

A number of conduct cases also provided an opportunity to appraise ethical ideas and standards.[56] These included party political activity and contact with parliamentarians with the then active question of the rights of public servants to speak out on public matters excluding those relating to their field of employment.

In this period there was much stress on the quality of heads of department, appointed by the Governor-General on the recommendation of the prime minister, often after discussion in the Cabinet. Department heads frequently spent a decade in the post. Known as permanent heads, they were indeed very permanent, not least because later ideas about mobility had not yet taken hold. Most appointees came from the public service, but not usually from the department itself (except where specialist qualifications were called for). Major sources of department heads with generalist backgrounds were the Treasury, Defence and, increasingly, External Affairs, and Trade. Quite a number naturally had distinguished war records. In this period, a small number came from outside the service.

A growing number had tertiary qualifications; and, not least because of the war, they had a range and variety of experience which heads in earlier times could not generally match. Even so, there were a small number of controversies throughout the Menzies years. One head of the Army department, Allan McKnight, had a major falling out with the Military Board over proposed amalgamation of the Defence and service departments; assigned to the Atomic Energy Commission he had major disagreements with the Chairman, Phillip Baxter, who was keen for Australia to develop an atomic bomb.[57] In another case, in order to bring new energy to the Defence Department, Sir Frederick Shedden was, with difficulty, persuaded to retire a year earlier than planned.[58] Much attention was given to encouraging the head of External Affairs, Sir Arthur Tange, to take a posting abroad; he eventually went to India as high commissioner in 1965.[59]

The Government made use of ad hoc bodies from time to time. Examples of committees of inquiry, apart from Morshead and Boyer committees referred to above, included the Murray Committee on university funding in 1957 and the Vernon Enquiry into the economy which reported in 1965. Several royal commissions were also established, the most famous being that into the Petrov defection, headed by Justice Owen of the Supreme Court of New South Wales and the Spicer Royal Commission into the sinking of HMAS *Voyager* ten years later.

Parliament[60]

Parliament was a central forum in Menzies' political life, though by no means the only one. He was a member of two parliaments (Victoria and the Commonwealth) and three houses (Legislative Council, then Legislative Assembly in Victoria; the House of Representatives in Canberra). When he addressed the United States House of Representatives in 1950, he told them he was a "House of Representatives man". This was correct in that most of his time as a parliamentarian was as a member of the House of Representatives; and most of his time in the Parliament of Victoria was in the Legislative Assembly; his time in the Council had been brief and part-time.

Parliament was the doorway through which executive office was reached. It was also the place where the statesman advocated policy, challenged that of opponents, and defended his own.

The houses of which Menzies was a member all had relatively small chambers. Political debate and discussion had an intimacy which the larger chamber now occupied by the House of Representatives lacks. Moreover, for most of Menzies' time in the House, its proceedings were broadcast.[61] Although he had doubts about the value of broadcasting, no-one exploited this facility with greater skill than he. Both as Leader of the Opposition, and later as Prime Minister, his preferred time of speaking was 8.00pm on broadcast nights. His mastery of parliamentary eloquence thus went beyond the chamber to the nation at large.

While for many people their main experience of Menzies' ascendancy was as the gifted parliamentary advocate, for Menzies this skill was deployed in the context of large strategic and tactical circumstances. Menzies rarely had an absolute security as a prime minister. As war-time prime minister he continually had to deal with a House of Representatives in which he had a majority only briefly. The post-war prime ministership was often shadowed by a Senate where the Coalition only had a slender majority if it had one at all. He was, indeed, the first prime minister to contend with the Senate elected by proportional representation, what he once called "the crazy voting system".[62]

Parliament, 1939-41

The problems Menzies faced when he first became prime minister were somewhat ameliorated by the relative infrequency of sittings (51 days in 1939 and 43 in 1940, an election year). The Country Party refused to join a coalition led by

Menzies so his first government was a minority. It was, unlikely, however, that the Country Party would join with Labor to defeat the Government, though Menzies, because of his experience in Victoria, was always wary. He kept the door open to a resumption of coalition which in fact came in March 1940. He also considered a national government with Labor, including one led by John Curtin, and made no fewer than four offers. Labor rejected them all; Curtin, in particular, apart from contending that there was only one thing worse than a coalition of two parties and that was a coalition of three, also had a strong philosophical commitment to the need, during war-time, for a strong Opposition. In the end, the Advisory War Council was, notwithstanding its longevity, a barely adequate substitute.

The main means Menzies employed to meet the parliamentary situation was creation of a range of committees, formal and informal, and most including both senators and members. Even this idea ran into difficulties, Menzies being strongly of the view that each committee should have a government supporter in the chair. The coverage of the committees was broad: war expenditure; social security; profits; broadcasting; rural industries; and apples and pears! Although the Senate already had a Standing Committee on Regulations and Ordinances, a special committee was also appointed to scrutinise regulations made under the *National Security Act* 1939. this committee was partly intended to allay concerns stemming from the Great War when there was no scrutiny of the profuse number of regulations made under the *War Precautions Act* 1914.

The committees, in the event, made little serious impact on the intense parliamentary politics after the 1940 election, but they did ensure that that parliamentarians had a larger role in government than they had had during the Great War.

Opposition, 1941-49

Once out of office in October 1941, Menzies had a rare period of virtual inactivity in the House. Appearances are deceptive: he remained a member of the Advisory War Council, and, when the Opposition eventually moved a no confidence motion in the Government in June 1943, foreshadowing what lay ahead, it was Menzies and not the ancient leader of the UAP, W.M. Hughes, who seconded Fadden in the debate. These were the years when Menzies, in the famous *Forgotten People* broadcasts, laid out the philosophical foundations of Australian Liberalism.

But in the task of resurrecting Liberalism as a political force, the House of

Representatives was his base. In the years, 1943 to 1949, he raised parliamentary opposition to a new level of potency and impact; in this endeavour, broadcasting of proceedings, which had commenced in 1943, was critical. Among a number of notable speeches, those opposing bank nationalisation and the associated politics have been long remembered.

As with so many aspects of his political life, his practice of Opposition was sustained by clear views about purpose. It was "to be not merely a period of frustration and dejection, but a splendid opportunity for a revival of the spirit and a replenishment of the mind." His first precept was that:

> [the role of Opposition was] not just to oppose for opposition's sake, but to oppose selectively. No Government is always wrong on everything, whatever the critics may say. The Opposition must choose the ground on which it is to attack. To attack indiscriminately is to risk public opinion, which has a reserve of fairness not always understood.

A second precept was that:

> An Opposition must always remember that it is the alternative Government; that it is unwise, when in Opposition, to promise what you cannot perform; that a quick debating point scored in Parliament against some Government measure will be a barren victory unless you are confident that in office, you would not be compelled to do, substantially, what the Government is doing.[63]

Another precept about Opposition was a strong preference for leading members to be "all-rounders, well informed on a wide range of topics, competent as flexible debaters, and able to make useful contributions to the formulation of general policy." He was thus hostile to development of the shadow cabinet. He had his own Opposition executive but its members "were not specifically attached to particular departments."[64]

Parliament, 1949-66: Senate matters

When Menzies won government in 1949 he faced problems quite different from those of a decade earlier. Whereas previously his situation in the House of Representatives was never comfortable, after 1949 it was the Senate which from the beginning presented significant strategic and tactical problems. Menzies was, in fact, the first prime minister of Australia to have persistent difficulties with the Senate.

After the war both sides of politics decided that the then method of electing senators, essentially a winner-take-all system, needed an overhaul. In his policy speech for the 1946 election, Menzies told the voters that, because of the way the Senate so often had a preponderance of one party or another, "we believe that an early attempt must be made to devise some new method of Senate election." Chifley said nothing about the matter; it had long been Labor's policy to abolish the Senate. But his deputy, Evatt, had long ago advocated proportional representation for the Senate in a prize-winning essay at university, Liberalism in Australia.[65]

The 1946 election amply demonstrated the need for a change. Labor, with 52.1 percent of the vote, secured 15 of the 18 seats contested and, having won all 18 at the 1943 election, it thus dominated the Senate, 33 to three.

In 1948 the Government decided to expand the House for the first time since federation. Expansion of the Senate was also necessary in accordance with the nexus requirement embodied in section 24 of the Constitution which specifies that the number of members of the House "shall be, as nearly as practicable, twice the number of the senators".

The opportunity was taken to introduce a proportional method of filling vacancies, five in each State at periodical elections, which, up to that time had always been held in conjunction with general elections for the House, and ten in the event of simultaneous dissolution of both Houses under section 57 (commonly called a double dissolution).

The innovation had two consequences for Menzies. In the first instance, it meant that, should the Coalition parties win in 1949, there was virtually no prospect that they would have a majority in the Senate. The very best they could hope for would be 27 seats in a Senate of 60 and that is how many they had. It was therefore unlikely that the House of Representatives would run the prescribed three years if the Coalition was victorious. In that circumstance the greater likelihood was that section 57 would be activated and there would be a double dissolution. (In the period, 1910-49, several newly-elected governments faced hostile Senates (Cook in 1913; Scullin in 1929); the Curtin Government, coming to office mid-term in 1941, also faced an Opposition majority in the Senate until mid-1944.)

Menzies unlike almost anyone else at the time saw that the new method of election would significantly alter the workings of section 57. As he observed at the time, it would make a double dissolution much less attractive for an incoming prime minister. The change had the unusual effect of making bicameral disagreement over legislation more likely but, contrariwise, making resolution less likely except by means of a joint sitting. (So it has proved to be: in the five double dissolutions after 1949-1951; 1974; 1975; 1983; and 1987 – only on two occasions has the result been majorities for the same side in each house.)

Section 57 was expressly concerned with adoption of legislation. Menzies' interest also embraced a view that it was generally desirable that a ministry should be supported in the parliament as a whole. He was not the only Westminster party leader at the time to contemplate questions of bicameralism. Across the Tasman, his counterpart, Sydney Holland, considered what to do about New Zealand's Legislative Council, membership of which was a life appointment; he had previously, by private member's bill, sought its abolition and, in 1951, it was indeed abolished. There is an anecdote that when Holland sought Menzies' advice, he replied: "Why don't you abolish it?"

And, in the United Kingdom, the Attlee Government had had to utilise the provisions of the *Parliament Act* 1911 to enact some of its nationalisation legislation which fell outside the Salisbury convention that the Opposition in the Lords would not impede legislation giving effect to proposals covered by Labour's manifesto; the *Parliament Act* itself was amended in these years to reduce the Lords' suspensory veto from two years to one. In his own State, Victoria, a Labor Government fell because it was unable to secure passage of its budget in the Legislative Council, a manoeuvre which Menzies supported publicly, as Malcolm Fraser pointed out to him in 1975. (When the Coalition first opposed finance legislation if the Senate in April 1974, Menzies had written to Heather Henderson: "I always like to remember that when Arthur Calwell was Leader of the Opposition, he would never tolerate the refusal of supply by the Senate; his view being, quite rightly, that the primary control of finances was with the Lower House and not with the Senate. His view was right, as the Liberal Party's view today is wrong."[66]

Menzies addressed what he saw as the general problems created by the new method of voting by some proposals for amending the Constitution. He sought to ensure that governments had a prospect of securing a majority in the Senate. This was to be accomplished by providing that, at periodical elections, the number of vacancies to be filled was always an odd number; and that at a double dissolution election, vacancies would be divided into two groups, one for long-terms (up to six years), the other for short terms (up to three years). The legislation was referred to an Opposition-only select committee in the Senate, which reported unfavourably. The proposal was not thereafter pursued (this matter is addressed more fully by Anne Twomey in chapter 11).

In the meantime Menzies, having won the 1949 election, had to deal with the immediate political situation. Throughout 1950 the Government assiduously pressed ahead with its legislative program ensuring that, when the opportunity arose, it had a bill meeting the requirements of section 57. The Opposition, which made the most of its Senate advantage, changed its position on the bill to ban the Communist Party, and passed it. Menzies accordingly relied on a bill re-establishing the board of the Commonwealth Bank as a vehicle for a double dissolution early in 1951.[67]

There are two noteworthy features of his handling of the double dissolution. The first was his attitude to the Governor-General's role. In his advice recommending the dissolutions, he emphasised that this was an occasion when the Governor-General had to act on his own discretion: the Prime Minister's advice, in this instance, was not advice which it was obligatory for the Governor-General to accept. Dr Evatt, the Deputy Leader of the Opposition, agreed that the Governor-General should make his own decision and contended that the grounds for a double dissolution did not exist.

Second, Menzies not only supported his advice with a full account of the relevant legislative history, he also included opinions by the Attorney-General, the Solicitor-General and a leading counsel, Garfield Barwick, KC.

In the double dissolution election which followed the Menzies Government was returned with a slightly reduced majority in the House and a sufficient majority in the Senate. It took three more elections, one for the Senate alone (1953), one for the House alone (1954), and eventually a conventional House/half-Senate election (1955) for the change of election methods in the Senate to be assimilated in the sense that elections for the House and periodical election of senators were realigned. But the Senate remained able to test the Government; during the 1956-58 parliament, the Government's legislation establishing the Reserve Bank was several times defeated; it was the first time that, though there was legislation meeting the requirements of section 57, no double dissolution followed; it was passed early in the next parliament when the Coalition recovered a small majority in the Senate.

Thus, following the 1955 election, a joint committee of the Senate and the House was created to review the Constitution with high level membership from both sides. A major reason behind its creation was Menzies' continuing, and active, interest in the consequences of the 1949 changes for the workings of bicameralism in the Parliament. It made little advance, proposing among other things that a joint sitting without an intervening double dissolution would be a possibility. No action was taken on the Committee's recommendations.[68] There was no further activity on this matter for more than a decade.

Another question arising from proportional representation was what to do about casual vacancies in the Senate, whether caused by death or resignation. This became a significant matter because it was very likely, most of the time, that the Senate would be evenly divided where, previously, as already observed, one side or the other would usually have a comfortable majority.

The first casual vacancy under the 1948 voting method arose when a Labor senator from Western Australia died. It was initially expected that the Liberal Government then in office would take advantage of the situation to add to Liberal numbers in the Senate, as would have been so prior to 1949. The Premier, Ross McLarty, however, appreciated that the new method of electing senators suggested a different approach to filling casual vacancies was required. He supported selection of a person nominated by the party of the deceased senator, the Labor Party. In doing so, he wrote to his counterparts in other States. What became known as the "gentlemen's agreement" was effectively adopted in all States with equivocation on its application in cases of resignation rather than death; later Coalition governments in Queensland insisted on occasion that a panel of names be submitted when a vacancy arose.

The "gentlemen's agreement" did not fully preserve the membership as determined at the relevant election. The vacancy was still subject to popular vote at the next Federal election and this could (but not necessarily) lead to the seat passing to a senator from the other side.

Menzies' handling of the casual vacancy question provides useful insight into his attitude to how the Federation should work. He treated the whole matter as one for State parliaments and governments. Copies of the premiers' correspondence were sent to him but otherwise he played no formal role in this instructive piece of constitutional arrangement.[69]

Parliament, 1949-66: other matters[70]

There were a number of other events during the Menzies years worthy of note. In 1950, the House of Representatives eventually adopted permanent standing orders. There was later a major rationalisation of the manner in which the Parliament handled appropriation legislation. These changes, which limited the committee-of-the-whole stage, reflected the growing complexity of government business. In retrospect, a preferable approach might have been to find other means of examining appropriations than in plenary session, perhaps by adopting estimates committees similar to those in use in the UK House of Commons since the end of the war. But such innovation was well ahead of most thinking then extant in Australia.

The early 1950s otherwise witnessed some modest developments in committee work reflecting a pattern observable in several other parliaments around the world. The Joint Committee on Public Accounts was re-established, very much a consequence of initiatives by Professor Bland who became the first chairman of the revived committee. The Government also established a Joint Committee on Foreign Affairs. Labor, however, objected to confidentiality conditions applying to its proceedings and refused to participate, espying in its proposed operations an endeavour by the Government to limit public debate on foreign policy; Casey, the Minister for External Affairs, saw it largely as a study group.

Menzies was not enamoured by committee activity and had very little direct experience of it. In retirement he looked askance at what he saw as proposals "to graft the United States committee system onto our own responsible system of government. . . . the United States Committee system and our system of Responsible Government are at opposite poles, and you cannot effectively establish a compromise between them."[71] He firmly opposed an attempt in 1950 by an Opposition-only Senate Select Committee on National Service to bring the Chiefs of Staff before it to give evidence on various defence policies of the Government.

1955 was the year of a famous case of parliamentary privilege, the Fitzpatrick-Browne case.[72] It is an illustration of how much opinion about parliamentary practice and customs can change. After an inquiry by the House Committee of Privileges and debate in the chamber, the two were imprisoned for three months for an article in the *Bankstown Observer*, "M.H.R. and Immigration Racket", attacking the Labor member for Reid, Charles Morgan. Menzies took an active lead in the matter, as also did Dr Evatt. Accounts of the case deriving from participants, including Menzies, and observers treat the matter largely in parliamentary terms. More recently, the case has been treated in legal terms; the Parliament itself has placed privilege on a statutory footing. Even as criticism mounted of how the case had been handled, Menzies remained unrepentant:

Looking back on it all, I think that what we did was right; . . . the House itself maintained a high standard of responsibility; and that the punishment inflicted served as a proper warning to people that the freedom of a newspaper or writer is freedom and not licence, and that it can be lost when it is abused.[73]

There was plenty of tough politics in the Parliament during the Menzies years, especially when Dr Evatt was leading the Labor Party. Menzies' comments, however, on the results of the 1966 election when the Coalition was returned with a record majority in the House give some insight into the softer and less public side of the battles and show an aspect of parliamentary life usefully borne in mind when observing such conflicts:

While I delighted in the victory, I must say that I am relieved Eric Costa [Labor member for Banks, NSW] managed to save his seat; just as I am sorry that my old sparring partner Reg Pollard [Labor member for Lalor, Victoria] was defeated.[74]

Endnotes

[1] Sir Robert Menzies, *Afternoon Light*, Cassell Australia, 1967, 236-7.

[2] Robert Menzies, *Forgotten People And Other Studies in Democracy*, Liberal Party of Australia (Victorian Division), 2011 [1943], ch XXIX; see also, David Lee, "States Rights and the Adoption of the Statute of Westminster, 1931-42", *History Australia*, 13 (2), June 2016 (forthcoming).

[3] Menzies, *Afternoon Light*, 243, 246.

[4] Ibid., 188.

[5] Ibid.

[6] See G.S. Reid, *Chronology of the Federal Parliament*, ch 1 (section sub-titled, "The opening of the first Parliament of the Commonwealth"), NLA MS, Box 41.

[7] J.R. Odgers, *Australian Senate Practice*, 6th ed, RAIPA, 1991, 234-5.

[8] Cited, ibid., 235.

[9] Heather Henderson (ed), *Letters to My Daughter*, Pier 9, 2011, 29.

[10] Ibid., 111.

[11] Menzies, op. cit., 253.

[12] A.W. Martin, *Robert Menzies: A Life*, Vol 2, Melbourne University Press, 1999, 64.

[13] Cited, *Afternoon Light*, 208.

[14] *Afternoon Light*, 24-5.

[15] Cited, *Letters to my Daughter*, 208.

[16] Ibid.

[17] Ibid., 206.

[18] Cited, ibid., 208.

[19] Phillip Ayres, *Owen Dixon*, Melbourne University Press, 2007, 286.

[20] A.W. Martin, *Robert Menzies – A Life*, Vol 2, Melbourne University Press, 1999, 528-9.

[21] *Letters to my Daughter*, 64.

[22] This section is based on Sir John Bunting, *R.G. Menzies – A Portrait*, Allen & Unwin, 1988, chs 4-5; L.F Crisp, *Australian National Government*, Longmans, 1965, ch. 10; Department of the Prime Minister and Cabinet, "History of the Department of the Prime Minister and Cabinet", Extract from Annual Report, 1978-79; Paul Hasluck, *The Government and the People, 1939-1941*, Australian War Memorial, 1952; David Lee, "Cabinet", Scott Prasser et al, *The Menzies Era*, Hale & Iremonger, 1995, 123-136; Patrick Weller, *Cabinet Government in Australia, 1901-2006*, UNSW Press, 2007.

[23] A.W. Martin, *Robert Menzies – A Life*, Vol 1, 1993, Melbourne University Press, 1993, 68-9.

[24] Crisp, *Australian National Government*, 339.

[25] Martin, Vol 2, 449; Graeme Starr, *Carrick – Principles, Politics and Policy*, Connor Court, 2012, 142-3.

[26] Geoffrey Sawer, *Australianj Federal Politics and Law, 1929-1949*, Melbourne University Press, 1963, 104.

[27] Weller, *Cabinet Government in Australia*, 66.

[28] Crisp, *Australian National Government*, 341.

[29] Ibid., 342.

[30] Ibid., 342-3.

[31] Ibid., 347.

[32] Ibid., 348.

[33] Department of the Prime Minister and Cabinet, "History of the Department of the Prime Minister and Cabinet", Extract from Annual Report, 1978-79, 59.

[34] Ibid., 60.

[35] Ibid.

[36] Ibid.

[37] Weller, op. cit., 100.

[38] Department of the Prime Minister and Cabinet, op. cit., 63.

[39] Ibid.

[40] Crisp, op. cit.

[41] Much information upon which this section is based has been derived from Annual Reports of the Public Service Board, Canberra, 1948-1966.

[42] See Samuel Furphy (ed), *The Seven Dwarfs and the Age of the Mandarins*, ANU Press, 2015.

[43] David Horner, *Defence Supremo: Sir Frederick Shedden and the Making of Australian Defence Policy*, Allen & Unwin, 2000.

[44] See generally Hasluck, Appendix 2, 582.

[45] See Stuart Macintyre, *Australia's Boldest Experiment: War and Reconstruction in the 1940s*, Newsouth Publishing, 2015.

[46] Hasluck, 565.

[47] See Tim Rowse, "Coombs the Keynesian," Furphy, up. cit., ch 7.

[48] Geoffrey Bolton, *Paul Hasluck: a Life*, University of Western Australia Press, 2014, 175.

[49] Sir Robert Menzies, *The Measure of the Years*, Cassell Australia, 1970, 149-50.

[50] Ibid., ch 17.

[51] Bunting, *R.G. Menzies*, 96-7.

[52] R.P. Deane, *The Establishment of the Trade Department: a case study in administrative reorganization*, ANU Press, 1963.

[53] F. Mediansky, "Defence Reorganisation 1957-75," W.J. Hudson (ed.), *Australia in World Affairs, 1971-75*, Allen & Unwin, 1980, 37-64.

[54] Menzies, *The Measure of the Years*, ch 11; John Howard, *The Menzies Era*, HarperCollins, 2014, ch 5; see also Selwyn Cornish, *The Evolution of Central Banking in Australia*, Reserve Bank of Australia, 2010.

[55] G.E. Caiden, *Career Service*, Melbourne University Press, 1965.

[56] See, in particular, R.S. Parker, "The Vow of Silence," *The Administrative Vocation*, Hale & Iremonger/RIPAA, 1993, .

[57] J.R. Nethercote, "McKnight, Allan Douglas," *Australian Dictionary of Biography*, Vol. 18, Melbourne University Press, 2012.

[58] Horner, op. cit.

[59] Peter Edwards, *Arthur Tange: Last of the Mandarins*, Allen & Unwin, 2006, 144-5.

[60] This section draws extensively on G.S. Reid, *Chronology of the Federal Parliament*, National Library of Australia, MS 8371, Box 41.

[61] Menzies, *Afternoon Light*, ch 13.

[62] Henderson, op. cit., 66.

[63] Menzies, *The Measure of the Years*, 15-16.

[64] Ibid., 17-18.

[65] H.V. Evatt, *Liberalism in Australia*, 1918.

[66] Henderson, op. cit., 262.

[67] See Menzies, *The Measure of the Years*, ch 37; for a lively account of the 1951 double dissolution, see Odgers, *Australian Senate Practice*, 6th ed, 1991, 36-43.

[68] Parliament of the Commonwealth of Australia, Joint Committee of Constitutional Review, 1958-59.

[69] Geoffrey Sawer, *Federation Under Strain*, Melbourne University Press, 1977, 130-3, 199-202.

[70] For more detail and analysis, see Reid, op. cit., ch 7.

[71] Henderson, op. cit., 133.

[72] Menzies, *Afternoon Light*, ch 13; for an account of an observer, see J.R. Odgers, op cit, 1038-9.

[73] Menzies, *Afternoon Light*, 304.

[74] Henderson (ed), op. cit., 132.

14

A Convert to the Faith
Menzies and Canberra

David Headon

In January 1966, Bob Menzies put his feet up for a well-earned rest after a record number of years in his second stint as prime minister. In the "afternoon light" of retirement from federal politics, he and his wife Pattie embarked on an enjoyable sojourn at the University of Virginia, and he settled down to write two volumes of memoirs.

The first of these memoirs, aptly entitled *Afternoon Light* (1967), provides a wealth of detail about his long and eventful life in the public sphere, and the significant individuals who impressed him along the way.[1] While a good read, with all sorts of interesting insights and quite candid memories, the book does follow a predictable path of recollection. It is only in the first and last chapters that Menzies bends sufficiently to allow more of his private side, the "interior," to surface.[2] The first chapter, "A Portrait of My Parents," reads as if it simply had to be the lead-off, one part affection, one part duty and one part confession; the last chapter, "Cricket – a Diversion," is popped in shyly at the end, our author perhaps diffident about the relevance of its inclusion in a work of purported significance.

The second volume of memoirs, *The Measure of the Years* (1970), published a few years later, presents us with more flesh and blood, more personality.[3] Cricket, one of the self-confessed loves of Menzies' life, now gets its own section of five. But the longest section in the book by far – and the most interesting for the historian keen to analyse and interpret – is Part II, "Some Highlights of a Long Term of Office, 1949-1966." One of these "highlights," "Canberra – The Making of a City," stands out from the rest because, better than any of the others, it shifts seamlessly from the public to the personal, on occasion invoking phrasing intentionally chosen for its Biblical resonance. Menzies details his own Damascus Road journey, from feeling an "exile" in Canberra in the bleak 1930s to becoming the unabashed zealot of the 1960s. As he expresses it, "Once I had converted myself to this faith, I became an apostle ... "[4]

There is no doubt that Menzies regarded the development in the 1950s and '60s of Australia's hitherto ailing national capital as one of his most important and enduring achievements. For an individual so entrenched as a young man in the delights of his home state of Victoria, a politician so often characterised as unbending, with a "streak of ruthlessness"[5] adding starch to a sense of life's certainties, such a dramatic transformation was extraordinary, by any measure of the years.

How did it happen? Menzies' Canberra story is one of the most compelling – and revealing – narratives of his second term in office.

* * * * *

Late in 1934, when a 40-year old Menzies arrived in Canberra for the first time as the new member for the blue-ribbon (United Australia Party) seat of Kooyong, it must have been a shock. Yes, he had been born in rural Victoria into a life that was hardly "to the purple" of privilege as he once put it.[6] In the decades that followed, however, as a quality, multiple prize-winning education led to a smooth progression to the law and then a successful entry into State politics, the stringencies of tiny Jeparit in the Wimmera district retreated into the past. The "civilised" life in marvellous Melbourne took hold. It was a lifestyle, a milieu that he revelled in.

When recoiling in those early years from the inter-state politician's compulsory Canberra experience, Menzies was no different from virtually all his Victorian fellow-travellers, either the public servants having to re-locate, or the parliamentarians embarking on their semi-regular commute. Contemporary journalist (and historian) Warren Denning, in *Capital City—Canberra Today and Tomorrow* (1938), observing the impact of this reluctant northern trek to rural New South Wales, cleverly captured the mindset of the public servant forced to uproot:

> Reality proved equal to their worst expectations. Desolation swept into many a heart when the first panorama of Canberra was viewed—a silent

valley mocking the efforts of men, symbolised in small settlements and public buildings striving to attain a grotesque dignity; lazy smoke curling above the bush-clad hill slopes, crows squawking in quest of carrion, sheep meandering along the meadows, and magpies nesting near the Parliament House—the hearts of the sophisticated Melbourne people failed them.[7]

The politicians sulked as well:

It would be pleasant to record that in the first difficult, formative years of Canberra's history the members of the National Parliament made an earnest, courageous and self-sacrificing effort to reconcile the conscript population to its new habitation, and to give the National Capital that dignity in their practical every-day lives that they willingly enough accorded it in most of their speeches. Unfortunately, if that were said it would be incorrect; for no specifically interested body of men – allowing for very definite and praiseworthy exceptions – ever have consistently done less for Canberra.[8]

Bob Menzies was no exception to the rule. Bush Canberra failed to stir any warm memories of his own bush childhood. It was a political destination, pure and simple, a place of work that was a cold, uncomfortable train ride away from his wife, family and friends. Indeed, when he accepted the nomination for Kooyong, as his biographer, A.W. Martin, puts it, Menzies "made plain the distastefulness to him of Canberra, both physically and professionally."[9]

The trouble was that Canberra, soon enough, made it abundantly clear that it didn't think much of Menzies either. Mutual distaste hardened. In the House of Representatives, Attorney-General Menzies almost immediately had to endure what Martin describes as "particularly virulent attacks," "especial vituperation" inflicted on him by a Labor Opposition still resentful of the unseemly pressure under which the government of James Scullin had been replaced by an emergent United Australia Party in the first years of the Depression. Menzies was targeted despite being in Victorian State politics in the Scullin years.[10]

As stressful as the initiation period was for the new minister, worse was to come. The year 1937 was something of an *annus horribilis*, as issues in the Canberra community, local workplace issues, demanded that the Commonwealth Attorney-General either pay attention to what was in front of him, or face the consequences. Some background is required here. In these fledgling years for Menzies in Canberra, the resident population was less than 10 000, most of whom were imported public servants (and their families) engaged in full-time work. They had secure jobs. However, the new national capital had begun to slip into depression by late 1927, with the first major construction phase coming to a close after the opening of the Provisional (now Old) Parliament House in May. The small yet militant population of manual workers bore the brunt of the economic downturn, and they were determined to make their predicament a public one. They knew their rights and were not afraid to assert them.

The group organised a number of deputations to the Federal minister, and a succession of demonstrations, the first of them in 1927. This was followed by further significant shows of strength in 1930, 1931, 1935 and 1937, the workers even obtaining a meeting with the Governor-General (in 1933) to air their grievances. The pattern of protest throughout the years was identical: all aimed at securing work for the local unemployed and/or preventing reductions in the allocation of relief work for the locals.[11]

One such cut-back occurred in June 1937, at the beginning of a Canberra winter, and it prompted a demonstration of about eighty-odd workers outside the Parliament building on 28 June. For the Lyons Government, already under national and international pressure because of the ongoing fall-out from the Egon Kisch case, and suffering sundry electoral and strategic setbacks, it was extremely poor timing.[12] Even more alarming for a United Australia Party (UAP) beginning to fray at the edges under a leader whose health was in decline, inside the House on the very same day as the worker demonstration, the Supply Bill was introduced. As one historian has observed, the Bill was "attacked with all the savagery that Labor could muster. A seventeen-hour session concluded at 7.55 in the morning ... the *Canberra Times* describ[ing] the temper of proceedings with the headline, 'Night of Storm—Disorderly Scenes in House'."[13] The day after the angry scenes both inside and outside the House, the Assistant-Secretary of the Attorney-General's Department despatched an *Unlawful Assemblies Ordinance* to the Government Printer. When it appeared in the *Commonwealth Gazette* with unusual speed on 22 July, it certainly looked like the local workers had become a convenient target for a government venting frustration for its troubles. If this was the case, the Government and the relevant minister would soon come to regret such a precipitate, clumsy response.

The *Ordinance*, probably authored by Menzies himself, prohibited meetings of more than twenty people within a triangular area bordered by Commonwealth Avenue, Kings Avenue and a straight line running parallel to King Edward

Terrace. The reason given for the *Ordinance*, the official line, was stated in an accompanying memorandum. Owing to the fact that "large bodies of persons ... have made demonstrations outside the Parliament House," the Government had introduced an *Ordinance* "to ensure that the business of the National Parliament is conducted without undue interruption."[14]

There were other potential explanations, and these pertained to the Attorney-General's own attitudes. Menzies felt nothing but contempt for mob behaviour. The fact that he had been the primary target of the rowdy group's vitriol, and right in front of the national Parliament no less, would have irked him. He had nothing in common with what he labelled "the unthinking and unskilled mass." In the same 1942 speech from which this description is taken, "The Forgotten People," he put it succinctly: "The moment a man seeks moral and intellectual refuge in the emotions of the crowd, he ceases to be a human being and becomes a cipher."[15]

When Menzies went searching for pretexts for the *Ordinance*, he inevitably called on his detailed knowledge of the British legal system, his admiration for "the Mother Parliament" and the satisfying bulwark against social unrest of Old World values and conditioning. "The man who goes into the Parliament of the United Kingdom," he trumpeted in January 1938 at the beginning of White Australia's sesquicentenary year, "goes to a Parliament which sits ... in London, at the very centre of the world."[16] With his *Unlawful Assemblies Ordinance*, Menzies sought to impose an English solution on an Australian problem and he found what he wanted in the *Imperial Seditious Meetings Act*, a statute with a history dating back to 1817. Determined to keep these local trouble-makers at a physical distance, he did not anticipate how quickly and dramatically the issue would escalate.

It seemed as if the whole community took him on – the *Canberra Times*, locally-elected Advisory Councillors and a host of outraged citizens, not just the original protesters, all spurred into action by what they characterised as patently anti-democratic measures. They would resist. The day after the gazettal, a *Canberra Times* editorial appeared under the heading, "Whom the Gods Wish to Destroy," using a damning quotation from Euripides. The paper sought to meet Menzies on his own British battleground: the *Ordinance* negated "one of those marks of British freedom that distinguishes British liberty from other brands," and it originated from a young minister wet behind the ears and so out of touch that he had forgotten the text of a speech he had given in the capital the previous year where he banged on about British tolerance. What irony! According to the editorial, this new *Ordinance*, "repressive, provocative and reactionary," was "the worst piece of legislation in Canberra's history."[17]

You did not have to be a genius to understand the broader implication of the newspaper's attack. Here was the nation's principal legal officer producing legislation that contradicted every Briton's eternal rights as spelled out in Magna Carta itself. The insults, implied and overt, kept coming. One letter to the *Canberra Times* advanced a distinctively Australian context, condemning Menzies as "descended politically from the Victorian administrators who provoked the Eureka Stockade,"[18] in the process unleashing a torrent of deeply personal abuse. The Attorney-General was solely responsible for a law "to repress the people of the territory [and] interfere with orderly and lawful gatherings at the very heart of Canberra and ... Australia"; his ignorance of Territory laws had made him a "laughing stock" as the nation's law-maker; he was "guilty of a clumsy blunder;" and he had a "poverty of public outlook."[19]

The hostility of this community crusade would subside when pragmatic government concessions were eventually made, but not before Menzies was forced to endure one of the most uncomfortable periods of his entire public life. No wonder he dismissed Canberra at this time as a place of exile. When he recalled the dark days of 1941, in the tranquillity of retirement decades later, Menzies confessed to some personal inadequacies in his leadership manner. I was "many years younger," he wrote in *Afternoon Light*, and "consequently more prone to intolerance and hasty judgements." These were "salad days" when, by his own mature assessment, he was "green in judgement."[20] His first reactions to Canberra and its residents were presumably shaped by the same flaws.

When Menzies became prime minister in April 1939, he could not possibly have anticipated the scale of the tumult that lay ahead, for himself and for the nation. With another global conflict looming, he and Pattie made the decision to live in Canberra. The couple did retain their Melbourne home, but they made the symbolically important decision to establish The Lodge as their primary residence. Within months of making this commitment, Menzies had the melancholy duty of telling the nation it was at war; shortly after, it became clear that his prime ministership threatened to be overwhelmed by a suffocating combination of both local and international events. Menzies could not even count on his own party's total support, much less that of the Labor Opposition, and when three of his strongest political allies – the Federal ministers Henry Gullett, Geoffrey Street and James Fairbairn – were killed in a tragic air crash near Queanbeyan on 13 August 1940, his political position deteriorated alarmingly.

Under these circumstances The Lodge, a brisk walk for Menzies away from the daily trials of the Parliament, must have seemed like a genuine refuge. A haven of tranquillity. Pattie ensured it was just that, despite inheriting a well-worn house that had changed considerably during the occupation of Joe and Enid Lyons, and their cricket team of young children. In her book, *Prime Ministers' Wives* (1992), Diane Langmore suggests that The Lodge in 1939 "was in much the same condition as it had been when the Bruces had occupied it in 1927 ..."[21] That is hardly likely. The Menzies' third child, author and Liberal Party grand dame, Heather [Henderson], can be regarded as a reliable (first-hand) witness on this, and she remembers "a certain amount of wear and tear over the years."[22] This is surely the understatement of a diplomat's wife because we know that, while not all the Lyons brood lived in Canberra during their father's term in office, enough of them did to necessitate converting the area at the top of the stairs, plus a small outside balcony, into what Heather remembers as "a sort of dormitory for the children."[23]

Pattie faced a monumental task of domestic economy but she went about it with typical resourcefulness, given the country's war footing and the budget cuts occurring in all areas except defence. We gain insight into her lot from an interview she provided for the *Sun* newspaper, reported on 28 October 1939, some six months into the first Menzies term: "It is hard enough for a home-loving woman to be the wife of a hard-working barrister but it is infinitely worse when the barrister becomes Prime Minister ..."[24] The "home-loving woman" went about her business methodically, in the process establishing the first links of emotional attachment to place in this new and very different environment, for herself and her sceptical husband.

First, she introduced some much-needed Lodge redecoration, dismantling the temporary partitions and removing the "soft furnishings" and carpets of the Lyons family. Then, as daughter Heather takes up the story:

> Mother enlisted the assistance of Dolly Guy Smith, from the Myer Emporium in Melbourne, who came to Canberra to help my naturally thrifty mother to do something about the furnishings.[25]

At Myer, Dolly Guy Smith had succeeded Ruth Lane-Poole, the remarkable woman responsible in the mid-1920s for the interior design and fit-out of The Lodge (with some 130 different pieces of furniture) for Prime Minister Stanley

Melbourne Bruce, and the Governor-General's Yarralumla residence. Lane-Poole's background comes straight out of Ripley's "Believe-It-Or-Not": she effectively disowned her wayward parents as a youngster and became a ward of her two older female cousins, Susan called "Lily" and Elizabeth called "Lolly" Yeats, sisters of renowned modernist poet, William Butler Yeats; in Dublin, she was given away in marriage by her cousin William to her husband Charles, who much later became the first head of the Australian Forestry School in Canberra; and she applied to all her design work the working principles and values of the famed Arts and Crafts Movement of William Morris, a close friend of the Yeats family and formative influence on Ruth.[26] During the war years of Menzies' first prime ministership, Ruth and Charles were still living nearby at Westridge House, not far from The Lodge, and Ruth ran a design shop in Kingston.[27] It is not too fanciful to consider the three women, Pattie, Ruth and Dolly, comparing notes in order to produce a budget-conscious makeover for The Lodge.

But Pattie did not stop with an interior refresh. She was a garden enthusiast as well. Initially in defiance of the head gardener's wishes she had additional plots established, some for the decorative flowers in constant demand for VIP visitors, and others chock full of vegetables of all kinds. Her ducks and chooks were good layers, too, so that when her often beleaguered husband came home for lunch – and he did come home as often as possible—he walked into the peace of unlikely bucolic surrounds.[28] It was a long way from inner city Melbourne, but in the circumstances some country comforts provided a solace that the Prime Minister needed more than ever before.

On 26 August 1941, Menzies adjourned a meeting of a Cabinet deeply divided over his leadership. Back he went as always to Pattie at The Lodge, and they went for their usual stroll to discuss the latest crisis. He always valued her advice and, when he returned to Parliament House later in the day, he informed his colleagues that he intended to resign – which he did on 30 August. The visitors' book of The Lodge contains two signatures for 5 September 1941, those of Pattie and Robert Menzies, followed by the rather poignant addition of one of Shakespeare's favourite usages, "Finis."[29] Courtesy of a contemporary newspaper report we know that Pattie "was unable to restrain her feelings when she said farewell" to those who had served her and her husband so dutifully. She "wept quietly," we are told, perhaps enough tears for the two of them.[30] They would be back.

"A period of at best tepid support for the nation's capital" is the way I describe the decade of the 1940s in *The Symbolic Role of the National Capital – from*

Colonial Argument to 21st Century Ideals (2003).[31] In the war years almost nothing occurred to alter the face of Canberra other than the emotional, long-overdue opening of the Australian War Memorial on Remembrance Day, 1941. During the post-war years, a few structures went up, such as the equally long-overdue Melbourne Building in Civic, and the Research School of Physical Sciences and University House that confirmed the Australian National University's central city location. But this was "small beer ... Canberra's overall appearance and social patterns hardly altered at all."

William (later Sir William) Dunk, appointed as the Chairman of the Public Service Board in March 1947, was so disheartened by the absence of commitment of his predecessors in the job that he removed their photographs from his new office wall.[32] One of the few prominent individuals at that time with a "consuming interest" in Canberra's development, Dunk would find his efforts to lure a fresh generation of public servants to the nation's capital thwarted at every turn. Major additions to the physical fabric were simply out of the question as the desire for change was just not there. For Canberra, these were dour years, "years of vacillation and transition," according to the title of one of *Symbolic Role*'s chapters.[33]

When Menzies was re-elected as prime minister in December 1949, his wife, "thrilled to the core" with a victory she regarded as "the high point of her political life," also felt "a little faint" at the prospect.[34] Memories of the ordeal of 1939-41 lingered, memories of a bitterly contested, truncated prime ministership considered by many to be a failure.[35] But this was a brand new page and the Menzies family approached the task with a sense of purpose. Daughter Heather remembers the initial re-engagement with the capital with clarity:

> [my parents] came back to virtually the same house they had left. We felt as if we were coming home when we came back to Canberra and I think the staff felt the same ...[36]

This time around, however, the Menzies took a symbolically significant step further, actually selling their Melbourne home.[37] There must have been a sense of satisfaction when the Menzies signed The Lodge visitors' book once again, this time on 17 February 1950, under the aspirational heading, "Advance Menzies."[38] They made their intentions plain. With the nation's continuing endorsement, they were in for the long haul.

It can be put no other way: the decade from 1950 to 1960 was *the* critical fulcrum in Canberra's history, a period during which lasting foundations were built that would give us the national capital as we know it today. Although the National Capital Development Commission would implement its plans for a massive expansion of the city in the following decade, the 1960s, none of this activity would have been possible were it not for what went before: a remarkable combination of visionary legislation, an evolution in the attitude of the Prime Minister, the wise appointment of key public servants, the new-found commitment of a critical mass of key politicians, the intervention of family, cricket, a Queen's visit and a prime minister's wife who became one of Canberra's most determined defenders. The importance of the '50s decade for Canberra cannot be overstated.

In *The Measure of the Years*, Menzies notes that "when I came back into office at the end of 1949 I began to think that I could see some renewed opportunity of doing something."[39] The evidence suggests otherwise – that he recognised such opportunity only gradually, over the next seven or eight years, persuaded by an accumulation of game-changing events, incidents, outspoken family members, talented peers and successful elections. The elements necessary for change steadily coalesced.

Let us start with Menzies' wife and partner, Pattie. We know she had established a close bond with Canberra and The Lodge years earlier, so it was an easy adjustment for her to take up where she had left off. Staff relationships were reaffirmed, garden plots reclaimed, flowers of choice refreshed and vegies of choice re-planted. If Menzies asserted himself with authority in the Parliament and within his party, post-1949, so, too, did Pattie in her patch. She was back, older and wiser.

Pattie left nothing to chance at this time. Always conscious of the need to spend public money prudently, she introduced a raft of small alterations designed to make The Lodge more comfortable, family-friendly:[40] toilet cisterns were modernised and seats replaced, ants extinguished, walls re-painted inside and out, and new wire netting put up to protect the chooks from the crows.[41] In later years she attended to bigger ticket items, having faulty electrical wiring fixed at last, cellar dampness eliminated and new furniture purchased commensurate with a Prime Minister's official residence. All this took place with a minimum of fuss because, last time at The Lodge, Pattie had proven herself a fast learner. One senior public servant, James (later Sir James) Scholtens, in a minute from 1952, revealed the no-nonsense strategy adopted by the Prime Minister's wife. When asked to transact the purchase of a new table, rug and settee, Scholtens suggested that he provide her with the official order forms, noting that:

> She thought the suggestion a good one … [but] I could not help thinking
> that this method detracted from the status of a Prime Minister's wife. The
> position arises largely because the wife of the present Prime Minister
> acts as her own Comptroller and Secretary.[42]

Scholtens mis-read both the situation and the lady in question. John (later
Sir John) Bunting, Secretary to the Prime Minister's Department, 1959-68, and
friend of the Menzies family, was a far more acute observer, full of admiration
for Pattie's capacity to stand up to the predominantly male world of the Prime
Minister's departmental staff. On matters directly concerning The Lodge, he
later wrote:

> … one was in for the occasional battle. It was likely to be a fair fight, but
> Dame Pattie … could deliver, verbally of course, a hefty blow when she
> came up against a resistance that she suspected of being unnecessary, or,
> worse, just humbug. It was a civilised sort of combat … but it was not
> wise to invite it, and if by chance or mishap you did, then best to keep
> out of range![43]

For the Lodge staff, it seems to have been a wholly different situation. There
was no standing on ceremony. Pattie's permanent staff of two was insufficient
yet, according to Bunting:

> … household work had to go on … what surprised me a little [on one
> of my visits] was that an extra staff member engaged specifically for
> cleaning was taking it easy in one of the chairs and … the cleaner on her
> knees with the scrubbing brush and soap was Dame Pattie![44]

The Lodge in the 1950s became in all senses a home, "very much part of the
neighbourhood" according to Heather,[45] with her mother – granny to an increasing
number of grandchildren – harvesting homegrown vegies, bottling fruit from
the garden and picking seasonal mushrooms in the vacant paddock behind The
Lodge. In the official prime ministerial dwelling, contentiously vacant during the
terms of far too many Australian prime ministers, Dame Pattie Menzies nurtured
an environment of domestic comfort and repose. As Diana, the daughter of the
Menzies' son, Ken, remembers:

> We had great times at The Lodge when we were little. Granny would take
> us out for long days at the river and then at night we would be allowed
> to have our choice of tinned spaghetti or baked beans or tinned sausages
> and beans while as a treat we watched Disneyland … With the exception
> of red meat, The Lodge seemed to be quite self-sufficient. I remember

the vegetable garden, the chickens (with heads on and off), the flowers, learning how to ride a boy's bike down the grassy slope (and falling onto the central bar). I remember the big laundry copper, the kitchen, Granny's preserved fruit ... she got involved in everything.[46]

Diana's childhood was the sort of settled upbringing that a whole generation of baby-boomer Australian kids had in the 1950s. No different, and this had its own charm for all members of the family.

Father Bob, grandfather Bob, despite the baggage of the political past, could not help but play a willing part in the maintenance of this warm, family atmosphere. The inviting dichotomy of public and private merging in an earlier Australia is wonderfully rendered by another of Heather's vivid recollections:

> My parents used to sit outside and have a drink (Vegemite glasses were favourites for this purpose) or a cup of coffee or tea. My mother kept a shanghai tucked into the wisteria nearby. From time to time she would leap to her feet, grab it and take a pot-shot at the currawongs, saying, "I can't stand those beastly creatures – they're always killing the baby birds."
>
> One day my father said, weakly: "Pat, for goodness' sake, sit down. One day you're going to hit a passing pedestrian and then we'll be in *real* trouble."[47]

He had a point to his mock-scolding: apparently buses full of curious sightseers were known to drive straight in the front of The Lodge, head round the house as the passengers craned for a sticky, and then depart out the back. Until a guardhouse was installed, there was no security whatsoever. On occasion this could be worrying, such as when Pattie, carving for dinner, was interrupted by a disturbed man who had walked right into the house and then took flight when he encountered a steely woman with a carving knife.[48]

There are so many stories which recall the pleasures of a calmer, more relaxed era. Heather again:

> If children kicked their balls into the garden they could easily nick through the useless wire fence and retrieve them. The Fishers, who lived near the back gate, often drove through because it was a short cut. In fact, the Fishers' young son, Bill, rang the bell one day and my mother went to the door.
>
> Dame P: "Hello, Bill, what do you want?"

Bill: "I'm doing a project at school and want to ask Mr Menzies some questions."

Dame P: "We're having lunch, but come in."

With great composure Bill came in and sat at the table, opened his exercise book, licked his pencil, asked his questions and wrote down my father's answers. Having got what he wanted, he very politely said thank you and went home to his stunned parents.[49]

Might the interface with a bold Bill Fisher (who went on to a distinguished career with the Department of Foreign Affairs and Trade) have been the kind of meaningful experience that confirmed Menzies' complete change of heart towards Canberra? This compelling combination of public life (down the road) and normal family pursuits that Canberra made possible? Most likely. Menzies' own family circle of parents and siblings stayed very tight throughout his life; despite the inevitable imbroglios of politics, he was able to embrace a lifestyle in Canberra in the 1950s and '60s that recreated the same closeness with his own children and grandchildren.

Menzies walked often, prodigious distances around Canberra according to Heather and her cousin, Bob Green.[50] One favourite wander took place of a Saturday afternoon, down to Manuka Oval to watch the grade cricket and sit on the hill by himself in the sun, either in his suit or coat off. Perhaps it was the subtle magic of those relaxing Saturdays that got him thinking, in October 1951, when he heard that the visiting West Indian cricket team had no game arranged in the first fortnight of their tour, that he should make a call to the Chairman of the Australian Board of Control. This was sufficient impetus to begin the fine tradition of the Prime Minister's XI games at Manuka.

Menzies loved these games, and they proved enormously popular with the Canberran public for most of the seven fixtures that he hosted between 1951 and 1965. Notably, in 1963, he enticed Don Bradman out of retirement to captain his side. The great Don managed only four runs, bowled by English fast bowler Brian Statham. The crowd, while obviously disappointed, could still feast that day on the shots of those elegant English stylists, Ted "Lord Ted" Dexter, Colin Cowdrey and Tom Graveney. The Prime Minister's games, especially in the early years, were more gala event than competitive contest. You were not allowed to get a duck, according to the protocols set down by the founder, and the emphasis was on a "carnival spirit" as he put it.[51] Each match featured a convivial dinner, with Menzies always one of the after-dinner speakers. Enthused by the success of the first match, at the celebration dinner he recited a couple of light-hearted poems he had written earlier in the day. This was not the expected behaviour of the patrician politician, "Pig Iron" Bob according to the popular sobriquet, who had begun to bestride the floor of the House of Representatives like a colossus. Cricket was his release, as Sir John Bunting puts it so elegantly in his Portrait. For Menzies, "cricket was a holiday."[52]

There is an abundance of anecdotes associated with the Prime Minister's fixtures during the Menzies era, particularly the first few games in the 1950s featuring some of Menzies' closest cricketing friends – great characters all, such as Jack Fingleton, Lindsay Hassett, Sam Loxton, Bill O'Reilly, Neil Harvey, Arthur Morris, Richie Benaud and Ian Craig, to mention only a few of the Australians participating.[53] The sheer fun of the occasions must have deepened Menzies' growing affection for Canberra, and we know that the games stayed in his memory forever. To the extent that he could ever let his hair down, at the PM's games he did. When reminiscing in *The Measure of the Years* about his passion for cricket, and these games especially, he said he was "sad to record" that there had been no Prime Minister's XI match since his retirement in 1966.[54] Bob Hawke, another mad-keen cricketer and cricket lover, re-introduced the concept in the summer of 1983-4 to a receptive Australian and Canberran public. Alas, the founder was not there to appreciate the gesture of solidarity from someone from the other side of the political divide. During their terms in office, Prime Ministers John Howard and Tony Abbott, also keen sport fans, continued to support the idea with enthusiasm. The games these days lack the joy and exuberance of Menzies' yesteryear celebrations but, on the bright side, the long-term future of the annual match is assured.

As the 1950s progressed, the slow yet distinct changes in Menzies' attitude to Canberra, at the personal level, were effectively complemented by several milestones in the city's unfolding public narrative: the convening of the Federal Congress of Regional and Town Planning, held at Albert Hall in Canberra, 9-12 August 1951, the Jubilee year of the Commonwealth of Australia; the historic Senate Select Committee (SSC) that met in 1954-55 "to inquire into and report upon the Development of Canberra," concluding that the "time has come to take the responsibility of building the National Capital from the unborn backs of future generations and place it firmly and squarely on the shoulders of people alive today;"[55] the invitation to William (later Sir William) Holford, eminent Professor of Town Planning at University College, London, to respond to the SSC's findings, and the impact he would have on the Prime Minister of Australia in an advisory role that lasted for some seven eventful years (1958-65); and, most important of all, the establishment of a National Capital Development Commission (NCDC) in 1958 to oversee the process of national capital expansion and enhancement.

A couple of years after he had been appointed to the position of Canberra's Senior Town Planner in 1949, the dogged Trevor Gibson played a prominent role in the Jubilee Federal Congress. The historian, Jim Gibney, states in *Canberra 1913-53* (1988) that "almost everybody of any standing in the Australian planning world" attended the Congress, and heard Gibson advance the case for immediate attention to the nation's shunned capital city: "Canberra is neither town nor country. A garden without a city, it is socially starved, wasteful and uneconomic in layout ... "[56] Utilising the title of a recent series of local broadcasts, he asserted that Canberra was "Everybody's Business."[57] The publicity generated by Gibson's exasperation must have caught Menzies' attention, given the status of the gathering. But a more influential catalyst for change was one of the Congress's two principal speakers, the debonair William Holford—South-African born, though for many of his professional associates more English than the English, complete with toffy accent. Impressively credentialled to provide an expert opinion on Australia's capital, and with loads of charisma, Holford made a big impression. He would return several years later and make a difference.

In the meantime, the visit of Queen Elizabeth II to Australia in 1954 fuelled Menzies' disillusionment with the present state of Canberra as national capital. First, he had to endure the political point-scoring of the combative Labor Premier of New South Wales, Joe Cahill, who insisted on strict protocols being followed when the Queen was in his State. This meant that the Premier would welcome the monarch when she stepped onto NSW soil. The Prime Minister did get to greet her first, but only after a compromise was reached and a special landing stage concocted, at Farm Cove on Sydney Harbour, for the arrival.[58]

Another dose of irritation for the Prime Minister occurred when the Queen departed NSW from Broken Hill. It would scarcely have been lost on Menzies that such humiliation would continue indefinitely while ever Canberra itself was regarded as second-rate. Menzies had the bitter-sweet privilege of escorting the Queen around his nation's capital city: sweet because the young monarch charmed him; bitter because Canberra resembled nothing so much as a big sheep station with a cluster of buildings in the middle, most of them the worse for wear.

In 1954, there was no shimmering lake, no bridges of any consequence, little commemorative fabric and no real population to speak of.

For a proud Prime Minister, the cumulative effect of these realities must have been exacerbated by his own entrenched monarchist sympathies, his effusive admiration for all things British. After all, this was the same person who, twenty-odd years earlier, on seeing the White Cliffs of Dover – and Britain – for the first time, could write in his diary that the "journey to Mecca has ended;"[59] this was the same person labelled "very pro-British" by highly-placed English bureaucrats in the 1930s when Menzies was a visiting Privy Councillor; the same person who, in his "salad days" when "green in judgement," openly expressed his admiration for the British civil service while condemning his own country's " 'democratic' stupidity;"[60] and, much later in life, this was the same person who, in November 1948, only six years before the Queen's first visit to Australia, in a crowd outside Buckingham Palace after hearing of the arrival of the Queen's first child, would later recall the moment as blissful:

> The excitement was intense. We were all friends, and slapped the backs of perfect strangers with complete abandon. For sound reasons we could not call out for the Princess, but we did, most lustily and senselessly, call out for the Duke. By the end of another hour we, thousands of us, changed our quarry and roared for the King. No result. The balconies of the Palace were untenanted. We then put it on a family basis. We, and nobody more vociferously than the ex- and future Prime Minister of Australia, cried in unison "we want grandfather!"[61]

In twenty-first century Australia, how does one begin to comprehend the depth and intensity of Menzies' monarchist feelings or the rationale for them – much less assess them objectively seventy years later? Fortunately, Menzies' primary biographer, Allan Martin, is as reliable as ever in his scholarly analysis of this substantive element of the Prime Minister's character:

> Menzies' Britishness was never a garment he consciously put on; his education and environment had made it a part of his very fibre ... He was an Empire man, British to his bootstraps, not just admiring turn-of-the-century imperial ideas, but imbibing and making them permanently his own.[62]

Menzies' speech in Adelaide in October 1954, six months after the Queen's departure, stated the case with typical economy: "We [Australians] are British through and through. We are for the Crown. We are the Queen's men and women."[63] Menzies' sovereign saw his Canberra at first-hand in a dire state. For this entrenched royal, anticipating future visits, something had to be done. Canberra was an embarrassment.

The Queen left Fremantle to return to Britain on 31 March. Just over seven months later Senator John McCallum, former State president of the Federal Labor Party turned-foundation-member of the Liberal Party (in 1944), moved a motion in the Senate to appoint a committee to report on Canberra's development. John Overall (destined to play an integral role in Canberra's future) has rightly described the resulting Senate Select Committee and its exemplary *Report* as "the defining moment in the city's history."[64] It is a conclusion impossible to argue with: 83 witnesses, 76 rigorous recommendations, and an 80 000-word set of findings that is as trenchant as it is visionary. When summing up decades of inactivity, stupidity, parochialism, wilful resistance and buck-passing, the select committee characterised its subject in words that have since taken on an oft-quoted life of their own:

> After 40 years of city development, the important planned areas stand out, not as monumental regions symbolising the character of a national capital, but more as graveyards where departed spirits await a resurrection of national pride.[65]

Of seminal importance, the committee recommended "a centralised authority with powers similar to those of the Snowy Mountains Hydro-electric Authority" under "a single commissioner with full executive powers."[66]

When the inaugural Commissioner of the ensuing National Capital Development Commission, John (later Sir John) Overall, published his memoirs in 1995 he summed up the social and cultural context in 1950s Australia:

> The country was entering its most stable period of government in its short history, and the longest economic boom this [twentieth] century. Home ownership increased sharply … There was a consumer revolution … There was also a huge increase in migration and a baby boom. And, crucially, it had a leader in Prime Minister Menzies who believed a strong and vibrant capital was needed to bring the six states together and give the country a national focal point.[67]

The Prime Minister, he acknowledges elsewhere in the memoir, was a "powerful champion."[68] He was that, but we need to understand exactly what took place in the two years, 1956 and 1957, that completed Menzies' conversion into an "apostle" for Canberra. For it is in these crucial years that (as daughter Heather has confirmed) there was a "big revolution" in her father's attitude.[69]

In January 1956, Allen (later Sir Allen) Fairhall, "no politician" by his own assessment, was elevated by his leader to head up the departments of the Interior and of Works.[70] Fairhall, Member for Paterson in the Newcastle coal-belt area of NSW, had acquired a reputation for fairness and efficiency in his seven years in Parliament. These were qualities that the portfolio would benefit from immediately. In the same month as the Fairhall appointment, a pregnant Heather Henderson returned to Canberra after spending some time in Indonesia with her husband, Peter Henderson, a diplomat. Heather remembers her return, and the net result of a campaign that she and her mother began vociferously to prosecute:

> I stayed at The Lodge with my parents. Every night, when my father came home for dinner, he would be lectured by either my mother or me. We pointed out Canberra's failings.
>
> "Bob, you try pushing a pram round these awful footpaths."
>
> "Dad, it's almost impossible to find somewhere to live here."
>
> On and on we went. In the end, he said: "Well, we're stuck with Canberra, whether we like it or not, so we might as well do it properly."[71]

This family memory, a staple anecdote these days for historians giving talks on Canberra folklore, does coincide with the chronology of Menzies' own recollections in *The Measure of the Years*. "In the homely phrase," he writes of his reformed position, "I thought that the buck was being passed too frequently."[72]

At a time ripe for decisive action, the now "impregnable" Liberal leader might well have been further mobilised by what happened in mid-April 1956.[73] In an event sure to have rekindled uncomfortable memories, the *Canberra Times* reported that some six hundred local day labourers gathered on the lawns of Parliament House to protest against government-imposed restrictions on a fragile Canberra building program. Was Menzies spooked by the demonstration, so similar to twenty years earlier? We do not know. What is certain is that in less than a fortnight he would write a long, detailed and disarmingly frank letter to his relatively new Minister for the Interior setting out his position on Canberra: "I am not very proud of what has happened to Canberra during my current period in office," he began. If the historian of today is looking for *the* pivotal moment of change in Menzies' attitude, the opening salvo of the revolution to come, then this letter is it:

> I am disappointed and amazed at some of the developments in the city ... Surveying Canberra, one gains an impression of flat-top roof buildings, squat with inevitable dullness within the plain and looking to some extent like a view of Cairo. It only required the odd goat or camel to make the view complete ... Whenever I have asked about the matters in the past, I have been told that it is someone else's business. I would now like you to look into the matter and give me your views and some answer to the problems where the city is going.[74]

Fairhall did look carefully into the matter over the coming months to determine an approach that he hoped might succeed where so many before him had failed. Menzies, anxious to get things moving, pre-empted his minister when he asked a trusted officer in the Prime Minister's Department, his Yarralumla neighbour, Ken Herde, to prepare a paper on Canberra's "future planning and development" while he (Menzies) was out of the country in June/July attending the Prime Ministers' Conference in London.[75] After his return, Menzies endorsed all the proposals and sought Cabinet's agreement. Given his unchallenged authority, this was a given. Fairhall, alert to Menzies' born-again position on Canberra (former Interior Minister, Wilfrid Kent Hughes, called him "virtually the lord mayor"[76]), was instructed to prepare the appropriate legislation. The minister had not been idle; he had done his homework as well, and initiated a one-on-one meeting in Newcastle, late in 1956, about the time of the Melbourne Olympics, that would assume its own significance in the story.

Fairhall had a meeting with John Overall, decorated Second World War paratrooper, architect, engineer and town planner and, by the mid-1950s, an individual with impeccable leadership experience within large organisations. The Minister for the Interior sought Overall's expert take on Canberra's future development. A veteran of El Alamein and Tobruk, who had first seen a fog-enshrouded Canberra as he parachuted in, Overall would soon make his own indelible mark on the national capital canvas. Menzies said he was "in no doubt that we could not possibly secure a better man."[77]

The momentum generated in 1956 increased the following year: William Holford was invited to Canberra and, in June 1957, he walked the city in order to produce a report containing a number of recommendations on what he felt should be done, starting with an independent commission; the Prime Minister of

Australia visited Holford, the "impressive and lively" Holford as he described him, in London just a few weeks later, their discussion confirming Menzies in his view that Canberra must have a "special and powerful new authority;"[78] Fairhall, with the complete support of his leader, guided the National Capital Development Commission Bill through the Parliament, August to October, and had the satisfaction of seeing it become legislation on 10 October; and Holford submitted his report in December, "Observations on the Future Development of Canberra, A.C.T." (published in May 1958), which emphasised the necessity for immediate creation of an independent commission, and stated unequivocally that Canberra could never reach its design potential while it remained geographically divided by the Molonglo River, "an open wedge between the federal town on the south bank and the municipality in the north."[79] Canberra must have the lake that it was gifted in the magnificent 1912 international competition-winning plan of Walter Burley Griffin and Marion Mahony Griffin.

The Prime Minister's own grasp of the range of issues and imperatives relating to Canberra firmed up exponentially at this time, solidifying an unfashionable commitment that was soon tested by some of his parliamentary colleagues. He knew well that "every penny spent on Canberra [was] grudged," so he could hardly have been surprised when covert attempts were made to water down the NCDC legislation in order to reduce the organisation's power and budget.[80] Menzies, with yet another election success under his belt (in November 1958, with an increased margin) stood firm. More humorously but no less significantly, the Prime Minister's strong support for the creation of the lake also came under pressure. He tells the story memorably:

> I went away to England once more very happy, because the estimates [for funding the lake] had been accepted; my dream had been given shape; but when I returned I found that Treasury (which in any country moves in mysterious ways its wonders to perform) had induced ministers to strike the item out. At the very first meeting after my return ... I turned to the Treasurer, who was a good friend and ultimate successor, the late Harold Holt, and said, with what I hoped was a disarming smile, "Am I rightly informed that when I was away the Treasury struck out this item of one million [pounds] for the initial work on the lake?" The reply was yes, and that Cabinet had agreed. I then said, "Well, can I take it that by unanimous consent of ministers the item is now struck back in?"[81]

Needless to say it was, and NCDC Commissioner Overall had his men on the Monaro plains early next morning digging up the first sods.

Menzies and Overall worked exceptionally well together, aided by the fact that the NCDC became a "favoured son" of the Prime Minister, as Overall put it.[82] There was deep mutual respect between the two men. Overall knew he could count on the Prime Minister's support when he needed it most, and Menzies knew that this was one public servant who would not be intimidated by anyone, himself included.[83] When Menzies tried to shoehorn a (for him, rare) captain's pick into an important NCDC job, Overall refused to countenance it and threatened to resign if he did not get his way. Menzies learnt a lesson, later stating with undisguised admiration that Overall "occasionally frightens me" with his dedication to the task and work ethic.[84] Overall for his part learnt on the job as well, realising that when seeking the Prime Minister's support for an initiative, a dry Noilly-Prat vermouth and gin, late in the day, did not hurt his chances of success.[85]

* * * * *

Analysts of Robert Menzies' two prime ministerships will remain forever divided on the ledger of achievements and failures. On at least one aspect of his many years in power, however, all can agree: the once reluctant "conscript" to Canberra became one of the national capital's most loyal and devoted servants. No-one has been more influential. Towards the end of his life, this thought thrilled him: "I am delighted in my old age to think that Australia's capital has now become an object of pride and pleasure. This was always a national conclusion devoutly to be wished." While it would only be attending to unfinished business for Canberra's Place Names Committee to name a suburb "Menzies"—despite his professed wishes to the contrary—the city itself will forever remain his lasting memorial.

Endnotes

[1] Sir Robert Menzies, *Afternoon Light – Some Memories of Men and Events*, Cassell Australia, 1967.

[2] Cameron Hazlehurst (ed.), *Australian Conservatism – Essays in Twentieth Century Political History*, Australian National University Press, 1979, 2.

[3] Sir Robert Menzies, *The Measure of the Years*, Cassell Australia, 1970.

[4] Ibid., 143.

[5] A.W. Martin, "Sir Robert Gordon Menzies", in Michelle Grattan (ed.), *Australian Prime Ministers*, New Holland Publishers (Australia) Pty Ltd, 2000, 178.

[6] See Hazlehurst, 2.

[7] Warren Denning, *Capital City – Canberra Today and Tomorrow*, "The Publicist", 1938, 50-1.

[8] Denning, 87.

[9] A.W. Martin, *Robert Menzies – A Life*, Vol. I (1894-1943), Melbourne University Press, 1993, 137.

[10] Ibid., 129.

[11] This section of the essay draws on information provided in: Kel Robertson, *The Federal Capital Territory Unlawful Assemblies Ordinance of 1937*, a thesis in partial completion of Master of Letters, Australian National University, 1995.

[12] See Robertson, 76.

[13] *Canberra Times*, 30 June 1937, 3. See Robertson, 80.

[14] "Explanatory memorandum accompanying the Unlawful Assemblies Ordinance (No. 9 of 1937)", National Archives of Australia (NAA), AA A432 37/694. See Robertson, 47.

[15] R.G. Menzies, "The Forgotten People", reproduced in Robertson, 90.

[16] Reproduced in David Headon, *The Symbolic Role of the National Capital – from Colonial Argument to 21st Century Ideals*, Commonwealth of Australia, 2003, 91.

[17] Editorial, *Canberra Times*, 23 July 1937, 4. Reproduced in Robertson, 98.

[18] *Canberra Times*, 28 July 1937, 1. Reproduced in Robertson, 100.

[19] *Canberra Times*, 3 August 1937, 2; *Canberra Times*, 4 August 1937, 2; *Canberra Times*, 6 August 1937, 4. Reproduced in Robertson, 102-4.

[20] Menzies (1967), 44-5.

[21] Diane Langmore, *Prime Ministers' Wives – the Public and Private Lives of Ten Australian Women*, McPhee Gribble, 1992, 184.

[22] Heather Henderson, *A Smile for My Parents*, Allen & Unwin, 2013, 88.

[23] Ibid.

[24] *Sun*, 28 October 1939. Reproduced in Langmore, 185.

[25] Heather Henderson, "Prime Minister's Daughter in Canberra", *Canberra Historical Journal*, New Series, 44, September 1999, 3.

[26] See John Dargavel, *The Zealous Conservator – a Life of Charles Lane Poole*, University of Western Australia Press, 2008, 3-4, 119-20, 123.

[27] Dargavel, 166.

[28] See Langmore, 185.

[29] National Library of Australia (NLA), MS 4936, Box 555. See Graeme Barrow, *The Prime Ministers' Lodge – Canberra's Unfinished Business*, Dagraja Press, 2008, 40.

[30] *Sunday Sun & Guardian*, 7 September 1941. Reproduced in Barrow, 40.

[31] Headon, op. cit., 99.

[32] See Eric Sparke, *Canberra 1954-1980*, AGPS Press Publication, 1988, 82.

[33] Headon, 98.

[34] *Sun*, 12 December 1949. Reproduced in Langmore, 188.

[35] See Martin, in Grattan, 186.

[36] Henderson, op. cit., 3-4.

[37] See Langmore, 188.

[38] NLA, MS 4936, Box 555. See Barrow, 48.

[39] Menzies (1970), 144.

[40] See Henderson, "Prime Minister's Daughter", 7.

[41] See Barrow, 49.

[42] NAA, A463, 1958/51, Part 1, J.H. Scholtens minute, 13 July 1952. Reproduced in Barrow, 49.

[43] Sir John Bunting, *R.G. Menzies – A Portrait*, Allen & Unwin, 1988, 133.

[44] Ibid.

[45] Henderson, *A Smile*, 94.

[46] Ibid., 95-6.

[47] Ibid., 92-3.

[48] Henderson, "A Prime Minister's Daughter", 4.

[49] Henderson, *A Smile*, 94.

[50] Henderson, "A Prime Minister's Daughter", 3.

[51] Menzies (1970), 271.

[52] Bunting, 166.

[53] See Menzies (1970), 269-75; see also Don Selth, *The Prime Minister's XI – the Story of the Prime Minister's XI Matches – Menzies to Hawke*, Woden Printers and Publishers, 1990, 66-71.

[54] Menzies (1970), 273.

[55] *Report from the Select Committee Appointed to Inquire into and Report Upon the Development of Canberra* (Chair: Senator J.A. McCallum), Government Printer, September 1955, 17.

[56] *The 1951 Federal Congress on Regional and Town Planning – Record of Proceedings*, 9-12 August 1951, 13.

[57] 1951 *Federal Congress Proceedings*, 17.

[58] See John Overall, *Canberra – Yesterday, Today and Tomorrow – A Personal Memoir*, Federal Capital Press of Australia Pty Ltd, 1995, 32.

[59] Reproduced in Martin, *Robert Menzies*, Vol 1, 148.

[60] Ibid., 152, 154.

[61] Menzies (1967), 237-8.

[62] Martin, in Grattan, 182, 204.

[63] Robert Gordon Menzies, *Speech Is Of Time – Selected Speeches and Writings*, Cassell & Company Ltd, 1958, 201.

[64] Reproduced in Headon, 108. This source provides detail of, and a broad context for, the *Report* and its public and political reception (see 103-15).

[65] [Senate] *Report*, 54.

[66] [Senate] *Report*, 23.

[67] Reproduced in Headon, 103.

[68] Overall, 29.

[69] Henderson, *A Smile*, 82.

[70] Reproduced in Sparke, 52.

[71] Henderson, *A Smile*, 145.

[72] Menzies (1970), 145.

[73] Sparke, 32.

[74] NLA, 4936/1/16/139, Menzies to Fairhall, 28 April 1956. A significant section of Menzies' letter is reproduced in Overall, 32-3.

[75] See Henderson, *A Smile*, 83-4.

[76] Reproduced in Sparke, 54.

[77] Ibid., 67.

[78] Ibid., 62.

[79] [Sir] William Holford, *Observations on the Future Development of Canberra, ACT*, Government Printer, 1957, 6.

[80] Menzies (1970), 147.

[81] Ibid., 146-7. See also Bunting, 191.

[82] Overall, 77.

[83] See Sparke, 68-9.

[84] Reproduced in Overall, 64.

[85] Overall, 47.

Index

United Nations, 22, 94, 97, 101, 107, 111-2, 117, 121

United States, 3, 12, 21-2, 35, 37-8, 46-50, 53, 57, 94-101, 104, 106-13, 117-20, 134-6, 140, 151, 156, 159, 164, 172, 181, 200, 204-7, 241, 261, 295, 327, 332, 349, 356

Vernon Committee, 16, 66, 318
Enquiry, 147, 165
Report, 145, 169-70, 174
Vietnam War, 55, 96, 101, 116, 119-20

War Precautions Act, 350
Watson, Chris, 27

Wedgwood, Ivy, 86, 88-9, 91

Wentworth, William Charles 'W C', 295, 305

Wheeler, (Sir) Frederick, 347

White, Thomas, 46

White Australia policy, 54, 133, 148

Whitlam, Gough Edward, 6, 55, 59, 73, 114-5, 122, 215, 290, 293, 303-4, 306

Whitlam Government, 59, 100, 138, 162, 174, 337

Wilson, (Sir) Roland, 141-2, 153, 340, 347

Women's Liberal League (NSW), 79-80

Yew, Lee Kwan, 22, 54, 115-6, 122
Young Nationalists, 9, 40, 77, 81

Acknowledgements

Many people have contributed and otherwise supported publication of this book. It marks the 50th anniversary of Sir Robert Menzies' retirement as Prime Minister of Australia in January 1966. The anniversary provided a timely opportunity to examine the record and achievement of Sir Robert's three and a half decades in Australian government and politics. He was, in those years, the paramount figure in Australia's public and political life.

Accomplishing this properly entailed a considered appraisal both of his own immense contribution, and that of the governments he led, particularly the post-war Liberal-Country Party Coalition Government, 1949-66.

Major credit inevitably and rightly belongs to the thirteen authors who readily agreed to write the essays which compose the book. They have come from diverse backgrounds in terms of experience and disciplinary disposition. The quality of the book owes much to their readiness to read essays of other contributors writing in related fields. The volume has likewise benefitted from two round tables at which most of the essays were discussed with the several authors and other experts in twentieth century Australian national politics and government. We much appreciate the participation of those who attended the round tables: Professor Geoffrey Blainey, AC; Professor Judith Brett; Professor Brian Galligan; the late Dr John Hirst; John Paul; the Honourable Dr Peter Phelps, MLC; and Dr Denis White. Bruce Edwards of the Federal Secretariat of the Liberal Party chaired the Melbourne round table, and assisted the project in numerous other ways.

Our thanks to Dr Phelps in Sydney and Simon Frost in Melbourne for arranging congenial rooms for the discussions and suitable hospitality during the day.

Several authors have acknowledged comments made by others on their papers during the course of writing; Lorraine Finlay, School of Law, Murdoch University, provided valuable advice on several essays as finished drafts came to hand.

I want to express particular thanks to Professor Jonathan Pincus. As the Table of Contents shows, he contributed one chapter and jointly authored another. From conception of the book until its finalisation, he was a constant source of advice and suggestion. He provided continuing assistance in appraisal of various essays as they were finalised. In a wide-ranging project of this character, any editor is indeed fortunate to be able to draw upon the wisdom of such an accomplished scholar. For his support and counsel in the year and a half during which the book took shape, and for much else besides in many years of friendship and conversation, I am deeply grateful.

In readying the book for publication, Michael Gilchrist has brought his great skills in preparation of text to the task, and, in addition, a great deal of patience upon which this project has made many calls.

As usual, Dr Anthony Cappello of Connor Court has overseen the processes of publication with his customary expertise and judgment.

As editor, I also owe many thanks to Professor Patrick McArdle and other colleagues and friends, especially Malcolm Mackerras, at the Canberra Campus, Australian Catholic University. They have provided a very congenial environment in which to work, without which this volume would have encountered many problems otherwise promptly resolved.

The book forms part of the publishing program of the Menzies Research Centre. It has enjoyed, throughout, the unerring support of the Executive Director, Nick Cater, and the very cheerful enthusiasm of the Deputy Director, Kay Gilchrist. Especially in the many labours of finalising copy the book has been fortunate in the various endeavours of Dr David Furse-Roberts, Scholar-in-Residence; and interns at the Centre, Hugh Evans and Pieter-Francois Schiefler.

Finally, many thanks to Heather Henderson for the Foreword and the Honourable Josh Frydenberg, MP, the member for Kooyong since 2010, for the Preface. The support they have given to the project as it progressed has been reassuring and constantly encouraging.

J. R. Nethercote
Canberra
March 2016